THE GREAT

General Editor ROBER'

C000263696

Imperial Apocalypse describes the collapse of the Russian Empire during World War One. Drawing material from nine different archives and hundreds of published sources, this study ties together state failure, military violence, and decolonization in a single story. Joshua Sanborn excavates the individual lives of soldiers, doctors, nurses, politicians, and civilians caught up in the global conflict along the way, creating a narrative that is both humane and conceptually rich.

The volume moves chronologically from the Balkan Wars of 1912–13 through the fierce battles and massive human dislocations of 1914–17 to the final collapse of the Russian Empire in the midst of revolution in 1917–18. *Imperial Apocalypse* is the first major study which treats the demise of the empire as part of the twentieth-century phenomenon of modern decolonization, and it provides a readable account of military activity and political change throughout this turbulent period of war and revolution. Sanborn argues that the sudden rise of groups seeking national self-determination in the borderlands of the empire was the consequence of state failure, not its cause. At the same time, he shows how the destruction of state institutions and the spread of violence from the front to the rear led to a collapse of traditional social bonds and the emergence of a new, more dangerous, and more militant political atmosphere.

Imperial Apocalypse

*The Great War and the Destruction
of the Russian Empire*

JOSHUA A. SANBORN

OXFORD
UNIVERSITY PRESS

OXFORD
UNIVERSITY PRESS

Great Clarendon Street, Oxford, OX2 6DP,
United Kingdom

Oxford University Press is a department of the University of Oxford.
It furthers the University's objective of excellence in research, scholarship,
and education by publishing worldwide. Oxford is a registered trade mark of
Oxford University Press in the UK and in certain other countries

Published in the United States of America by Oxford University Press
198 Madison Avenue, New York, NY 10016, United States of America

British Library Cataloguing in Publication Data
Data available

Library of Congress Cataloging in Publication Data
Data available

ISBN 978–0–19–964205–2 (Hbk.)
ISBN 978–0–19–874568–6 (Pbk.)

Table of Contents

Preface

I began researching this book more than a decade ago with a study of everyday life in the war zones of the Eastern Front during World War I in mind. I wanted to restore the humanity of the voiceless men and women who figure in most histories of the war only as archetypes of the primitive Russian peasant-soldier or the suffering victims of modern war. Most of my initial archival forays were dedicated to the excavation of their stories through police reports, censored letters, telegrams from army officers, and the memoir and diary literature. It was only later, as I began writing articles based on my research, that I saw more clearly the trajectory of events I was describing. A different sort of history now emerged, one that linked military violence, state failure, social collapse, and the end of empire together in an overlapping but causal chain. This process bore such a striking resemblance to the world-historical process of twentieth-century decolonization that I reframed my project to suggest that Russia's apocalyptic experiences during the Great War and the Civil War represented an early phase of a dramatic but painful global story. The phenomenon of decolonization places the Great War even more centrally in the narrative of twentieth-century world history. This book thus has two aims: to describe the lives of a wide variety of actors on the Russian Front and to analyze the way the Russian Empire decolonized.

These two aims structured most of my authorial choices. I linger on descriptions of the lives of soldiers and nurses, recount in some detail how Osip and Mariana lost their cows, uncover the desperate and sordid endeavors of El'za Vimba near the Apollo Theater in Riga, and tell of Doctor Mirotvortsev's frantic travels through the war zone not just because of the intrinsic interest of these small-bore histories, but because these unknown stories help to flesh out the story of the war as a whole. English-speaking readers have long been able to grasp the humanity of those fighting on the Western Front. I hope this book introduces them to others who lived through those awful years on the other side of the continent. Similarly, I came to share the view of many military historians that accounts of war that ignore combat leave out something essential. As a result, there is a good deal more on the battles of the war than I had envisioned at the start of the process. At the same time, the desire to follow the unraveling thread of empire in Eastern Europe determined choices as well. The story of the Balkan Wars took on added importance as an introduction to the events of the Great War, and the sad tale of the Russian Civil War provided a concluding bookend. Events in Ukraine in the summer of 1917 seemed much more important as I finished this book than they did when I began. It turned out that the stories of life in front-line zones and of the collapse of the empire were much the same story, viewed from different angles. They belong together in the same study.

Finally, I wrote this book for multiple audiences. I have tried always to keep in mind non-specialist readers interested in enlarging their knowledge about the Great

War or Russian history. I do not expect readers to be scholars either of this time period or of the history of Russia and Eastern Europe. For the same reasons, I trust that students will find this text engaging and accessible. This accessibility does not have to come at the expense of scholarly rigor. While there are some tensions involved, I hope that specialists will find both that I have incorporated the latest research into my argument and that I have new contributions of my own to make, both factually and analytically. I particularly hope that non-Russianist historians of the Great War find this work useful and stimulating. If general readers profit from the discussions of state failure and decolonization, and specialists can forgive the abbreviated treatment of some issues and the absence of others, then I will consider this book a success.

All books on this topic must deal with the troublesome issues of dates and names. The Julian calendar used by Russia prior to 14 February 1918 lagged thirteen days behind the Gregorian calendar used on the rest of the continent. To assist those who wish to fix Russian events on the broader European timeline and to minimize confusion, I give both dates each time I use a date in the text. In the footnotes, however, I retain whatever date is used in the documents themselves. Names are trickier. For locations, I mostly use the place names used today, so I refer to L'viv rather than L'vov, Lwów, or Lemberg. If for no other reason, this will help readers who may want to find these locations on Google Maps. I do make exceptions for names familiar in English, such as Moscow, Warsaw, Kiev, and the Vistula River. Most personal names are rendered in the standard Library of Congress transliterations from Russian, even if the name is plainly of some other ethnic origin, so it is General Ianushkevich rather than General Januszkewicz. Exceptions are made in footnotes, where I use whatever spellings are in the documents themselves, transliterating directly from the Russian where necessary.

I have benefitted from the wisdom of so many people over such a long period of time that I know I cannot acknowledge them all here. Let me give special thanks to the students involved in Lafayette College's wonderful EXCEL program, which allows undergraduates the opportunity to work as research assistants for professors at the college. These young women and men worked with me in a variety of ways for time periods ranging from a couple of months to a couple of years: Maria Azimova, Carla Benedek, Martin Chojnacki, Ivan Dimitrov, Daniel Faulkenberry, Diana Galperin, Brian Geraghty, Milos Jovanovic, John Raymond, Christine Shanahan, Hannah Smock, Zsuzana Vojtekova, Lori Weaver, and Sandamali Wijeratne. I also benefitted greatly from Vasilii Kashirin's assistance over the period of several years. Other scholars have been particularly helpful. Andrew Janco alerted me to the possibility that I might find useful manuscripts at the Biblioteka-fond "Russkoe Zarubezh'e," and Brigid O'Keeffe and Eric Lohr very kindly and thoughtfully read a full draft of the final manuscript. I will not list the many other specialists on the Great War who have influenced my thinking and have read parts of this work. So many have shaped this book that there would scarcely be anyone left to review it if I were to mention them all.

It is a challenge to conduct a major research project while not at a research university, but Lafayette College has been very supportive throughout the process.

In addition to funding the EXCEL scholars mentioned, the Academic Research Committee provided several grants to conduct research in Moscow, Kiev, Riga, St. Petersburg, Washington DC, and Stanford, California. Karen Haduck and the rest of the interlibrary loan staff at Skillman Library worked very hard to fulfill my many challenging requests. John Clark, another outstanding librarian, refashioned the maps at the last moment, for which I am tremendously grateful. This book would not have been possible in this form without their diligence and professional excellence. Several former and present Lafayette colleagues have shaped my views of empire or have otherwise given thoughtful feedback on my work: Paul Barclay, Bill Bissell, Emily Musil Church, Neil Englehart, Rebekah Pite, Deborah Rosen, and Andrea Smith have been particularly important in this regard. I also received extensive and generous support from external grants and fellowships. Work on this project began in earnest when I was a visiting fellow at the Shelby Cullom Davis Center for Historical Studies at Princeton. Further fellowships from the American Council of Learned Societies and the National Endowment for the Humanities allowed me to spend extended periods abroad for research.

Finally, I deeply thank Robert Gerwarth for inviting me to submit a book proposal for inclusion in this series, and Christopher Wheeler, Robert Faber, and Cathryn Steele for their assistance and judgment at OUP. Last, but not least, I give my love and thanks to my wife Kim and my children Clayton and Grace. It is a cliché to remark that the book took me away from them physically and mentally at various times over the years. It is also true.

I have made use of selections from several previous articles when composing this text. I thank the publishers listed below for permission to reuse them here.

- Joshua Sanborn, "Unsettling the Empire: Violent Migrations and Social Disaster in Russia during World War I," *Journal of Modern History* 77, no. 2 (June 2005): 290–324, © 2005, reprinted with permission of the University of Chicago.

- Joshua Sanborn, "The Genesis of Russian Warlordism: Violence and Governance during the First World War and the Civil War," *Contemporary European History* 19, no. 3 (August 2010): 202–207, © 2010, reprinted with permission of Cambridge University Press.

- Joshua Sanborn, "Military Occupation and Social Unrest: Daily Life in Russian Poland at the Start of World War I," in *Writing the Stalin Era: Sheila Fitzpatrick and Soviet Historiography*, Palgrave Macmillan, 2010, reproduced with permission of Palgrave Macmillan. The full published version of this publication is available from: http://us.macmillan.com/writingthestalinera/ GolfoAlexopoulos and <http://www.palgraveconnect.com/pc/doifinder/10. 1057/9780230116429>.

List of Maps

Sources for Maps

Department of Military Art and Engineering, at the U.S. Military Academy (West Point), *Eastern Front, 1917*, Wikimedia Commons, retrieved from http://en.wikipedia.org/wiki/File:EasternFront1917.jpg, May 20 2014.

Gilbert, Martin. *Atlas of Russian History*. Oxford: Oxford University Press, 1993. ("War and Revolt under Peter the Great, 1695–1723," pp. 37–8).

Gorlitskaia operatsiia: manevrennyi period 1915 goda. Moscow: Voenizdat, 1941 (pp. 24–5).

Lincoln, W. Bruce Red Victory: *A History of the Russian Civil War*. New York: Touchstone, 1989 ("The Russian Civil War, 1918–1921. The War in European Russia," front piece).

Magocsi, Paul R. *Historical Atlas of Central Europe*. Seattle: University of Washington Press, 2002. ("World War I, 1914–1918," p. 122).

Natural Earth. *Free vector and raster map data at naturalearthdata.com*, retrieved from http://www.naturalearthdata.com, March 2014.

Podorozhnyi, N. E. *Narochskaia operatsiia v marte 1916 g. na Russkom fronte mirovoi voiny*. Moscow: Gosizdat, 1938 (p. 13).

Stone, Norman. *The Eastern Front, 1914–1917*. New York: Charles Scribner's Sons, 1975 (p. 83).

USGS, Center for Earth Resources Observation and Science, *30 arc-second DEM of Europe* (uploaded to Data Basin by Conservation Biology Institute on July 29, 2010), retrieved from http://app.databasin.org/app/pages/datasetPage.jsp?id=7a286ca8a7fa492a9f95d58324ca918c May 20, 2014.

USGS, Center for Earth Resources Observation and Science, *30 arc-second DEM of Asia* (uploaded to Data Basin by Conservation Biology Institute on July 29, 2010), retrieved from http://app.databasin.org/app/pages/datasetPage.jsp?id=7a286ca8a7fa492a9f95d58324ca918c May 20, 2014.

Introduction: Imperial Challenge

The 100th anniversary of the beginning of World War I is upon us. Scholars, journalists, social commentators, and politicians from around the world are gathering together in the summer months of 2014 and reflecting upon the many ways that the Great War helped define the century that followed it, just as many did upon the 50th anniversary of the war in 1964 and on the occasion of the passing of the twentieth century. Most of them are traveling to the battlefields of France, where the German army fought French, British, and American armies for four bloody years. The titanic clashes there mesmerized a century's worth of Europeans and North Americans. The Marne, the Somme, Verdun, and a host of other place names symbolized slaughter and despair, just as Versailles would come to represent the postwar political failings of European statesmen. Every educated European and North American citizen for the past century has been expected to know these names and to be able to interpret their significance.

That same expectation has not held for the places of conflict in Eastern Europe and Eurasia. German schoolchildren between the wars were expected to learn of the great victory at Tannenberg in 1914,[1] but what of Gorlice, Przemyśl, Trabzon, Ivangorod, or Bolimów? Europeans know of the "Rape of Belgium," but what of the shelling of civilians in the border town of Kalisz or of what contemporaries called the "Polish Exodus"—the flight of millions of civilians away from the fighting and into the Russian heartland? These disappeared from the annals of European remembrance so quickly that Winston Churchill was able to claim with justification as early as 1931 that it was an "Unknown War."[2] It was neglected not only by populations who never fought in the east, but by many of the combatant countries as well, particularly in the lands of the Russian Empire, where the events of the Russian Revolution of 1917 and the Civil War that followed it took the center stage of historical memory.[3] When the collapse of the Soviet Union initiated a resurgence of interest in pre-revolutionary events, World War I got some scholarly

---

[1] Dennis Showalter, *Tannenberg: Clash of Empires* (Washington DC: Brassey's, 2004 [1991]), 351–3.

[2] Winston Churchill, *The Unknown War: The Eastern Front* (New York: Charles Scribner's Sons, 1931).

[3] Daniel Orlovsky, "Velikaia voina i Rossiiskaia pamiat'," in *Rossiia i pervaia mirovaia voina (materialy mezhdunarodnogo nauchnogo kollokviuma)*, ed. N. N. Smirnov (St. Petersburg: Dmitrii Bulanin, 1999), 49–57; Aaron J. Cohen, "Oh, That! Myth, Memory, and World War I in the Russian Emigration and the Soviet Union," *Slavic Review* 62, no. 1 (Spring 2003): 69–86. Note, however, that the war still played a role in unexpected ways. See Karen Petrone, *The Great War in Russian Memory* (Bloomington: Indiana University Press, 2011).

attention, but it barely made a ripple on popular consciousness. Historians have diligently studied these events over the years, but their findings have not fully been integrated into broader historical narratives.[4] One recent author, justifying his own focus on the Western Front, writes "[f]or many, myself included, the First World War means Ypres, the Somme, and Verdun, not Tannenberg. . . . The First World War is Versailles, not Brest-Litovsk."[5] There are almost no Russian monuments to the fallen, no television extravaganzas, and little public attention. It is a sign of the rupture of memory and history that, when some enthusiasts attempted to begin a tradition of commemoration for the Russian war effort, they chose 11 November, a date central for many combatant countries because of the armistice signed on that day in 1918, but much less important for Russia, which had signed a separate peace eight months earlier.[6]

Have we lost anything of substance in this process of forgetting? Or was the rapid eclipse of the Eastern Front an indication that the events that took place there were of little or no long-term historical importance? Were those events so similar to those that took place on the Western Front that learning about them would be redundant for those familiar with the events in France, significant for those who were directly involved perhaps, but otherwise the proper domain of trivia-seekers? Churchill had an answer, couched in his usual grandiose prose. It was, he said,

> the most mournful conflict of which there is record. All three empires, both sides, victors and vanquished, were ruined. All the Emperors or their successors were slain or deposed. The Houses of Romanov, Hapsburg and Hohenzollern woven over centuries of renown into the texture of Europe were shattered and extirpated. The structure of three mighty organisms built up by generations of patience and valour and representing the traditional groupings of noble branches of the European family, was changed beyond all semblance. These pages recount dazzling victories and defeats stoutly made good. They record the toils, perils, sufferings and passions of millions of men. Their sweat, their tears, their blood bedewed the endless plain. Ten million homes awaited the return of the warriors. A hundred cities prepared to acclaim their triumphs. But all were defeated; all were stricken; everything that they had given was given in vain. Nothing was gained by any. They floundered in the mud, they perished in the snowdrifts, they starved in the frost. Those that survived, the veterans of countless battle-days, returned, whether with the laurels of victory or tidings of disaster, to homes engulfed already in catastrophe.[7]

One need not adopt Churchill's heroic and elegiac framework to appreciate his basic point that the extirpation of three empires woven into the texture of Europe was an event of deep importance.

---

[4] As the notes and bibliography to this work attest, there is actually an enormous amount of material available on the conflict on the Eastern Front.

[5] Leo van Bergen, *Before My Helpless Sight: Suffering, Dying and Military Medicine on the Western Front, 1914–1918*, trans. Liz Waters (Farnham: Ashgate, 2009), 18.

[6] Cohen, 85. It was also no doubt chosen as part of a general post-Soviet attempt to keep the Revolution Day holiday (7 November) on the calendar without actually commemorating the Bolsheviks.

[7] Churchill, 1.

WAR AND THE PATTERN OF DECOLONIZATION

This book proceeds from the premise that the collapse of empire in Europe was indeed a significant historical event. This process took place over the whole duration of the war, not simply during the peace conferences that ended it. The Great War was a war of European decolonization. The trajectory of decolonization affected the conduct of the war, and the fact of decolonization in Eastern and Southeastern Europe was one of the most tangible and significant outcomes of the conflict. As a result, focusing on the Eastern Front allows us to see a dynamic of the war that might be missed otherwise and that had implications for the rest of the twentieth century.

Decolonization was a crucial aspect of the war from its beginning right through to its end, but it continues to be largely ignored by mainstream scholarship. The events of the summer of 1914 have been exhaustively studied, yet no author to my knowledge has attempted to use decolonization as a lens upon the Sarajevo assassination or the July Crisis. Indeed, scholars have generally ignored the dynamic of decolonization even for the later stages of the conflict, such as the period leading to the Paris Peace Conference, when the process became virtually impossible to miss. Erez Manela's recent book is a welcome contribution to this field, but even he restricts his scope to Africa and Asia, which prompts him to link the upsurge of anticolonial rhetoric to the "Wilsonian Moment" in late 1918 and 1919.[8] He is aware of the significance of the slogan of national self-determination in Eastern Europe in 1917, but nevertheless Poland is touched on only tangentially, and Ukraine is mentioned only in the context of the Ukrainian diaspora in the United States.[9] Wilson borrowed the slogan of the self-determination of nations from Eastern Europeans rather than the other way around, and this fact deserves closer study.

Instead, the debate has focused on the dynamic of competitive imperialism among the Great Powers. The question of war guilt led the combatants on the Western Front to point fingers at one another as the main instigators of the conflict, and as a result far more attention has been paid to developments in Berlin, Paris and London than to those in the Balkans, where the crisis developed.[10] Scholars shifted their focus north and west not only for historiographical reasons (having to do with the pressing demand of assigning blame for the war), but also for good historical

---

[8] Erez Manela, *The Wilsonian Moment: Self-Determination and the International Origins of Anticolonial Nationalism* (Oxford: Oxford University Press, 2007).

[9] Manela recognizes that the language of self-determination had been enthusiastically adopted by Lenin and the Bolsheviks earlier in the war and that the Russian Revolution allowed for the spread of this ideal in 1917 to the extent that he speaks of a "dual challenge of Lenin and Wilson to the old ways of European politics." Nevertheless, Europe is not studied as a zone of "anticolonial nationalism" in his work. Manela, 38.

[10] For an excellent analysis of the gargantuan literature on the outbreak of the war, see Annika Mombauer, *The Origins of the First World War: Controversies and Consensus* (Harlow, UK: Longman, 2002). A recent corrective, which devotes significant attention to the Balkans, is Christopher Clark, *The Sleepwalkers: How Europe Went to War in 1914* (New York: Harper Collins, 2013).

ones. Most statesmen and later historians assumed that a massive war between the Great Powers would be fundamentally rooted in the massive political conflicts that had developed between them. Events on the periphery might act as sparks, but there was little reason to assume that they would be anything more than that. Thus, European diplomats in July 1914 normally (but, as we shall see, not always) treated the crisis as one between the imperial powers. They declared war and ordered military mobilizations in August within the context of the imperial system that had governed their actions for the previous century. But wars are frequently about many things at once, and great wars are almost by definition conglomerations of multiple conflicts that proceed simultaneously. One of those conflicts during the war was about the existence of imperial control as such, not just about which empire would do the controlling. This aspect of World War I existed at the very beginning of the war, and it developed rapidly over the following years.

Just as shifting to the model of colonization and decolonization rather than great power imperialism allows us to see the events of the war in a new light, so too does this model give us new insights into developments normally classed as the "rise of nationalism" in Eastern Europe. Again, the study of nationalism in Eastern Europe has long occupied an important part of the war literature. In particular, treatments of the Habsburg Empire in the period before and during the war regularly discuss the restiveness and political aspirations of particular ethnic groups, and many conclude that the multiethnic empire was ultimately untenable as a modern state.[11] Scholars make similar assessments regarding the Russian Empire as well.[12] In this reading, the rise of nationalism put such intense pressure on imperial states that those states had to take ever more desperate measures to contain nationalist movements. The war deferred these aspirations for independence, but when the imperial states went down to defeat, nationalist groups deployed the language of self-determination to gain political recognition in Paris.

This interpretation is not so much wrong as incomplete. It overemphasizes the early formative processes of developing ethnic consciousness and overvalues the role of the articulate and published promoters of the national idea. Above all, however, the model of national liberation is problematic because it is founded on the assumption that the process is primarily one of moving from colonial dependence to national sovereignty, and that therefore the primary struggle is between the nation seeking liberation and the empire that seeks to maintain control.

This general framework, as we shall see, is not robust enough to explain the complicated political and military processes that lead to independence, which are

---

[11] There are many instances of this in the twentieth-century literature. For a twenty-first-century example, see Robin Okey, *The Habsburg Monarchy: From Enlightenment to Eclipse* (New York: St Martin's, 2001), vii, 400–1. Mark Cornwall offers the nuanced view that the national question in the army was overstated early in the war by self-serving generals but that it grew more important in the last two years of the war as Habsburg subjects mobilized against both the war and the old regime. Mark Cornwall, "Morale and Patriotism in the Austro-Hungarian Army, 1914–1918," in *State, Society, and Mobilization in Europe during the First World War*, ed. John Horne (Cambridge: Cambridge University Press, 1997), 173–90.

[12] A. Iu. Bakhturina, *Okrainy rossiiskoi imperii: gosudarstvennoe upravlenie i natsional'naia politika v gody Pervoi mirovoi voiny, 1914–1917 gg.* (Moscow: ROSSPEN, 2004), 3.

powerfully influenced both by vicious fighting between purported co-nationals and by deep engagement with regional and global powers other than the imperial state most directly affected. The model of national liberation helps even less when attempting to explain why conflict continues, indeed frequently intensifies, after the achievement of national independence. We might also note that many of the actual states that emerged from the process in World War I were actually multi-national. As the names suggest, Czechoslovakia, the Kingdom of Serbs, Croats, and Slovenes, and the Union of Soviet Socialist Republics all incorporated multiple politically conscious nationalities. Despite its name, Poland too was a multinational state (especially in the interwar period). It is true that virtually every political movement interested in decolonization over the past century adopted the national idiom, and this choice of idiom had powerful consequences for political beliefs and political practices everywhere it was deployed. Nevertheless, we should distinguish between the core political processes of decolonization and the ideology that imperfectly structured those political interactions.

One of the reasons why scholars of the Great War have paid so little attention to the concept of decolonization is that politicians established the terms of the debate regarding the causes and consequences of the war before commentators had a chance to see the pattern that emerged over the course of the twentieth century. Historians know that hindsight is never actually twenty-twenty. Still, the capacity to take the long view is one of the great advantages that historians enjoy over the people who lived through historical events. Over the course of the twentieth century, we have had ample opportunity to see the emergence of nationalist movements and the collapse of imperial rule. These historical processes took place on a continental scale in the wake of World War II, and when discussing events in Africa and Asia commentators regularly discuss them both in terms of national liberation and through the lens of decolonization. In the Americas and Europe however, where anti-imperial independence movements took place earlier in the modern era, scholars use the concept of decolonization less often. It is worth asking, therefore, whether the revolutions and rebellions of the late eighteenth and early nineteenth centuries in the Americas and the rise of new states in the wake of World War I in Europe were decolonizing movements before their time.

As we engage in these comparisons, it might be helpful to identify a general historical pattern and logic of decolonization. I will suggest that the process of decolonization takes place in four basic stages. Phase one is the *imperial challenge* stage. In this formative period of decolonization, certain members of colonized communities build anti-imperial political movements that have the capacity to grow in their legitimacy and authority in the region in question. It helps, but is not necessary, for a corresponding movement to be developing in the metropole that casts doubt on the usefulness or morality of the imperial project.[13] Nationalism has historically been a powerful contributor to these calculations of legitimacy and

---

[13] On the impact of this process in the metropole in the early modern period, see Anthony Pagden, *Lords of All the World: Ideologies of Empire in Spain, Britain, and France, c.1500–c.1800* (New Haven: Yale University Press, 1995).

authority in both the metropole and the periphery in the modern era, but again it is not logically necessary. It also helps if the imperial state sees a reduction in its capacity to physically control or effectively govern the areas under its rule, either as a result of economic crisis, military defeat, or some other event.

Phase two is the *state failure* stage. Here we should note that decolonization necessarily entails state failure. Revolutionaries frequently imagine that they can simply take over the apparatus of the state, seize the "commanding heights," engrave new nameplates for their offices, and make the bureaucracies function as they desire. They are always disappointed. States are much more than formal positions and capital city office buildings. They are also systems of personalized networks of power and of routinized authority and submission. Just as importantly, states are defined by their capacity to legitimate and control violence. As a result, independence requires the demise of one set of personalized networks, the end of habitual authority and submission, and the delegitimization and loss of control over violence before a new "state" can be built. There need be no causal relationship between imperial challenge and state failure. As we will see in this book, state failure does not need to be brought on by anti-imperial revolutionaries. Imperial states can self-destruct, either knowingly or unintentionally.

The outcome of state failure is, if not inevitable, at least predictable. With the collapse of previous legitimating mechanisms for violence, the scope for "violent entrepreneurship" is greatly enhanced.[14] Aspirants for power, wealth, or pleasure can create or utilize organizations of violence in the period of open and violent competition that accompanies the process of state failure and attempts at state building. These violent organizations may be formal military units, but they are just as frequently loosely organized paramilitary units or even what are best described as gangs. The rise of competitive violent entrepreneurs, in turn, deeply affects economies, since the role of violence in the economy, hidden, legitimated, and routinized under successful states, now assumes a much more prominent role, tilting the economic balance towards those who are expert in violence and away from those who are expert in managing capital, engaging in commerce, or performing peaceful labor. This shift toward non-productive extraction and the crippling of existing economic systems does not lead to general prosperity. At the same time, the rise of the class of violent entrepreneurs transforms social relations. Fear and insecurity lead many citizens to withdraw from public spaces and social interactions. Many others evacuate zones in which conducting a normal life has become nearly impossible and exceedingly dangerous.

Thus the phase of state failure frequently leads to a *social disaster* phase of decolonization. People abandon their jobs, flee their homes, join up with organizations of violence, and fight for a share of what has now become a rapidly dwindling resource base of economic goods and political support. As poverty spreads and whatever social or state institutions responsible for providing relief or

[14] I borrow this term from Vadim Volkov. See his insightful and stimulating volume on violence in the Russian economy during the 1990s. Vadim Volkov, *Violent Entrepreneurs: The Use of Force in the Making of Russian Capitalism* (Ithaca, N.Y.: Cornell University Press, 2002).

health care crumble, famine and pestilence often make their presence felt. These, in turn, destroy social relations even more, as neighbors hoard food, hospitality carries risk of mortal illness, and desperate people sever their social ties with their fellow townspeople or villagers in order to seek a better place. Unless arrested quickly, this social disaster phase can lead to an apocalyptic death spiral, as the experience not only of Russia during the Civil War attests, but also of places like Congo and Somalia in our own time.

The question then becomes, how and when does phase four, the *state-building* stage, take place? The cynical answer might be: we don't know yet. Decolonization severely damaged European polities and societies, and the process of state-building in Eastern Europe during the seventy years following the end of the war was, as a result, marked by an unusually high prevalence of bloody political factionalism and outright dictatorship. This dark period is one that many peoples in Africa and Asia are still experiencing, which again suggests a strong parallel between these separate episodes of imperial collapse. Less cynically, we might note that all states are works-in-progress and that state institutions of course emerged and strengthened in Eastern Europe in the 1920s. Nevertheless, I suggest that we might understand these new states more fully if we classed them not only as revolutionary, or democratic, or national, but also as postcolonial. This book, in any case, is concerned with the first three phases of decolonization, and it focuses on the ways that war and decolonization overlapped in areas on the Eastern Front. That front was a zone of vibrant diversity, as it had been for many centuries.

IMPERIAL BORDERLANDS ON THE EVE OF THE WAR

Medieval Eastern Europe was a patchwork of independent kingdoms and mostly autonomous principalities. The early modern age of empire laid waste to nearly all of them. The list of vanquished countries includes some later resurrected into modern states, such as the kingdoms of Georgia, Serbia, and Armenia, and others whose names only reappear in moments of international crisis: Courland, Livonia, Galicia, the Khanate of Crimea. Between the fourteenth and eighteenth centuries, these lands were fought over, traded back and forth, and incorporated into one of the six great imperial states of Eastern Europe: the Ottoman Empire, Russia, Austria, Prussia, Sweden, and the Polish-Lithuanian Commonwealth. At the turn of the seventeenth century, it appeared that Russia might not survive this political jostling. In 1603, Poland invaded a Russia mired in dynastic crisis and civil war and established a puppet government there. Violent revolts by the occupied Russians proved successful, however, and by 1613 a new dynasty (the Romanovs) had been installed. Poland remained a major player throughout the seventeenth century, famously sending emergency troops to Vienna in 1683 to break the Ottoman siege of the Habsburg capital city. This event proved to be the high-water mark for both the Ottomans and the Poles, however. Over the course of the eighteenth century, the Prussians, Austrians, and Russians continued to gain power and territory, while the Poles, Swedes, and Ottomans weakened. The Russian army under

Peter the Great (r. 1682–1725) and Catherine the Great (r. 1762–1796) drove this dramatic shift of regional power.

Peter was the author of Russian success in the north. The Great Northern War (1700–1721) was ruinously expensive in lives and treasure, but the defeat of Sweden allowed Russia to annex the lands on the eastern and southeastern shores of the Baltic (a territory that ranged from St. Petersburg to Riga and which is now part Russian and partly in Estonia and Latvia). Peter's attempt to achieve a similar victory in the south against the Ottoman Empire failed, however. Another fifty years elapsed before the great breakthroughs along the northern shore of the Black Sea occurred, with a series of victories over the Ottomans and their allies (such as the Crimean Khanate) in the 1760s and 1770s. The Treaty of Kuchuk–Kainarji in 1774 consolidated these gains, opening up new lands for Russian colonization in what is today mostly southern Ukraine. These victories also allowed Russia to move along both the western and the eastern shores of the Black Sea. In the west, they created a land bridge to the Balkans. In the east, the victories not only over the Ottomans but over the Persians as well led to the annexation of Transcaucasia (Georgia, Armenia, and Azerbaijan) by 1828.

The most dramatic shift, however, was the utter destruction of the Polish state. In 1700, Poland was one of Eastern Europe's powerhouses. In 1800, it no longer existed. The Great Northern War was devastating for the Poles. Swedish armies invaded Poland during the war, capturing Warsaw in 1702 and forcing the abdication of August II in 1704. Russian troops soon drove away the Swedes, and when August II was reinstalled on the throne in 1715, the Polish state became a "Russian puppet."[15] This puppet state was enormous, stretching from the Oder River in the West to the Dnipro in the East—from the gates of Kiev to Kraków and beyond. It incorporated not only all of modern-day Poland and Lithuania, but Belarus and large chunks of Ukraine, Latvia, Moldova, Germany, and Russia as well. Almost immediately, the Austrian and Prussian governments, along with Polish elites, contested Russian dominance. The result of this struggle was a series of partitions of Poland that, between 1772 and 1795, divided the country three ways, with Russia getting roughly the eastern half of the old Polish empire and Prussia and Austria splitting the west. The territory of the old Polish-Lithuanian Commonwealth would comprise, almost completely, the war lands of the Eastern Front (see Map 1).

This history of states tells only part of the story of these imperial borderlands. The social dynamics of the region were just as important. Class, religious affiliation, and ethnicity merged in unusual ways. Very frequently, nobles spoke a different language from their peasants. German landowners in the Baltic region governed estates composed of Latvians, Estonians, and Lithuanians. Polish nobles owned Ukrainian serfs, colonizing Russian nobles in the nineteenth century exploited Polish peasants, and even in Russia, the Russian nobility felt more comfortable speaking French than the language of their field hands. Commercial occupations

---

[15] Anita J. Prazmowska, *A History of Poland* (New York: Palgrave Macmillan, 2004), 119.

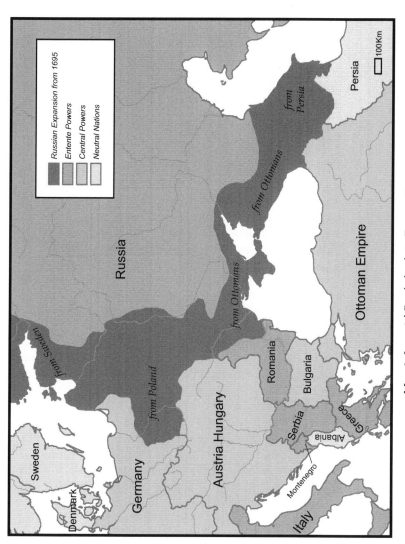

Map 1 Imperial Borderlands in Eastern Europe

were similarly ethnicized. Armenians and Greeks were significant players in the Ottoman trading system, and Jews played a similar role in Russia. The Russian Empire largely confined Jews to the Pale of Settlement and restricted their ability to own land. Jews therefore dominated retail enterprises in vast swathes of the region, buying and selling from Slavic peasants. The social conflict inherent in the trading relationship only exacerbated the anti-Semitism that was endemic throughout Eastern Europe.

Religion played a large role not only in the development of anti-Semitism, but also in the broader social and cultural world in which people lived. The pagan communities that occupied the region were targeted for conversion in the tenth century. Eastern Orthodox Christianity was the most successful enterprise, extending from Greece through much of the Eastern Balkans and Ukraine into Russia. The predecessor state to both modern Ukraine and modern Russia, the state of Kievan Rus', adopted Orthodoxy in 988. A couple of decades earlier, in 966, Piast Poland had adopted Roman Catholicism. In the succeeding centuries, Islam and Protestantism (mostly in the form of Lutheranism) would also gain adherents in the region. Religious community, even more than linguistic or political community, provided the basis for self-identification for most residents in the region well into the modern era.

Finally, it was important that serfdom had dominated the lands of the Russian Empire until the 1860s. Serf owners (including the Romanov family and the Russian state itself) had encouraged agriculture far more than industry, and they had thwarted educational initiatives, civic development, and urban growth. The specter of serf revolt left them fearful of mass action and resistant to the trend toward social homogenization developing in nascent nation-states in Western Europe. As a result, it was only after the serf emancipations that the great underlying social motors of nationalism—primary schooling, mass media, industrial economies, and universal military conscription—would begin to develop in the Russian Empire. Simultaneously, the decision of the imperial state to prevent the establishment of elected local government and the reformed court system in the borderlands created a tangible differentiation between "core" and "periphery" in the empire that had previously been much more difficult to define.[16] For all of these reasons, mass anti-imperial movements were slow to develop in the Russian Empire. Religious communities were difficult to politicize, linguistic communities were separated by physical and social space, and the state consciously thwarted mechanisms of mass mobilization. In 1860, it was impossible to conceive of a

---

[16] Alexander Morrison, "Metropole, Colony, and Imperial Citizenship in the Russian Empire," *Kritika: Explorations in Russian and Eurasian History* 13, no. 2 (Spring 2012): 341. On indeterminacy of core and periphery in the Russian Empire and the late nineteenth-century efforts to define this distinction more clearly, see Jane Burbank and Mark von Hagen, "Coming into the Territory: Uncertainty and Empire," in *Russian Empire: Space, People, Power, 1700–1930*, ed. Jane Burbank, Mark von Hagen, and Anatolyi Remnev (Bloomington: Indiana University Press, 2007), 1–32; Leonid Gorizontov, "The 'Great Circle' of Interior Russia: Representations of the Imperial Center in the Nineteenth and Early Twentieth Centuries," in Burbank, von Hagen, and Remnev, *Russian Empire,* 67–93.

successful independence movement by Latvians, Estonians, Lithuanians, or Ukrainians. Only Poles (and then largely the Poles in the "Congress Kingdom," shorn of the Lithuanian, Belorussian, and Ukrainian populations of the old Commonwealth) had the capacity for nationalist rebellion. Poles demonstrated this capacity repeatedly, not only in the fighting that surrounded the partitions, but also in major rebellions in 1830–1831 and in 1863. In each case, the insurrections fell victim to the last factor that inhibited independence movements—the might of the Russian army. When serfdom ended, therefore, there was little fuel for the nationalist fire.

That situation would begin to change in the fifty years between the end of serfdom and the outbreak of World War I. All of the great Eastern European empires saw significant industrial growth in this period. Education levels rose even in the most benighted territories of the Russian Empire. Each state adopted universal conscription (Russia was the last to do so, in 1874), thereby sending millions of young peasant men into a nationalizing institution, and political figures took ever more account of a widening "public" that threatened to encompass the whole "people."

Nationalist movements therefore grew quite rapidly during the pre-war era. Ukrainian nationalism first took hold in the Habsburg domains of western Galicia, but nationalist activism among a thin educated elite soon crossed the border into the Russian Empire. Similarly, in different ways and at different paces, the national idea developed in Belarus, Lithuania, Latvia, Estonia, Finland, Georgia, and Armenia. Officials in the Ministry of Internal Affairs also observed with concern an "exceptional rise in the religious and national-cultural self-consciousness" of the Muslim population.[17]

Just as nationalism grew among colonial peoples in the periphery, so too did it strengthen among Russians. The Russian Empire had become the most extensive empire in the world in large part due to a high level of flexibility in its administration of new territories and peoples. Ever since the sixteenth century, empire-builders had favored the policy of co-opting local elites and delegating significant political responsibility and cultural authority to the "native chiefs." This strategy fit well with a conservative, dynastic empire, and it was accompanied by a "non-uniform and inconsistent governance" that proved able to manage "a multiplicity of social arrangements within a single state."[18] Inconsistent governance did not mean weakness. To the contrary, the techniques employed to bind these imperial intermediaries to the autocrat were remarkably effective.[19] In the second half of the nineteenth century, however, these traditional bases of rule were being challenged from within as surely as they were from without. The Russian imperial elite

[17] Letter from A. A. Makarov to N. V. Pleve (Minister of Internal Affairs), 13 August 1912, in D. Arapov, "'Vo vsem musul'manskom mire nabliudaetsia chrezvychainyi pod"em religioznogo i natsional'no-kul'turnogo samosoznaniia': Ministerstvo vnutrennykh del i 'musul'manskii vopros'," *Istochnik* 55, no. 1 (2002): 61.

[18] Burbank and von Hagen, 15.

[19] Jane Burbank and Frederick Cooper, *Empires in World History: Power and the Politics of Difference* (Princeton: Princeton University Press, 2010), 193.

became more and more nationalistic as the nineteenth century progressed, and calls grew louder with each passing year for the Russian Empire to openly trumpet its Russian nature, to create a "Russia for the Russians," and to "tilt in the direction of uniformity as a new principle of state."[20]

Again, the Great Reform era surrounding the emancipation of the serfs provided the turning point. The Polish insurrection of 1863 was the most important catalyst for change, because it convinced the tsar and his advisors that the co-optation of the Polish elite was impossible. The Polish gentry would never become reconciled to Russian rule. When the military gained the upper hand, the state therefore embarked on a systematic effort to eviscerate the upper-class base of Polish nationalism. In addition to executing 400 of the top leaders, Tsar Alexander II exiled over 20,000 nobles and confiscated roughly 3,500 of their estates. Russian administrators took over Polish universities. Even the name "Poland" was eliminated in favor of the euphemistic designation of the "Vistula region" (*Privislinskii krai*).[21] If this was not yet Russification, it was a very conscious de-Polonization of the cultural, economic, social, and political elite.

The insurrection also forced state officials to consider how the Great Reforms would affect imperial power. Most importantly, the measures taken to improve education and to relax censorship of both books and periodicals forced Russian imperialists to squarely face the political aspects of language questions. The response, which unfolded fitfully and inconsistently over the course of twenty years, was to embark on a program of cultural Russification. Russification extended far beyond Poland. In the summer of 1863, the government moved to ban books written in the Ukrainian language. The Ministry of Internal Affairs insisted that such a language did not exist—that normal peasants in the region were Russian-speaking Russians who had simply been linguistically compromised by their Polish neighbors. A large campaign to convert Catholics to Orthodoxy also took place at this time, with the result that nearly 60,000 Catholics from Belarus were pressured into adopting a new faith. These repressive measures continued, indeed intensified, during the reign of Alexander III (1881–1894) and together constituted the new policy of Russification. Alexander III extended these policies northward, where the privileges of the Germanic nobility in the Baltic provinces came under assault. The state made Russian the language of schooling in the region for the first time, and the German university in Dorpat was Russified in 1893.[22]

In certain respects, these Russification policies succeeded. Preventing nationalist intellectuals from reaching their nations through schools or the press undoubtedly hindered the activities of anti-colonial activists as they sought to build mass movements. Overall, however, Russification proved counterproductive. In 1860, few lower-class people in the Russian Empire thought of their ethnicity as an important political fact. To the extent they were politicized, it was regarding issues

---

[20] Burbank and von Hagen, 17.

[21] Andreas Kappeler, *The Russian Empire: A Multiethnic History*, trans. Alfred Clayton (Harlow, England: Longman/Pearson, 2001), 253.

[22] Kappeler, 258.

surrounding social estate and economic condition. Their political opponents were local ones, not bureaucrats in faraway St. Petersburg. In 1863, when nearly all of the Polish nobility and intelligentsia rebelled, very few Polish peasants joined them. Peasants further to the south rarely used the word "Ukrainian" as a self-designation, and most other national movements remained stuck at the stage of gathering folklore and founding small national societies. In 1860, nearly all Eastern European national movements were still in a very early phase of cultural awakening.[23] Absent the collision between the two national movements that had become openly politicized—the Polish and the Russian—it is difficult to imagine a widespread nationalist challenge to the Romanov throne that would have any chance of success.

Russification was on balance a gift to nationalists. It provided a concrete political program that fellow nationals up and down the social ladder could understand. Russification entailed assaults on churches, languages, and schools at the precise moment when the Great Reforms were creating conditions in which the social bases of nationalism could develop. Almost immediately, throughout the region, national movements saw greater and greater success as they moved from cultural collection to political agitation. This agitation coincided with similar efforts to reach "the people" by the left-wing intelligentsia, a group that moved from populism to Marxism over the course of the last two decades of the nineteenth century. Socialism and nationalism therefore shared some important goals, and several different groups experimented to find the right balance, from the independence-seeking Social Democratic Mensheviks in Georgia to the Polish Socialist Party (PPS) led by Józef Piłsudski. Nationalism and socialism symbiotically grew together throughout the period.

Both movements developed yet further in the final decade before the war. The revolutionary events of 1905 clearly demonstrated the capacity of nationalist politicians to mobilize crowds. Nearly all indicators of political engagement and revolutionary violence were higher in the borderlands than they were in central Russia. Not all of this activity was directed against the tsarist state—intense violence between Armenians and Azerbaijanis left thousands dead, and a wave of anti-Jewish pogroms swept across the western empire, for instance—but most of it was. There were more strikes, more uprisings, and more executions of rebels in Poland and Georgia than there were in other parts of the empire.[24]

The 1905 Revolution also laid the basis for further nationalist development in structural ways. Most importantly, the creation of an imperial parliament (the Duma) allowed for open political campaigning and the creation of nationalist political parties.[25] Poland again took the lead, with the PPS signing up more than 50,000 members by 1906, but nationalist agitation occurred nearly everywhere.

---

[23] In Miroslav Hroch's formulation, nearly all were still in Phase A of national development. Miroslav Hroch, *Social Preconditions of National Revival in Europe: A Comparative Analysis of the Social Composition of Patriotic Grounds among the Smaller European Nations* (Cambridge: Cambridge University Press, 1985).

[24] Kappeler, 333.

[25] See here Rustem Tsiunchiuk, "Peoples, Regions, and Electoral Politics: The State Dumas and the Constitution of New National Elites," in Burbank, von Hagen, and Remnev, 366–97.

Russia was once more no exception. The most important political figure of the Duma period, Prime Minister Petr Stolypin, repeatedly tapped into the reservoir of Russian nationalism for support, promoting policies that favored the development of a "Great Russia," while keeping the far-right Russian nationalists at arm's length. Right-wing Russian nationalists of both the radical and conservative sort also struggled openly with the tension between empire and nation in the last decade before the war.[26]

In many respects, then, the colonial spaces that formed the imperial borderlands in 1914 seemed ripe for the maturation of independence movements. Nationalist elites existed throughout the region, the population was beginning to see the world in nationalist terms, and politicians forwarded concrete political parties and political programs. But for all of this, political independence for the Poles, much less for the Ukrainians, Latvians, or Georgians, was nearly as far away as it had been in 1860. None of these movements was even close to garnering the political and military power it would need to defeat the Russian Empire. The uprisings in 1905 had proven this just as surely as the failed uprisings of 1830 and 1863 had. The Russian state was strong and growing stronger, and imperialism was becoming more and more popular amongst the increasingly influential Russian public. Stolypin's political program in the western borderlands, which sought to strengthen the state while continuing to Russify it, provided evidence of the vitality of Russian imperialism in its very last years. Indeed, the parliamentary period represented its own type of elite co-optation. As nationalists were elected to office and sent to St. Petersburg, they learned to work within the system. They knew as well as anyone how futile an armed uprising would be, and they normally sought to achieve incremental gains of autonomy by playing the game the right way in the metropole and hoping to leverage the proximity of the German and Austro-Hungarian empires to their own benefit. Few nationalists ringing in the new year in 1914 would have predicted that within four years, their chance for independence would be upon them. The catalyst for decolonization would have to come from elsewhere.

THE BALKAN BEGINNINGS OF THE GREAT WAR

As it turned out, that "elsewhere" was the Balkan peninsula, where imperial rivalries had reached the crisis stage and the process of decolonization had matured. Recent scholarship has begun the process of restoring Balkan history to a central rather than epiphenomenal place in the history of the Great War, and with good reason. As Alan Kramer has noted, the well-documented fact that certain predispositions for war existed among certain key constituencies in the Great Powers "does not explain why war broke out in 1914, rather than 1910 or 1918, or why it became a European and world war." For that, he claims, one needs to seek answers in the

---

[26] M. N. Luk'ianov, " 'Rossiia – dlia russkikh' ili 'Rossiia dlia russkikh poddannykh'? Konservatory i natsional'nyi vopros nakanune pervoi mirovoi voiny," *Otechestvennaia istoriia* no. 2 (2006): 36–46.

Balkans.[27] Events on that peninsula moved quite quickly in the early years of the century. The successful coup of radical Serbian nationalists in 1903 and the large uprising against Ottoman rule in Macedonia in the same year changed the political landscape on the ground quite substantially, mainly by demonstrating the strength of anti-Habsburg and anti-Ottoman sentiment. Then, the weakening of Russia as a result of the Russo-Japanese War and the Revolution of 1905 transformed the international balance of power once more. In the summer of 1908, the Young Turk revolution in Macedonia further destabilized the sultan's regime, leading many to expect a major political transformation throughout the region.

The accelerating Ottoman collapse led the Russian foreign minister, Aleksandr Izvol'skii, to make a risky play from a poor position. The Habsburgs had been granted a thirty-year term of occupation of Bosnia-Herzegovina by the 1878 Treaty of Berlin, and all the Great Powers knew that Austria-Hungary wanted to annex the region permanently upon the expiration of that term in 1908.[28] Izvol'skii, knowing that his weakened army was in no position to stop them, sought to leverage his position by offering to acquiesce to an Austro-Hungarian annexation of Bosnia if the Habsburgs stood by quietly while the Russians expanded their access and influence in the Turkish Straits. However, the announcement that the Austrians were annexing Bosnia so angered Russian (and Serbian) public opinion that Izvol'skii had to pivot and publicly denounce the annexation he had just secretly endorsed. Russia issued partial mobilization orders and rattled its sabers, but to little effect. In March 1909, Germany threatened both military action and the exposure of Izvol'skii's back-room diplomacy. The French proved justifiably reluctant to launch a continental war to expand Russian naval power or to save Izvol'skii's reputation. Unable to rely on its allies, its still crippled army, or even its own foreign minister, Russia backed down. Among the sobering lessons of the crisis was that Austria enjoyed more reliable support from Germany than Russia did from France and Britain. As a result, Russian foreign policy experts were ironically drawn even closer to the Balkan states, which they hoped they could depend on more when the chips were down.[29] At the same time, the "almost unprecedented debate" regarding imperial policy showcased the much more prominent role that Duma figures and "public opinion" played in the post-1905 order.[30] Russian policy, as a consequence, tilted more toward the romantic views of nation and empire shared by much of the educated elite.

The Austrian diplomatic success not only humiliated the Russians, but it also angered the Serbian government, which had been on increasingly bad terms with the Habsburg Empire and was locked in a crippling tariff war with it. Dreams of a

---

[27] Alan Kramer, *Dynamic of Destruction: Culture and Mass Killing in the First World War* (Oxford: Oxford University Press, 2007), 72. Christopher Clark takes this observation even further and spends most of the early sections of his book on the July Crisis exploring Balkan histories. See Clark, *The Sleepwalkers.*

[28] Clark, 83.

[29] Andrew Rossos, *Russia and the Balkans: Inter-Balkan Rivalries and Russian Foreign Policy, 1908–1914* (Toronto: University of Toronto Press, 1981), 6.

[30] Rossos, 8.

Greater Serbia depended on acquiring Bosnia, Macedonia, and Albania (also still part of the Ottoman Empire). The Bosnian annexation demonstrated the continued strength of Austria-Hungary in the region, but it did nothing to prop up the Ottoman state. With Russia chastened and the Habsburgs satisfied, the young Balkan states took the lead in bringing about an end to the "Eastern Question" and launching an intensive wave of decolonizing activity. Bulgaria, which had been functionally independent since 1878, took advantage of Ottoman weakness by demanding full independence and formal recognition, which it received after some hasty trilateral monetary negotiations with St. Petersburg and Istanbul in 1908.[31] In 1910, Nicholas of Montenegro had himself declared a constitutional monarch and intensified his activity in the neighboring Ottoman domains of Albania. Albania, long a multiethnic and polyglot province on the edge of the Ottoman Empire, was prime territory for such adventurism. King Nicholas promised the (largely Catholic) population of northern Albania that he would support them if they were to rebel against the Ottoman state, and the rebellion duly occurred in early 1911. The Ottomans responded with force, and Nicholas permitted the overmatched rebels to cross the border to safety in his realm. The Ottomans threatened to cross the border themselves to attack the insurgents, an event that would have meant war. Russian mediation prevented war from occurring, as Russian diplomats calmed down the Montenegrin king and forced the Ottomans to make such substantial concessions toward autonomy for the Albanian rebels that they could return home feeling secure and vindicated. This was neither the first nor the last time that political actors in the Balkans forced the pace of change well beyond what was desired by their nominal patron, Russia. The Russian Foreign Ministry was locked in a reactive mode, scrambling to respond to actions taken without its support and frequently without its knowledge.

No sooner had this crisis been resolved than the Ottomans were forced into further territorial concessions, this time by a much larger party than Montenegro. Italy occupied the North African Ottoman province of Tripoli in the late summer of 1911, and the Ottomans declared war that September. This Tripolitan War immediately changed the political calculations of Balkan politicians. The leaders of Serbia, Bulgaria, Montenegro, and Greece, who had watched each other warily for the better part of the past decade (in particular in Macedonia), now quickly hammered out a series of bilateral military and political conventions. In March 1912, Serbia allied with Bulgaria. In May 1912, the Greeks and the Bulgarians did the same. In the late summer, Montenegro joined the group with a series of oral and written agreements that were finally ratified on 13 September/2 October, less than a week before Montenegro declared war on the Ottoman Empire. The sum of these agreements was an alliance called the Balkan League.

Russia, which had long desired such an alliance to counterbalance Austro-Hungarian power on the peninsula, lent its considerable diplomatic support to the formation of the Balkan League. As the negotiations progressed, however,

---

[31] Edward C. Thaden, *Russia and the Balkan Alliance of 1912* (University Park, PA: Penn State University Press, 1965), 39.

Russian officials grew increasingly concerned. The Foreign Ministry knew that Russia was not militarily or diplomatically ready for a Balkan conflict and continually reminded its Balkan clients that all of these new alliances should be strictly defensive in nature. In 1912, however, Balkan leaders openly threatened to ignore their patron. The Bulgarian finance minister informed Izvol'skii (who had been demoted to ambassador to France in 1910) that Russia had to allow Bulgaria "freedom of action" at such an auspicious moment of Ottoman weakness. Izvol'skii duly warned his boss, S. D. Sazonov, that the new military convention between Serbia and Bulgaria was in fact an "offensive" alliance.[32]

The final collapse of Ottoman power in Europe, so long predicted, now seemed imminent. Powerful politicians across the continent were unsettled by these developments, which promised to recalibrate the relationship between the Great Powers. For Russia and Austria-Hungary in particular, victory in the scramble for Southeastern Europe promised continued prestige and power for future generations, while defeat might mean dropping out of the club of imperial giants and deeply weakening the prospects of their allies in the process. In retrospect, it is easy to see why diplomats were so concerned by the flow of events. A war in the Balkans clearly had the potential to create a new imperial pecking order. What those diplomats did not see was that the Balkan Wars would launch an era of conflict that would do much more than unbalance the existing system of imperial power relationships; it would destroy them entirely. The venerable old states continued to treat the new Balkan nations as children, though by now, in Tsar Nicholas II's memorable words, they viewed them as "well-behaved youngsters . . . grown up to become stubborn hooligans."[33]

Those "hooligans" turned out to have strong and effective armies. In 1912, they quickly routed Ottoman forces. Greek troops took Salonika just hours before the Bulgarians arrived. Montenegrin troops pushed southward along the Adriatic. Serbia moved into western Macedonia as the Bulgarians pushed the Ottomans nearly back to Istanbul. These rapid successes sent the Great Powers into a frenzied tizzy of activity. In contrast to 1878, however, when Great Power noncombatants had benefitted from the Balkan Wars, the most they could do at this stage was to contain Serbian ambitions on the Adriatic by insisting on the establishment of an independent Albania. The Second Balkan War broke out in 1913, when Bulgaria, seething about Serbian advances in Macedonia, launched an ill-considered attack on its erstwhile ally. The Second Balkan War ended quickly, as all of Bulgaria's neighbors pounced on it and carved off territories for themselves.

The two Balkan Wars had removed the Ottoman factor from the political equation on the Balkan peninsula, but from the Serb perspective they only served to heighten emotions regarding Austro-Hungarian rule over Slavs in the region. All Serb politicians knew that a reckoning with the Habsburg Empire would require strong Russian support, and the Serbian government did its best to maintain

---

[32] E. G. Kostrikova, *Rossiiskoe obshchestvo i vneshniaia politika nakanune pervoi mirovoi voiny, 1908–1914* (Moscow: IRI RAN, 2007), 196–7.
[33] Cited in Clark, 275.

excellent relations with its large eastern ally. Even Austrophiles such as the former Serbian prime minister Vladan Georgievic lobbied visiting Russian military figures, assuring them that the "whole Serbian people" would rise up against Austria, while chiding them for the "timid waverings of Russian policy."[34] Still, most Serb leaders knew that their depleted army needed time to recover and that they needed a period of peace to consolidate their remarkable gains.[35] Prime Minister Nikola Pašić believed that it was in Serbia's best interest for the Austrians to be regional players for the next twenty-five years or so, as this would give Serbia time to consolidate its gains in the south.[36] Even the Central Executive Committee of the radical nationalist group called the Black Hand, when learning ahead of time of the covert operation to assassinate Franz Ferdinand sponsored by its own members, tried to squash the plan. As Joachim Remak noted, "The Committee members were not exactly squeamish – many of them had been among the regicides of 1903, and all of them were satisfied that the pan-Serb aim justified violence. Yet when confronted with this bald plan for killing the Austrian heir to the throne, they sobered, for it was plain that they might be inviting war."[37] Pašić was in fact so concerned about the prospect of provoking Austria that when he learned that young men armed with bombs and pistols (including Gavrilo Princip) had been smuggled across the border, he tasked his subordinates with stopping them and preventing further bands from infiltrating Bosnia on the eve of the archduke's visit.[38] But neither the leaders of the Black Hand nor the leader of the Serbian government were willing to betray their comrades or the fact of their knowledge by alerting the Austrians, not least because they had no stomach for appearing to side with the imperial power rather than with young nationalist radicals.[39] Pašić, notes Christopher Clark, had "an intense sensitivity to public opinion, a need to feel attuned to the Serb nation in whose cause he had suffered and worked."[40] All the Central Committee could do was order the mastermind of the plot, Col. Dragutin Dimitrijević, to contact his subordinates and call it off. He did not do so.

On 15/28 June 1914, Princip fired the shots that would start the Third Balkan War, killing Franz Ferdinand and his wife Sophie in the Bosnian capital of Sarajevo. The assassination of Franz Ferdinand was not just a pretext for an already inevitable war. It engaged European leaders and citizenries at multiple levels. There was the question of imperial rivalry, of course, as always. So too was this an instance of uncoordinated action by a small group of violent political entrepreneurs. As we

---

[34] E. I. Martynov, *Serby v voine s Tsarem Ferdinandom (zametki ochevidtsa)* (Moscow: P. P. Riabushinskii, 1913), 13–14.

[35] James M. B. Lyon, "'A Peasant Mob': The Serbian Army on the Eve of the Great War," *The Journal of Military History* 61 (July 1997): 499.

[36] Iu. A. Pisarev, *Tainy pervoi mirovoi voiny: Rossiia i Serbiia v 1914–1915 gg.* (Moscow: Nauka, 1990), 30.

[37] Joachim Remak, *Sarajevo, the Story of a Political Murder* (New York: Criterion Books, 1959), 77.

[38] Vladimir Dedijer, *The Road to Sarajevo* (New York: Simon and Schuster, 1966), 390; Clark, 57.

[39] Dedijer, 395. There has been significant dispute regarding the question of whether Pašić tried to warn the Austrians about the plot in either general or specific terms. Dedijer believes he did not, while Clark suspects that he did.

[40] Clark, 19.

have seen, the plot was far from being part of a master plan of liberation on the part of the Serbian elites, who did not want to take their battered army into the field while hoping for the support of a Russian military machine that was in a period of significant transition. But it mattered that the July Crisis began with a terrorist act committed by a conspirator linked to the boldest representative of decolonization—Serbia—for the cause of a Greater Serbia. The response of many important actors, in particular Kaiser Wilhelm, was quite visceral.[41] The assassins were savages and Serbia simply had to be put in its place.

Radical Serbs did not view the act as barbaric. To the contrary, they cheered its cool, self-sacrificial martyrdom and saw it as a reasonable and productive instance of what we would today call asymmetrical warfare on the part of the oppressed against an imperial machine that commanded far more resources than they did. In Russia, feelings about the assassination were mixed (often within the same person), but in Germany and Austria the horror over the murder helped those who sought war win the very contentious struggles within the policy elite. The importance of the discourse on atrocity reached all the way down to Gavrilo Princip, the assassin himself, who maintained throughout his interrogation and trial that the killing of Franz Ferdinand was a legitimate political act. But Princip had also killed the archduke's wife Sophie. When asked why he had done this, Princip claimed that he had been aiming at General Potiorek (the regional commander in Bosnia who was riding in the same car) but had been jostled during the shot. He was almost certainly telling the truth. Still, for most of the time he appeared to shrug off Sophie's death as an instance of acceptable collateral damage. During the trial, however, it emerged that Franz Ferdinand's last words had been an anguished and futile plea: "Sophie dear! Sophie dear! Don't die! Stay alive for our children!" After this testimony, the moved court took a brief recess so that all parties could retain their composure. One of the defense lawyers approached the normally imperturbable Princip during the break to ask whether the testimony had left an impression on him. Princip, flustered, threw up his hands and asked "Do you think I am an animal?"[42]

This was a question that much of Europe had already asked and answered in various ways by the time of Princip's trial in October 1914. It would, indeed, become a question that would be asked of many other Europeans in the following years, as the issues of terror and atrocity rose to such significance. The ground for the accusations of barbarism in Belgium, France, East Prussia, Galicia, Armenia, and Serbia itself was well laid. The war itself was not inevitable, but it was inevitable that once the war came it would be a war "for civilization" in which atrocity would play an important role. Just as importantly, Princip's radical act had exposed the volatile relationship between imperial competition and anti-colonial activism at the

---

[41] See here the Kaiser's marginalia on two key memos in June and July 1914, the tenor of which (i.e. "The Serbs must be disposed of, and that right soon!") left no doubt in ministerial minds that he desired war. These memos are translated in Imanuel Geiss, ed., *July 1914, The Outbreak of the First World War: Selected Documents* (New York: Charles Scribner's Sons, 1967), 60–1 and 106–7.

[42] Remak, 222.

moment when both of these carried extremely explosive potential. The process of decolonization had moved well into a mature phase in the Balkans by June 1914. The Austrian assault on Serbia in July not only internationalized the conflict between those two states but allowed decolonization to move beyond the imperial challenge stage throughout Eastern Europe as a whole.

1

The Outbreak of War and the
Transformation of the Borderlands

Throughout the month of June, 1914, forest fires raged out of control near St. Petersburg. The smoke from the trees and peat bogs infiltrated the capital city, making it difficult to breathe.[1] In the middle of this hazy context, news of the Sarajevo murders on 15/28 June 1914 came to Russian policymakers unexpectedly. Nikola Pašić, the Serbian prime minister, quickly assured St. Petersburg that the Serbian government had not ordered the assassination, and the Russian government took him at his word. Indeed, Russian officials, as most leaders around Europe, thought it unlikely that the crime would lead to war. It was only weeks later, on 10/23 July, that the Austrian ultimatum to Serbia made clear the full seriousness of the crisis.[2] The Austrian note demanded the throttling of anti-Austrian propaganda, the arrest of all the figures already implicated in the plot (including two of the primary conspirators, Voja Tankosić and Milan Ciganović), and explanations for the continued hostility expressed by the Belgrade government. More provocatively, it also required Serbia to "agree that organs of the Imperial and Royal [Austro-Hungarian] Government assist in Serbia in the suppression of the subversive movement."[3] This struck many observers, including the British Foreign Secretary Edward Grey, as an unacceptable violation of Serbian sovereignty, and Vienna in fact assumed and hoped that the Serbs would reject the Austrian demands.[4] The ultimatum kicked off a week of intense diplomatic and military activity. On 13/26 July, the tsar ordered military districts in European Russia to move to a war preparation footing.[5] That process accelerated with the news that Austria had declared war on Serbia on 15/28 July. At this point, the tsar ordered a

---

[1] Z. G. Frenkel', "Zapiski o zhiznennom puti," *Voprosy istorii* no. 1 (2007): 79.

[2] Barbara Jelavich, *Russia's Balkan Entanglements, 1806–1914* (Cambridge: Cambridge University Press, 1991), 252–3.

[3] The text of the ultimatum may be found in Annika Mombauer, ed. and trans., *The Origins of the First World War: Diplomatic and Military Documents* (Manchester and New York: Manchester University Press, 2013), 291–5.

[4] Christopher Clark, *The Sleepwalkers: How Europe Went to War in 1914* (New York: Harper Collins, 2013), 451–7. Clark also points out, however, that the demand for a joint investigation was not as terrible as it might have appeared, as sovereignty had been quite conditional in the dramatic reshuffling of borders in the Balkans in recent years.

[5] Lieutenant-General Lukomskii, secret telegram to military district commanders in European Russia, 13 July 1914, in *Vostochno-Prusskaia operatsiia: sbornik dokumentov* (Moscow: Gosudarstvennoe voennoe izdatel'stvo Narodnogo Komissariata Oborony SSSR, 1939), 75.

partial mobilization of four military districts to be directed at Austria. Most of Nicholas' advisors by this time believed that war with Germany was unavoidable, and they urged the tsar both for technical and principled reasons to announce a general mobilization, but Nicholas held out hope until late on 17/30 July, when he finally accepted the need for the general mobilization. The next day, military officials posted call-up announcements around the empire, and the general mobilization began in earnest.[6]

The Russian people, however, only began concentrating on the international crisis a few days before the mobilization was announced. The mainstream Russian press, especially those newspapers read by non-elites such as *Gazeta kopeika* and *Russkoe slovo*, sharpened its focus with the news of Austria's ultimatum, so the reading public became aware of the danger starting on 11/24 July.[7] Those outside of this "public sphere" only realized that war was imminent when mobilization began. The reaction to the news of impending conflict varied from person to person, but it was strong everywhere. Large patriotic demonstrations took place in many areas of the country, though mobilization riots exploded as well.[8] Pessimists expected the Germans to be in Petrograd by September, while optimists up and down the social ladder thought a quick victory would allow Russians to even the score with the Teutonic states on their border.[9]

This was a war that Russian politicians, primary among them Nicholas II, hoped to avoid, or at least to defer. In contrast to their Germanic counterparts, Russian military men also preferred a diplomatic solution, hoping that Vienna could be made to back away from its maximalist position regarding Serbia. Officers pressed a hard line only after they were unpleasantly surprised by Nicholas' initial order to scuttle their mobilization plans in order to mobilize parts of four military districts against Austria.[10] Since everyone in Europe agreed that there was a question mark over Russian mobilization, even under ideal circumstances, the last thing the General Staff needed was to have a wrench thrown in the machinery at the very outset of the process. The rescinding of that order and the ordering of a general mobilization the following day was what top staffers successfully pressed for, but still they feared that the confusion in the four crucial districts in question (Kiev, Odessa, Moscow, and Kazan') would literally derail their ambitious plan to be prepared for battle within fifteen days. Some misunderstanding did occur. War Minister V. A. Sukhomlinov received complaints from some reservists who had only seen the original announcement that they had been illegally inducted, and the

---

[6] Copies of the string of telegrams sent out to military districts regarding mobilization may be found in RGVIA f. 2000, op. 3, d. 1154.

[7] Eric Lohr, "The Russian Press and the 'Internal Peace' at the Beginning of World War I," in *A Call to Arms: Propaganda, Public Opinion, and Newspapers in the Great War*, ed. Troy Paddock (Westport, CT: Praeger, 2004), 101.

[8] Josh Sanborn, "The Mobilization of 1914 and the Question of the Russian Nation: A Reexamination," *Slavic Review* 59, no. 2 (2000): 267–89.

[9] Mikhail Konstantinovich Lemke, *250 dnei v tsarskoi stavke: vospominaniia, memuary*, 2 vols. (Minsk: Kharvest, 2003), 1: 9–10. St Petersburg was rechristened Petrograd on 18/31 August 1914 in order to give the capital a less German, more Slavic name.

[10] The best account of Russia's road to the war remains D. C. B. Lieven, *Russia and the Origins of the First World War* (New York: St Martin's Press, 1983).

commander of the Turkestan Military District became so befuddled that he telegrammed back to Petersburg asking whether he should move south to commence hostilities on "another front."[11]

But the initial missteps only modestly affected mobilization. Nearly 4,000,000 men were called up on schedule, and General Pavel von Rennenkampf's First Army marched across the German border within fifteen days of mobilization, just as they had promised their French allies. Though not all of their men and equipment were firmly in place on that date, the First Army was sufficiently prepared to win the first major battle on the Eastern Front just nine days later at Gumbinnen. Given the decision of the Central Powers to send large numbers of their forces elsewhere (Belgium, France, and Serbia) in the first days of the war, Russia enjoyed numerical superiority and (as was then thought) the advantage of being on the offensive and fighting the war in enemy territory. The problems that would soon strike the army were not connected with their mobilization schedules.

Likewise, given the sour public response and mobilization difficulties associated with the Russo-Japanese War, it is difficult to characterize the national response to the declaration of war as anything other than a success. Even skeptical observers marveled at the difference between the mobilizations ten years apart.[12] Twenty-four of every twenty-five reservists responded to the call of the government, and every quarter of Russian society offered the army and the government its support.[13] As I have argued elsewhere, this public demonstration of loyalty did not entail enthusiasm for the war as such. Many Russians violently protested the war and the mobilization of men (and horses), but most of the public activity during the mobilization period supported the government. Power flowed out into the streets in these days, a somewhat scary but also intoxicating feeling for those who participated. Even the government, to its delight in the wake of the events of 1905, saw crowds without seeing revolution. In retrospect, we can see that a switch had been flipped in Russian politics. Mass patriotic demonstrations proliferated, crowds of villagers flocked to makeshift libraries to read war news, publishers focused on the heroic deeds of common Russians, and the tsar himself seemed briefly to understand that nothing would be the same again. But throughout these heady scenes, there was an undercurrent of briefly silent tension and a recognition that a powerful force had emerged on the Russian political landscape.[14]

[11] Evgenii Styrkas, Semen Novenkov, and Arsenii Shurduk, Telegram to War Minister, 19 August 1914, RGVIA f. 2000, op. 3, d. 1159, ll. 55–56. General Poslavskii, Telegram to Mobilization Department, 20 July 1914 RGVIA f. 2000, op. 3, d. 1194, ll. 143–143ob.

[12] Lemke, *250 dnei*, 1:13.

[13] Raymond Pearson, *The Russian Moderates and the Crisis of Tsarism, 1914–1917* (Basingstoke: Macmillan, 1977).

[14] Josh Sanborn, "The Mobilization of 1914"; Scott J. Seregny, "Zemstvos, Peasants, and Citizenship: The Russian Adult Education Movement and World War I," *Slavic Review* 59, no. 2 (Summer 2000): 290–315; Hubertus Jahn, *Patriotic Culture in Russia during World War I* (Ithaca: Cornell University Press, 1995).

THE FIRST MONTHS OF WAR

Germany declared war on Russia on 19 July/1 August and promptly prepared its troops for defensive action, while Russia initiated its defense by launching a two-pronged attack on both Germany and the Habsburg Empire. This confusion of assault and protection was one of the key features of the military and diplomatic situation in 1914. Every state perceived its own actions in defensive terms, and every state also thought that aggressive action was the best means of providing security for the country. The Habsburgs, fearful of Balkan decolonizers, demanded a war, got one, and invaded Serbia. German military leaders, Moltke in particular, expressed anxiety about growing Russian strength and urged the Foreign Secretary Gottlieb von Jagow in the spring of 1914 to initiate a "preventive war in order to defeat the enemy while we still stand a chance of victory."[15] Russia, for its part, was no different. Convinced of a Teutonic plan to reduce the empire to a second-rate power, military planners and political leaders designed a strategy to fend off the threat with a large invasion.

Why did a state that felt so vulnerable adopt such a risky strategy? First, there was the question of geography. Russian Poland bulged in the gap between German East Prussia and Austrian Galicia. Few felt that this strategic position was ultimately tenable. Either Russian armies had to use Poland as a staging area for attacks into the flanks of their enemies, forcing them to retreat, or they in turn would have to abandon the territory to avoid losing their armies in a pre-war pocket. Second, there was the question of supplies. By the turn of the century, Russian logistical experts planning for the contingency of war in Eastern Europe had discovered that it would take them fifty-seven days to move each month's worth of food into the combat zone. Before long, the army would either have to starve or would have to begin living off the land. Officers took the position that it was better to ravage the territory of the enemy than to bleed dry one's own population, so carrying the fight into enemy lands seemed the best option.[16] Third, Russian military and political leaders subscribed as fully to the cult of the offensive as their counterparts did in the rest of Europe. They, like so many others, understood the terrifying strength of modern weaponry. They drew the conclusion not that mass infantry action had become suicidal, but that success would require uncommon élan and self-sacrifice. Morale of this sort was best developed, they believed, in offensive actions. Finally, there was the question of alliances. Russia needed France fully engaged in the war, and the price of the alliance was a commitment to relieve pressure on the Western Front (where Russian and French military planners correctly believed the main German assault would come). This not only meant that they had to take the more concentrated strategy of limiting the invasion to

---

[15] Cited in Annika Mombauer, *Helmuth von Moltke and the Origins of the First World War* (Cambridge: Cambridge University Press, 2001), 172. The broader context for the quote is provided by Mombauer on pp. 172–4.

[16] William C. Fuller, Jr., *Strategy and Power in Russia, 1600–1914* (New York: Free Press, 1992), 390.

Austria off the table, but also that they were obliged to promise to invade East Prussia within fifteen days of the start of mobilization, more than ten days before all of their military pieces would be fully in place.[17]

As a result of all of these pressures, the General Staff quickly repudiated the cautious (and perhaps more prudent) strategic "Plan 19" implemented in 1910, whereby Russia intended to mothball its expensive fortresses in central Poland, to withdraw at the start of the conflict to a strong line of defense anchored by the Kovno–Grodno–Belostok–Brest line of fortresses, and to consolidate their forces for a massive counteroffensive weeks after fighting began.[18] In 1912, they altered Plan 19, creating a new Plan 19A with two variants "A" and "G." Variant G was a contingency plan that was to be used in case the Germans began the war by launching a massive attack on Russia rather than France. Since the Germans, as expected, began their offensives in the west, the General Staff ultimately deployed variant "A." The official goal of this invasion plan, even in these top secret documents, was "going over to the offensive against the armed forces of Germany and Austria-Hungary with the goal of transferring the war into their territory,"[19] as if it were already assumed that the Germans would get the better of the first battles. The General Staff reiterated this logic in March 1914 in a mostly accurate assessment of the likely array of forces that would face Russia in the event of war. The generals expected "very significant forces" to cross the border before Russian mobilization had finished, but they also expected that the German attention to the conflict with France and England would allow for the "fastest possible going over to the offensive" by Russian troops.[20] Anticipating this counteroffensive, they set aggressive tasks for their own forces at the very outset of the conflict. The First and Second Armies were to encircle German forces in East Prussia in the region of the Masurian Lakes, while the Third, Fourth, and Fifth Armies were to invade Austrian Galicia, coming together on the line of L'viv–Przemyśl and preventing the escape of Austrian forces either behind the Dniester or to Kraków (see Map 2).[21] This was the strategy set in motion in August 1914.

The war began according to plan. The two armies probed each other carefully in the first few days, as each empire shuttled millions of men to the war zone. Each side sent spies across the border to gather intelligence, and there was some early small-scale fighting. German troops took expeditions down the Vistula, the Russian

---

[17] Full mobilization was expected to take twenty-six days; forty-one days if troops from Central Asia and the Caucasus were included. Bruce W. Menning, "The Offensive Revisited: Russian Preparation for Future War, 1906–1914," in *Reforming the Tsar's Army: Military Innovation in Imperial Russia from Peter the Great to the Revolution*, ed. David Schimmelpenninck van der Oye and Bruce W. Menning (Cambridge: Cambridge University Press, 2004), 224.

[18] Menning, "The Offensive Revisited," 222.

[19] The Russian reads: "переход в наступление против вооруженных сил Германии и Австро-Венгрии с целью перенесения войны в их пределы." I. I. Rostunov, *Russkii front pervoi mirovoi voiny* (Moscow: Izd. Nauka, 1976), 92.

[20] "Vyderzhki iz zapiski glavnogo upravleniia general'nogo shtaba o veroiatnykh planakh troistvennogo soiuza protiv Rossii po dannym na 1 marta 1914 g.," in *Vostochno-Prusskaia operatsiia: sbornik dokumentov*, 70.

[21] *Vostochno-Prusskaia operatsiia: sbornik dokumentov*, 92–5.

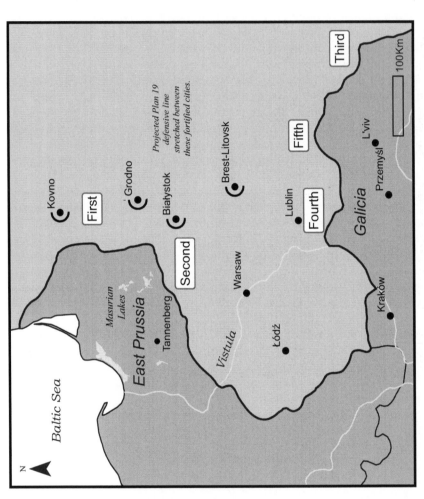

Map 2 Russian Forces in Poland, Plan 19 and 19A

cavalry launched several border raids, and there were some skirmishes between patrols.[22] The most significant military event of this first week was the German occupation and then sacking of the border town of Kalisz on 20–21 July/2–3 August, which will be described later in this chapter, and the occupation of the town of Częstochowa (with its important Catholic shrine), but these attacks paled in comparison with the war raging on the Western Front. As France and Belgium absorbed the shock of the first battles, the Russians mobilized as quickly as they could, urged on by their Francophile commander-in-chief, Grand Duke Nikolai Nikolaevich.[23] On 28 July/10 August, General Nikolai Ianushkevich (the chief of staff at General Headquarters or "Stavka") telegrammed General Iakov Zhilinskii (the commander of the Northwestern Front), indicating that both the First and Second Armies should be up to fighting strength by the twelfth day of mobilization in order to relieve pressure on the western allies. He further urged Zhilinskii to ensure tight communication between the two armies so that the offensive would result in the envelopment of German forces in East Prussia from both flanks.[24] Zhilinskii responded that while some units were ready for action, many others still had marching to do before they got into position. As a result, he envisioned a full-scale assault only on the twentieth day of mobilization.[25] In the event, the timing of the invasion reflected both the desire to attack early and the need to mobilize further before undertaking large battles. Rennenkampf's army crossed the border in force on 29 July/11 August,[26] but the first large engagement took place at Stallupönen on 4/17 August. This was a murderous but inconclusive battle that led in short order to the battle of Gumbinnen roughly twenty-five kilometers to the west on 7/20 August. Gumbinnen had a rather more direct outcome: a clear Russian victory. On the same day, as Zhilinskii had promised, General Aleksandr Samsonov's Second Army invaded East Prussia from the south.

This was a dangerous moment for the Germans. On paper, the two Russian armies had nearly thirty divisions to throw at the thirteen divisions of General Maximilian von Prittwitz's Eighth Army. An encirclement of the Eighth Army would entail a serious crisis, as most of the rest of Germany's armed forces were urgently attempting to reach Paris, and the road to Berlin would be relatively clear. Prittwitz, fearing the worst, proposed a retreat back to the west bank of the Vistula River, roughly 250 kilometers away. Prittwitz proposed, in essence, to save

---

[22] P. N. Bogdanovich, *Vtorzhenie v Vostochnuiu Prussiiu v avguste 1914 goda: Vospominaniia ofitsera general'nogo shtaba Armii generala Samsonova* (Buenos Aires: Dorrego, 1964), 45; Major-General Sir Alfred Knox, *With the Russian Army, 1914–1917: Being Chiefly Extracts from the Diary of a Military Attaché*, 2 vols. (London: Hutchinson & Co., 1921), 1: 41.

[23] On the Francophilia of the grand duke and his personal commitment to start operations early, see Paul Robinson, *Grand Duke Nikolai Nikolaevich: Supreme Commander of the Russian Army* (DeKalb: Northern Illinois University Press, forthcoming).

[24] Telegram from General Ianushkevich to General Zhilinskii, 28 July 1914, in *Vostochno-Prusskaia operatsiia: sbornik dokumentov*, 85–6.

[25] Telegram from General Zhilinskii to General Ianushkevich, 30 July 1914, in *Vostochno-Prusskaia operatsiia: sbornik dokumentov*, 87.

[26] Dennis Showalter, *Tannenberg: Clash of Empires* (Washington, DC: Brassey's, 2004 [1991]), 137.

Germany by sacrificing East Prussia. Much has been made about the emotional and monetary investment many of Germany's most notable landed elites had made in East Prussia, and this attachment no doubt played a role in the shock experienced in Berlin when Prittwitz's orders became known. But we should also note that this withdrawal would have had devastating and immediate military consequences for the Austro-Hungarian forces in Galicia as well.[27] Russia's invasion of Galicia proceeded far more slowly and ineffectively than it might have done, in large part because of the continuing German presence and pressure from the north.

The Russian victory at Gumbinnen had not been so devastating and demoralizing that it had to produce such a significant strategic outcome, however. The Germans had been defeated, but they had hardly been destroyed. General von Moltke therefore resolved to risk the survival of the Eighth Army by ordering the fight to be continued. Relieving Prittwitz, he appointed General Paul von Hindenburg as commander of the Eighth Army and named General Erich Ludendorff as his chief of staff. Arriving on the scene, Hindenburg and Ludendorff discovered that the Russian army was rather less formidable in the staff room than it was in the field. Coordination between the First and Second Armies had broken down, with the First Army refusing to follow up its victory at Gumbinnen by chasing the Germans and the Second Army bulging dangerously deep in the center of the line. The opportunity presented by these failures of command was too clear and too tempting to pass up. Moving forces quickly from Gumbinnen to the southwest, the Eighth Army attacked the exposed flank of the Russian Second Army, encircled it, and took most of its soldiers prisoners on 16/29 August. General Samsonov, fleeing in pain with his staff, committed suicide before reaching safety. Wheeling back to the north, the Eighth Army now smashed into the First Army, driving it back across the border on 31 August/13 September and completing the rout. The defeat of the Second Army (The Battle of Tannenberg) and of the First Army (The Battle of the Masurian Lakes) ended the existential threat to Germany.

These initial battles in East Prussia revealed a great deal about how the war would proceed on the Eastern Front. In the first place, soldiers on both sides fought hard and well, even in exceptionally trying circumstances. Older romantic notions of warfare, with clean columns of men marching into the fight or of immense cavalry waves deciding the outcome of the battle, were quickly and brutally dashed, not only on the Russian side, but on the German side as well. Nevertheless, enlisted men on both sides were able to hold firm in the face of artillery bombardments, move where they were ordered, and to assault positions in frightful conditions. In the second place, despite this relative parity at the level of the soldier, a clear superiority had emerged for the Germans at the level of command. This was not simply a question of "blundering" by particular generals such as Samsonov, but a systemic issue. The Russian army did an unusually poor job of putting together all the complicated pieces of military puzzles. This problem of "linkages" had plagued the military for more than a generation, but it had clearly

---

[27] This was the fear of the German High Command as well. Mombauer, *Helmuth von Moltke*, 247.

not been resolved.[28] Russia would have won the battle (and perhaps the war) in East Prussia if Rennenkampf had relentlessly pursued his beaten foe after Gumbinnen, a point that Ludendorff admitted as well.[29] He did not, in part because the men charged with coordinating the actions of the two armies (primarily General Zhilinskii and Grand Duke Nikolai Nikolaevich) were unable to persuade or force him to do so. Rennenkampf also had his own concerns about a shaky supply train, another area of linkage that was already fraying in the first days of the war. Finally, the Russian army was unable to deploy intelligence effectively to clarify the nature of the situation that Rennenkampf faced. Here, too, the lack of proper vertical and horizontal links between the many different units of the Russian military proved problematic.[30]

The battles also showed the limits of how far Germany could exploit these Russian weaknesses. Ludendorff tried to duplicate the destruction of the Second Army further north when fighting the First Army, but to no avail. When Rennenkampf retreated, he got closer to his supplies, while the Eighth Army went further out on a limb. The final attempts to destroy the First Army were fruitless and had to be called off. At the end of the day, the forces were more or less back to their pre-war positions. Two attempts by Germany to invade Russian Poland in November and again in January 1915 both had initial success before sputtering out as well. With only one exception (the topic of Chapter 2), the Great War armies fought essentially tethered to a pole.[31] The length of rope varied from a kilometer to more than a hundred, but every commander found it difficult to extend too far beyond the railheads that supplied him with food and shells. A slow repositioning of poles and ropes was always possible, and occasionally achieved, but this was beyond the patience and endurance of most of the belligerent powers. Already by the time the snows fell in 1914, it looked as though the war would have no clear military resolution.

We see further evidence of these dilemmas in the Russian invasion of Galicia. Just as Germany had been able to exploit weaknesses of the Russian command, so too was Russia able to do the same to Austria-Hungary. The Austrian war effort was hampered from the outset by the mismanagement of General Franz Conrad von Hötzendorf, the Austro-Hungarian chief of staff. Conrad was one of the men most responsible for the decision to turn the assassination of Franz Ferdinand into a continental war. He had pressed vociferously for war against Serbia ever since 1906, arguing more than twenty-five times for war in 1913 alone.[32] It was this obsession with dealing with the Serbian imperial challenge that crippled Austria's mobilization. Conrad held two urgent imperatives as the war began: first, to defeat Serbia, and second, to defend his country and participate in his alliance's titanic struggle for dominance in Europe by fighting the Russians in Galicia. In principle, these two goals were not contradictory, but in practice Conrad had to decide where to send his soldiers once they hopped on their trains. The plan worked out in early 1914

[28] Bruce W. Menning, *Bayonets Before Bullets: The Imperial Russian Army, 1861–1914* (Bloomington: Indiana University Press, 1992), 3.
[29] Rostunov, 128.   [30] Showalter, 207.
[31] For this image of "tethering," see Menning, "The Offensive Revisited," 231.
[32] Hew Strachan, *The First World War* (New York: Penguin/Viking, 2003), 11.

was to commit a large force to Galicia, a small force to Serbia, and to have a third force whose destination would be determined by the political flow of events. Conrad, to the shock of both his German allies and his own mobilization experts, sent this third force to the Balkans rather than Galicia. Under heavy pressure, he relented, but only after it was too late to change the train schedules. As a result, seven corps of soldiers spent the first month of the war on trains to the Serbian border before reboarding those trains to cross the entire length of the empire back to Galicia. Other aspects of the mobilization were similarly uninspiring, and as a result, Russia had the chance to organize its offensive.

The Russian invasion of Galicia began on 7/20 August, on the same day as the Battle of Gumbinnen. On the northern end of the front, the armies matched up relatively evenly. Conrad sent his First and Fourth Armies with relatively full complements to the border just in time to fight off the Russian Fourth and Fifth Armies. Both sides had roughly 350,000 men, and the initial battles (Krasnik and Komarów) went in favor of the Austrians. Russian forces retreated nearly to Lublin, and the commanders immediately began working to get one another sacked for incompetence. To the south, however, Conrad's mobilization failures were more evident. Only a single undermanned army (Third Army) faced two Russian armies (Third and Eighth Armies). Those armies slowly (probably too slowly) but surely marched westward, winning their engagements, and making it to the Galician capital of L'viv on 19 August/1 September. The Austrians promptly withdrew, leaving the city in Russian hands on 21 August/3 September. Conrad by this time had devised a plan to take advantage of his own weakness— he would allow the Russian Third and Eighth Armies to advance quickly so as to open the possibility for an attack on their northern flank. This was not totally foolish. General Nikolai Ruzskii, the commander of the Third Army, had been implored on multiple occasions to help the Fifth Army to his north and had refused, leaving a potentially dangerous gap to be exploited. But Conrad's move was too late. After taking L'viv, Ruzskii relented and sent reinforcements northward. At the same time, the Russian Fourth and Fifth Armies in the north were filling up with men still arriving from the depths of Russia, including a whole new Ninth Army that was formed and ready to move into action. In the first week of September, these new forces attacked the Austrian forces that had occupied the positions near Lublin and drove them relentlessly back into Austrian territory. One by one, Austrian corps began to crumble and retreat. Conrad asked for help from his German allies on 27 August/9 September, but he received none. On 29 August/11 September, fearing encirclement, Conrad ordered a significant retreat. The Russians pursued them deeper into Galicia. On 8/21 September, the grand duke ordered General Nikolai Ivanov, the commander of the South-western Front, to bypass the fortress of Przemyśl and to drive towards both the Carpathians and Kraków.[33] A meager attempt at a joint German–Austrian

---

[33] Telegram from Grand Duke Nikolai Nikolaevich (Stavka) to General Ivanov (Southwestern Front), 8 September 1914, HIA, Collection: Russia—Shtab Verkhovnogo Glavnokomanduiushchego, box 1, folder "Osnovnye direktivy," n. p.

counteroffensive in October failed, and by November the Austrians had been pushed more than 100 kilometers to the west of their border. Russia now controlled all of Eastern Galicia, had moved into Western Galicia all the way to the Tarnow–Gorlice line, and pressed in on the ancient Polish capital of Kraków from the north and from the east. In Tarnow, deep in Galicia, anxious civilians displayed icons in their windows to "demonstrate that Christians lived there, not Jews."[34] The remainder of the troops on the Southwestern Front took the fight to the slopes of the Carpathian Mountains. By the middle of November, they had reached and taken several of the most important passes, including Dukla and Uzsok. Virtually all that remained of Austrian Poland were the environs of Kraków and the besieged fortress of Przemyśl (see Map 3).

The Carpathians are the longest mountain range in Europe. Though not as imposing as the Alps (the highest point is 2655 meters on the current border between Poland and Slovakia), they nevertheless formed the largest natural barrier between the invading Russians and the Austrian and Hungarian homelands. They were difficult to cross in good weather and nearly impossible to force in winter. Nevertheless, this imposing landscape would be the major battlefield during the winter of 1914–1915. The Russians had good cause to press onward, as they knew that victory in the Carpathians would leave them fighting downhill all the way to Budapest, where they hoped they could force the Habsburgs out of the war. Surprisingly, however, it was the Austro-Hungarian forces that pressed the issue. After the embarrassments of 1914, when the Austrians had been beaten both by Russia and by Serbia, Conrad felt that he needed a victory. He thought that his best chance would be to reverse the Russian gains through a counteroffensive that would drive the Russians out of the Carpathians and relieve the siege of Przemyśl.

Conrad's attack began on 10/23 January 1915, and it flailed from the start. Men and supplies could barely move in the icy ranges, whole units froze to death in their tents, and the whole effort resulted in little more than a retaking of the passes. The Russian counterattack in February erased those gains and garnered thousands of prisoners besides, but the Russians could no more advance rapidly in the snows than the Austrians had. Another round of attacks and counterattacks would follow in February with little to show for either side other than the deaths of men. Roughly 800,000 men were casualties in the Austro-Hungarian army, most from sickness.[35] The line moved nowhere, and the Przemyśl fortress finally surrendered on 9/22 March, taking away the final impediment to a massive concentration of a Russian invasion force in the Carpathians. The spring looked ripe for the knockout blow.

In a similar fashion, the winter battles between Russia and Germany were far more devastating in terms of casualties than they were in strategic importance. In September, Germany tried to follow up the Tannenberg victory with an invasion of

---

[34] N. A. Bobrinskii, "Na pervoi mirovoi voine. Iz zapisok grafa Nikolaia G. Bobrinskogo," *Dvorianskoe sobranie* no. 3 (1995): 179.

[35] Graydon A. Tunstall, *Blood on the Snow: The Carpathian Winter War of 1915* (Lawrence: University Press of Kansas, 2010), 12.

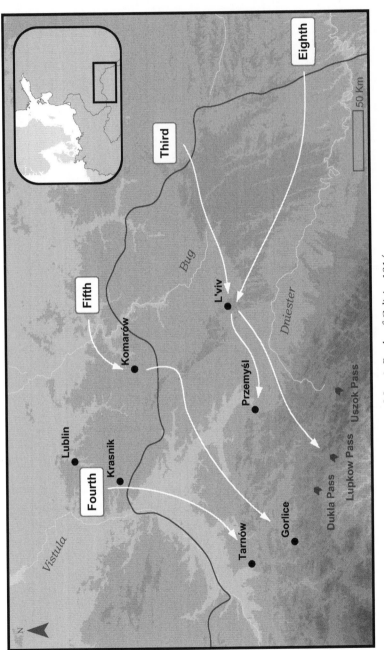

Map 3 Battle of Galicia, 1914

Russian Poland. The Russians beat them back across the border in relatively short order thanks to a successful counteroffensive by the Tenth Army. Another attempt at a combined offensive by the Central Powers in central Poland failed in October. Russia planned a similar offensive in the center aimed directly at Germany, but the planning never led to action. Once more a failure to coordinate the war effort left army commanders unsure of their strategic aims and their men to wait, fight a bit, and cause trouble with civilians. Warsaw, the hub of much of this staff and supply activity, rapidly became ungovernable, as masses of wounded soldiers and frightened civilians overwhelmed the city's capacity to provide urban services.

The sense of imminent danger intensified in November, when the Germans launched a more successful invasion of northern Poland on 29 October/11 November, moving more than seventy-five kilometers into Russian territory after winning border clashes that forced the Russian Second Army to fall back all the way to the industrial town of Łódź within a week. The Russian armies were dangerously undermanned, with many battalions staffed with only 300 men, a third of their normal complement. With winter now upon them, the troops on the Northwestern Front lacked 500,000 pairs of boots, and rifles and artillery shells were virtually gone as well.[36] On the northern edge of the new front line, the Germans were only fifty kilometers from Warsaw. The Russian armies seemed close to disaster once more, but the Germans again faced the difficulties of developing a successful offensive. The skilled retreat of the Second Army had saved Łódź, and with it a city full of supplies. As German munitions and other goods ran low, the Russians brought additional forces to bear in the form of units from the First Army from the north. What had looked like victory nearly turned into disaster for Germany, which had to fight a bloody retreat to avoid being trapped. Once more, the two sides had traded blows nearly evenly with little to show for it other than destruction. The Russians suffered 100,000 casualties in the battle, devastating not only the rolls of its divisions but the infrastructure that supported them. Łódź had only 5,000 hospital beds ready for the wounded; 50,000 men had to be sent elsewhere for care.[37] In the event, none of them could stay very long. Feeling weak and exposed, General Ruzskii decided in early December to withdraw further back into Poland to positions along the Bzura and Rawka rivers, abandoning the city so many had fought to defend.

The German Ninth Army, under the command of General August von Mackensen, tried several times to dislodge Ruzskii's troops from these positions. In December, all attempts failed. On 18/31 January 1915, the Germans unleashed a new weapon—poison gas—for the first time on any front in the war, near the Rawka river town of Bolimów, only fifty kilometers west of Warsaw as the fumes fly. This attack failed—the wind changed direction, and it was too cold for the gas

---

[36] "Zhurnal soveshchaniia sostoiavshagosia v Brest 30 Noiabria 1914 goda," 30 November 1914, HIA, Collection: Russia—Shtab Verkhovnogo Glavnokomanduiushchego, box 1, folder "Osnovnye direktivy," n. p.

[37] Norman Stone, *The Eastern Front, 1914–1917* (New York: Penguin, 1999 [1975]), 107.

to work properly—but the Russian counterattack sputtered just as badly, leading to 40,000 Russian casualties in three days.[38]

Soldiers got no respite in February. Stymied in central Poland, Ludendorff resolved to attack out of East Prussia from the north instead, launching the "Winter Battle of Masuria." Once more, poor Russian linkages caused untold suffering for the men. In this case, the great failure was one of intelligence. The major offensive aimed at destroying the Russian Tenth Army was launched on 25 January/ 7 February, but Russian commanders confusedly mistook it variably as a diversion, a flanking maneuver, a drive due east to Kovno rather than south towards Warsaw, virtually anything but what it was. Still, Russian soldiers fought well enough to preserve the army in retreat, with the exception of the XX Corps in the center of the line, which received orders to stay put to assist in a counteroffensive that would never come. The Germans trapped them in the Augustów Forest and took them prisoner. Over the course of the entire battle, 110,000 men were taken prisoner and another 100,000 were wounded.[39] This was another clear German victory, but as Norman Stone rightly points out, it was "a tactical success like many others in the First World War—barren of strategic consequence."[40] They could go no further without endangering their flanks, and continued fighting over the next two weeks demonstrated that even their new positions were unsupportable. Early in March, the Germans returned to the frontier.

The Masurian battles sent the Russian elite into a vicious cycle of recrimination fueled by public discontent. The command errors had been so profound that the rumblings of treason on the part of the command staff grew louder. A scapegoat was soon found—Colonel Sergei Miasoedov, a one-time corrupt border guard with tight connections to General Sukhomlinov, the Minister of War. Miasoedov had been disgraced after a public tiff with Aleksandr Guchkov, a prominent member of the Duma, but he rebuilt his career during the war as an interpreter in the Tenth Army before being arrested for treason. Though convicted only of "marauding" the civilian population (not selling secrets), he was executed on 19 March/1 April 1915. The most recent account of these sordid events makes a convincing case for the innocence of Miasoedov.[41] At the time, however, his guilt was widely assumed.

As the spring of 1915 approached, Germany and Russia were close to the borders on which they had begun the war. Germany had been utterly unsuccessful in winning the war, but Russia was setting itself on the path of self-destruction. The war took place within the context of the major military engagements, but already it looked as though the conflict would not be decided by troop movements. Instead, the war transformed the behaviors and outlooks of such a wide group of imperial subjects that cracks appeared throughout the edifice of the *ancien régime*. The first bits of evidence of state failure and social collapse—the two core phases of the decolonizing process discussed in the introduction—were visible already in 1914.

---

[38] Stone, 112.

[39] William C. Fuller, *The Foe Within: Fantasies of Treason and the End of Imperial Russia* (Ithaca and London: Cornell University Press, 2006), 132.

[40] Stone, 118.   [41] Fuller, *The Foe Within, passim.*

One of the most affected and most important groups of these subjects were the soldiers of the Russian Imperial Army.

THE SHOCK OF COMBAT

For combat soldiers, the first days of fighting were stunning. The stories they told to family members and readers expressed shock and surprise, but historians of combat soldiers in the twentieth century are more likely to notice how similar those stories were to those told by combatants throughout Europe. Their combat experience consisted of a common mix of fear, guilt, and excitement. Here is one typical account, given by Aleksandr Uspenskii, a company commander in Rennenkampf's First Army in 1914:

> I remember my personal impressions and feelings in that first moment of baptism by fire. The enemy was not visible, but his fire was terrifying: exploding fragments of shells rained down on you from above, with a sort of special bleating audible in the air (Lieutenant Colonel Solovev called this sound their "goat trumpeting") . . . the tender, plaintive sounds of flying bullets tearing through the air, the whistle of grenades, exploding on contact with a special crackling. Enormous fountains of earth, stone, sand, and smoke from the explosion of "suitcases" [the largest German shells], the cries and groans of the wounded, the contortions and agony of the dying. And yes, the feeling of horror and fear of death involuntarily overcame me. I consciously said good bye to my life and prayed to God (how clearly faith sprang up then!) that if it were God's will, then please take my life quickly, so as not to suffer as the severely wounded did.[42]

These terrifying impressions combined with rather more positive ones for Uspenskii, as he lovingly remembered his thrill about their initial victory, his awe at the sight of Russian soldiers in the distance running "beautifully" into the line of battle, and the hearty exchanges of war stories with his comrades after the battle. Within days, too, the nightmares had begun, as visions of the dead and maimed reappeared late in the evening. Uspenskii spent one awful night in a barn, watching his soldiers screaming and thrashing in their dreams as they slept, producing an unwelcome feeling that their lodging had become a mental hospital.[43]

The comment about "suitcases" is one of the most common in Russian battle accounts and it highlights another understandable but overlooked fact about Russian soldiers—they well knew that victory would depend not on an idealized rustic bravery but on their weapons. Soldiers had their own catalog of fear and sense of danger. Bullets were almost musical as they whistled through the air, shelling was terrifying, and extended pounding by the German "suitcase" shells was almost unendurable. Moreover, they learned that the same was true for the Germans. As

---

[42] A. A. Uspenskii, *Na voine: Vostochnaia Prussiia—Litva, 1914–1915 g.g., Vospominaniia* (Kaunas: n. p., 1932), 28.
[43] Uspenskii, *Na voine*, 32–7.

the war began there was some nervousness about the enemy. Russian soldiers liked stereotypes as much as anyone, and the German reputation for precision, orderliness, brutality, and military effectiveness certainly preceded them. Had the Russians lost all their early battles, it might well have led to a permanent inferiority complex. Some soldiers, of course, did succumb to this complex, which then grew as the war progressed. But most learned that the Germans, in the end, were just soldiers, too. This revelation was striking enough that several memoirists and diarists pointed to the moment when this realization was made most clear to them. For those in the First Army, the rout of Mackensen's XVII Corps at Gumbinnen was especially memorable. Mackensen's men marched into them, the Russians remembered, almost as if on a parade ground, in the open and in formation, a sort of twentieth-century Pickett's Charge with the same degree of success. The Russian artillery blew them apart, riflemen picked them off, machine-gunners mowed them down, and then all the Russian soldiers saw how much easier it was to kill men who were retreating rather than staying put.[44]

The lessons for the Russians were clear but increasingly painful. They could beat the Germans if they were well commanded and well armed, but they lacked both of these assets.[45] Significant ammunition deficiencies emerged in the first battles, and these legendary shortages would grow much worse before they got better in late 1915. The story for soldiers in the first year of war was of increasing concern. They spent too many days being shelled without seeing enough shells going the other way. They had too many rifles without bullets and men without rifles. The army overcame some of these problems when battling the Austro-Hungarian army, but the combination of shortage and poor leadership proved bitter very early on for those in East Prussia. Soldiers in the First Army, who had fought hard to enter the region and rejoiced mightily at the sight of fleeing Junkers, grew angry when their generals' mistakes forced them to retreat almost without a fight. The days of devastating, demoralizing defeat on the battlefield would come later, in 1915. Dennis Showalter, in his magisterial work on the Battle of Tannenberg, also observes that any detailed look at combat in the first battles of the war shows no innate German superiority. The Germans developed a narrative of natural superiority as part of the myth-making of Tannenberg, but as combat troops the Russians consistently impressed not only Showalter but the Germans who faced them. Leadership and supply were the areas in which the Germans demonstrated superiority, not in how well they shot, much less their level of courage.[46]

Another simple myth that one can readily dismiss is that Russian soldiers, accustomed to a lower standard of living in the first place, were less put out by the rough and changed circumstances of life on the march than their more cultured counterparts on the other side of the lines were. As one might expect, no one likes

[44] Uspenskii, *Na voine*, 46–50.
[45] This feeling only intensified as the war went on. Even in the darkest days of the retreat of 1915, soldiers maintained that they could win the war if they had sufficient armaments. See "Obzor pisem iz deistvuiushchei armii," 24 August 1915, RGVIA f. 2067, op. 1, d. 3845, l. 66.
[46] Showalter.

to be lice-ridden, cold, hungry, and footsore. Russian soldiers complained about these deprivations (and persisted nevertheless) at about the same level as other combatants in the war—no one described these conditions as "just like home." To the contrary, all accounts stress the different fabric of life that emerged. That fabric was conditioned by combat and by the discomforts of life, but there were also opportunities for the expansion of a certain sort of male sociability that overstepped all pre-war constraints and wartime disciplinary measures. This new social formation highlights an important fact about the decolonizing process in the Russian Empire during World War I. At the same time that the war was destroying the traditional political and social relationships in the empire, it was generating new forms of politics and social interaction. This was certainly true for the men in uniform, who busily created their own new society at the front with its own practices, norms, and expectations. Some of those practices are evident in the military events discussed throughout this book: marching, digging, hiding, robbing, eating, killing, dying. One other practice conditioned army life: waiting. Stuck in muddy fields and damaged little towns across the front, soldiers drank, gambled, sang, and played, tightening the bonds with one another and increasing the separation between their society and the rest of the world.

Alcohol played a particularly important role in lubricating and solidifying the brotherhood at the front, despite the fact that the government, in a burst of progressive enthusiasm, fiscal irresponsibility, and unrealistic expectations, had forbidden the sale and consumption of alcohol. Technically, the law was supposed to apply to civilians and soldiers alike, but enforcement was haphazard. Officers, the worst offenders, did virtually nothing to impose this ban in most units. Alcohol was a traditional and functional part of Russian military society, and military men drank when they could obtain liquor, which normally meant either purchasing or looting in the territories they occupied. The other common soldier drug of choice—tobacco—was not prohibited (except on sentry duty, though sentries smoked often enough to get either written up or shot on a fairly regular basis). Indeed, this was one of the items sent from the rear in patriotic care packages or handed to troops on the march by local civilians.

The other prohibited activity that flourished during the war was gambling. One need not be a psychologist to see the attraction of high stakes gambling for men living in the kingdom of chance and death, nor need one know much about Russian culture through the great novels of the nineteenth century to realize that gambling was a common elite pastime. But still, virtually every writer and stacks of disciplinary reports mention the enormous scale and scope of gambling among soldiers and officers. Here are two fairly representative examples, the first from a censored letter by Ensign Bogoiavlenskii writing to a friend in Moscow in late 1915:

From 7 November to 16 November [20–29 November] we stayed in one village and rested there: wine, vodka, cognac and other spirits, anything you wanted, since *popoiki* (parties) happened every day. We played cards all night, and I won 950 rubles and wanted to send the money home...but I sat down to play on the next day, and, as usually happens, lost not only this but another 260 of my rubles and stopped playing for good. But I found another pleasure – there are many "special" sisters – they come to every *popoika* and drink alone; in addition, there are many Warsaw wives and so forth, they are building rear trenches and they have supervisors who aren't commoners, but high school and college girls from Warsaw and other cities. The supervisors are for the officers and the workers for soldiers. They are all pictures of beauty, like Polish girls are in general.[47]

This commingling between Russian soldiers and Polish girls was frowned upon both by the army command and by local Poles, and it was feebly prohibited by both, but to little effect. As Bogoiavlenskii makes clear, wine, women, and cards were staples of soldier entertainment.

Song was also popular, both on the march and in camp, and some took the trouble to learn local folk songs as part of their repertoire.[48] Sports and games were also common. One observant visitor cataloged the activities of a unit he visited. Soldiers engaged in many different sorts of games, Olympic ones such as the high jump and long jump, and rather more carnivalesque ones such as the "greasy pole," the sack race, smashing pots with cudgels, and a variant of a jousting game in which men drove carts under an arch capped with a bucket of water. A soldier had to try to put his lance through a hole, and failure to do so led to "cooling results."[49]

Still, these leisure pursuits were often desperate ones, born of emptied souls and deep soldier ennui, as a rather less upbeat letter from the Eighth Army in 1916 shows:

> I'll describe for you our unenviable life in the trenches and the mood, both among officers and soldiers. At the present time, there's a short break in the action, which won't last long, as it always does. We sit and smoke or reread old newspapers, when suddenly a sentry will burst into our dugout and announce that the Germans are firing canisters of poison gas. Of course we leap up and put on our masks, this is a so-called "indication of attack," and of course [we start firing] to try to prevent the attack. Then we sit and wait from minute to minute for some sort of trick from the Germans. Everyone's mood is depressed and sad, although sometimes we do get together for good times. We get a couple of bottles of something or other, make a bad dinner, but of course after dinner we want to fool around with cards if nothing gets in the way. In general we don't get any calm, there's always the noise of exploding shrapnel or grenades. . . . The soldiers are all tired and are requesting leaves. One and a half arshins [about one meter] of snow just fell, it got cold and melancholy is seeping through our souls. Everything would be fine if we just had some sort of success.[50]

---

[47] Ensign Bogoiavlenskii, Censored letter to V. A. Velichkin, 11 December 1915, RGVIA f. 2067, op. 1, d. 3845, l. 355ob. "Sisters" refer to nurses attached to the Red Cross or to the medical units run by the Union of Towns and the Union of Zemstvos (Zemgor), who were called "Sisters of Mercy." Whether these "special" sisters were actually attached to the nursing services is of course a different matter.

[48] J. Y. Simpson, *The Self-Discovery of Russia* (New York: George H. Doran Company, 1916), 146.

[49] Simpson, 145.

[50] Military Censorship Department of the Quartermaster General of the Staff of the Eighth Army, "Svodka otchetov voennykh tsenzorov 8-i armii za period s 31-go oktiabria po 15-e noiabria s.g.," 15 November 1916, RGVIA f. 2067, op. 1, d. 2937, l. 188.

The mood of Russian soldiers thus depended on the usual factors: weather, food, and combat success. They were neither more nor less prone to being stoic or enthusiastic than other soldiers. They were also quite typical in their desire to find someone to blame for their misfortune. Here many soldiers were comparativists. Early in the war, soldiers had a great many legitimate complaints. They muttered bitter oaths as they watched (and shot at) German medics on the field of battle while their own medical staffs were so small as to be virtually insignificant. As we will see in Chapter 4, civilians and soldiers alike quite correctly blamed the government and military for the failure to prepare medical services properly. Similarly, many Russian soldiers, both in and out of prisoner-of-war (POW) camps, knew that Russian POWs had the roughest lot because the government had no mutual agreement with hostile armies. The Red Cross proved able to improve the situation slightly as time progressed, but many POWs were shocked by the relative lack of concern the government expressed in their fate.[51] Finally, and most importantly, soldiers were comparativists on the question of supplies. They knew that they could compete in a fair fight, but they also knew that they had had almost no fair fights (at least against Germany) from the end of Tannenberg until 1916, and they blamed their leaders for this problem as well.

CIVILIAN LIFE AT THE FRONT LINE

Russia's move to a war footing affected political structures just as it did social life.[52] The Russian General Staff realized in the midst of the mobilization crisis that the existing field regulations needed immediate revision. Thus, on 16 July/29 July, just as Nicholas issued and retracted several mobilization orders, he signed into law a set of guiding principles that were at once incomplete and breathtakingly ambitious. These new rules established a broadly defined front-line zone that came under the direct control of the leaders of the active army, imposing martial law on all territories west of the Dnipro River and as far east as St. Petersburg itself.[53] Other important ports, such as Arkhangel'sk and Vladivostok, were also placed under military rule.[54] Though the tsar apparently envisioned assuming the role of supreme commander-in-chief himself, he was eventually persuaded to stay in St. Petersburg and to appoint his cousin, Grand Duke Nikolai Nikolaevich, to the new position. It took two weeks for the Supreme Headquarters (Stavka) to get up

[51] These issues are discussed at greater length in Chapter 3.

[52] Parts of this section are taken from Joshua Sanborn, "Military Occupation and Social Unrest: Daily Life in Russian Poland at the Start of World War I," in *Writing the Stalin Era: Sheila Fitzpatrick and Soviet Historiography*, ed. Golfo Alexopolous, Julie Hessler, and Kiril Tomoff (New York: Palgrave Macmillan, 2010), 43–58.

[53] Daniel W. Graf, "Military Rule behind the Russian Front, 1914–1917: The Political Ramifications," *Jahrbücher für Geschichte Osteuropas* 22, no. 3 (1974): 390.

[54] Daniel W. Graf, "The Reign of the Generals: Military Government in Western Russia, 1914–1915," (Ph.D. diss., University of Nebraska, 1972), 10.

and running, leaving a window of time in which civilian officials had to report to the commanders of regional military districts rather than to their ministry chiefs.[55]

Even after Stavka began functioning regularly, the lines of authority were not particularly clear. The grand duke and his chief of staff, General Ianushkevich, were in charge, but they clearly focused their attentions on combat operations, not civilian administration. In September 1914, Nikolai Nikolaevich finally got around to appointing Prince N. L. Obolenskii as the point man for civilian affairs and then creating a Chancery for Civil Administration for him in October. Obolenskii, two other officials, an enlisted clerk, and two orderlies then began trying to govern civilian life across a territory larger than Germany.[56]

It therefore goes without saying that civilian administration did not end at the doors of Stavka. In the first place, employees of civilian ministries were supposed to remain in place and continue performing their jobs as they had done before the war. As we shall see, this expectation was not always met, but enough stayed on to provide some continuity. In addition, a wide variety of military officers now enjoyed governance rights in the areas where their troops were stationed. Front commanders, army commanders, corps and divisional commanders could all issue edicts, as could the chiefs of supply and fortress commanders. In enemy territory occupied by Russian officers, depot officers exercised similar rights. These military men created regulations to enforce security in the zones of their authority, which they could do by imposing curfews, conducting searches of homes and businesses, and deporting undesirables. They sought to control economic life by fixing prices, forbidding trade in certain goods, and requisitioning labor. They endeavored to suppress political life by imposing censorship, dismissing local officials, and occasionally harassing civilian relief agencies. All of this was done by decree, with no right of remonstrance on the part of affected civilians or outraged civilian bureaucrats.[57] The result was confusion, indeed anarchy. The chain of command looked clear enough, as each of the men in uniform existed in a hierarchical system headed by the grand duke, who in turn answered only to the tsar. But the fact that civilian administration was at best an afterthought meant that communication, authority, and responsibility for these affairs during the war were unclear. Exigency—and its twin arbitrariness—were the only common features of political life in the front-line zones. No single act did more to lay the conditions for comprehensive state failure in the borderlands than the edict of martial law.

This drastic weakening of governmental authority and competence coincided with the massive disruptions occasioned by modern war. As we have seen, armies were quite mobile on the Eastern Front. They regularly advanced more than fifty kilometers during offensives, occupying towns and villages across East Prussia, Poland, and Galicia as they did so. Even outside of the major offensives, each army sent patrols behind enemy lines and even occupied frontier towns such as Kalisz and Częstochowa with very modest troop concentrations for weeks at a time.

[55] Graf, "The Reign of the Generals," 11–14.
[56] Graf, "The Reign of the Generals," 30.
[57] Graf, "The Reign of the Generals," 22–37.

The Germans even temporarily seized towns much further from the border, for example Pruszków, and cavalry patrols and marine expeditions down the Vistula regularly appeared without warning (see Map 4). Persistent physical insecurity therefore defined civilian life in the border zones on the Eastern Front from the very first days of the war. Civilians and soldiers alike knew that the trenches they constantly dug were porous, frequently overrun, and no guarantee of safety for those huddling within or behind them.

Unexpectedly, this insecurity in many ways invigorated civic life in the region. After all, the tsar had declared martial law in part to prevent civic activism of any sort. Military officials hoped and expected that the civilian population would remain docile and fully obedient while troops occupied their cities, towns, and villages. The armed forces were utterly unprepared to actually govern in the zones of their authority, however. In occupied enemy territory in German Poland and East Prussia, they had no real plans and indeed appear simply to have requested civilian police officials to serve in these new areas.[58]

As we saw earlier, the occupation of German territory was brief. In Galicia, by contrast, military and state authorities controlled new territories for several months at a stretch. The victory in September 1914 over Austria-Hungary put new men in control of an ethnically diverse and politically explosive region. The tenor of wartime Galician ethnopolitics had been set by the Habsburgs, who launched a massive campaign against suspected Russophiles in the first month of the war. Austrian officials arrested tens of thousands of Ukrainians, most of them politically innocent, and sent them to concentration camps, most notably the notorious Talerhof camp, where they languished and perished en masse during the ensuing years of the war.[59] The sudden Russian victory led to fears that the ethnic tables would simply be turned and that only those local actors sympathetic to Petrograd would be tolerated in the occupied zone. Many officials and Austrian sympathizers fled along with the Habsburg armies as they retreated.

At first, the army command was interested primarily in maintaining quiet. Early edicts imposed curfews, confiscated weapons, and promised stern punishment for any violation of the peace, calling on the "urban and rural population of the province to restore a calm life of peaceful labor and to support complete public order."[60] General Aleksei Brusilov, the commander of the Eighth Army, appointed one of his colonels as commandant of the city of L'viv and instructed him "to demand no more than perfect order and the fulfilment of all the requirements of the military authorities, and as far as possible to allow the normal life of the city to continue." He told the inhabitants to "stay quietly at home, satisfy all the demands of the military authorities, and live as tranquilly and peaceably as possible." In

---

[58] Governor Kupreianov (Suwałki), Telegram to N. V. Kharlamov, 17 August 1914, GARF f. 215, op. 1, d. 174, l. 487.

[59] See *Galitskaia golgofa: voennye prestupleniia Gabsburgskoi monarkhii, 1914–1917* (Trumbull, CT: Peter S. Hardy, 1964).

[60] State Councilor Chartorizhskii (Tarnopol' governor), "Ob"iavlenie," 25 August 1914, RGVIA, f. 2005, op. 1, d. 12, l. 21, 28; Lieutenant-General Count Bobrinskii (Military Governor General of Galicia), "Obiazatel'noe postanovlenie," 31 August 1914, RGVIA f. 2005, op. 1, d. 12, l. 15.

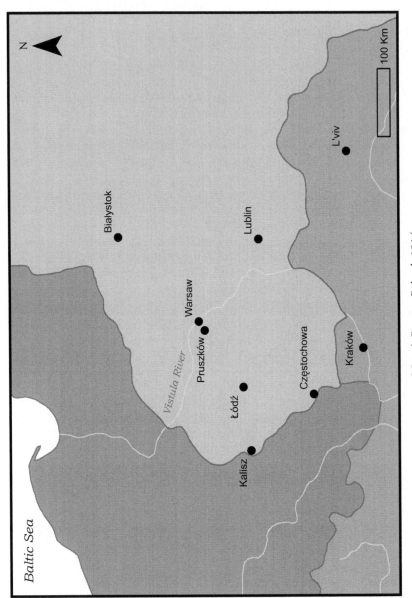

Map 4 Russian Poland, 1914

return, he promised payment for goods and services and announced that "at the moment the races, religions and political views of the citizens were of no concern to me."[61]

Governing was not quite this easy, however. Economic problems arose immediately. Inflation, a problem that would bedevil authorities throughout the war, prompted rapid action from Russian authorities. State Councilor Chartorizhskii warned inhabitants of Ternopil' as early as 26 August/8 September 1914 that all "artificial and unconscientious raising of prices" would be punished by fines and imprisonment.[62] Three days later, he issued additional regulations that required merchants to accept Russian money at the decidedly non-market rate of 30 kopecks for every Austrian crown. He also published a *taksa*, or list of fixed prices, on key goods, "with the goal of protecting the population of the city of Tarnopol' from the corruption of salespeople." Black bread, for instance, could not be sold for a price higher than 3 kopecks.[63] Count Bobrinskii, the Governor-General of Galicia, issued the same regulations for all of Galicia just a few weeks later.[64] The Russian state would use these mechanisms to combat inflation for the rest of the war. In provinces near the war zone, such as Kaluga, officials followed the 31 July/13 August 1914 advice of the Ministry of Internal Affairs and instituted the *taksa* in the first month of the war.[65] Other towns followed suit according to their own lights, and by 1915, 228 of the 250 cities polled by the Union of Towns had taken measures against inflation, usually by publishing a *taksa*.[66] Some recent historians have praised price controls as an effective and necessary method of dealing with price-gouging speculators,[67] but the relentless rise of inflation even in the face of violent administrative measures taken against Russian commercial figures suggests otherwise. Indeed, the record shows that these crude economic regulations worked no better in Russia than they did in other countries at war, and they raised expectations that the government would be able to control the faceless "market"

---

[61] General A. A. Brusilov, *A Soldier's Notebook, 1914–1918* (Westport, CT: Greenwood Press, 1971 [1930]), 57.

[62] State Councilor Chartorizhskii (Tarnopol' Governor), "Obiazatel'noe postanovlenie," 26 August 1914, RGVIA, f. 2005, op. 1, d. 12, l. 27.

[63] State Councilor Chartorizhskii (Tarnopol' governor), "Ob"iavlenie," 29 August 1914, RGVIA, f. 2005, op. 1, d. 12, l. 22–23.

[64] Lieutenant-General Count Bobrinskii (Military Governor General of Galicia), "Obiazatel'noe postanovlenie," 17 September 1914, RGVIA f. 2005, op. 1, d. 12, l. 16–16ob.

[65] Irina Belova, *Pervaia mirovaia voina i rossiiskaia provintsiia, 1914-fevral' 1917 g.* (Moscow: AIRO-XXI, 2011), 64. Price controls were a very popular measure for wartime governments across the continent. France, for instance, was just as quick to regulate the price of bread as Russia was. Tyler Stovall, "The Consumers' War: Paris, 1914-1918," *French Historical Studies* 31, no. 2 (Spring 2008): 304.

[66] Thomas Fallows, "Politics and the War Effort in Russia: The Union of Zemstvos and the Organization of the Food Supply, 1914–1916," *Slavic Review* 37, no. 1 (March 1978): 73; Mark Baker, "Rampaging 'Soldatki,' Cowering Police, Bazaar Riots and Moral Economy: The Social Impact of the Great War in Kharkiv Province," *Canadian-American Slavic Studies* 35, no. 2–3 (2001): 150, fn. 36.

[67] Belova, 64. Belova's own subsequent account of several failed measures taken by the Kaluga and Orël governors, along with her observation that virtually every issue of provincial newspapers during the war held accounts of the state punishing merchants who violated the *taksa*, likewise suggests that these economic policies were failures.

when times got bad. These were expectations that the Russian state could not meet.[68] Local governance devolved to district chiefs, many of whom had been sent by governors of other provinces because they were incompetent. Count Bobrinskii was aware of this problem, and also that competent administration was necessary in those regions devastated by combat, but he worked too slowly to overcome it, probably because he too was overwhelmed by responsibilities that were beyond him.[69]

State interventionism did not stop in the economic realm. The dominant strand of Russian nationalism held that all of Galicia was truly Russian and that all "Ruthenians," "Ukrainians," and speakers of various "dialects" were Russian too. They harkened back to the medieval state of Kievan Rus' and claimed that all of the political complications were simply Austrian oppression, all of the religious diversity was a papal plot, and all of the languages were corruptions of the true Russian tongue. This was "Carpathian Rus'," or, more tendentiously, "oppressed [*pod"iaremnaia*] Rus'."[70] All that would be necessary to reunite this lost province to its true home would be an energetic policy to remove the Germans and Poles who dominated politics, the Uniate priests who owed allegiance to the Vatican, and the nationalist Ukrainians who annoyed them with their linguistic demands. These nationalists overturned the pre-war policy of caution and ignored men like Ivan Shcheglovitov, the Minister of Justice, who warned that the wholesale destruction of civilian institutions in wartime violated international law.[71] The authorities transformed the court system, requiring Russian to be the primary language of justice. They closed all the schools in Galicia before reopening them with a Russian-language curriculum.[72] A concerted campaign was launched against Galician Jews, whom they felt had been coddled by their Austrian overlords. They targeted many for deportation, allowed the troops to abuse and lynch them, and consciously pursued a campaign of revoking the civil rights enjoyed by Jews under the Habsburg Empire.[73] Finally, they allowed the Holy Synod to send Archbishop Evlogii, a strident proponent of mass conversion, to the region to conduct repressive policies against the Uniate Church and local priests. The tsar and Stavka did

---

[68] For a discussion of price controls and politics in Germany during the war, including the similar observation that the German state took the blame for market problems, see Robert G. Moeller, "Dimensions of Social Conflict in the Great War: The View from the German Countryside," *Central European History* 14, no. 2 (1981): esp. 147–51.

[69] Letter to General N. N. Ianushkevich (Stavka), from Count Bobrinskii (Military Governor General of Galicia), 23 October 1914, RGVIA, f. 2005, op. 1, d. 1, l. 44ob. On Bobrinskii's "lack of experience and his ignorance of the country," see Brusilov, 69.

[70] A. Iu. Bakhturina, *Politika rossiiskoi imperii v vostochnoi Galitsii v gody pervoi mirovoi voiny* (Moscow: AIRO-XX, 2000), 42.

[71] Bakhturina, *Politika*, 55; Mark von Hagen, *War in a European Borderland: Occupations and Occupation Plans in Galicia and Ukraine, 1914–1918* (Seattle: University of Washington Press, 2007), 26.

[72] von Hagen, *War in a European Borderland*, 26–7.

[73] For explicit orders in these regards, see letter from General Ianushkevich (Stavka) to Count Bobrinskii (Military Governor General of Galicia), 19 March 1915, RGVIA, f. 2005, op. 1, d. 12, l. 110ob. See also Peter Holquist, "The Role of Personality in the First (1914–1915) Russian Occupation of Galicia and Bukovina," in *Anti-Jewish Violence: Rethinking the Pogrom in East European History*, ed. Jonathan Dekel-Chen et al. (Bloomington: Indiana University Press, 2011), 52–73.

not fully control this process. Indeed, the actions taken by the Orthodox Church directly contravened the orders to observe religious tolerance issued by Count Bobrinskii, orders that made clear that Orthodox priests could only be sent to a village if 75 percent of the population requested one.[74] Instead, the occupation was driven by enthusiastic actors on the ground who had a "complete lack of perspective."[75] This was further evidence of a weakened imperial state, as political entrepreneurs hijacked state policy and district chiefs devised their own policies.[76] The result was catastrophic. The heavy-handed assault on churches and religious leaders outraged local residents. Ukrainian activists were upset by the campaign against the Uniate Metropolitan Andrei Sheptits'kyi, and the international community protested the violation of international law and the persecution of Galician Jews.[77] The predations by unrestrained soldiers and the increase in crime unnerved everyone.[78] The Russian Empire gained few civilian friends in the region and made many enemies.

In Polish regions on the Russian side of the border, the army was also in practice an occupying force that replaced civilian authorities and requisitioned large amounts of labor and merchandise, but army officials, to the extent that they thought about it at all, appear to have believed that life would continue as normal. They imagined that local officials would continue to serve, currency would be protected and respected, and goods would be available for sale or for orderly requisition.[79] It turned out, however, that these local officials (mostly from the Ministry of Internal Affairs and the Ministry of Finance) were not very enthusiastic about being military lackeys in combat zones. These stranded bureaucrats quickly abandoned their virtually indefensible customs posts, packed up currency stores and other valuables in provincial centers, and fled to Warsaw in order to avoid capture.[80] Those who stayed sometimes faced extremely dangerous situations. State Councilor Agafonov, the head of the district of Nieszawa, a border town on the Vistula, was taken hostage by a small German landing force. The enemy commander compelled him to issue German decrees over his own signature for several days before retreating beyond the river. Agafonov left town quickly as soon as he could.[81] In some particularly threatened areas, gendarmes even fled or changed into civilian clothes to avoid German capture.[82] Those who stayed were often left without any supervision or oversight, with predictable results. At the Otwock railway station, an abandoned gendarme grabbed himself a healthy supply of

---

[74] Count Bobrinskii (Military Governor General of Galicia), Circular to governors, 27 October 1914, RGVIA f. 2005, op. 1, d. 12, l. 11.

[75] Bakhturina, *Politika*, 69, 144.   [76] Bakhturina, *Politika*, 215.

[77] von Hagen, *War in a European Borderland*, 41.   [78] Bakhturina, *Politika*, 103–4.

[79] Warsaw Governor, Secret letter to Warsaw Governor General, 6 August 1914, GARF f. 215, op. 1, d. 167, l. 11.

[80] Warsaw Governor, Secret letter to Warsaw Governor General, 6 August 1914, GARF f. 215, op. 1, d. 167, l. 11.

[81] "Dokladnaia zapiska Nachal'nika Neshavskago uezda Statskogo Sovetnika Agafonova," n.d. (but after 16 August 1914), GARF f. 217, op. 1, d. 304, ll. 213–215ob.

[82] Warsaw Governor, Secret letter to Warsaw Governor General, 10 August 1914, GARF f. 215, op. 1, d. 167, l. 15.

vodka, drank himself into a stupor, and imposed a one ruble "tax" on every passenger heading toward the ticket booth.[83] In practical terms, this departure of officials from the Ministry of Internal Affairs and the Ministry of Finance left a gap of authority. When armed troops arrived they ruled with varying degrees of arbitrariness. In the first months of the war in particular they clearly had no plan, much less training, for civilian administration. As a result, they did very little of it. When they did try their hand at organizing, they typically botched the job. When army officials took over the crucial task of railway administration, for instance, they slowly drove the rail network into the ground while civilian railway experts twiddled their thumbs.[84] This lack of coordination between civilian and military authorities was ubiquitous. In one notorious instance, the Minister of Internal Affairs learned of a new labor law issued by the Petrograd military chief only when finding a copy of it posted on the fence of his summer home one morning.[85]

Much of the day-to-day governance in these regions, ranging from fire prevention to trade to policing, thus fell to local notables.[86] Take, for instance, the city of Włocławek, which was occupied by a German detachment for three weeks immediately following the outbreak of the war. The Germans arrested the captain of the police, disarmed the rest and told them to leave the district or be detained. Other local citizens who showed insufficient enthusiasm for the occupiers were also imprisoned. Volunteers from the fire brigade carrying sabers maintained order in the town. After the German departure, only these lightly armed men served as police, a situation that obtained in other cities such as Lubień and Kowal as well. For all of these border cities, the only Russian army presence was a detachment of Cossacks that had eighty kilometers to patrol, looking mainly for German scouts rather than civilian criminals.[87] Even in towns like Kutno, where local officials neither fled nor were driven away, new institutions of local self-government sprang up immediately. Within the first two weeks of the war, Kutno residents established a committee to assist families of mobilized reservists and a citizens' committee to assist the "most needy residents of Kutno."[88] Again, we see wartime events undermining the traditional state while providing an opportunity for a re-envisioning of political practices and relationships in the empire.

These new political forms, however, were ad hoc and poorly supported both materially and in terms of the people needed to run them. As one group of new

---

[83] "Resident of Otwock," Letter to the Gendarme Administration, 3 August 1914, GARF f. 217, op. 1, d. 304, l. 135ob.

[84] Knox, 1: 195.   [85] Graf, "Reign of the Generals," 88.

[86] On this, see too Jan Molenda, "Social Changes in Poland during World War I," in *East Central European Society in World War I*, ed. Béla K. Király and Nándor F. Dreisziger (Boulder: Social Science Research Monographs, 1985), 187–201. This was true far from the front as well. Arkhangel'sk lacked any government at all for several months as the military and imperial governments dropped the ball. Graf, "Reign of the Generals," 89.

[87] Warsaw Governor, Secret letter to Warsaw Governor General, 22 August 1914, GARF f. 215, op. 1, d. 167, l. 21–22ob.

[88] Warsaw Governor, Secret letter to Warsaw Governor General, 22 August 1914, GARF f. 215, op. 1, d. 167, l. 21–22ob.

Polish committeemen dryly observed, they were not prepared for this sudden authority and responsibility, since they had been deprived of the opportunity to develop institutions of local self-government in the pre-war period.[89] One can hardly blame Polish organizers for reminding the imperial government of the costs of its repressive pre-war policies in Poland. In terms of local governance, this repression had taken the form of delaying the introduction of elected local institutions (zemstvos) to the "Western Provinces" as long as possible for fear of abetting the development of Polish nationalism. The tsarist Ministry of Internal Affairs then made matters worse by insisting that the new Polish zemstvos be dominated by ethnic Russians.[90] Still, what was done was done. The facts on the ground were that imperial officials had evacuated, military officials were indifferent to civilian administration, and local officials were complete novices.

As if that were not bad enough, the new local administrators now had a whole set of problems that even experienced men would have struggled with, such as finding housing for makeshift military hospitals, feeding and sheltering residents whose houses had been destroyed, and attempting to regulate trade in very volatile circumstances. Providing security was even more difficult, since the most dangerous troublemakers were literally outside of the law—those members of the rival armies whom the firemen and shop owners could not even hope to contain. However, the services of these locals were important. As the Płock governor attested, they helped resolve disputes between landlords and tenants, between estate owners and laborers, and between businesspeople. They established systems of temporary credit, protected state property, and enforced basic food safety regulations in urban markets.[91] As these tasks grew more complicated during the first turbulent months of the war, members of several of these urban committees joined together to plead for the creation of a whole system of local "resident committees" supported from above by a "central resident committee."[92] The proposal was met with hesitance in Warsaw and St. Petersburg. The emergence of the political vacuum and the troubled experience of nearly a decade of Duma politics in the empire had made the tsar's servitors wary of local political participation, much less proposals to crown the edifice of resident committees with a central body of politically active Poles. Nevertheless, in the first days of September Roman Dmowski's National Democrats formed just such a central committee.[93]

Instead of fully engaging with these local initiatives, army officials ordered civilian administrators to return to endangered areas and strengthened martial

[89] Central Society of the Rural Economy in the Kingdom of Poland, Letter to Warsaw Governor General, 22 August 1914, GARF f. 215, op. 1, d. 174, l. 172–173.

[90] Theodore R. Weeks, *Nation and State in Late Imperial Russia: Nationalism and Russification on the Western Frontier, 1863–1914* (DeKalb, IL: Northern Illinois University Press, 1996), 131–51.

[91] Płock Governor, Secret letter to Warsaw Governor General, 30 August 1914, GARF f. 215, op. 1, d. 167, l. 26.

[92] Central Society of the Rural Economy in the Kingdom of Poland, Letter to Warsaw Governor General (22 August 1914), GARF f. 215, op. 1, d. 174, l. 172–173.

[93] Norman Davies, *God's Playground: A History of Poland*, 2 vols. (New York: Columbia University Press, 1982), 2: 380–1.

law in the region.[94] They concerned themselves not only with law and order but also with transforming economic behavior in the war zone. As a consequence, they systematically and consciously disarticulated traditional imperial trading patterns. Prior to the war, the Polish frontier had buzzed with international trade. Migrant workers crossed the border frequently, both legally and illegally. Roughly 400,000 seasonal laborers made the trip from the Russian Empire to the German Empire annually in the final years of peace.[95] Goods flowed through the zone at a rate high enough to ensure healthy profits not only for merchants but also for the officials who supplemented their incomes by easing bureaucratic regulations at the border.[96]

The outbreak of hostilities logically shut down this entire network of economic activity. In the empire as a whole, the export trade plummeted to 13.3 percent of its pre-war total in the first year of the war and recovered only slightly thereafter.[97] Domestic trade took a beating as well, again largely due to state controls. Army edicts dating from the very first month of the war prevented trade with the rest of the empire for many key goods. Grain, flour, livestock, and leather had to be sold within provincial borders.[98] The same went for fuel, and the trade in liquor was, as in the rest of the empire, forbidden for the duration of the war. The rationale for these edicts was clear: the army desperately needed a constant source of goods of all sorts from the regions where its troops were stationed, and it could not or would not tolerate a system in which it had to compete for those goods either with private economic actors or with state organs in the rear. The only way to establish the military as a monopoly consumer in the war zone was to use the mechanisms of martial law to compel producers and traders to give them the right of first refusal.

The attempt to impose a system of economic autarky for each separate province was bad enough. But army commanders also disrupted normal economic operations within provincial towns. Most notably, the pathological suspicion of merchants in general and Jews in particular led to ill-advised assaults on simple practices such as warehousing bulk goods. Building stocks of supplies to hedge against severe shortages at some later date was criminalized. News that merchants were doing exactly this in December 1914 led army officials to believe that the Jews had banded together to form a large conspiratorial plot to raise prices through speculation.[99] Sixty-four men were arrested in Warsaw, most of them Jewish. Their protestations during interrogation were quite convincing. One detained man held that he had brought salt all the way from Odessa but couldn't sell it because of the Christmas holiday and warehoused it instead. A merchant from Pruszków explained that he had

---

[94] General Zhilinskii, Telegram to General Ivanov (30 August 1914), GARF f. 215, op. 1, d. 174, l. 227.

[95] Eric Lohr, *Russian Citizenship: From Empire to Soviet Union* (Cambridge, MA: Harvard University Press, 2012), 68.

[96] Fuller, *The Foe Within*, 23, 29.

[97] Michael T. Florinsky, *The End of the Russian Empire* (New Haven: Yale University Press, 1931), 33.

[98] Lieutenant General Danilov, Mandatory decree to the city of Vil'no, 6 October 1914, GARF f. 217, op. 1, d. 437, l. 2.

[99] Head of supplies for armies of the Northwestern Front, Telegram to Warsaw Governor-General, 5 December 1914, GARF f. 215, op. 1, d. 201, l. 1.

a large storehouse of sugar because he had evacuated all of it on the eve of the Germans taking the city. Even the local gendarmes came to the realization that there was no criminal intent in the activities of the merchants. The logical conclusion was that merchants were helping the war effort by bringing goods into the war zone, not only from other provinces, but also from the grasp of the enemy.

The high command did not accept this logic, however, and overrode the objection of the police. Gendarmes arrested the merchants and confiscated their goods. With peacetime networks disrupted, warehousing difficult, trading danger-ous, and armed men roaming the land, price instability in Poland was inevitable. The authorities responded as they had in Galicia, by attempting to fix prices on key goods. Again this was driven by army officials with only the slightest notions of how economic and social systems operated.[100] As Mikhail Lemke noted in the diary he kept at Stavka during the war, the General Staff Academy had done nothing to prepare its officers for the demands of civilian governance they were sure to face in zones of martial law. Graduates had no coursework on "state law and the economy, nothing on fundamental legal codes and administrative organs . . . nothing on finance, they don't have a clue on anything of the kind." As a result, he concluded, "they go on blindly, simply not even suspecting anything about the life of the country."[101]

A group of key financial actors in Warsaw saw the danger immediately. Less than two weeks after the bullets started flying, they pleaded with top officials to adopt immediate measures to stabilize the war zone economy by underwriting reliable emergency institutions for the extension of credit and protecting property rights (from military depredations above all). They warned that in existing conditions the only reasonable economic decision left for many in the area was "liquidation."[102] The Polish businessmen were ignored. Instead, the high command continued to issue punitive regulations (don't export, don't raise prices, don't stockpile) and did nothing positive to support local economies in the midst of catastrophic change. Already in August 1914, the army was helping to create the "overarching anti-market consensus" that Peter Holquist has identified as being a crucial develop-ment within Russian political culture during the war years as a whole.[103]

As usual, the bureaucratic inclination to think that lots of regulations would correspond to lots of orderliness was mistaken. To the contrary, the true economic story was one of near anarchy. Ham-handed, overbearing officiousness by a deeply understaffed and inexperienced administration led not to a rational utilization of local resources but to the instantaneous emergence of new forms of economic

---

[100] Lieutenant General Danilov, Mandatory decree (n. d. but 1914), GARF f. 215, op. 1, d. 873, l. 87ob.

[101] Lemke, *250 dnei*, 2: 625.

[102] Warsaw Stock Market Committee, Report to Ia. G. Zhilinskii (head of armies on the Northwestern Front) (15 August 1914), GARF f. 215, op. 1, d. 174, l. 159ob.

[103] Peter Holquist, *Making War, Forging Revolution: Russia's Continuum of Crisis, 1914–1921* (Cambridge, MA: Harvard University Press, 2002), 44. One might note too, as Thomas Owen does, that the ideological building blocks of anticapitalist thought had quite deep roots within both Russian officialdom and the Russian intelligentsia. Thomas Owen, *Russian Corporate Capitalism from Peter the Great to Perestroika* (Oxford: Oxford University Press, 1995), 116.

practice that did even more to bewilder the administration. The second economy of the black market hummed with activity. Traders moved between army camps and towns selling not just food, liquor, and cigarettes, but also army uniforms, rifles, revolvers, overcoats, and boots. Some of this was clearly the result of scavenging battlefields, as men arrested with contraband near engagement sites had up to ten times as much material as those away from the fighting.[104] But soldiers also regularly sold their gear to local merchants. In Płock, authorities arrested several enlisted men for selling away winter clothes, for instance, and leakage of state property remained an issue throughout the war.[105]

What we might call a "third economy" also emerged in the form of looting, which was quite widespread. Individually, in small groups, as parts of full units, on both sides of the pre-war border, and by both armies, soldiers simply took advantage of their strength to take what they wanted. In one very typical case, the residents of an estate near the Vistula returned to the premises they had fled during an artillery barrage in late September to find Russian soldiers milling about, eating vegetables, and pointlessly destroying furniture. When one of the bailiffs complained, a soldier struck him, threatened him with a bayonet, and told him to shut up. The estate was stripped bare, as were neighboring ones in the region.[106] Looting occurred both near the front lines (as in this case) and well in the rear. Indeed, in October 1914, the new commander of the Second Army (General Sheideman) noted that most of the reports that soldiers were "offending" and "robbing" the locals came from regions well east of the Vistula River.[107]

Robbery was a constant threat in border zones, and though most perpetrators were in uniform, civilian gangs soon appeared as well. In early 1915, for instance, four bandits from Warsaw, acting on a tip that a wealthy family had been left without male protection, invaded the home of Marianna Sopievskaia. They stole fifty-three rubles in cash and sixty rubles in goods, raped Sopievskaia's two teenaged daughters, and shot a neighbor whose dogs raised the alarm during the attack.[108]

As the Sopievskaia attack demonstrates, Christian families were not immune from attack. Nevertheless, Jews were the favorite targets of violence throughout the region. On 31 August/13 September 1914, for instance, the 235th Belobeevskii Infantry Regiment had a two-hour layover at the Tlusz railway station. Many enlisted men hopped off the train to visit local Jewish merchants. Upon finishing

---

[104] See for instance Governor Papudolgo (Łomża province), Telegram to Warsaw Governor-General, 27 November 1914, GARF f. 215, op. 1, d. 192, l. 61; Chancellery Director for the Warsaw Governor General, Secret letter to the supply chief of the Dvinsk Military District, 15 December 1915, GARF f. 215, op. 1, d. 192, l. 66.

[105] General von Rennenkampf, Order no. 226 to troops of the First Army, 31 October 1914, GARF f. 215, op. 1, d. 192, l. 37.

[106] Warsaw Province Gendarme Administration, Report to the Chancellery of Police Units under the Warsaw Governor General, 10 November 1914, GARF f. 217, op. 1, d. 1152, l. 337–338.

[107] General Sheideman, Order no. 121 to troops of the Second Army of the Northwestern Front, 10 October 1914, in *Prikazy po 2 Armii, 1914* (Bound collection of orders held in the Military Section (Voennyi Otdel) of the Russian State Library (VO-RGB), Call number D 157/22). Many thanks to Vasilii Kashirin for informing me of the existence of these volumes.

[108] Warsaw Governor, Letter to Warsaw Governor General, 28 April 1915, GARF f. 215, op. 1, d. 873, l. 56–56ob.

their "shopping," however, many refused to pay for the goods they had collected. In response, the shopkeepers closed their doors and began conducting trade only through the windows of their shops. The soldiers reacted by breaking down the doors and "violently taking various goods." The officers of their regiment stood by passively during the robberies, which would have gone unnoticed in the documentary record (as so many others obviously did) if a general from the Second Army Staff hadn't happened by and been outraged by the "disorder."[109] These more isolated attacks always had the potential to spread and develop into full-scale pogroms, as events in Lublin on 19 August/1 September had demonstrated. Twenty Jewish stores were robbed and destroyed, with total losses of more than 20,000 rubles.[110]

Hunger did not prompt the looting. Most units were in fact quite well, if monotonously and blandly, fed in the first few months of the war.[111] If there was an economic reason behind the violence, it was instead that supply agencies could not deliver visible and desirable goods promptly. Supply troops were supposed to purchase chickens and apples, for instance, to feed to the soldiers, but they moved slowly, didn't carry enough money, and generally stumbled on the job, so soldiers quickly resorted simply to taking what they saw. But the thefts cannot be explained simply in economic terms, for much of the problem was plainly one of thuggish criminality, the abuse of the weak by the strong, a fact that is attested to by the overwhelming number of Jews victimized by army troops in these regions. Soldiers knew that their word would be honored over that of a Jew, and even the murder of robbed Jews went largely unpunished.[112]

Again, however, the extent of victimization went well beyond the Jewish community. Take, for instance, the sad story of Osip's stolen cows. On 6/19 February 1915, as part of their winter offensive against the Tenth Army, German troops appeared in the Augustów district of Suwałki province, prompting a local lord, Tomashevskii, to order the evacuation of all local livestock in a single herd back to the town of Kuźnica, about fifty kilometers away. When two local peasants, Osip Iakubchik and Mariana Mikhnevich, arrived in Kuźnica, they discovered their cows had been taken. Upon further investigation, they discovered that Lieutenant Nemilov of the 5th Caucasian Convoy Battalion had taken their cows from the herd driver (greasing the way with a five-ruble note), claiming that he had seized them in Germany and brought them back to Russian soil. Aggrieved, they went to Nemilov's commander, who told them it was none of his business and to bring it

---

[109] Chief of the Warsaw Province Gendarme Administration, Telegram to military district commanders and Governor General, 26 August 1914, GARF f. 217, op. 1, d. 1152, l. 276.

[110] Captain Vavilov (chief of the Gendarme Administration of Lublin District), Secret telegram to the chief of the Gendarme Administration of Lublin Province, 20 August 1914, GARF f. 238, op. 1, d. 144, l. 3.

[111] When armies were on the move, however, logistical difficulties frequently left men hungry and angry. See Knox, 1: 131.

[112] Governor of Płock, Secret letter to Warsaw Governor General, 20 January 1915, GARF f. 215, op. 1, d. 877, l. 1. For more detailed descriptions of assaults on Jews by occupying armies, see S. An-sky, *The Enemy at His Pleasure: A Journey Through the Jewish Pale of Settlement during World War I* (New York: Henry Holt, 2002), 5–7.

up with Nemilov. This they did, with predictable results—a barrage of invective and a rapid shove out the door. Osip and Mariana were persistent. As they noted, these cows represented their only assets. They went to the local police chief, who sympathetically took depositions but informed them that he had no power over military personnel, indeed quite the opposite. Martial law had made local authorities irrelevant in cases of this sort. They had just one last resort—to go over Nemilov's head to the staff of the Tenth Army with a sad, woeful petition. This had the desired effect, as Nemilov was forced by superiors to write his own justification, which no one, apparently, believed. As a result he was ordered to return the cows or pay the villagers off. The case ended on 6/19 May, with a formal request from Nemilov to the Tenth Army staff for the money to reimburse Osip and Mariana, just in time, it seems, for them to flee the German offensive with the rest of the army and population. One assumes the story ended badly for the cows as well.[113]

The travails endured by Osip and Mariana show not only the instances of thievery by Russian army personnel, but also the labyrinthine structure in place to deal with the broader problems of looting. Both the lengthy process involved and the final compensation coming from the high levels of the Tenth Army command suggest that the widespread marauding was the result of a systematic failure of leadership on the part of the army command, which dealt ineffectively with uniformed bandits. Top military officials understood that the war effort depended to a great degree on the cooperation of the local Polish population and might well come down to the ability of one side or the other to enlist the active support of key Polish constituencies. Army commanders were therefore quite disturbed by the frequent complaints coming from civilian populations, and they issued numerous edicts demanding that soldiers be restrained. But they were unable to stop the depredations, no doubt because the only strategy they deployed was to order their subordinates to punish their soldiers severely for violating orders. As early as 19 August/1 September 1914 General von Rennenkampf (commander of the First Army) was instructing officers to stop their troops from "marauding" by threatening them with summary execution.[114] On 23 August/5 September, he put teeth into the order by announcing that four men had been shot for robbing local civilians.[115] As usual, however, swinging big sticks from far away could not substitute for strong leadership by junior officers on the ground, and that leadership was clearly missing in many units of the Russian army. Circumstances did not improve after the ghastly losses of cadre officers in the first months of fighting. In one regiment analyzed by David Jones, 40 percent of the colonels and 50 percent of the captains were killed in the first battle in August 1914 alone. By the end of that month, only 23 officers (of 77 at the start of the war) remained (though some

---

113 See set of documents on this case in RGVIA f. 2106, op. 3, d. 175, ll. 116–128.
114 General von Rennenkampf, Order no. 23 to troops of the First Army, 6 August 1914, *Prikazy po 1 Armii* VO-RGB, D 157/20.
115 General von Rennenkampf, Order no. 34 to troops of the First Army, 10 August 1914, *Prikazy po 1 Armii* VO-RGB, D 157/20. See too Knox, 1: 75.

wounded officers eventually returned).[116] Their replacements, called the "kids from the train stations" by now-grizzled vets, had short and often deeply deficient courses of training. As one recalled, he was trained as if in peacetime, "without links to the front, as if the war didn't exist." He went just once to the firing range and saw a machine gun once as well, though he was not allowed to touch it.[117] These green officers were the only power enforcing the boundary between atrocity and proper behavior in zones occupied by the Russian army.

ETHNOPOLITICS

If the martial law regime did more to intensify the economic disruption that the war brought than to mitigate it, much the same can be said of the impact of military rule on the political life of the region. Whatever positive (and unintended) outcomes there may have been as the result of the development of local civic activism were far outweighed by the poisonous brand of ethnopolitics practiced by the Russian military. Many Russian officers were already inclined to look at the world through ethnic lenses in 1914, but the usual political nightmares of military occupation (unreliable collaborators, hidden insurgents, and widespread espionage in particular) prompted the high command to almost universally deploy an ethnic grid of reliability in the regions they occupied. Officers and soldiers automatically suspected Germans and Jews of treason or espionage, while they treated Russophone and Ukrainophone populations as natural allies.[118] As Eric Lohr has demonstrated most exhaustively, these ethnopolitical initiatives were both mistaken in their assumptions and profoundly destabilizing in their outcomes.[119] The botched occupation of Galicia demonstrated the many problems with the new brand of ethnopolitics in Ukrainian lands, but even these complications paled in comparison with the ethnopolitical riddles posed by the Poles. Optimists in the Russian administration saw Poles as natural Russian allies, and several of these men were deeply annoyed when they realized that most Polish civilians saw them as foreign oppressors.[120] Some appealed to high-minded Slavophile ideas, but most hoped that anti-German and anti-Jewish sentiment would provide sufficient support for the Russian cause. Officials were quick to report the evidence for this, however shaky. In October 1914, for instance, one local official informed the local gendarme administration that "according to reports from Pruszków, a certain Jew named Berson was sending telegraphs reporting troop movements to the enemy. In

---

[116] David R. Jones, "The Imperial Russian Life Guards Grenadier Regiment, 1906–1917: The Disintegration of an Elite Unit," *Military Affairs* 33, no. 2 (October 1969): 292–3.

[117] S. V. Vakar, "'Eto vam ne universitet, a eskadron'," *Voenno-istoricheskii zhurnal* no. 2 (2000): 50–1.

[118] I have addressed some of these issues elsewhere: Joshua Sanborn, "Unsettling the Empire: Violent Migrations and Social Disaster in Russia during World War I," *Journal of Modern History* 77, no. 2 (June 2005): 290–324.

[119] Eric Lohr, *Nationalizing the Russian Empire: The Campaign against Enemy Aliens during World War I* (Cambridge, MA: Harvard University Press, 2003), *passim*.

[120] Knox, 1: 232.

addition, in private conversations with local residents, Berson said that if the Germans entered Warsaw they would build a bridge with the skulls of peasants."[121]

This notion that Jews reveled in the prospect of the German army inflicting bloody punishment on their Slavic tormentors was widespread. One group of Jews, who gathered secretly in an apartment on Kholodnaia Street in Warsaw in October 1914, so frightened the Poles in the building that they immediately called the police. The Poles were convinced that the Jews were planning to "dismember" them. Instead, it turned out that the Jews had gathered to share information on the best route to escape to the German side of the line without running into Russian troops.[122] These fears of Jewish retribution were also linked to the rapid expansion of spy mania in the region. Soldiers and Polish civilians alike saw espionage in nearly every strange occurrence, in nearly every odd congregation of Jews or strangers, and in nearly every misfortune of the war. This wartime phenomenon has been well chronicled in various recent works,[123] and it is striking how quickly it developed in the war zone. Soldiers and civilians alike wrote denunciations of residents with suspiciously German names, of those who fed invading German troops, even of women who expressed their fears of German attacks while helping to care for wounded soldiers.[124] Soldiers regularly detained curious civilians who asked too many questions, to the extent that even their officers complained that they had become "afflicted with a sort of spy mania."[125] As with economic disaster, political suspiciousness occurred well before anyone had time to become weary with the war.

The fear of spies was not totally baseless. The Germans and the Austrians did set up intelligence operations in Russian Poland, just as the Russians tried to send agents to the other side of the line. It is difficult to determine how successful and widespread those enemy spy networks were.[126] German intelligence in the area was certainly far better than Russian intelligence, and this contributed decisively to their military victories, though much of this advantage was probably due to superiority in technical espionage. It does, however, seem clear from the archival files that Russian counter-intelligence was not very talented and tended simply to round up people with German and Jewish names while scores of Polish agents operated among them. As Mikhail Lemke put it, counter-intelligence operations were run by people

121 Chief of Warsaw Province Gendarme Administration, Secret letter to chief of the Gendarme Administration of Grójec and Błonie districts, 22 October 1914, GARF f. 217, op. 1, d. 304, l. 487.
122 Chief of Warsaw Province Gendarme Administration, Secret letter to superintendent of the 7th District of the Warsaw Police, 21 October 1914, GARF f. 217, op. 1, d. 546, l. 516.
123 The most systematic attempt to deal with the question is Fuller, *The Foe Within*, esp. 172–83.
124 Unsigned postcard sent to Warsaw Province Gendarme Administration, 16 September 1914, GARF f. 217, op. 1, d. 304, l. 306; report of the chief of the Gendarme Administration of Grójec and Błonie districts to Warsaw Province Gendarme Administration, 14 November 1914, GARF f. 217, op. 1, d. 304, l. 484a; Captain Budakovich (6th Siberian Rifle Regiment), letter to Warsaw Province Gendarme Administration, 8 October 1914, GARF f. 217, op. 1, d. 304, l. 484.
125 Simpson, 149–50.
126 Russian counter-intelligence did discover some spy networks, such as the one run out of Kraków by the Austrian army. Chief of Łomża Province Gendarme Administration, Completely secret circular to chiefs of district gendarme administrations in Łomża province, 5 January 1915, GARF f. 1669, op. 1, d. 88, l. 2.

who displayed an "indifference to the fate of the country and the army, laziness and an inability to get down to hard work."[127] Ethnic profiling was the result both of the conceptual apparatus of Russian officialdom and of incompetence. It was easier to arrest Jews than it was to infiltrate spy networks. As a result, Jews were deported, and Russia's enemies got good information.

Not surprisingly, in conditions of wild instability in the security situation, these real and imagined political sympathies took on greater dimensions when the military lines were moving. When German troops retreated from the border districts in Piotrków province soon after occupying them, in the middle of August 1914, for instance, every changed military disposition struck fear in at least part of the population. The Piotrków governor urged the front commander to send him troops, field courts, and other punitive mechanisms to round up Germans and Jews denounced for espionage and treason. Among the accusations leveled at these populations was the charge that when Russian troops retreated, the Germans and Jews felt a "malicious joy" and "terrorized the Poles, promising them the fate of Kalisz for their loyalty to the Russians."[128]

The fact that these threats of retribution mentioned Kalisz is significant for understanding both civilian insecurity and the correspondingly quick rise in the politics of fear during the war period. Kalisz was a city of about 70,000–80,000 people on the Russo-German border. German troops occupied the city on 20 July/ 2 August, a day after the German declaration of war on Russia. On the following day, the German commander (Major Preusker) put the city under martial law.[129] That evening, things began to fall apart. In a pattern that would be repeated many times in Belgium and France in the next few weeks, a group of nervous, trigger-happy German soldiers led by officers fixated on the danger of civilian snipers (*francs-tireurs*) got into a firefight in the dark and lashed out at an entire city.[130] It is still unclear what set off the gunfire. The first official German report blamed civilians, a second allowed for the possibility that Russian provocateurs had ambushed the troops, and Polish residents thought it was a case of friendly fire.[131] In private correspondence, Russian officials were convinced that the incident began when a group of Russian army reservists returning from Łask marched singing into the darkened town, not knowing it had been taken by the enemy.[132] The phenomenon of both hostile and friendly troops stumbling into one another at

---

[127] Lemke, *250 dnei*, 2: 545.

[128] Governor Iachevskii (Piotrków province), Telegram to Zhilinskii, 18 August 1914, GARF f. 215, op. 1, d. 174, l. 470.

[129] The martial law order is included in Lawrence R. Flockerzie, "Poland's Louvain: Documents on the Destruction of Kalisz, August 1914," *The Polish Review* 28, no. 4 (1983): 78.

[130] The definitive study of the assaults on civilians on the Western Front is John Horne and Alan Kramer, *German Atrocities, 1914: A History of Denial* (New Haven and London: Yale University Press, 2001). A recent account of the Kalisz incident is provided in Laura Engelstein, "'A Belgium of Our Own': The Sack of Russian Kalisz, August 1914," *Kritika: Explorations in Russian and Eurasian History* 10, no. 3 (Summer 2009): 441–73.

[131] Flockerzie, 79–87.

[132] State Counselor Tolmachev, Report to the Warsaw Governor General, 27 July 1914, GARF f. 215, op. 1, d. 174, l. 65ob–66.

night and firing at each other was quite common, especially in these early probing days of the war. What made this incident special was the fact that it happened in an urban center and that German troops quickly became convinced that locals had taken up arms against them.

The German response was excessive, a point that even the German commandant of Kalisz in November 1916 came to admit.[133] German troops shot suspected ringleaders, took the town government and religious leaders (and at one point 750 other men) hostage and promised to execute them if further assaults occurred, levied a 50,000-ruble fine, and then withdrew from the town in order to punish it with an artillery barrage. The Germans admitted to killing eleven people, other sources estimate the figure was over 100, and one local priest reported that he buried 500 people by the time the smoke had cleared. German soldiers also engaged in widespread raping, pillaging, and arson.

There are two points to be made about the Kalisz atrocities. First, this sort of attack, though not unique, was unusual. The German army did assault civilians in several locations in Poland, but there was no concerted terror campaign. Second, the fact that these atrocities were not widespread did not matter a great deal. News of Kalisz spread quickly by word of mouth, as more than 50,000 residents fled the city and sought refuge in communities across Russian Poland. Poles even helped hide normally despised Russian bureaucrats from the German invaders. Refugees spread tales of woe far and wide.[134] The story was soon developed in other media as well. Propagandists quickly produced a film entitled *Krwawe dni Kalisza* (Kalisz's Bloody Days) and showed it in Warsaw to highlight the atrocities.[135] It did not take long for the Russian and Polish press to use Kalisz as an example of innate German barbarism and to argue that the war was being fought for the sake of civilization.[136] The anger was very real. Even in private, figures such as Grand Duke Nikolai Nikolaevich became upset when speaking of Kalisz.[137] Those few observers who chalked the murderousness up to the nature of war rather than the nature of the German army were ignored.[138]

One particularly graphic and personal account of life in Kalisz was told by a "Mrs Gust," who had survived the assault and was attending a school for Sisters of Mercy in Riga. *Petrogradskii kur'er* published her story on 28 August/10 September and touted it as a first-hand view of "all the horrors of Teutonic bestiality." When the German assaults began, Gust, her husband, and her son fled the city. On the first day, her husband had gone off to look for a cart and had never returned. She feared the worst as she waited several days for him to come back. She finally decided

[133] Flockerzie, 87.

[134] State Counselor Tolmachev, Report to the Warsaw Governor General, 27 July 1914, GARF f. 215, op. 1, d. 174, 66.

[135] Harold B. Segal, "Culture in Poland during World War I," in *European Culture in the Great War: The Arts, Entertainment, and Propaganda, 1914–1918*, ed. Aviel Roshwald and Richard Stites (Cambridge: Cambridge University Press, 1999), 69.

[136] See sample press clippings on German atrocities (especially in Kalisz) in GARF, f. 215, op. 1, d. 185, ll. 20–36.

[137] Knox, 1: 44.   [138] Frenkel', 87.

to take her son to Łódz, but no sooner had she got there than she decided that she had to return to look for her spouse. She went through several German checkpoints, where she had all her silver money taken from her, but made it back to a devastated city where dead bodies lay uncollected and rotting on the streets. When she got back to her apartment building, the neighbor's sobbing maid approached her. The maid reported that her boss had fled and left her alone in the house with her daughters, fifteen-year-old Anela and twelve-year-old Zosia. Before long seven drunken German soldiers arrived, held down the mother and then raped her two girls, leaving them "bloody and disfigured" on the floor. Zosia had fallen into a "nervous fever" and was near death when Mrs Gust left them.[139]

This story highlighted two of the major propaganda themes of the war: the need to fight Teutonic barbarism, and the dangers that would befall defenseless women and children if Russian and Polish men failed in their military missions. These themes were picked up quickly by journalists. Upon entering L'viv on 23 September/8 October 1914, one reporter noted that "at the same time as the German horde, when passing by enemy cities and towns, put everything to fire and the sword and the whole world cried out about their barbarism, our troops, our soldiers and officers, were true knights, true gentlemen, and beautiful L'vov remained completely untouched, continuing its life just as if nothing had happened."[140] Russian propagandists clearly believed that this type of story would convince scared Polish civilians to support the Russian war effort. Indeed, most Polish historians now agree that the Kalisz episode strengthened the position of pro-Russian politicians, at least in the short term.[141] German commentators reached similar conclusions both directly after the war and long after it. In the words of one author in 1920, the events in Kalisz were the "darkest page in the history of the entire campaign."[142] Another commented that the human and public relations disaster occasioned by the massacre equated to a "lost battle."[143] The politics of fear, in other words, worked quite well.

This hope that shared anti-Semitism and a shared terror at the German army's reputation for barbarism would create a durable alliance between Poles and Russians was not fully borne out. Plenty of Poles on both sides of the pre-war border urged resistance toward foreign occupiers. One flyer posted in Warsaw in August from the "National Workers Union, National Peasant Union, the Editorial Board of 'Pol'sha,' and the Union of Independence" urged Poles to stay out of the war and allow their "enemies to weaken themselves." They noted that it didn't make sense from a Polish nationalist standpoint for "Poles to fight with Poles under the banners

---

[139] "Poezdka v Kalish, zaniatyi nemtsami," Clipping from *Petrogradskii Kur'er* no. 213, 28 August 1914. GARF f. 215, op. 1, d. 185, l. 8.

[140] Report from reporter (signature illegible), 23 February 1915, RGVIA f. 2005, op. 1, d. 12, l. 274.

[141] Davies, 2: 389.

[142] Georg Gothein, *Warum verloren wir den Krieg?* 2nd ed. (Stuttgart and Berlin: Deutsche Verlagsanstalt, 1920), 182. Cited in Heinz Lemke, *Allianz und Rivalität: Die Mittelmächte und Polen im ersten Weltkrieg (Bis zur Februarrevolution)* (Berlin: Akademie-verlag, 1977), 23.

[143] Count Hutten-Czapski, cited in Lemke, *Allianz und Rivalität*, 23.

of our enemies."[144] Authorities also ran down accusations that young men were agitating among students to develop armed cells, but these investigations usually came to naught.[145] Those who were actually arrested for espionage or treason tended to be social marginals, ethnic enemies, and women identified as prostitutes.[146]

These small groups of hidden spies and revolutionaries apparently did not succeed in convincing the population to abandon the reasonable "wait and see" policy adopted by most Polish citizens in the early phase of the war. At the start of 1915, the Warsaw Province Gendarme Administration sent out questionnaires to local gendarmes asking very pointed questions about local political attitudes, including whether any attempts were made to commemorate the November 1830 Polish uprising, how Poles treated Russian troops, and so forth, and the response from virtually every district was similar. There were no attempts to agitate in 1914 for immediate independence, and Poles related to the Russian army quite well. Still, local populations were very interested in the development of Polish Legions, they followed military and political events with great enthusiasm, and above all they had taken the 1/14 August declaration of Grand Duke Nikolai Nikolaevich that promised autonomy for Poland after the war quite seriously, coming out in rallies 20,000-strong in cities such as Łódź the day after the proclamation was issued.[147] As 1914 came to a close, it seemed clear that there would be no nationalist Polish uprising to contend with, at least not in the immediate future, but that big political outcomes were envisioned for the end of the conflict.[148]

COSSACKS AND INSECURITY

If imperial officials were calmed by the news that no rebellion was forming, they ought not to have been. The first months of the war had deeply destabilized the borderlands. The destruction of trade networks and the expansion of the role of violence in the economic system through looting and requisition resulted in an unstable official economy suffocated by regulations and a vibrant but lawless

[144] Natsional'nyi Rabochii Soiuz, Natsional'nyi Krest'ianskii Soiuz, Redaktsiia "Pol'shi," Soiuz Nezavisimosti, "Poliaki!" (Translated from Polish by Warsaw gendarmes) (8 August 1914), GARF f. 217, op. 1, d. 304, l. 94.

[145] See the case of Eduard Iozefov Reshke (1915), GARF f. 217, op. 1, d. 315, l. 1–5.

[146] See list included in: Chief of Łomża Province Gendarme Administration, Completely secret circular to chiefs of district gendarme administrations in Łomża province (4 February 1915), GARF f. 1669, op. 1, d. 88, l. 91.

[147] Bakhturina, *Okrainy rossiiskoi imperii: gosudarstvennoe upravlenie i natsional'naia politika v gody Pervoi mirovoi voiny, 1914–1917gg.* (Moscow: ROSSPEN, 2004), 29. This declaration, which had been drawn up at Sazonov's request, was ambitious enough to make the tsar nervous about issuing it over his own signature. The grand duke cut through the emperor's vacillation by issuing it himself, against the protests of several ministers. Needless to say, cautious Poles also noticed the lack of the emperor's signature and calibrated their expectations accordingly. Graf, "Reign of the Generals," 173.

[148] Chief of the Gendarme Administration of Pułtusk and Płońsk districts, Secret letter to chief of the Warsaw Province Gendarme Administration, 12 January 1915, GARF f. 217, op. 1, d. 546, l. 649.

unofficial economy. The weakening of imperial political administration likewise created space for new forms of political activity even as it generally meant a decline of order and security. Finally, the explosion of international conflict in a multi-ethnic and colonial space led to both the ethnicization of politics and deep fears and paranoia expressed in spy mania, pogroms, and various other expressions of violent ethnopolitics.

These processes were colored throughout by the insecurity produced by military assaults upon civilian populations. In contrast to John Keegan's quaint vision of the Great War as "curiously civilized" in this respect,[149] the Eastern Front saw a great deal of inhumanity on the part of combatant armies, not least the Russian army. Indeed, the focus of a great deal of the most recent literature on Russia's war experience has been on the troubling relationship between armed formations and (largely) unarmed civilian groups from the Baltic to the Black seas. Peter Gatrell's award-winning book on refugees, Eric Lohr's work on ethnic assaults, deportations, and property seizures, the ongoing research of Mark von Hagen, Peter Holquist, and Aleksandra Bakhturina on Russian occupation policies in Galicia, and a welcome mixing of the largely unconnected literatures of Jewish history and Russian history in recent years have transformed the study of World War I in Russia.[150]

The firm conclusion reached by all of these authors is that the Russian army not only took on the formal right of governance in the war zone, but also actively pursued an increasingly radical line toward civilian populations in their zones of authority. Gatrell is clear that the high command "jealously guarded" their new civilian powers and that this new dynamic was "one of the main impulses behind population displacement."[151] Lohr goes even further, arguing that the army "drove" deportation orders well beyond the limits civilian officials wanted to uphold, that army policies "allowed socioeconomic and national tensions to become important factors in the emergence of radical violence" toward Jews in particular, and that army commanders even "tolerated the participation of soldiers in pogroms, looting, and rape of Jews and other local civilian populations in the front zones."[152]

In broad strokes, these accounts are true. There can be no doubt that the high command in the first year of the war not only sanctioned, but ordered, mass population movements that fall under the rubric of "ethnic cleansing" ("cleansing," (Russ. *ochishchenie*) was exactly the term they used in their orders). General Ianushkevich, the chief of staff at Stavka until summer 1915, was particularly guilty in this regard. Shloyme Rappaport (better known by the pseudonym

---

[149] John Keegan, *The First World War* (New York: Vintage, 1998), 8.

[150] See Peter Gatrell, *A Whole Empire Walking: Refugees in Russia during World War I* (Bloomington: Indiana University Press, 1999); Lohr, *Nationalizing the Russian Empire*; Viktor Kel'ner, "The Jewish Question and Russian Social Life during World War I," *Russian Studies in History* 43, no. 1 (Summer 2004): 11–40.

[151] Gatrell, *A Whole Empire Walking*, 16.

[152] Eric Lohr, "The Russian Army and the Jews: Mass Deportation, Hostages, and Violence during World War I," *Russian Review* 60 (July 2001): 405; Lohr, *Nationalizing the Russian Empire*, 17.

S. An-sky) saw much of the devastation in person, but he first saw its results when he visited Warsaw in November 1914. The city, he writes, was "still reeling" from the German assault in October and swamped by displaced Jews. Thousands of refugees arrived daily to join the more than 50,000 already there.[153] The refugees he visited "spoke softly, in a monotone, with stony faces. It was as if these people had lost themselves as well as all hope." What they spoke of was violence and forced migration. "It was the same story everywhere: Cossacks had ridden in with swords and sticks, driven the Jews out of their homes and ordered them to leave town."[154] The evidence of a massive assault on the empire's Jewish population was there for anyone to see, and many did. But Ianushkevich was one of those many twentieth-century true believers, for whom reality had little purchase over their toxic imagination. Thus, in the midst of another wave of Jewish deportations in February 1915, he chastised Count Bobrinskii in the following way: "Stavka has received reports that Jews are continuing to terrorize the Russian and Polish population, and that your treatment of them, despite this, continues to be too delicate. In view of this, I beg you to take measures for the strictest execution of existing orders, without allowing any weakening of them."[155]

It is also clear that Russian soldiers, on their own initiative, launched vicious anti-Jewish and anti-German pogroms both in the occupied territories and in the borderland regions of the Russian empire.[156] More generally, as we have seen, they indulged in plunder operations. However, as we have also seen, the incidents of looting and other forms of civilian abuse caused great consternation among many other Russian soldiers and commanders. If, by 1917 (and into the Civil War), violence against civilians had become commonplace, even accepted and laudable in certain circumstances, the same was not yet true in 1914. It would take years of internal and external war to break down the conviction of most officers and a great many soldiers that abusing civilians destroyed discipline, created more dangerous conditions for the troops, and fomented instability.

Take, for instance, the important figure of General Aleksei Brusilov. Brusilov's hands are far from clean in regard to ethnic cleansing and the later decision to undertake scorched earth policies, but his records are filled with concern over the undisciplined looting of his soldiers, a fixation that indicates that looting was a widespread phenomenon, but also leaves no doubt as to Brusilov's own desire to stamp it out. As early as 9/22 September 1914, he complained to one of his corps commanders about soldiers robbing the people with whom they were quartered and ordered courts martial to punish the perpetrators.[157] At about the same time,

---

[153] The Warsaw refugee problem was already international news by then. See "Refugees Warsaw Problem: Halls and Warehouses Filled with Homeless Victims of the War," *New York Times* (16 October 1914), 3.

[154] An-sky, 12–14.

[155] Telegram from Ianushkevich to Bobrinskii, 1 February 1915, RGVIA f. 2005, op. 1, d. 12, l. 89.

[156] Dzh. Klier [John Klier], "Kazaki i pogromy: chem otlichalis' 'voennye' pogromy?" in *Mirovoi krizis 1914–1920 godov i sud'ba vostochnoevropeiskogo evreistva*, ed. O. V. Budnitskii (Moscow: ROSSPEN, 2005): 47–74.

[157] Telegram from Brusilov to the commander of the XXIV Corps, 9 September 1914, RGVIA f. 2134, op. 2, d. 580, l. 12.

he also urged his superiors to treat the issue seriously by taking the "most decisive and stern measures of struggle against marauding," including the establishment of military police inspections up to 100 kilometers from the front line.[158] Even Ianushkevich, in the very document cited previously, wrote that "the interests of our army and the Russian population come first, but of course only in conditions that forbid robbery and marauding, which in any instance is unacceptable."[159]

Brusilov and Ianushkevich had reason to be concerned. The reports that they were reading indicated that the poor treatment of civilians might lead to a much more difficult occupation. As the L'viv governor wrote in October 1914, he was receiving daily reports from local residents "on the continuous robbery and violence performed by the Cossacks, both by those passing through the district towards their positions and those stationed in the district." Cossacks sometimes took the last bits of property from local residents, especially livestock and grain. The fear that resulted led many local peasants to keep their livestock hidden inside, and the harvest was consequently ungathered, leading to food shortages and higher prices. As the governor warned, "this attitude on the part of enlisted men is eliciting the most extreme irritation towards Russian troops on the part of the local population and in the future threatens serious impoverishment and even famine both for people and animals."[160]

The accused parties in this case came from Cossack units, whose reputation for wild brutality was so well established that it behooves historians to be skeptical of constant claims that the "Cossacks did it." Even the most ardent skepticism, however, cannot fully overcome the impression on the part of nearly all parties involved that Cossacks (and their counterparts in the so-called Savage Division of men from the Caucasus) were indeed far more likely to commit crimes against civilians than regular enlisted men were. Again, a systematic examination of assaults upon civilians on the Eastern Front would be helpful to establish the different forms and perpetrators of violence, but there is sufficient evidence to suspect that Russian military occupation of both foreign and domestic regions would have been far milder if Cossack units had been absent. One analysis of a sample of fifty-four pogroms notes that nearly all (fifty-one) began with soldiers present and that "more than four-fifths of the reports explicitly identify the appearance of Cossacks in the area as the key event spurring the pogrom."[161]

We can start from the top, again with Brusilov. In early November 1914, he received a very explicit report from the commander of a convoy unit who visited the city of Sanok soon after Russian troops occupied it. While this convoy commander was posting notices demanding the collection of weapons from citizens, he learned

---

[158] Telegram from Brusilov to Stavka, n.d. (but late August or early September 1914), RGVIA f. 2134, op. 1. d. 534, l. 28.

[159] Telegram from Ianushkevich to Bobrinskii, 1 February 1915, RGVIA f. 2005, op. 1, d. 12, l. 89.

[160] Letter from the Governor of L'vov (Ministry of Internal Affairs) to the Military Governor General of Galicia, 4 October 1914, RGVIA f. 2134, op. 2, d. 580, l. 81.

[161] Eric Lohr, "1915 and the War Pogrom Paradigm in the Russian Empire," in *Anti-Jewish Violence: Rethinking the Pogrom in East European History*, ed. Dekel-Chen et al. (Bloomington: Indiana University Press, 2011), 42.

that many residents had already fled the city because of Cossack robberies. He then went to the town of Rimanuv and saw the following scene: "Cossacks of the 2nd Cossack Line Regiment were coming out of stores with bags, accompanied by local peasant Ruthenians with bags robbed from the stores and apartments. On the square 10–12 Cossacks of the Orenburg Regiment were standing around doing nothing to stop the robbery." Wanting to do something, the convoy commander shot his revolver in the air and began to beat the looting soldiers he could get his hands on, leading to a brief dispersal. But many drunken Cossacks continued their activities, so he sought out the Cossack commander, whom he forced to take control of the situation. When the drunken soldiers had disappeared, the local Polish and Jewish merchants came bearing complaints that they had been "totally ransacked." Their stores and apartments had been looted of all money and valuables, and then, for good measure, the Cossacks had broken their plates and furniture before departing.[162] In response, Brusilov's staff wrote up a draft order noting the widespread marauding and chastising officers for not taking decisive measures. Tellingly, though the order began by talking broadly about "enlisted men," the language slipped later in the document to simply talk about the "complete destruction of apartments and stores by Cossacks."[163]

The second reason to suspect that Cossacks treated civilians worse than their regular army counterparts was that civilians commonly turned to regular officers for protection or recompense from Cossacks. In Anatolia in 1916, Ensign Romanov was approached by peasants from the village of Ki who complained that Cossacks of the Fifth Hundred of the 4th Don Battalion had punched them and threatened them with bayonets when stealing a bull from them. Romanov promptly investigated and found conflict rather than satisfaction on visiting the Cossack unit. In the acting commander's (Golubintsev's) account, Romanov entered swearing and calling them "forty year old thieves, robbers, and marauders" before rounding on Golubintsev in a "most inappropriate and rude way." Golubintsev refused to believe that his Cossacks would do such a thing, since they got plenty of food in the mess, and used as his proof the fact that no one had come to him with a complaint. The conclusion of the Cossack commanders was that Romanov should be punished for being rude to an officer and that they should be left alone. It appears from the file that no one was in fact punished for this incident.[164]

Nevertheless, we might be forgiven for believing Romanov rather than Golubintsev, since existing evidence also indicates that few Cossacks thought that looting enemy populations was wrong; indeed, most appear to have taken the spoils of war as a Cossack entitlement.[165] One Cossack from the Caucasian Front testified to that effect: "That a Cossack can steal something from a Turk is normal.

---

[162] Report from commander of the 193rd etap to Colonel Zabolotnyi, 5 November 1914, RGVIA f. 2134, op. 2, d. 153, l. 157–158.

[163] Draft order of Eighth Army, November 1914, RGVIA f. 2134, op. 2, d. 153, l. 162.

[164] Reports of Romanov and Golubintsev, July 1916, RGVIA f. 2294, op. 1, d. 282, ll. 765–767.

[165] These questions of plunder, exemplary punishment, and the concept of "civilized" war were much in the air just before the war, especially in the wake of the repression of the Boxer Rebellion, where the Cossacks also built a rather nefarious reputation for themselves. On this, see James Louis

In war many rob, but under the name 'requisitions'—forage for the horses, livestock for the feeding of people, and so on—this is the psychology of war, after all war itself is violence. But to hand over a Cossack for this to military field court . . . was simply unfair."[166] Others were equally clear. One officer recounted asking a Cossack whether they had taken any prisoners in a recent raid and was met with the display of a bloody knife and the retort, "Why prisoners? Smash their brains!"[167]

Finally, enemy commanders observed a difference. Here is Hindenburg, commenting obliquely on the common practice of all combatant sides to execute men who surrendered.[168] "It was only against the Cossacks that our men could not contain their rage. They were considered the authors of all the bestial brutalities under which the people and country of East Prussia had suffered so cruelly. The Cossack apparently suffered from a bad conscience, for whenever he saw himself likely to be taken prisoner he did his best to remove the broad stripe on his trousers which distinguished his branch of the service."[169] From the testimony of the victims, the perpetrators, and military witnesses from both sides of the conflict, then, we have evidence that Cossack units were the primary (though certainly not the sole) culprits in the widespread abuse of civilian populations that occurred on the Eastern Front in the first year of the war. At the end of the day, however, it mattered little to civilians whether they were being abused by Cossacks or regular army troops. For many communities on both sides of the front line, martial law brought not order but a thinly veiled savagery. Civilians were left defenseless in the face of unprecedentedly destructive forces, and the state had abandoned them to their fates.

CONCLUSION

Armchair mapgazers following the progress of the first months of the Great War may have come to the conclusion in March 1915 that the Russian Empire was strengthening and expanding as a result of the war. The Russian invasion of East Prussia had of course failed, but the Russian army had made significant progress in the south. Much of Galicia had been conquered in the fall and winter campaigns, and those lands were slated for rapid annexation to the Romanov Empire. Tsar Nicholas II himself went on a controversial visit to the Galician capital of L'viv in April 1915 in order to solidify this claim, and little in the conflict between the

Hevia, *English Lessons: The Pedagogy of Imperialism in Nineteenth-Century China* (Durham, NC: Duke University Press, 2003), esp. 78–81.

[166] F. I. Eliseev, *Kazaki na kavkazskom fronte 1914–1917* (Moscow: Voenizdat, 2001), 228.

[167] Diary entry of S. An-sky, 23 January 1915, manuscript copy of diary translation by Polly Zavadivker, 31. Many thanks to the translator for providing me with a copy of her work.

[168] For a recent examination of this practice, see Niall Ferguson, "Prisoner Taking and Prisoner Killing in the Age of Total War: Towards a Political Economy of Military Defeat." *War in History* 11, no. 2 (2004): 148–92.

[169] Marshal Paul von Hindenburg, *Out of My Life*, trans. F. A. Holt (London: Cassell and Co., 1920), 97; for more on Russian (and Cossack) atrocities in East Prussia, see Knox, 1: 62, 68.

Russians and Austro-Hungarians suggested that L'viv would soon revert to Viennese control. In the north, though the Germans had won most of the battles, those victories had brought little strategic consequence. Armies stood roughly at the prewar border, and the fully mobilized German Empire now had to face a set of enemies that was growing stronger each day. New soldiers kept filling the Russian ranks, and the British continually increased the size of their armed forces and tightened the noose of the economic blockade. Perhaps even more surprisingly, there was even less chance of ethnic unrest in the western empire than there had been on the eve of the war. There was no Polish rebellion, no Latvian rebellion, no Georgian rebellion, and no Ukrainian rebellion anywhere to be seen. Russophiles in the region worked actively to support the Russian war effort, Russophobes helped the Austrians and the Germans. Most nationalists tried to figure out which way the wind was blowing on any given day and trimmed their sails accordingly.

But neither the map nor the military outlook told the true story of the empire's fortunes. Behind the scenes, the Russian Empire had laid the basis for its own self-destruction. The imposition of martial law severed the links between governance and authority throughout the entire western empire. Experts in local affairs melted away, some picking up guns, some fleeing eastward, many others disappearing without leaving a historical trace. The men charged by the high command with civilian administration were few in number and poor in qualifications. The task of imperial administration, tricky at the best of times, was virtually abandoned. In its place was raw power—men with guns. Some of these men behaved well, others were inclined toward atrocity, but military discipline everywhere proved a thin reed. By spring 1915, what we can call the "state" and "society" in the borderlands stuck together mostly out of habit and a lack of alternatives. Trust, legitimacy, prosperity, reliability, accountability, and above all hope for the future were deeply weakened. The state and an empire teetered on the verge of collapse. The Germans were about to push it over the edge.

2

The Front Migrates

Gorlice is a small, pretty Polish town of about 28,000 people situated in the foothills of the Carpathian Mountains, roughly thirty kilometers north of the current Slovakian border. In the center of town stands an aging museum devoted to the battle that put the town on the world map in the spring of 1915. The curators have displayed photographs and artifacts from the battle, have built a three-dimensional relief map of the town's environs showing troop locations and movements, and have even created a wax museum of notable figures from the era ranging from General Mackensen to the town's mayor. The museum gets visits from local schoolchildren on field trips and from Poles with the right guidebooks, but most travelers go elsewhere. Foreign tourists are small in number, according to the museum administrators. There is a thin stream of Germans, a handful of others, but almost no Russians ever come to the spot. Even fewer make it to the hilltops and forests surrounding the town, where dozens of military cemeteries lie mostly unobserved in varying degrees of repair or disrepair. Judging by the material evidence at these sites, they are used mainly by teenagers seeking seclusion.[1] The memorials are sobering. Some indicate German soldiers by name, others mark the locations of mass graves of Austro-Hungarian soldiers, and still others show where Russians are buried. But these cemeteries do not contain all of those killed in battle, for many corpses went unburied or were hastily covered with dirt. Local residents still find the bones, bullets, and shell fragments from those days of destruction today. The truth is that Gorlice is a graveyard, not just of men, but of the Russian Empire as well.

RETREAT FROM GALICIA

In 1915, Gorlice was a small town in the Austro-Hungarian Empire, more than 300 kilometers from the pre-war Russian border. Despite its distance from Russia proper, this region held a special place in the Russian nationalist imagination. It is believed that the great Slavic migrations of the sixth century began from these northern slopes of the Carpathians, and it was to this region that the Slavic world (or at least Slavs in arms) had returned, fighting on both sides of the conflict. In Aleksei Ksiunin's first dispatch from Gorlice in 1915, he told of passing a small

[1] For a catalog of these cemeteries (including pictures), see <http://www.cmentarze.gorlice.net.pl/Gorlice/Gorlice.htm> (accessed 23 March 2013).

village funeral with a wooden coffin and a pretty young girl in mourning. "If not for the mountains," he wrote, "you could have thought that you were travelling through one of our villages near Moscow or Kostroma. Even the faces of these peasants were the same—round and simple. The huts were the same too."[2]

Ksiunin, a Russian journalist, was able to visit Gorlice because the Russian invasion of Galicia had forced the Austrian army to retreat all the way back to the Gorlice–Tarnow line by the autumn of 1914. From these lines, the Russian army was well positioned to either make an assault on Kraków or across the Carpathians and onto the Hungarian plains. As we saw in Chapter 1, Russian efforts to accomplish the latter task were mired in ice and snow during the winter of 1914–1915. The effort to take Kraków likewise sputtered out after the Battle of Limanowa in December 1914. As spring arrived and the snows melted, however, these opportunities presented themselves anew. Przemyśl surrendered to the Russians on 9/22 March 1915, and there was now no threat from the rear. Austrian armies had suffered terribly over the winter campaigns, and Romania and Italy were engaging in talks to join the Entente. In early April, Russian troops from the Third and Eighth Armies seized the peaks of the Beskids and seemed poised to go further.[3] Indeed, on 29 March/11 April, Grand Duke Nikolai Nikolaevich impatiently grilled General N. I. Ivanov at the Southwestern Front, asking why he was not energetically pursuing their enemies in the mountains.[4] Internally, the Habsburg army was becoming increasingly demoralized, with low supplies and high ethnic tension. The Austro-Hungarian Empire found itself facing the possibility of defeat, a prospect that spelled doom for the war efforts of the Central Powers as a whole. Austrian policymakers begged and cajoled Germany for greater military support on their front, and these entreaties soon turned to threats. Even Conrad thought it wise to frighten his German counterparts in April with the prospect of making a separate peace, telling Erich von Falkenhayn, the chief of the German General Staff, that he would rather give up Galicia to the Russians than lose Trieste to Italy.[5]

For all of these reasons, the German high command made the decision to propose a joint operation with their Austro-Hungarian colleagues in mid-April. They would send one of their most accomplished field commanders—General Mackensen—along with a newly formed Eleventh Army to join the Austro-Hungarian Fourth Army in an assault on the center of the Russian lines. Mackensen would be in command of both armies but would be subordinate to the high commands of both the Austrians and the Germans. He planned to drive through the gap between the northern slopes of the Carpathians and the Vistula River by opening up an attack across a wide fifty-five-kilometer front from Gorlice to

[2] Aleksei Ksiunin, *Narod na voine: iz zapisok voennogo korrespondenta* (Petrograd: Izd. B. A. Suvorina, 1916), 191.

[3] I. I. Rostunov, *Russkii front pervoi mirovoi voiny* (Moscow: Izd. Nauka, 1976), 231.

[4] Telegram from General Ianushkevich (Stavka) to General Ivanov (Southwestern Front), 29 March 1915, HIA, Collection: Russia—Shtab Verkhovnogo Glavnokomanduiushchego, box 1, folder "Osnovnye direktivy," n. p.

[5] Norman Stone, *The Eastern Front, 1914–1917* (New York: Penguin, 1999 [1975]), 128.

Tarnów. This sector seemed vulnerable not only for geographic reasons, but also for reasons of troop deployment. Russian authorities, planning to attack in the Carpathians, had stationed forty-four of the sixty-seven divisions on the Southwestern Front in the mountains rather than in the lowlands.[6] The remaining twenty-three divisions would be easier to outnumber and outgun. Consequently, the Central Powers concentrated superior forces (about ten more divisions and 140,000 more men than were present on the Russian side) and superior firepower (roughly double the number of artillery pieces) in the hopes of saving the alliance and the war effort.[7]

The attack began at 10 a.m. on the morning of 19 April/2 May with an artillery barrage that lasted all day and well into the night. Hour after hour, the Germans pounded the insufficiently prepared Russian defensive lines. Troops were poorly entrenched and protected for a number of reasons. In the first place, officers and soldiers alike held widespread contempt for the building of field fortifications, which they associated with the failures in Manchuria during the Russo-Japanese War and with a lack of élan.[8] The spring melt had left many trenches half-filled with water, and other defenses had been hastily put together in the period of invasion the previous year. Efforts to improve defenses had not gone far, in part because when the X Corps had asked for help earlier that spring to build entrenched reserve positions, the high command responded that if they had enough manpower to worry about these issues then they had enough to give to other sectors of the front. Two regiments were peeled off from the Corps to give to the armies planning the invasion in the Carpathians.[9] General Radko Radko-Dmitriev, the commander of the Third Army, knew that he had insufficient reserves and that the enemy was massing on the other side of the line. General Ivanov, the commander of the Southwestern Front, ignored Radko-Dmitriev's requests for help and continued to pour men into the Carpathian armies for the spring invasion.[10] Shell shortages were also a problem. The Third Army had, on paper at least, a reserve for each gun of about 400–500 shells. This number, though lower than the Germans had at the time, was not catastrophic. Other combatant forces could and did mount successful defenses with less during the war. But separate units and different batteries tended to hoard materials during the war. As a result, guns placed in the busiest parts of the battle did run out at inopportune times.[11] Enemy artillery, now safe from counter-battery fire, rained down ever more murderous barrages on the Russian infantry. To make matters worse, the Russian army had adopted the practice of staffing first-line

[6] Neil M. Heyman, "Gorlice-Tarnow: The Eastern Front in 1915," *The Army Quarterly and Defence Journal* 109, no. 1 (1979): 61.

[7] Rostunov, 236.

[8] General A. A. Brusilov, *A Soldier's Notebook, 1914–1918* (Westport, CT: Greenwood Press, 1971 [1930]), 142–3.

[9] Stone, 135–6.   [10] Brusilov, 126.

[11] Even Norman Stone, generally skeptical about Stavka's constant complaints of munitions shortages, concedes that even though the role of the lack of shells in the Russian defeats of 1915 has been "exaggerated," there is "little dispute" about the scale of the problem in the spring of 1915 and that "[s]hell shortage could not have been more clearly documented than by Russian abandonment of Poland that summer." Stone, 144–7.

trenches quite heavily rather than leaving thin screens in the front in favor of a stronger reserve system in fortifications further behind the line. The first day was thus extremely bloody, as indeed the whole battle would be.

German and Austrian units began combined artillery and infantry assaults at one in the morning on the next day, 20 April/3 May, at the very northern edge of the battle zone, near Tarnów. These attacks did not succeed, in part because Russian artillery had survived the initial barrage in this sector and sprang into action to defend the infantry below them. Other sectors were less fortunate. Later that day, German and Austrian troops broke through near Gromnik (thirty-five kilometers north of Gorlice) and in Gorlice itself. Radko-Dmitriev begged for reserve forces, but all that Ivanov had to give was the III Caucasian Corps. Ivanov in turn requested support from the other fronts, but he was given only the 13th Siberian Division from the Northwestern Front. After that, Grand Duke Nikolai Nikolaevich informed him, "you must search for means of strengthening the threatened sectors with your own resources from the Southwestern Front."[12] With the line broken and no reserves able to stop the incursion of the enemy, Radko-Dmitriev and Ivanov either had to order a retreat or risk the encirclement of neighboring units to the north and south. They chose the former, retreating on 23 April/6 May to a new line along the Wisloka River about twenty-five kilometers east of the previous line. The key to the initial defeat at Gorlice was not the shells or morale, but the staff room. The mismanagement of reserves was, in the opinion of General Brusilov at least, an act of "criminal carelessness."[13]

The leadership at Stavka was outraged by the order to retreat, and it insisted that the line must be held in little towns along the Wisloka such as Pilzno and Jasło. Radko-Dmitriev resolved that the best way to stop the retreat was to launch a counterattack, which he did on 24–25 April/7–8 May. The maneuver was a disaster. Cavalry units rode into the teeth of the storm, never to return. Fresh German reinforcements clobbered Russian forces along the whole front. The XXIV Corps, normally staffed with 40,000 men, emerged from the battle with less than 1,000.[14] Now retreat was the only option, but Stavka still insisted on staying put and even launching new counterattacks. Ivanov's entreaties to withdraw were met with the grand duke's "categorical order . . . not to undertake any retreat whatsoever without my express permission."[15] The Third Army suffered for two more days before being given permission to retreat another fifty kilometers to the San River. Their presence did not slow the enemy advance, as German and Austro-Hungarian troops crossed the Wisloka with ease up and down the river by 26 April/9 May.[16] Of 250,000 Russian soldiers in position a week earlier, only 40,000 men made it

---

[12] Cited in Rostunov, 240.

[13] Brusilov. In fairness, most Russian generals were quite bad at deploying reserves throughout the war. See Major-General Sir Alfred Knox, *With the Russian Army, 1914–1917: Being Chiefly Extracts from the Diary of a Military Attaché*, 2 vols. (London: Hutchinson & Co., 1921), 1: 222.

[14] Stone, 138.   [15] Stone, 139.

[16] Richard L. DiNardo, *Breakthrough: The Gorlice-Tarnow Campaign, 1915* (Santa Barbara: Praeger, 2010), 70.

back to the San unharmed on 30 April/13 May 1915.[17] In addition to the tremendous number of dead and wounded, hundreds of thousands of men simply disappeared from the army as deserters, prisoners, or missing in action. More than 100,000 men were lost in this way in May 1915 alone, and more than 500,000 vanished from May through August.[18] The Third Army was no more than a "harmless mob" by 6 June.[19]

Stavka had held out so long in the face of the unwelcome news because the retreat to the San made the Carpathian positions (and therefore the invasion of Hungary) untenable—exactly the reason why the Central Powers had launched the offensive when and where they did. The Russian invasion force in the mountains simply had to pack up and retreat, much to the dismay and confusion of the enlisted men, who had fought hard battles in ice and snow to make it to the peaks by spring only to give it all back over the period of a couple of marches. Leonid Andrusov was a medical worker stationed on the peaks of the Carpathians near the present-day Ukrainian village of Rozhanka with the Eighth Army in those spring days. On 30 April/13 May, rumors spread that their regiment was about to be replaced on the front. "Then the secret came out that it would be the Germans who would replace us. . . . No one knew the reasons for the retreat."[20] Ordered to pack up all their gear immediately and conduct a night march, they were fortunate that the enemy units facing them did not realize that they were retreating. Even the companies ordered to cover the retreat fled. Instead, Andrusov's unit got a head start and marched eighty kilometers through a landscape that alternated between bucolic spring scenes and the burning oil fields of Drohobych to a line of defense in the village of Bratkovichi near the town of Stryi before digging in to defend. Similar scenes played out all over the Carpathians, as all Russian units save one made it to the new line of defense unmolested. That one unit—the 48th Infantry Division— was captured more because its impetuous commander Lavr Kornilov recklessly counterattacked than because of severe pressure from the enemy.

The Russians had drawn their line in the San, but it too was soon obliterated. Two weeks of battles raged along the river during 1–7/14–20 May before the high command once more realized the need to retreat. The Italian entry into the war on the side of the Entente on 10/23 May caused the Central Powers to halt the offensive for a time to assess the situation, but the attacks resumed with success three weeks later at the beginning of June. On 9/22 June, the Austrians marched down the streets of L'viv, having almost completely reversed the Russian success in Galicia from the year before. In contrast to 1914, however, the success in Galicia brought strategic gains across the entire front. Romania, spooked, did not (yet) enter the war on the side of the Entente. Even more significantly, with the Southwestern Front in apparently endless retreat and a simultaneous German

---

[17] Stone, 139.

[18] Report of the Duty General at Stavka, cited in Mikhail Lemke, *250 dnei v tsarskoi stavke: vospominaniia, memuary*, 2 vols. (Minsk: Kharvest, 2003), 1:52.

[19] Knox, 1: 287.

[20] Leonid N. Andrusov, manuscript of memoirs, Biblioteka-fond "Russkogo Zarubezh'ia" (BFRZ), d. E-134, l. 9.

offensive successfully proceeding along the Baltic coast, Russian Poland became ever more exposed. The Russian dream in 1914 of a two front attack that would force its enemies to abandon their territories east of the Danzig to Kraków line had been reversed. If a straight line were to be established in 1915, it would leave Poland in the hands of the Central Powers.

The Central Powers did not pause long to consolidate their spring gains. Predictably (and not unreasonably), Hindenburg and Ludendorff pushed for a decisive blow, perhaps even toward Petrograd. Falkenhayn, however, was just as reasonable in his conviction that a decisive invasion was impossible against an enemy that had so much space to retreat. They decided in the end to rehabilitate the war plans of 1914 by planning a pincer movement that would trap the Russian forces fighting in Poland in an enormous encirclement. If successful, the maneuver would bottle up five Russian armies, or half of their fighting forces along the front. This would of course represent a major victory, but it would not entail an invasion of the Russian heartland. The end game was to force Russia to sign a separate peace, not to conquer and occupy the whole country.

The prospects for German success were greater in 1915 than they had been a year earlier. In the first place, they had momentum, and they had it for a reason. Russian men fought with insufficient supplies, and Russian generals maneuvered with insufficient skill. There seemed no particular reason why either of these conditions would change in the short term. Secondly, the price of German support for the Austrian cause earlier in the year was putting Germans in control of the southern part of the front as well as the northern. Mackensen's group was a combined force of the German Ninth Army and Austro-Hungarian Fourth Army, and in June he assumed control over the Austro-Hungarian Second Army and the newly formed German Army of the Bug (River) as well. Austria had complete control only over the far south of the line, and those forces had the least success of any over the course of the summer. As General Brusilov put it, the Austrians "caused us very little trouble," in part because they used little artillery.[21]

The broader plan of encirclement was relatively simple. Mackensen would wheel due north from his positions along the San, while the German Eighth and Ninth armies would push southward from East Prussia, hoping to meet either at Siedlce, the old 1914 target, or perhaps as far east as Brest-Litovsk. At the far northern end of the front, the German Tenth and Niemen armies would drive eastward out of East Prussia into Lithuania (see Map 5). If Russian generals behaved as they had done during the Gorlice campaign, by fighting too long in ravaged forward positions, the plan would likely succeed.

The German offensive thus put the Russian high command in a difficult spot. They either had to fight to save Poland and risk losing the heart of their armed forces, or they had to sacrifice Poland by executing a complicated fighting retreat. The threat was real enough that they began the process of evacuating Warsaw quite early, on 20 June/3 July. Historical valuables, families of state and military officials,

---

[21] Brusilov, 167.

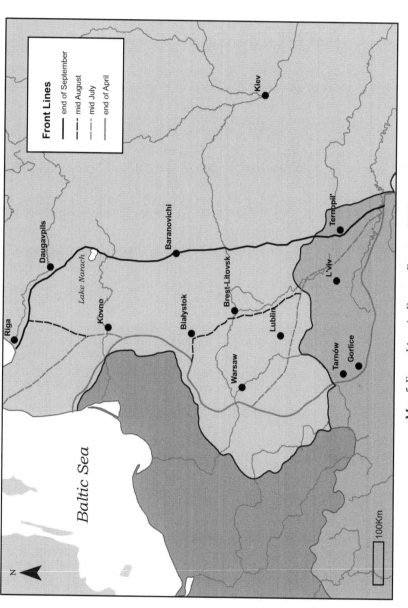

Map 5 Front Lines in Eastern Europe, 1915

and all factories not directly serving the needs of the city or the army were packed up and began moving eastward. Food reserves for one month were to be left in Warsaw and on the left bank of the Vistula. All the rest was to be requisitioned and moved across the river. On 25 June/8 July, they made preparations for destroying the bridges across the Vistula. In the rural regions around Warsaw, the Second Army began implementing plans for mass requisitions and destruction of property.[22]

Despite these preparations in the rear for retreat, Stavka continued to order combat troops to stand and fight. In the south, Mackensen hammered his way northward, perfecting the "Mackensen Wedge." A hurricane of shells would pulverize the exposed, barely entrenched Russian forces, and then the infantry would march in to take the new lines. They would then bring the artillery up and start all over again. Andrusov described the impact of such an attack. His line of forces was breached when two companies of the 312th Vasil'kovskii Regiment, "unable to bear the shelling, put their hands in the air and surrendered. The Germans immediately sent strong forces into the breach and within an hour or so had taken the town of Stryi."[23] From his vantage point at a dressing station on a hill on the end of a line, Andrusov described what came next:

> I saw how the Germans drove a large herd of livestock out of Bratkovichi. Then a mob of our prisoners went through. Soon the enemy line stretched from Bratkovichi to the nearest grove, and they began to rush forward toward Falish (the next village). All at once the 12-pounders that had been silent in recent days spoke up, and all along the village enormous fountains of earth began to soar into the air. Dirt, wood, and enormous shell fragments rained down everywhere.... One after another, huge suitcases [shells] flew in with a horrible howl, shaking the earth with their explosions. It was a real hell all around, since virtually the whole civilian population had remained in the village up until this point. With howling and crying, women and children were racing about the village, not knowing where to run; the livestock were bellowing.[24]

This was what the Mackensen Wedge looked like at the ground level throughout Poland and Ukraine.

Mackensen's tactics, tried so often on so many fronts during the war, were defeated elsewhere by multiple, extensive lines of deep fortifications and the rapid deployment of reserves once a breakthrough occurred. Russian generals, however, continued to focus on holding forward positions rather than trying to fortify lines deeper to the rear, so when the inevitable falling back occurred it was to insufficiently prepared places. As a result, fewer and fewer men had the luxury of falling back. Mackensen simply ground entire armies into dust with his multiple armies moving forward in major battles. The Army of the Bug won at Hrubieszów on 8/21 July and Chełm on 19 July/1 August. The Fourth and Ninth armies succeeded at Krasnystaw on 9/22 July and at Lublin on 23 July/5 August.[25] Some engagements

[22] Commander of Second Army, Telegram to Warsaw Governor General, 20 June 1915, GARF f. 215, op. 1, d. 174, l. 304.

[23] Andrusov, manuscript of memoirs, BFRZ, d. E-134, l. 11.

[24] Andrusov, manuscript of memoirs, BFRZ, d. E-134, ll. 12–13.   [25] Rostunov, 256–7.

ended with enormous numbers of prisoners (15,000 in one day at the Battle of Krasnystaw), but mostly the dead and wounded piled up. By late July, roughly a month since Mackensen's pincer had moved north, the two Russian armies facing him were short 180,000 men.[26] Mackensen, whose troops had been slaughtered in retreat in the very first engagement of the war at Gumbinnen, was now getting his revenge. The only downside to this method, one that would turn out to have significance, was that it was slow.

RETREAT FROM POLAND

The other half of the pincer came down from East Prussia. The German Twelfth Army led by General Max von Gallwitz struck at the hinge of the Russian First and Twelfth armies on 30 June/13 July near Przasnysz. Once more Russian commanders tried to hold their forward positions, once more it was in vain. The two Russian armies communicated poorly, fought one another for reserves, and tried to rely on bravado for victory. General Litvinov, the commander of the First Army, ordered "categorically that all troops should hold their lines." The artillerymen of the First Army had fewer shells than the units in Gorlice had had, bullets were running out, and thousands of infantry lacked rifles.[27] Most of them died cowering in ditches, and 24,000 more were soon taken prisoner. In four days, the two Russian armies took a 70 percent casualty rate and had to retreat several kilometers. Seeing the difficult situation, General Alekseev (the front commander), ordered a retreat to the Narew River (roughly fifty kilometers away).[28] The smaller German concentrations to the north and between the two pincers also had a relatively easy time, in part assisted by gas attacks during an advance on 25 June/8 July.[29] The northern arm made it nearly to Kovno by 30 June/13 July.

While the positions along the Narew were relatively well prepared for a Russian defense, it had become clear that the tactic of staying put and fighting was leading to catastrophe. Hundreds of thousands of men were casualties in those early days of July, and the Germans seemed poised to finish the rest of them off. Finally, on 9/22 July, Stavka ordered retreat eastward to a line centered on Siedlce. The goal, as Front Commander M. V. Alekseev said to General Palitsyn on the morning of 10/23 July, was to "lead our troops out of the cauldron."[30] The battle along the Narew, which began later that day, was thus mainly a covering action from the perspective of the Russians, who fought to allow the central armies and the population of Warsaw to evacuate the Polish pocket. The Germans forced their way across the Narew on the first day of fighting, but the Russian armies fought long and hard enough to delay the German entry into Warsaw until 22 July/4 August, by

---

[26] Stone, 178.   [27] Rostunov, 258.   [28] Stone, 180.

[29] "O rasprostranenii germantsami udushlivykh gazov v raione Gumin-Berzhimov," RGVIA f. 12651, op. 1, d. 1152, l. 95–96.

[30] Quoted in Vera Alekseeva-Borel', *Sorok let v riadakh russkoi imperatorskoi armii: M. V. Alekseev* (Sankt-Peterburg: Bel'veder, 2000), 387.

which time the evacuation was mostly complete. These rearguard units displayed the same strengths and weaknesses that the Russian military had displayed over the course of the first year of the war. Units fought hard and inflicted serious casualties on German troops, but they were short on supplies. Ensign A. I. Todorskii noted in his diary that after several days of a fighting retreat, his men nearly ran out of bullets and were saved only by timely artillery support and scavenging the bodies of their mates for rifle ammunition.[31]

The last hope for the defense of Russian Poland was the string of fortresses that had been constructed and maintained at great cost prior to the war and had been supplied with scarce men and munitions during it. The citadels fell like a house of cards instead. In Ivangorod, the fortress commander begged for a proper garrison, but his reeling bosses at Stavka and in the Fourth Army could not bear to spare them until it was too late. The soldiers manning the fortifications were not supplied with sufficient bullets, with one crucial brigade having only 90 bullets per man at the start of the defense. Further miscommunications doomed the position. Just as the Russians had stabilized their defenses in Ivangorod on 11/24 July, Stavka demanded that they retreat. Eleven days later, on the same day that Warsaw surrendered, German and Austrian troops entered the fortress.[32] Other fortresses met the same fate. Kovno collapsed on 5/18 August, Novogeorgievsk surrendered on 6/19 August, Osowiec gave way on 9/22 August, and Brest-Litovsk capitulated on 13/26 August. By the end of August, the Russian Empire's rule in Poland, present since the days of Catherine the Great, was over.

The Great Retreat meant not only a military withdrawal but also a massive dislocation of civilian populations.[33] As we saw in Chapter 1, both forcible deportations and voluntary flight had been occurring since the start of the war. The declaration of martial law facilitated these deportations, as Stavka gutted Russia's already weak judicial protections when it took control. Legal procedures were streamlined, particularly in cases of suspected espionage, treason, or sabotage. The practices prescribed soon after the declaration of war mandated automatic deportation to the interior of the empire for suspicion of participation in troublesome activities.[34] In some cases, these regulations worked to soften the blows of military justice. Being convicted of many of these crimes meant death; if forced to choose simply between conviction and acquittal, authorities would as a matter of course convict and execute a number of people whose guilt remained in some doubt. Deportation offered officials an easy way out. They did not need to find

---

[31] "'Okopy eti okhrainiat Varshavu, k kotoroi tak neravnodushen nemets . . .': dnevnik nachal'nika sapernoi komandy 24-go Sibirskogo strelkovogo polka praporshchika A. I. Todorskogo, iiun'-sentiabr' 1915 goda," *Voenno-istoricheskii zhurnal* no. 9 (2004): 23–4.

[32] Lieutentant General A. V. fon Shvarts, *Ivangorod v 1914–1915: iz vospominaniia komendanta kreposti* (Paris: Tanais, 1969), 127–66.

[33] Much of this section is taken from an earlier article: Joshua Sanborn, "Unsettling the Empire: Violent Migrations and Social Disaster in Russia during World War I," *Journal of Modern History* 77, no. 2 (June 2005): 290–324.

[34] Circular to district court prosecutors in Warsaw province from the Ministry of Justice, 6 August 1914, GARF f. 217, op. 1, d. 1147, l. 50.

guilt, but they also did not need to release potential spies back into the combat zone. They ordered deportations frequently.

Many innocent civilians suffered. Take for instance the case of Iosif Kliapchinskii. In October 1914, a Russian counter-intelligence agent reported to the staff of the Second Army that he had heard that Kliapchinskii had eagerly awaited the arrival of the Germans and had "joyfully" greeted them when they marched into his hometown of Pruszków. He then allegedly told the Germans where the local factory director had stashed the firm's money and helped them rob it. This was clearly enough evidence to start an investigation, but every piece of evidence that the gendarmes uncovered contradicted the assertions of the army's agent. Three signed depositions by local residents convinced even the chief of the gendarmes that Kliapchinskii was innocent. Nevertheless, in the end the Warsaw Governor General erred on the side of caution and deported him for the duration of the war.[35] The number of deportees, unsurprisingly, continued to rise over the winter of 1914–1915.

Not all deportees were treated as individuals and given the dubious protection of kangaroo courts, however. Very early in the war, the army began to systematically target Germans and Jews for exile. Lists of members of suspect nationalities and their places of residence were drawn up immediately after the declaration of war.[36] The next stage came quickly. On 27 December 1914/9 January 1915, a directive of the Second Army ordered all male German colonists older than fifteen years of age to be deported beyond the Vistula River; a month later the order came to do the same with "all Jews and suspicious people."[37] The explicit reason for these deportations was that the "removal of Jews from these places is done with the goal of preventing them from getting definite information for spying."[38] In addition, the army used deportation as a political tool in foreign territories under its control in Eastern Anatolia (Batum and Kars provinces), East Prussia, and, especially, Galicia.[39]

The number of people affected by this policy of ethnic cleansing is still unclear, but the totals probably reached the hundreds of thousands by the end of the winter. In Warsaw alone at the end of January 1915, about 80,000 new Jewish refugees arrived. Later calculations for expelled and deported Jews, for the war as a whole, range between 500,000 and 1,000,000. The more ambitious effort to cleanse the

---

[35] This case, which started with the accusation on 15 October 1914 and ended with the deportation order on 5 February 1915, is in GARF f. 217, op. 1, d. 1184.

[36] List of German residents compiled by Warsaw gendarmes, 26 July 1914, GARF. f. 217, op. 1, d. 540, ll. 7–8.

[37] Order to the troops of the Second Army, 27 December 1914, GARF f. 217, op. 1, d. 437, l. 24; telegram from the chief of the convoy-supply division of the staff of the Second Army to the Warsaw Governor General, secret, 24 January 1915, GARF f. 217, op. 1, d. 437, l. 29ob.

[38] Telegram from staff of Second Army to Warsaw Governor General, n.d., GARF f. 217, op. 1, d. 437, l. 30.

[39] S. G. Nelipovich, "Naselenie okkupirovannykh territorii rassmatrivalos' kak rezerv protivnika: internirovanie chasti zhitelei Vostochnoi Prussii, Galitsii i Bukoviny v 1914–1915 gg.," *Voenno-istoricheskii zhurnal* no. 2 (2000): 60–9; Daniel W. Graf, "The Reign of the Generals: Military Government in Western Russia, 1914–1915," (Ph.D. diss., University of Nebraska, 1972), 120.

Jewish population from the Pale of Settlement would not occur until the retreat of Russian armies in the spring, but the process was already well advanced by the time of the military setback. The same was true for the ethnic German population in the region.[40]

Finally, of course, many civilians willingly fled the screaming shells and armies on the hoof. These "voluntary" refugees appeared early in the war and never disappeared. In October 1914, for instance, a wave of refugees from the environs of the besieged Austrian fortress of Przemyśl nearly overwhelmed other small Galician villages nearby after the Austrians destroyed all buildings within five kilometers of the fortress walls in order to clear their field of fire. The refugees were almost completely ruined, left "without a piece of bread and without any property at all." Claiming to be "Russian," they begged for help from the commander of the XII Army Corps, who reported on their "horrible situation" to General Brusilov, the commander of the Eighth Army. Brusilov, in turn, ordered their relocation to the rear under the supervision of a civilian official supplied by the Governor General of occupied Galicia.[41] Thus did improvisation result in a nascent bureaucratic structure for dealing with the many dislocations of war. Similar patchwork processes were happening up and down the front throughout 1914 and 1915, but they did not come together as a coherent refugee policy. Despite the lack of an organized policy initiative, however, hundreds of thousands of people had hit the roads in the context of direct violence or barely veiled force.

The situation on the Eastern Front prior to May 1915 was thus marked by rather more soldier–civilian interaction than military planners had hoped or anticipated. This interaction was brutal on some occasions, as in the case of the ethnically cleansed Jews and Germans, and compassionate on others, as with the "Russian" refugees in Galicia. Even a mix of these two relationships in the same village setting was not uncommon. But everywhere, a condition of mutual dependence arose. As we have seen, the war had completely transformed the economic lives of all individuals in the war zone. Soldiers, now completely divorced from economic production, relied fully on the military supply system for survival. That supply system, in turn, depended heavily on local populations for goods and services ranging from bread to shoes to local cart transportation. That the home economy could not produce and supply sufficient materials was evident from difficulties planners had in providing those few goods—ammunition and military hardware in particular—that they were unable to acquire in the zone of military occupation. By the same token, the occupied areas did not have enough resources to fully supply the army either. The result was an army that drew grain, clothing, and many other necessities both from the center of the empire and from the war zone.

Even Slavic civilians found their traditional economic practices completely disrupted. The military conscripted large portions of the labor force, both the

---

[40] See here Eric Lohr, "The Russian Army and the Jews: Mass Deportation, Hostages, and Violence during World War I," *Russian Review* 60 (July 2001): 404–19.

[41] See reports of commander of XII Army Corps and of Eighth Army, both on 28 October 1914, in RGVIA f. 2134, op. 1, d. 1153, l. 6, 8.

urban and rural economies saw rapid ownership transfers (and shutdowns) as the result of the ethnic nationalization of what had been a multiethnic community of property owners, and the vibrant international market for labor and goods in these borderland regions came to a halt.[42] The new economic system was completely dominated by the army, which acted as a monopoly consumer in many respects. Not only were prices fixed for goods and labor throughout the economy, but supply officials occasionally had to resort to forced requisitioning to meet the demands of the millions of men in their care. These requisitions were almost always accompanied by compensation, but this was often insufficient, not only because of low fixed prices and inflation, but also because the value of the last horse on a farm dependent on animal power for operation was much higher than the value of one horse among ten. Finally, as we have seen, the army became the welfare organization of last (and sometimes first) resort for people ruined by the war. A system of near complete codependency had developed, a situation that mysteriously escaped the attention of military planners.

This codependency represented a new front-line society of sorts. That society was obliterated in the spring of 1915. The collapse of the front at Gorlice forced army commanders to decide what to do with local civilians as they retreated from Galicia and Poland, and they responded cruelly and foolishly. Reasoning that the fields, factories, and military and civilian labor capacity of the population were resources that could not simply be handed over to the enemy, officers in the field began to implement a scorched earth policy. Top staff officers had already introduced the notion of "cleansing" war zones of populations earlier in the year, when Stavka had ordered several military districts "for reasons of military security" to carry out a "complete cleansing" of all German, Austro-Hungarian, and Turkish subjects in areas under martial law.[43] General Ianushkevich, who was supreme commander Grand Duke Nikolai Nikolaevich's chief of staff, used the same language when informing army commanders in February 1915 of the further tightening of his paranoid security regime. "The Jewish population, regardless of age or sex, in the region of military activity, is to be expelled to the side of the enemy. Regions occupied by rear units of the army are to be cleansed of all suspicious and unreliable people."[44] When the order to retreat came, top officers expanded the notion of population cleansing again, moving to a full-on scorched earth policy.

The orders themselves were sweeping. General Ivanov, the commander of the Southwestern Front, had his chief of staff order the evacuation of all men aged eighteen to fifty on 24 May/6 June and personally gave the order two weeks later to send "the whole population by whatever means necessary" to the rear in the

---

[42] The process of economic nationalization during the war is dealt with in depth in Eric Lohr, *Nationalizing the Russian Empire: The Campaign against Enemy Aliens during World War I* (Cambridge, MA: Harvard University Press, 2003).

[43] Telegram from Stavka to the commander of the Dvinsk Military District, 9 January 1915, GARF f. 217, op.1, d.1147, l. 100.

[44] Ianushkevich order cited in telegraph from General Alekseev to the commander of the Eighth Army, 20 February 1915, RGVIA f. 2134, op. 2, d. 542, l. 88.

midst of the retreat.[45] When it became clear that retreats across the whole front might become necessary, Ianushkevich gave explicit direction to all of his army commanders:

> When retreating, remove all resources intensively and early, especially railways, destroy crops by mowing or by other means, move all men of military age other than yids to the rear so as not to leave them in the hands of the enemy. You are required to remove all reserves of livestock, bread, fodder, and horses. It will be easier to supply the population from scratch upon our offensive than to leave material to the enemy that we could have carried away.[46]

In several regions directly threatened by attack, the military deported the entire population, men and women, children and the elderly.[47] According to Russian entry visa records, nearly 26,000 people fled Galicia on a daily basis during May 1915.[48] Lines of refugees trudging down roads stretched to thirty kilometers long in places.[49]

These hasty orders produced panic and a patchwork tableau of deportation and terror. Some villages were swept clean, while others, lying in the path of a different army corps, were left with residents and food supplies. Indeed, we should think of these more as multiple scorched earth directives than any kind of coherent policy. As Grand Duke Nikolai Nikolaevich complained to the head commanders of each army on 20 June/3 July, "I have gotten reports of the destruction of entire settlements by several corps, of unsystematic evacuation directives, and of the incorrect belief that has been created both among the population and the troops that these are repressive measures."[50] Especially destructive actions were apparently taken by the Third Army on the Southwestern Front and the Tenth Army on the Northwestern Front.[51]

Wealthy and connected residents could and did escape some of this damage by appealing to local army commanders.[52] This protection was not universal however. Andrusov recalled the scene when soldiers came upon the castle of a wealthy Polish noble:

> When we arrived there, the castle was completely intact. However, our soldiers tried to quickly turn it into a stable. They traipsed around the castle in a mob. Every item had to be examined, touched, and hurled about. As a result, all the rooms soon were filled

---

[45] Telegram to Stavka from Southwestern Front, 26 August 1915, RGVIA f. 2005, op. 1, d. 42, l. 170.

[46] Ianushkevich, telegram to army generals, 11 June 1915, GARF f. 215, op. 1, d. 249, l. 7–8.

[47] See for instance report of the head of the echelon supply department of the Second Army to the Warsaw Governor General, 15 June 1915, GARF f. 215, op. 1, d. 249, l. 24.

[48] A. Iu. Bakhturina, *Politika rossiiskoi imperii v vostochnoi Galitsii v gody pervoi mirovoi voiny* (Moscow: AIRO-XX, 2000), 187.

[49] Knox, 1: 322.

[50] Cited in Prince Obolenskii (Head of Stavka's Department of Civilian Affairs), report to Council of Ministers on "refugee question," 30 August 1915, RGVIA f. 2005, op. 1, d. 42, l. 8ob.

[51] Obolenskii, report to Council of Ministers, RGVIA f. 2005, op. 1, d. 42, l. 7.

[52] For an example of a (granted) request for armed protection of an estate, see telegram from Prince Liubomirskii to General Brusilov (27 August 1915) and positive response. RGVIA f. 2134, op. 2, d. 545, ll. 28–29.

with broken furniture, smashed dishes, and so forth. A luxurious library, in which there were a great many valuable ancient manuscripts, was soon turned into a heap of paper. No one tried to stop the disorder, since the command staff was occupied with other things.[53]

Andrusov makes no mention of whether the owner witnessed these events or had fled long before the armed men pounded on his castle door. A group of landowners in Volhynia also petitioned Stavka for relief, asking Grand Duke Nikolai Nikolae-vich to rein in the decrees, which created an "untimely panic among the local population" and made the harvest impossible.[54]

Though exact numbers of forced migrants are impossible to determine, the scale was enormous. German troops entering the region found the population cut by more than half in some provinces.[55] As many as 400,000 people fled Lithuania alone.[56] At the same time, relief organizations started counting the displaced in the millions. More precisely, officials counted over 3,300,000 refugees by the end of 1915, and the most careful calculation of registered and non-registered refugees at the start of 1917 had the number nearer to 6,000,000.[57]

Soldiers gave residents subject to evacuation a short period of time to collect whatever belongings they could carry and to leave their homes. Upon their departure, soldiers often first looted what was left and then burned homes and fields before following behind the slow-moving, dispirited, and vulnerable people they had uprooted. The scenes in war zones were painful and perplexing. As one soldier in the Russian army, Richard Boleslavski, remembered, orders to evacuate their position, burn the village in which they had been staying, and retreat 100 kilometers to the east came suddenly. The order came in the morning, and the village was to be destroyed by nightfall. Residents were confused. One nervously smiling woman thought at first that the soldiers were playing some sort of cruel joke. "Why do you have to burn this house?" she asked. "It's my house." "It's orders," was the simple response. Still unconvinced, she asked whose orders they were with a "plaintive, pitiable defiance in her voice." The soldiers answered again that they had orders from above, but the woman was uncomprehending. She returned to her cooking. Boleslavski understood the confusion. "We had been friendly with these people," he remembered.

> They had treated us as well as they could. Their stock of potatoes, which was all the food they possessed, had been buried to keep during the winter, but they had dug the potatoes and shared them with us. We had given them salt and canned salmon and buckwheat. Now we told them that they would have to collect what they could and

---

[53] Andrusov, manuscript of memoirs, BFRZ, d. E-134, l.14.

[54] Telegram from gathering of the Starokonstantinovskii Agricultural Society to Grand Duke Nikolai Nikolaevich, 30 June 1915, RGVIA f. 2003, op. 1, d. 39, l. 24.

[55] Vejas G. Liulevicius, *War Land on the Eastern Front: Culture, National Identity, and German Identity in World War I* (Cambridge: Cambridge University Press, 2000), 20.

[56] Piotr S. Wandycz, *The Lands of Partitioned Poland, 1795–1918* (Seattle: University of Washington Press, 1974), 347.

[57] Peter Gatrell, *A Whole Empire Walking: Refugees in Russia During World War I* (Bloomington: Indiana University Press, 1999), 3.

move anywhere they wanted to, preferably to the east. They could not understand. They did not want to understand; they did not want to believe.

Finally, as night came, the cavalry saddled up, and the painful reality set in. "One by one they dribbled out, still not quite believing: in couples, in threes and fours, moving slowly away and disappearing under the trees in the evening shadows." Boleslavski and the rest of his platoon then gathered straw and laid a combustible path from house to house. A single match was enough to set the whole village aflame. As the platoon mounted up and moved on, they passed the villagers, "sitting on the ground, or standing about, facing the crimson flare. All of them, especially the women and children, were sobbing."[58]

Elsewhere in Poland, the earth was just as scorched. As Count Roniker reported to the Warsaw Governor General days later, "troops burned all of the villages in their path in Płock, Płońsk and Pułtusk districts, drove out the whole population, and took their cows and horses without compensation." Russian cavalry had gone house to house, poured kerosene into the root cellars, and lit the homes on fire, one by one. German troops arrived quickly enough to douse the flames in some villages, but the rest perished. "The population," Roniker claimed, "everywhere and without exception did not want to leave their homeland, but their wishes were ignored and they were moved out by force with the threat of being shot on the spot. . . . They didn't have the chance to gather up their necessary belongings, since in the majority of cases the burnings were begun without warning. The fires consumed art, family documents, and even money." As a result, these districts had been turned into a complete "desert," and cholera began to rip through the new refugee communities. Forty-four cases had been reported in Włodawa, and mass graves sprouted along the roads upon which the refugees had fled.[59] Between the destruction of the German Mackensen Wedge and the catastrophe of the Russian retreat, Poles suffered tremendous losses. Over the course of the war, nearly two million homes and farm buildings were destroyed.[60] Thus were the fragile, immature ties between soldiers and local civilians brutally severed. Soldiers and civilians desocialized once again, destroying many of the economic and social resources necessary for resocialization as they did so.

---

[58] Richard Boleslavski, *Way of the Lancer*, in collaboration with Helen Woodward (New York: The Literary Guild, 1932), 23–5. Richard Boleslavski was the stage name of Bolesław Ryszard Srzednicki, a young Polish actor who moved from Odessa to Moscow to work at the Moscow Art Theater on the eve of the war. After his army service, he escaped to the United States in the midst of the Civil War and became a noted theater and film actor there.

[59] Count Adam Roniker (Chairman of the Executive Committee of the Warsaw Province Residents Committee), report to Senator Liubimov (Warsaw Governor General), 11 July 1915, GARF f. 215, op. 1, d. 249, l. 96ob. Roniker claimed to base his report on conversations he and his fellow committee members had with "hundreds" of former residents of these districts and their families. For good measure, he appended a list of fifty-three settlements he was sure had been destroyed by retreating troops.

[60] Jan Molenda, "Social Changes in Poland during World War I," in *East Central European Society in World War I*, ed. Béla K. Király and Nándor F. Dreisziger (Boulder: Social Science Research Monographs, 1985), 188.

Refugees continued to be victimized even after their initial dislocation. Military officials soon discovered that the mobs of refugees they had created did not simply disappear away from the front, as many of the deportees from the first months of the war had. Instead, they competed for food, fodder, and space on the roads. The military responded by using yet more force on them, as the poignant example of Polish refugees caught up in the midst of the Narew operation demonstrates. In the midst of the Battle of Przasnysz, as the need for retreat became evident, echelon commanders in the First Army were told to take "stern measures" to ensure that refugees stayed on the side of the road at all times, so that troops and transport vehicles could have unhindered passage. At the same time, all of these refugees were to be moved quickly to the far side of the Narew River (the intended new line of defense). The first draft of this order said that the refugees were to be "driven" (*gnat'*) across the river, but someone softened this to "directed" (*napravliat'*) in the final version.[61] The army did not record whether this fine distinction was observed during the "direction" of these civilians across the Narew, but it did note the catastrophic results:

> Just behind the front lines, there is a mass of refugees with small children and their domestic baggage. Their position is very difficult and unhappy. They are without shelter, are starving, and don't know where to go. Civilian authorities are absent, and help from those authorities is not evident. We need a proper and immediate organization of this business. We should create a whole string of feeding stations and let refugees know where those are so that the population doesn't get their baggage tangled up with military transports, and we should direct them to predefined places. Otherwise epidemic diseases and the unhappiness of a population humbly bearing its cross may arise. Extreme and energetic measures on the part of the administration are necessary.[62]

As if this situation were not bad enough, reports started pouring in that Cossack troops had taken to abusing the refugees near Wyszków, about twenty-five kilometers behind the Narew. These refugees were hoping to move further east, but they were being robbed of their money, their horses, and especially their livestock. They begged for protection from the military commandant of Wyszków, who was "ashamed" by the situation but had no forces with which to patrol outside of the city. He begged the staff of the First Army to give him troops and to authorize courts martial, but got no response.[63] At the same time, local peasants complained that swarms of deserters infested the woods in the immediate rear, coming out only to pillage.[64]

All of these depredations were even worse for Jews in Poland and Galicia. Across the war zone, from the very start of the retreat, pogroms, rapes, and armed robberies

[61] Order to commanders of echelon units of the First Army, 2 July 1915, RGVIA f. 2106, op. 3, d. 176, l. 1.

[62] Telegram from Ziborov (handwriting unclear) to General Rychkov, 6 July 1915, RGVIA, f. 2106, op. 3, d. 176, ll. 3–4.

[63] General Bolzhin, telegram to staff of First Army, 14 July 1915, RGVIA f. 2106, op. 3, d. 176, ll. 5–6.

[64] Knox, 1: 349.

defined the Jewish experience.[65] The treatment of Jews was far from uniform. Early on, there were moves toward ethnic cleansing. When the front approached the fortress of Kovno in May, the Kovno commandant (General Grigor'ev) ordered all 300,000 Jews in the area expelled. This order extended to soldiers in the vicinity of the fortress, who were to be arrested, stripped of their military uniforms and gear, and sent shoeless and half-naked to jail, first in the Kovno provincial prison and then further to the rear in Vilnius.[66] These expulsions raised concerns both in Russia and abroad. At a meeting of the Council of Ministers, even right-wing anti-Semites were appalled. "I'm no Judeophile," said Minister of Internal Affairs Nikolai Maklakov in an understatement, "but I disapprove. There are internal dangers—pogroms and feeding revolution. There is an international danger as well. It would be better to take hostages." The minister of finance chimed in that it would be nearly impossible to float the planned one billion dollar foreign loan in the midst of a mass persecution of this sort, and Krivoshein, the minister of agriculture, sputtered that it was a measure both harmful for the government and "medieval" in inspiration.[67] An-sky had a somewhat different interpretation of the Great Retreat, however. He considered the scorched earth campaign a real "turning point" in the wartime Jewish question. Whereas prior to the Great Retreat, all the misfortunes had been blamed upon the Jews, now "the catastrophe was too enormous and its causes too obvious for anybody to blame it on 'Jewish espionage.'"[68] Perhaps this was so, but the fact that Jewish misery now had more company did nothing to stop the ravages of the retreat. Nor did anti-Semitism or suspicions of Jewish spying abate. To the contrary, they persisted to such a degree that Krivoshein would snap at his colleagues in frustration in August that "we can't fight a war against Germany and another one against the Jews at the same time."[69] But powerful anti-Semites in the Russian army and the Russian government kept doing their best to fight precisely this dual war: soon after the front stabilized, observers reported that targeted Jewish deportations had resumed in places like Minsk province.[70]

Getting away from the multiple dangers of the front was only the first step for refugees. Russia's transportation infrastructure cracked under the strain of the emergency, and local authorities could not deal with the crisis with their limited experience and even more limited resources. Already by 20 June/3 July, the

[65] Alexander Victor Prusin, *Nationalizing a Borderland: War, Ethnicity, and Anti-Jewish Violence in East Galicia, 1914–1920* (Tuscaloosa: University of Alabama Press, 2005), 54.

[66] Untitled document among typescript descriptions of Jewish persecutions in papers of P. N. Miliukov, GARF f. 579, op. 1, d. 2011, l. 54.

[67] Notes of meeting of Council of Ministers, 8 May 1915, in *Sovet ministrov rossiiskoi imperii v gody pervoi mirovoi voiny. Bumagi A. N. Iakhontova (zapisi zasedanii i perepiska)* (St. Petersburg: Bulanin, 1999), 163.

[68] S. An-sky, *The Enemy at His Pleasure: A Journey Through the Jewish Pale of Settlement during World War I* (New York: Henry Holt, 2002), 129–30.

[69] Notes of meeting of Council of Ministers, 6 August 1915, in *Sovet ministrov rossiiskoi imperii v gody pervoi mirovoi voiny*, 211.

[70] Letter from Duma members Bomash, Fridman, and Gurevich to Alekseev, 29 November 1915, RGVIA f. 2134, op. 2, d. 542, ll. 123–125.

governor of Minsk counted hundreds of thousands of refugees in his territory and pleaded for them to be sent south to provinces along the Dnipro.[71] On 23 June/6 July, the governor of Smolensk wrote his counterpart in Warsaw, more than 800 kilometers away, that Smolensk was "overcrowded" with refugees and that there were no more living spaces for them to occupy in the city.[72]

In Vitebsk, more than 200,000 refugees had come through by 30 August/12 September. Diligent officials there tried to organize feeding stations and housing, but they could not do so on this scale, given the fact that they had only 129,615 rubles at their disposal and only a few people who could work full time. The provincial government had organized fifteen sanitary feeding stations in the area, but this still left refugees with hundreds of kilometers to traverse without help. Starving refugees stripped all edible materials from a swath of territory several kilometers wide along the roads. Not surprisingly, a cholera epidemic developed, though its scale was unclear because no one was there to register or treat the fleeing families.[73] An "enormous quantity of corpses" lay rotting alongside roads and at train stations, unburied because there was no one to do the work.[74] Throughout the zone of martial law, refugees turned to army officials for help and even for direction. Alekseev noted this phenomenon, remarking to army commanders that "they don't know where to go, no one is giving them guidance, and no one is regulating their movements."[75] Alekseev's staff tried to mobilize local policemen to assist in organizing refugee movements, but to little discernible effect.

The violent migration of humans was the most notable outcome of the Great Retreat, but other migrations happened at the same time. Since the beginning of the war, Russian authorities had endeavored to move economic resources out of harm's way during German incursions. The evacuation of Łódź in November 1914 presaged far more extensive transfers in 1915. Already by 7/20 June, the orders had gone out in Poland to start withdrawing goods from "inactive factories," especially copper goods.[76] As noted previously, the planning for the evacuation of Warsaw began more than a month before troops abandoned the city, and it took place before most soldiers even knew that a further retreat had been contemplated. Industrial equipment, precious metals, and other urban goods were shipped out of the war zone as soon as the possible ramifications of the Galician disaster had become clear.

Most of the Polish economy was agricultural. As with industrial property, the army high command preferred moving agricultural goods to destroying them or leaving them for the enemy. In Poland, orders from the staff came as early as 15/28

---

[71] Telegram from Baron Raush (Minsk) to Warsaw Governor General, 20 June 1915, GARF f. 215, op. 1, d. 249, l. 43–43ob.

[72] Governor Bulgakov (Smolensk), Telegram to Warsaw Governor General, 23 June 1915, GARF f. 215, op. 1, d. 249, l. 34.

[73] Report of Leib-Kirurga Vel'iaminova, 9 September 1915, RGVIA f. 2005, op. 1, d. 42, l. 19.

[74] Telegram to Stavka from Count N. A. Tolstoi, 22 August 1915, RGVIA f. 2005, op. 1, d. 42, l. 138.

[75] General Alekseev, Telegram to Danilov and all army commanders, 3 August 1915, secret, RGVIA f. 2106, op. 3, d. 176, l. 38.

[76] Danilov, Telegram to First Army, 7 June 1915, RGVIA f. 2106, op. 3, d. 168, l. 329.

June to use requisitioning as much as possible for seed, grain, fodder, and livestock. Hay was to be sent to Siedlce, livestock to the army herds in Kobrin, and grain to the Vokovyskii storehouse.[77] Machines, lathes, and other production materials were to be sent to Moscow; copper was sent to Petrograd. All of this had to be done expeditiously in order to allow troops to blow up the railway lines in good time.[78] Requisition prices were set by the army, and the price lists allowed for variation by province and by the quality of the goods. Prices for horses would range from 115 rubles for a poor beast in Płock to 300 for a riding mount in Warsaw. Supply officers reimbursed peasants between fifty-seven and sixty-one rubles for carts with iron wheels, while they paid only thirty-nine to fifty rubles for ones with wooden wheels.[79] At first the requisitions were conducted by a four-man team established by the echelon supply departments in the region of each given army,[80] but these teams had nowhere near the time and money needed for the task. As one official noted in the midst of the July retreats, there were insufficient resources available to conduct orderly requisitions. At the speed of doing one square kilometer per day and quadrupling the number of requisition teams, it would take more than a year and more than 15,000,000 rubles to requisition all the goods in the territory of the Second Army alone. As a result, "it is apparent that the work of requisition teams has no real meaning and only serves as a demonstration of concern for the population necessitated by the current political moment and mood."[81] This disjuncture between the desire for well-disposed Polish citizens and the state's inability to treat them fairly became more and more acute as the summer progressed. Aware of impending disaster, the Council of Ministers suddenly began efforts to make the 1914 political promises of Polish autonomy a reality. In late May 1915, the Council ordered the formation of a committee to begin work on the Polish political project that would have equal representation by Russians and Poles.[82] This decree was literally too little and too late. However, the refugee crisis did contribute toward decolonization in significant ways. In the first place, the army and imperial government found it impossible to deal locally with evacuation and refugee relief without the assistance of local authorities. Since zemstvos had been thwarted in the western borderlands, Stavka was forced to turn to the resident committees formed at the start of the war in places such as Grodno and Vilnius.[83] Tens of thousands of rubles were given by the Ministry of Internal Affairs to an array of residents' committees, and other major imperial

---

[77] The cattle never made it to Russian stomachs, as the Germans took Kobrin and those vast herds in August. Knox, 1: 328.

[78] Danilov, Telegram to Litvinov, 15 June 1915, RGVIA f. 2106, op. 3, d. 168, l. 352–352ob.

[79] Chief of the echelon supply department of the First Army, report, 14 July 1915, RGVIA f. 2106, op. 3, d. 168, l. 358.

[80] "Instruktsiia dlia proizvodstva rekvizitsii iz Polozhenie o rekvizitsiiakh pri po. V. V. 1914 gg.," RGVIA f. 2106, op. 3, d. 168, ll. 3–4.

[81] Warsaw Governor, Letter to Warsaw Governor General, 21 July 1915, GARF f. 215, op. 1, d. 174, l. 315.

[82] "Osobyi zhurnal soveta ministrov," 29 May 1915, GARF f. 215, op. 1, d. 174, l. 279.

[83] Obolenskii, report to Council of Ministers, RGVIA f. 2005, op. 1, d. 42, l.11.

relief organizations such as the Tatiana Committee gave even more.[84] As we saw in Chapter 1, these resident committees actively forwarded the cause of self-determination and they continued to do so as the disaster unfolded. Prince Lubomirskii's Central Residents' Committee became a key institution on Russian soil in the wake of 1915.[85] Secondly, refugee relief in the center of the empire was heavily ethnicized, with each national group forming agencies to take care of "their own" misfortune.[86] Public welfare and local governance were increasingly out of the hands of the government. For the vast majority of residents, the troubled relationship between the imperial state and its colonial periphery was growing ever more sour by the day, as Stavka well knew.[87]

Goods flowed eastward too. The most impressive planned effort was the evacuation of key factories and industrial workers from Riga. City officials had started planning for this contingency earlier in the war, and preliminary steps began in May. On 27 June/10 July, Polivanov ordered a full evacuation of defense industries and workers. Thirteen factories and more than 75,000 workers and their families were sent in thousands of train cars to more central locations.[88] Most economic relocation happened haphazardly however, some on the backs of the refugees themselves, some escorted by the military. Over a two-week period in the late summer, despite the fact that many of the requisitions and retreats had already occurred, a single echelon battalion escorted more than 53,000 head of cattle, 23,000 chickens, and assorted other livestock away from the front.[89] These massive herds posed problems of their own. The army intended to drive them about 400 kilometers in a bit more than a month, but the livestock wranglers were deeply concerned that they would lose tens of thousands of these animals because of a lack of forage. Hopes to lay in stores of forage along the way for the herds do not appear to have materialized, and the size of these herds grew daily as the army scooped up every animal not taken by fleeing residents.[90]

Cleansing turned out to be extremely dirty work, and it did not take civilian and military authorities long to realize what an enormous mistake they had made. Already by 20 June/3 July, Grand Duke Nikolai Nikolaevich was telling commanders that the population was viewing the policies undertaken during the retreat as "repressive measures" and that procedures had to change. Three days later, he convened a special conference at Stavka to discuss the situation. The issue was not simply a humanitarian one. Pressures of refugees and retreating armies

---

[84] Marius Korzeniowski, "Rejon Zachodni Centralnego Komitetu Obywatelskiego-powstanie i początki działalności," *Studia z dziejów Rosji i Europy Środkowo-Wschodniej* 29 (1994): 44–5.

[85] Gatrell, *Whole Empire Walking*, 155. [86] Gatrell, *Whole Empire Walking*, 141–70.

[87] Telegram from Ivanov (Chief of Supplies, Southwestern Front) to Chief of Staff at Stavka, 30 August 1915, RGVIA f. 2005, op. 1, d. 42, l. 200.

[88] Lieutenant-General Kurlov, "Zapiska ob evakuatsii iz goroda Rigi pravitel'stvennykh i obshchestvennykh uchrezhdenii, naseleniia, zavodov, fabrik i drugikh promyshlennykh zavedenii," n.d., GARF f. 601, op. 1, d. 549, ll. 299–314.

[89] "Svedenie o priniatom na etapy ot 4 sibirskago etapnago bataliona i sdannom rekvizirovannom skote. ot 22 avg. 1915–7 sept. 1915," RGVIA f. 2106, op. 3, d. 168, ll. 250–251ob.

[90] Chief of the echelon supply department of the First Army, report, 15 July 1915, RGVIA f. 2106, op. 3, d. 168, l. 359.

overwhelmed the capacity of transport officials to deal with them. The mobility of the army slowed to a crawl; far from simplifying the conduct of war by clearing battle areas of civilians, the retreat and evacuation policy of the military authorities had severely complicated their tasks. The conference resolved on several measures to reverse course. First, they ordered commanders not to engage in mass deportation. German colonists had to be cleansed, but others should remain. Jews were to be left for the enemy to deal with, and others could make their own decisions. Wanton destruction of property of little or no military use (such as homes for instance) had to stop. Useful goods such as food were to be requisitioned, but with payment and leaving a month's worth of supplies (as before). Draft-age men, who had previously been forcibly swept eastward, were instead to be asked to volunteer for work brigades at a wage of 1.8 rubles a day. Above all, the violence had to cease. Commanders would be held accountable for the actions of their soldiers. These orders were approved by Nikolai Nikolaevich on 24 June/7 July and sent immediately to field commanders.[91]

This directive had virtually no effect. The wave had already begun, and it would not reverse its course now. As even Stavka admitted, "these were the directives, but nevertheless the phenomenon of 'refugeedom' not only did not cease, but, growing and spreading, it acquired its present anarchic force."[92] Desperate troops continued to ravage the countryside. With the supply system in a state of crisis and the local economy in cinders, methodical pillaging, long a habit, became a necessity. As "locusts or the army of Tamerlane," soldiers and refugees swarmed eastward, devouring everything in their path.[93] Local notables continued to beg Stavka to stop the madness, one of them telling Alekseev that he now had displaced refugees from burned out villages living on his property because "the forcible deportation of residents is continuing, along with the burning of villages and estates."[94] This telegram and others like it prompted Alekseev to bring the treatment of civilians to the attention of his generals once more. Civilians, he wrote, were still "forcibly, against their will, required to leave their homes and move out ahead of the troops, and if they didn't leave, their villages were simply burned. There are reports that this was to hide looting on the part of certain military men and groups." He again urged that commanders inform residents that they should stay in their homes and not join the wave of disruptive sickly people dragging themselves eastward.[95] His commanders responded that the lurid reports were either exaggerations or isolated incidents and suggested that most of the evacuations were voluntary.[96]

---

[91] Obolenskii, report to Council of Ministers, RGVIA f. 2005, op. 1, d. 42, l. 7ob.

[92] Obolenskii, report to Council Ministers, RGVIA f. 2005, op. 1, d. 42, l. 7.

[93] This was the characterization given at the time by A. V. Krivoshein, the minister of agriculture, in a closed meeting of the Council of Ministers on 4 August 1915. Michael Cherniavsky, *Prologue to Revolution: Notes of A. N. Iakhontov on the Secret Meetings of the Council of Ministers, 1915* (Englewood Cliffs, NJ: Prentice Hall, 1967), 46.

[94] Shchitt (Justice of the Peace in Kobrin), telegram to Stavka, 5 September 1915, RGVIA f. 2005, op. 1, d. 42, l. 233.

[95] Telegram from Alekseev to the commander of the Western Front, 5 September 1915, RGVIA f. 2005, op. 1, d. 42, l. 220.

[96] Telegram from Evert to Alekseev, 6 September 1915, RGVIA f. 2005, op. 1, d. 42, l. 259.

In part, this was true. As General Arsenii Gulevich, Alekseev's chief of staff, reported in August, the shifting front had prompted the movement.[97] Enemy artillery destroyed many villages, and rumors that the Germans were "brutal" occupiers led many to take their chances on the road. Ever since Kalisz, atrocity stories regarding the German troops had been a staple of front-zone rumor mills, and these stories intensified in 1915. Official internal military reports from debriefed POWs and refugees suggested that the Germans confiscated everything, forced men into labor brigades, raped women in front of their relatives, and even burned villagers inside their houses, shooting any who emerged.[98] Soldiers wrote home with stories of their own. "A scout from our neighboring regiment was taken prisoner by the Germans, but was able to escape thanks to a happy accident. He returned covered in blood. He said that the Germans interrogated him about the disposition of our troops, but he was silent, and then they began to cut off his ears and fingers with a knife. Now I have become convinced of German atrocities with my own eyes."[99] In any case, the order to take or destroy all reserves save a one-month food supply per person made staying put nearly as unattractive as leaving, even without the extra factor of an invading army. Gulevich claimed that "only force would compel the population to remain in place,"[100] a statement that was not so much false as it was misleading. The combined pressures of military activity, advancing German armies, and Russian scorched earth practices had made the front zone nearly uninhabitable. There was no contradiction to the propositions that many civilians fled before being forced to leave, while others were burned out of their homes. Both of these processes happened simultaneously. Nevertheless, Stavka adopted Gulevich's assessment and forwarded it to the Council of Ministers as a defense of army behavior. As Obolenskii put it, "in these conditions, fulfilling the desires expressed by the Council of Ministers would lead to . . . forcible prevention of the population from saving itself from the threatening danger to its existence posed by the invasion of the enemy."[101] Instead, he urged increased monetary support to feed, transport, and provide security for the refugees.[102]

WAR AND GENOCIDE IN THE CAUCASUS AND ANATOLIA

In the meantime, events of a different sort on the Caucasian Front had unleashed a massive refugee crisis there as well. Hostilities between Russia and the Ottoman

[97] Telegram from General Gulevich to General Alekseev, 24 August 1915, RGVIA f. 2005, op. 1, d. 42, l. 255.

[98] Telegram from General Baiov to General Gulevich and Stavka, 29 August 1915, RGVIA f. 2005, op. 1, d. 42, l. 256.

[99] Letter from soldier in 55th Infantry Regiment to Kriukov (Moscow), excerpted by the military censorship bureau of Moscow and Khar'kov Military District, 11 December 1915, RGVIA f. 2067, op. 1, d. 3845, l. 355–355ob.

[100] Gulevich, telegram, RGVIA f. 2005, op. 1, d. 42, l. 255.

[101] Obolenskii, report to Council of Ministers, RGVIA f. 2005, op. 1, d. 42, l. 13.

[102] Obolenskii, report to Council of Ministers, RGVIA f. 2005, op. 1, d. 42, l. 14.

Empire had begun on the night of 16/29 October 1914, when Ottoman (and reflagged German) ships shelled several Russian ports and sank part of the Russian navy.[103] The bulk of the fighting took place on land, however. A week later, fierce fighting began, as Russia's General Georgii Bergmann took territory surrounding the village of Köprüköy and was then forced, over the course of days of battle, to retreat, with large numbers of casualties on both sides.[104] The decisive battle on the Caucasian Front would take place in December, when Enver Pasha, the Ottoman war minister, sought to destroy the Russian Caucasian Army with an encircling maneuver at Sarikamiş. His plan relied on surprise, so he ordered the bulk of his forces to move rapidly across unguarded mountain tracks as wintry conditions set in. Russian commanders received intelligence reports from local residents and Armenian volunteer units about Ottoman troop movements, and some Russian troops began retreating as a result. Nevertheless, Enver did manage to get his army between the front-line armies and the city of Kars as he intended. But the surprise was in vain, for the forced marches and overnight camping in heavy snow ravaged his army. Some men slipped away to commandeer the warm huts of locals, while others froze to death on barren, windswept ridges. About 25,000 men (out of 95,000) had become casualties even before the assault on the town of Sarikamiş began. The successful Russian defense of the town and the succeeding counteroffensive crippled the Ottoman Third Army even more. Only 18,000 men remained in the line by the middle of January 1915. Russian troops had suffered too, with 16,000 dead or wounded and 12,000 sick, but their army was intact and clearly had the initiative in the region.[105]

The consequences of Sarikamiş were significant. The Ottoman defeat spurred the British to accelerate their plans for an assault on the Dardanelles, and it prompted the Entente powers to reconsider their strategy in the Middle East as a whole. Though new vistas of power and opportunity were emerging, the front line in early 1915 remained the same: the borderland of the Ottoman and Russian empires. As the winter wore on, Russian generals planned a small operation in the spring and a larger one in the summer that would push Ottoman forces back and prevent any unification of effort with Azerbaijan and Persia. The Ottomans, for their part, scrambled frantically to mobilize their population for the next phase of the war. They quickly took the decision to empower Turkish paramilitary groups and Kurdish irregular forces to assault Armenian communities throughout Eastern Anatolia. The Armenian population living under Ottoman control was disarmed in February and, beginning on 26 March/8 April 1915, deported from their places of residence. In contrast with the Russian deportations, which did not have extermination as their goal, the Ottoman leadership used forced marches as an explicit "death warrant to a whole race."[106] Kurds savaged some villages, Ottoman troops

---

[103] W. E. D. Allen and Paul Muratoff, *Caucasian Battlefields: A History of the Wars on the Turco-Caucasian Border, 1828–1921* (Cambridge: Cambridge University Press, 1953), 239.

[104] Allen and Muratoff, 247.   [105] Allen and Muratoff, 249–85.

[106] These are the words of Henry Morgenthau, the American ambassador to Constantinople, cited in Leo Kuper, "The Turkish Genocide of the Armenians, 1915–1917," in *The Armenian Genocide in Perspective*, ed. Richard G. Hovannisian (New Brunswick and Oxford: Transaction Books, 1986), 48.

attacked others, and members of the paramilitary "Special Organization" connected to the Ottoman Young Turk leadership did the bulk of the work. They arrested or shot Armenian community leaders. Those who survived the initial attacks were captured and driven without food or water to their deaths. In Bitlis, the process began on 9/22 June 1915, when Ottoman troops began an operation aimed at arresting all able Armenian men. That assault wrapped up three days later, and the massacres began the following day, on 13/26 June. The Ottoman battalion led chained lines of men to neighboring villages, where they shot and then burned their victims. Within a week, the Armenian women and children of the city were arrested and forcibly deported. Only 2,500 of a pre-war population of 18,000 Armenians remained in the city, all of them under the protection of the American mission. Most of these also perished, either early on from sickness, or later when the American compound was liquidated and its director, Reverend G. P. Knapp, was shot.[107]

When Russian troops moved into Ottoman Armenia, they found the region depopulated. As one official commented, "Turkey has left us an Armenia without Armenians."[108] Most of those Armenians had perished, but thousands had fled to the Russian Empire for safety. In 1917, after two years of poverty, disease, war, and persecution, there were still 153,762 Armenian adults and 12,435 Armenian children on the refugee rolls in the Caucasus region alone.[109] The refugee crisis in the Caucasus was not limited to Armenians. As the lines shifted, Armenian militias proved able and willing to exact revenge on Kurdish and Turkish communities. Thousands of them fled the carnage as well.

Indeed, even after the Russian army established an occupation regime in Eastern Anatolia in 1915, it proved unable to successfully maintain order and defuse the murderous interactions between these groups. One important example of this complicated situation was in the city of Van. Van was the site of the most important Armenian uprising in 1915, which took place between mid-April and mid-May. The uprising coincided with a general Russian offensive into Anatolia, and advancing Russian troops forced the lifting of the Ottoman siege of the Armenian quarter of the city and a retreat from the area as a whole. Russian troops found a scene of disaster when they entered. Ruined buildings loomed open-mouthed and desolate in the town. "The houses there were all large two-story structures," one Russian nurse wrote, "but they were terrible: I didn't see a single intact window or door. . . . Not a single human being was visible anywhere." Outside of town, feral children orphaned by the siege, the Ottoman deportations and killings, and the Kurdish assaults on Armenian villages wandered in the mountains unattended.[110]

---

[107] See "The Murder of Reverend G. P. Knapp, Head of the American Mission, Bitlis," 16 October 1919, author (an Armenian from Bitlis) unknown. Hoover Institution Archives (HIA), Ernest Wilson Riggs papers, box 1, n.p.

[108] Report from Prince Gadzhemukov (chief of Dersim district) to General Iudenich (commander of Caucasian army), 14 March 1917, RGVIA f. 2168, op. 1, d. 274, l. 2.

[109] For numbers, see "Svedeniia o kolichestve bezhentsev na 1-oe marta 1917 na Kavkaze i v mestnostiakh Turtsii i Persii, zaniatykh russkimi voiskami," RGVIA f. 2168, op. 1, d. 288, l. 25.

[110] Christine D. Semine, *Tragediia russkoi armii Pervoi Velikoi Voiny 1914–1918 g.g.: zapiski sestri miloserdiia kavkazskogo fronta* (New Mexico: n.p., 1964), 28–34, quote on 28.

Local Armenians pressured the Russian commander, Major General Nikolaev, to arrest all the perpetrators he could lay his hands on. Instead, he decided to release most of the Kurds back to their villages, keeping a few as hostages subject to the death penalty in case of Kurdish sedition. In addition, he ordered the local Armenian population to leave the Kurds alone: no attacks on them, their livestock, or any of their property were to be countenanced.[111]

Aram Manougian, the leader of the Van resistance and governor of the territory, protested loudly. Local Kurds, he pointed out, had been behind the murders and rapes of many Armenians in recent months, assaults that the Russian troops themselves could verify. He urged Nikolaev to treat them as prisoners of war. Failing that, "we should look on them as ordinary criminals (murderers, bandits, and robbers), and they should suffer the appropriate punishment." The Armenian population, he warned, would not look dispassionately on the return of men responsible for victimizing 28,000 local Armenians, especially since many of them had expropriated Armenian property in the process.[112] Nikolaev was sympathetic to Manougian's point, and he replied that the governor should present him with a list of those to be prosecuted.[113] Indeed, many figures in the Russian chain of command thought that the empire should use the Armenian militias to their advantage. The penchant of those militias to massacre Muslims clearly raised the risk of an insurgency against the Russian occupation, however, so the army moved within months first to sideline and then to disband Armenian volunteer formations operating in the region.[114] By then, however, the damage to civilian populations had been done, with widespread disease, starvation, decimation, and flight.

The disasters of 1915 across the entire front focused the attention of military officials on the problem of population movement; so too did migration become a top priority for civilian leaders. The basic functions of the state were not being fulfilled, and imperial society was in a state of deep crisis. As one official noted in September 1915, "the victims of the war—refugees—currently represent no less an awful occurrence in Russian life than the war itself."[115] Very quickly the question of refugees and of forced deportations became one of the major issues in the politically volatile summer of 1915. In closed and open meetings alike, the newly invigorated mass politicians who sought control over the destiny of the nation and the war effort lambasted the tsar's bureaucrats and his military staff for their inhumane policies. As the chairman of the Council of Ministers complained to Grand Duke Nikolai Nikolaevich, "the daily inquiries in Duma commissions regarding the

---

[111] Major General Nikolaev, Order to detachment in city of Van, 22 June 1915, GARF f. 1791, op. 2, d. 179, l. 3.

[112] Aram Manougian (governor of Van), Telegram to head of the Baiazetskii Detachment, the commander of the Army of the Caucasus, and the commander of the Fourth Caucasian Army, 26 June 1915, GARF f. 1791, op. 2, d. 179, l. 4ob.

[113] Major General Nikolaev, Telegram to governor of Van and Van Okrug (Manougian), 4 July 1915, GARF f. 1791, op. 2, d. 179, l. 7–7ob.

[114] Michael A. Reynolds, *Shattering Empires: The Clash and Collapse of the Ottoman and Russian Empires, 1908–1918* (Cambridge: Cambridge University Press, 2011), 156–8.

[115] Order of the main commander for the relief of refugees on the Northwestern Front, 15 September 1915, RGVIA f. 2005, op. 1, d. 42, l. 284.

actions of civil and military authorities in the zone of military activity, primarily in regards to measures to help refugees, have put the government in an exceedingly difficult position."[116] By August, even moderate ministers were warning that "the naked and hungry spread panic everywhere, dampening the last remnants of the enthusiasm which existed in the first months of the war. They come in a solid phalanx, trampling down the crops, ruining the meadows, the forests.... The second great migration of peoples arranged by Headquarters is dragging Russia into the abyss, into revolution, and into destruction."[117] These were heartfelt and prophetic words.

Despite these bitter recriminations, both civilian and military officials worked hard over the summer of 1915 to devise a workable bureaucratic structure that could deal with the refugee problem. Army commanders soon realized that cash was among the most important assets they could utilize. Their troops needed meat and supplies; refugees needed a way to make their cumbersome and easily stolen assets more portable. As a result, requisitions, which had stirred local residents to anger in the first year of the war, suddenly became more popular. Indeed, many civilians now begged army officials to requisition their goods (at fixed prices now higher than the unstable wartime market could provide).[118] When the front line stabilized in the late summer of 1915, it became possible to organize a circle of transportation. Food and weapons came west, the empty wagons filled with "valuable items, belongings, [and] refugees" on their way east.[119] The upsurge of civic activism that had accompanied the war and had initially been thwarted by anxious conservative monarchists, now found work on a new social problem that the government and military authorities were unable to handle on their own. "Public" (*obshchestvennye*) organizations largely took over the relief, sanitation, feeding, and medical efforts aimed at refugees.[120] This new constellation of forces changed Russian politics for good. It ended the autocracy's monopoly on power and brought the war home in a tangible way. The fact that the new political structure arose in response to massive population dislocation also had important implications. Whatever else changed in Russia after the Great Retreat, the possibilities for organized population movements now expanded greatly. Having proven in 1914 that they could move millions of soldiers across the empire, they showed in 1915 that it was also thinkable, if more problematic, to do the same with civilians. This was yet another example of the way that the failing traditional state found ways to pioneer new practices to deal with the catastrophe that had befallen the empire.

---

[116] Telegram from Goremykin to Nikolai Nikolaevich, 22 July 1915, RGVIA f. 2005, op. 1, d. 42, l. 59.

[117] Comments of A. V. Krivoshein at meeting of the Council of Ministers on 4 August 1915. Cherniavsky, 46.

[118] See telegram from Podpolkovnik Nikandrov to Polkovnik Adzhiev (General Staff), 5 August 1915, RGVIA f. 2106, op. 3, d. 168, l. 52.

[119] M. N. Gerasimov, *Probuzhdenie* (Moscow: Voenizdat, 1965), 56.

[120] Telegram from General Danilov to General Alekseev, 25 August 1915, RGVIA f. 2005, op. 1, d. 42, l. 174; Gatrell, *Whole Empire Walking*, esp. 49–72.

THE GREAT RETREAT COMES HOME

The retreat of the Russian army and the flight of the civilian population of the Polish, Ukrainian, and Armenian borderlands utterly transformed Russian political life. Ever since the heady days of mobilization and the demonstrations (and riots) that accompanied it, Russian citizens and politicians had observed a political truce. Workers went on strike infrequently—the number of strikes in the last months of 1914 was lower than at any point in the previous decade[121]—and popular demonstrations were rare. The political opposition proudly withdrew from the public stage, granting war credits in the Duma in July 1914 and holding just one more brief meeting of that legislative body in January 1915. The tsarist government welcomed this apparent change in disposition, but the police continued to suspect that an improbable cross-party coalition between the liberal Kadets, the peasant-based Social Revolutionary Party, various "regional" nationalist parties, and the communist Bolsheviks and Mensheviks was lying in wait, hoping to replay the revolutionary events of 1905. The chief policeman of the empire ordered all party leaders in the metropole and the periphery to be watched closely with the objective of "decisive and active measures for paralyzing their maliciousness" when the time came. The Kadets, the chief of police wrote, were the most dangerous party, followed by the workers' movement. Nationalists, he thought, simply gravitated to the class-based metropolitan political parties.[122] Those leaders had displayed no open maliciousness whatsoever prior to the Great Retreat.

The events of 1915 forced many Russian leaders to change their tactics. As we have seen, the façade of unity began to crack as early as February, when the destruction of the XX Corps of the Tenth Army in the Augustów Forest provided the backdrop for the spectacular court martial of Colonel Miasoedov.[123] The quiet grumblings of treason in high places grew louder, and the Petrograd elite watched aghast as well-connected men from the capital began to hurl ever deadlier accusations at one another. At the same time, dissatisfaction regarding the supply situation produced new political formations of industrialists and progressive factions in the military and the Duma. None of this led to open opposition, however. As late as April, the American journalist Stanley Washburn wrote hopefully that "throughout Russia, the cause in which her Armies are engaged has come to be more nearly understood than any war she has ever engaged in . . . with the fall of Przemysl, we find Russian sentiment and confidence in Russia at probably the

---

[121] Diane P. Koenker and William G. Rosenberg, *Strikes and Revolution in Russia, 1917* (Princeton: Princeton University Press, 1989), 58.

[122] V. A. Briun-de-Sent-Ippolit (Director of the Ministry of Internal Affairs' Department of Police), circular to the chiefs of all provincial gendarme administrations, completely secret, 2 September 1914, GARF f. 217, op. 1, d. 304, ll. 526–531.

[123] The most comprehensive account of the Miasoedov Affair and the political conditions in which it took place is William C. Fuller, Jr., *The Foe Within: Fantasies of Treason and the End of Imperial Russia* (Ithaca: Cornell University Press, 2006).

highest point that has ever been reached in the history of the Empire."[124] Though Washburn was perhaps a bit too exuberant in his analysis (and though he missed some of the simmering dissatisfaction mentioned previously), he was not totally wrong. The contrast with the mood and behavior during the summer was therefore all the more striking.

The real fracture of the political system occurred during the summer of 1915. The initial Galician setbacks prompted Rodzianko to initiate discussions with the high command and with the tsar, and he forced a general meeting between Sukhomlinov and leading political figures in May that left Sukhomlinov holding the political bag for the shell crisis.[125] In general, however, the politicians were behind the curve of popular dissatisfaction, as the Kadet Prince Mansyrev explained to a fellow centrist in late May:

> Events are developing more quickly than you might think, and not in a direction that will lead us to the place we want to go . . . This movement is accelerating thanks to our failures in the Carpathians. Now everyone knows that we don't have enough guns, enough bullets, or enough shells, that we're sacrificing hundreds of thousands of people . . . Everyone sees and knows this, both the soldiers themselves and the civilian population; they know it in cities and in villages. They even know who is to blame for this lack of preparedness, and therefore dissatisfaction is growing not by the day but by the hour. It has already taken on real forms. But who is leading it, who stands at the head of this movement? Well, nobody, it's running itself somehow, without organization, without a plan or system, and thus it's even more terrifying, since it could lead not only to undesirable, but even to directly horrible or even unthinkable, results.[126]

Military defeat destroyed the last vestiges of tsarist legitimacy, and with it the Sacred Union that had governed political life in the first ten months of the war. The political events and solutions devised over the course of the summer (and the rest of the war) would bear the imprint of the new forms of political, social, and economic life developed in the front zone prior to the retreat.

In regions now much closer to the front, such as Kiev province, the open disposition of people turned from hopeful patriotism to a warier appraisal. One gendarme noted: "The mood of the peasant population is depressed. There is still no ferment among the people, but the earlier high spirits have disappeared. A lack of faith in the success of our arms has appeared. The failures and retreat of our troops have produced a notable change in the mood of the population."[127] Inflation riots grew larger in early April, with the Ministry of Internal Affairs warning governors on 12/25 April that inflation was "especially heavily felt by the poor, whose unhappiness has already begun to appear in several places in the

---

[124] Stanley Washburn, *The Russian Campaign, April to August 1915, Being the Second Volume of "Field Notes from the Russian Front"* (New York: Charles Scribner's Sons, 1915), 7–8.

[125] F. A. Gaida, *Liberal'naia oppozitsiia na putiakh k vlasti (1914–vesna 1917 g.)* (Moscow: Rosspen, 2003), 74.

[126] Diary entry of I. S. Kliuzhev relating a conversation with Prince Mansyrev, 21 May 1915, excerpted in Gaida, 75.

[127] "Svedenie o nastroeniia naseleniia Kievskago uezda za iiul' mesiatsa 1915 goda," TsDIAK f. 274, op. 4, d. 463, l. 164.

form of attempts to launch street disorders and pogroms of the trading establishments of merchants suspected of artificially raising prices."[128] "By 1915," notes Corinne Gaudin, "it was almost impossible to open an issue of a provincial newspaper without coming upon at least one article lamenting artificially inflated prices and the harm allegedly done by speculators."[129] Significantly, the oppositional labor movement revived as well. There had been an average of less than twenty strikes and less than 12,000 strikers per month across the empire over the first eight months of the war, but in April 1915, there were 111 strikes and 38,590 strikers, in May 165 strikes and 63,008 strikers, and in June 164 strikes and 80,054 strikers.[130]

This bubbling social unrest found its most visible outlets in two deadly events: a massive set of riots in Moscow in the last days of May and the violent repression of a growing strike wave in Kostroma in the first days of June. Both of these events gained immediate notoriety across the country and served as triggers for other strikes and riots in the late spring and early summer.

The unrest in Moscow began on 26 May/8 June, less than a week after the Austrians recaptured Przemyśl.[131] A group of roughly 100 women who showed up for their weekly appointment to receive sewing work for the army at the Committee of the Grand Duchess Elizaveta Fedorovna were turned away with the explanation that there was no material to give out. This upset the group of seamstresses, some of whom began shouting that their work had been given by the "German" grand duchess to the German sewing firm of Mandl. The crowd grew in size and belligerency, but the military governor of the city pacified them by promising to look into their complaints. On the same date, printers at the Giubner factory went on strike demanding the firing of Alsatian employees. Once again, the anti-German sentiment proved popular, and the police barely avoided the spreading of the strike to the nearby Prokhorov munitions factory. On the next two days, the police ran out of luck, as crowds successfully attacked factories and stores, first those with German names, then eventually those with foreign names, and finally virtually anything they saw. The city governor, Adrianov, feared that the situation could escalate into revolution and refused to order the police to shoot the rioters. Finally, however, he gave the order on 29 May/11 June to begin shooting into the rioting crowds, at which point the uprising subsided. By the end of the conflict, eight civilians and seven policemen had been killed, with at least forty other civilians seriously injured. Over 300 firms and many private residences had been destroyed, with damages totaling over 72,000,000 rubles. In terms of monetary damages, it was the largest pogrom in Russian history to date.

---

[128] Cited in Iu. I. Kir'ianov, "Massovye vystupleniia na pochve dorogovizny v Rossii (1914–fevral' 1917 g.)," *Otechestvennaia istoriia* no. 3 (1993): 4.

[129] Corinne Gaudin, "Rural Echoes of World War I: War Talk in the Russian Village," *Jahrbücher für Geschichte Osteuropas* 56, no. 3 (2008): 397.

[130] I. I. Mints, "Revoliutsionnaia bor'ba proletariata rossii v 1914–1916 godakh," *Voprosy istorii* no. 12 (December 1959): 23–40, here at 24.

[131] All this material comes from Lohr, *Nationalizing the Russian Empire*, ch. 2.

Eric Lohr has convincingly refuted the argument popular at the time that the government sanctioned or organized this pogrom. The unusual reluctance of the police to shoot into the crowds, he argues, was not a sign of complicity but a sign of caution. The Ministry of Internal Affairs had made a decision in April, following a string of demonstrations against price increases, that they would not transform economic grievances into dangerous political ones by killing civilians, and Adrianov followed that protocol. The Moscow riots demonstrated how quickly economic complaints could escalate into general disorder, however, and this policy was rescinded immediately. The message quickly went out from governors to police officials to be more forceful. Already on 3/16 June, the Governor of Chernihiv (Lavrinovskii) was telling his police chiefs that "in the present circumstances . . . representatives of state power must act decisively and quickly on the spot . . . don't allow any marches or demonstrations, even patriotic ones . . . If there is even the slightest resistance from the crowd, decisively take extreme measures, including the use of weapons."[132] Crowds of any sort were to be feared, not encouraged, and the temporary caution regarding the use of violence against civilians while the army was at war was thrown to the wind.

Lohr's treatment makes clear that if we take away the argument that the pogrom was officially directed, then we are left with the argument that this was a popular explosion of ethnic violence. The rioters came from different classes, different sexes, and different age groups, and once the anarchy developed, there were different targets of violence as well, but there is no doubt that the ideological character of the beginning stages was dominated by ethnic antagonism toward Germans. This antagonism had been present in central Russia and elsewhere in the empire before the war. But the ethnic antagonism of the war period was of a different sort. As we have already seen, an increasing number of people were growing exponentially angrier and more hostile toward the German element in their midst. Unhappy workers had frequently demanded that all Germans be purged from their firms well before the Moscow events. In February 1915, for instance, a crowd of mainly women workers in Kharkiv left their factory benches and demanded that the director of the factory, a certain Sonnenberg, be fired. "We don't need Germans!" they cried, but their demands were not met. They eventually dispersed without bloodshed.[133]

After the defeats in Galicia, however, crowds turned to violence in central Russia. Antipathies had been developing for some time, but the military retreat triggered mass outrage and increased violence on the home front. As Lohr puts it, "the link between events at the front and anti-alien sentiment at home appears to have been crucial."[134] What looked to some contemporaries to have been the re-emergence of

---

[132] Circular from the governor of Chernigov (Lavrinovskii) to police chiefs in Chernigov province, 3 June 1915, TsDIAK f. 1439, op. 1, d. 1667, l. 43.

[133] Major General Rykovskii, "Donesenie nachal'nika Khar'kovskogo GZhU departmentu politsii o zabastovke rabochikh kanatnoi fabriki v sl. Grigor'evke Khar'kovskogo uezda," secret, 13 February 1915, in *Rabochee dvizhenie na Ukraine v period pervoi mirovoi imperialisticheskoi voiny, Iiul' 1914 g.– fevral' 1917 g.: Sbornik dokumentov i materialov* (Kiev: Izd. "Naukova Dumka," 1966): 40.

[134] Lohr, *Nationalizing the Russian Empire*, 43.

a certain type of pre-war violence—the pogrom—in fact had assumed a different political mode colored by wartime circumstances and exacerbated by two factors: economic crisis and military defeat. Crowds on the street still beat minorities and destroyed property, but now the trigger was a shortage of supplies and work, the ideological content of the riot was linked to military conflict, and the violence itself was akin to the ethnic violence in the combat borderlands earlier in the war.

We can see the same phenomenon occurring in the context of a different sort of pre-war violence—the labor strike—before the smoke had even dissipated from the streets of Moscow. This time the site of the action was Kostroma. The cause of the strike was the same one that had stimulated nearly all of the economic unrest during the war—inflation.[135] Constantly rising prices, especially for staple goods such as food, prompted labor leaders to go to factory administrators time and time again with requests for wage hikes. At the Great Kostroma Linen Factory, however, managers resisted the latest demands, agreeing to increased wages only if apartment subsidies were reduced by the same amount. Management, not workers, linked the strike directly to the war, telling them on 2/15 June that "the terrible period that the fatherland is living through demands intense work and complete calm in the interior of the country. It's not the time to strike, it's necessary to work."[136] When the linen workers went out on strike the following day, the government reinforced this connection once more, saying that since the factory was fulfilling state orders "for the needs of the Russian soldiers fighting for faith, tsar, and motherland," strikers would be breaking the law and "helping only our enemy."[137]

This language had been deployed to good effect for the first nine months of the war, but the defeats and intensified economic disruption had eroded whatever patriotic good will had been present in July 1914. The strikers ignored the chest-thumping officials and marched through the city trying to build support for their cause. When the police tried to stop them, the crowd threw stones at them. The police commander responded by ordering his troops to fire at the crowd. The troops fired clear of the strikers, and once more the events of the retreat played a role. Some in the crowd took the empty shots as evidence that the police, like the soldiers at the front, had run low on munitions, and they shouted to their comrades "Don't worry, they don't have anything to shoot with, they're out of bullets!"[138]

---

[135] There were in addition a great many "pogroms" against shopkeepers because of inflation, sometimes with thousands of participants, most of them led by women. Iurii Kir'ianov counted a minimum of 17 of these in 1915 and 288 in 1916. See Kir'ianov, 9–10. On the numbers of women, see especially Barbara Alpern Engel, "Not by Bread Alone: Subsistence Riots in Russia during World War I," *Journal of Modern History* 69 (December 1997): 696–721. See also Mark Baker, "Rampaging 'Soldatki,' Cowering Police, Bazaar Riots and Moral Economy: The Social Impact of the Great War in Kharkiv Province," *Canadian-American Slavic Studies* 35, no. 2–3 (2001): 148–52.

[136] "Ob"iavlenie administratsii rabochim tovarishchestva Bol'shoi Kostromskoi l'nianoi manufaktory ot 2 iiunia 1915 g.," in E. V. Gorelkina ed., "Iz istorii rabochego dvizheniia vo vremia mirovoi voiny (Stachochnoe dvizhenie v Kostromskoi gubernii)," *Krasnyi arkhiv* 67 (1934): 5–27, here at 8.

[137] "Ob"iavlenie glavnonachal'stvuiushchego Kostromskoi gubernii," 3 June 1915, in Gorelkina ed., "Iz istorii rabochego dvizheniia," 8–9.

[138] "Iz protokola pokazanii pomoshchnika kostromskogo politseimeistera sudebnomu sledovateliu Kostromskogo okruzhnogo suda po vazhneishim delam ot 6 iiunia 1915 g.," in Gorelkina ed., "Iz istorii rabochego dvizheniia," 10.

This assessment was incorrect, as the next moments would prove. Police killed several strikers with their next volley, including several women and children.

Now it was the turn of labor activists to link the war and the Kostroma strike. Kostroma Bolsheviks issued a "Proclamation of Kostroma Women Workers to Soldiers" which read

> Soldiers! We are turning to you for help. Defend us. Our fathers, sons, and husbands were taken away and sent to the war, but healthy well-fed policemen are shooting us defenseless, weaponless women ... They say to us: work peacefully, but we're hungry and can't work. We made requests, but they didn't listen, we began to demand, and they began shooting. They say there's no bread. Well where is it? Can the Russian land bear fruit only for the German?[139]

The next day several more Kostroma factories went out on strike to protest the detentions and shootings, and the unrest soon spread to neighboring districts. The factory administration quickly acceded to the workers' demands, but the strike continued for several more days and became a key moment in the resuscitation of the strike movement in Russia. Within weeks, serious strikes would develop again in the region (in Ivanovo-Voznesensk) which would then boomerang back towards Moscow.[140]

The events in Moscow and Kostroma were just two (though an important two) of the events of the summer of 1915 that show how the eastward movement of the Russian armies sent not only soldiers and refugees in motion to the east, but wartime social dynamics as well. Ethnic conflict, rapid inflation, and open violence had developed first in the war zones. These had infiltrated, conceptually at least, the societies of central Russia as well, but they were not made manifest until the crisis situation brought on by the Great Retreat. Hope for victory dissipated, inflation increased much faster than wages, and discontent rose to a significant level. Someone would have to bear the blame. That someone was largely the Germans and the Jews in the first year of the war, but as time went on, this explanation grew less and less convincing to increasing numbers of people. Even in places close to the front (and rife with anti-Germanism and anti-Semitism), such as Kiev, blame shifted elsewhere. Educated society was "frightened by the indecisiveness and instability of the government," while among local peasants, the most prominent rumors were that "all our military failures were due to the treason of the high command."[141] In Petrograd, educated society fretted even more. Rumors spread of an imminent palace coup, depressed citizens spoke openly of a broken political and military system and the likelihood of German victory, and even the rich and

---

[139] "Proklamatsiia kostromskikh zhenshchin-rabotnits k soldatam," June 1915, in Gorelkina ed., "Iz istorii rabochego dvizheniia," 12.

[140] M. G. Fleer, ed., *Rabochee dvizhenie v gody voiny* (Moscow: Voprosy truda, 1925), 90.

[141] "Svedenie o nastroenii naseleniia Kievskago uezda v Avguste mesiatsa 1915 goda," TsDIAK, f. 274, op. 4, d. 63, l. 178; Timofei Smazheniuk, District Gendarme Watchman (Cherkassk district, Kiev province), report to the Kiev Province Gendarme Administration, 4 November 1915, TsDIAK f. 274, op. 4, d. 463, l. 228.

powerful, such as the wealthy industrialist A. I. Putilov, confided to foreign consuls that "the days of tsarist power are numbered."[142]

THE END OF THE SACRED UNION

The political landscape had indeed been transformed by the military defeats and the social unrest that came in the wake of those defeats. As noted previously, the recriminations over the munitions shortages led to a successful campaign by moderates to scapegoat the war minister Sukhomlinov, and he was forced to resign on 12/25 June. The same critical issue of shell shortage also forced the government to create a new "Special Commission for State Defense" in May.[143] This commission was still a state organ, subordinated to the Main Artillery Administration, but it included Duma members and a handful of key businessmen from Petrograd. The chairman of the Duma, Mikhail Rodzianko, had been the key figure in lobbying Stavka for these concessions to public opinion.

These maneuvers were not enough to save the Sacred Union of Russia's political parties with the tsar. In early June, the Kadets held a party conference at which delegates from the provinces savaged the leadership and political stance taken by men such as their primary spokesman Pavel Miliukov. The idea for the conference, Miliukov admitted, came from the "depths of Russia," and those delegates made sure that their dissatisfaction with both the government and the party leadership would be on the table.[144] The agenda for the meeting, however, deferred discussion of "tactical" political questions until the third and final day. The conference began with substantive discussions of key questions facing the nation. The list of these questions is a good barometer of what liberal elites saw as the most important political topics of the day: (1) the agrarian question, (2) inflation, (3) finance and taxation, (4) helping war victims, and (5) nationality questions (especially Jewish, Ukrainian, and Polish, though they would consider others (for example the Armenian question) if time permitted).[145] The reports and discussions on these issues were thoughtful. Some, for example A. I. Shingarev's report on the causes and consequences of inflation, were far better than anything floating around at the top of the tsarist government at the time. Nevertheless, there was impatience on the part of many delegates to get to the question of tactical politics. As A. S. Bezchinskii from Taganrog put it, "I don't understand how we are supposed to decide scholarly questions of the global causes of inflation and so forth at this conference . . . it's time to stop the debate, since it all leads to the same dead end—the fact that everything is in a state of disorganization at the very top. And we need to address that as soon as

---

[142] Gaida, 76.

[143] Peter Gatrell, *Russia's First World War: A Social and Economic History* (Harlow, UK: Pearson Longman, 2005), 90.

[144] Speech of P. N. Miliukov, 6 June 1915, in *S"ezdy i konferentsii konstitutsionno-demokraticheskoi partii. V 3-kh tt.*, t. 3, kn. 1 (vol. 3, bk. 1) (1915–1917 gg.) (Moscow: ROSSPEN, 2000), 12.

[145] *S"ezdy i konferentsii konstitutsionno-demokraticheskoi partii*, t.3, kn. 1,13.

possible."[146] Miliukov balked at this attitude, but he couldn't keep it repressed for long; the conference turned to political questions by the evening session of the second day, ahead of schedule.

Miliukov issued the report of the party's central committee on the current political situation and opened the floor for debate. Virtually every speaker urged the leadership to take a stronger position. G. D. Romm (from Vilnius) exclaimed that the resolutions of the central committee "failed to call things by their true names. It's too little to say that the government in the present war has turned out to be incompetent; we have to talk about the criminal activity of the government."[147] N. P. Vasilenko (Kiev) insisted that the overly diplomatic and conciliatory phrasing of the political program was the result of the leadership being out of touch with the country:

> This moment is critical for the Kadet party: either it helps save the country or it will perish itself. The imprint of old tactics lies upon the theses of the Central Committee...Already in August [1914] we in Kiev were more closely aware of the true state of affairs and already in December urgently pressed to convene a conference in order to tell you those things that you only now are understanding. And if you had listened to us, maybe things would have turned out differently.[148]

In this respect, as in the others already discussed in the chapter, those closer to the front had seen the dark new era very soon after the war began, but it was only after the Great Retreat that the full extent of the danger became apparent to those in central Russia.

The Kadet leaders were not alone in facing the wrath of their junior members. Even the party of principled cooperation with the government—the Octobrists—faced internal dissension. Both Rodzianko and Guchkov, the two most visible figures of the party, struggled to chart a course through the dangerous political waters of 1915, and both failed. By the end of June, they even ceased publishing their official newspaper, *Golos Moskvy*.[149]

With the government adrift and political parties in disarray, the need for new political approaches became apparent. Prior to the military retreats, Russia's top business leaders gave little thought to the potential need for massive economic mobilization. After them, they could think of little else.[150] Military and political failure led to military and political innovation. In late May, captains of industry and the leaders of the rapidly growing public organizations led by the Union of Towns and the Union of Zemstvos began fumbling their way toward one another. On 24

---

[146] Speech of A. S. Bezchinskii, 6 June 1915, in *S"ezdy i konferentsii konstitutsionno-demokraticheskoi partii*, t.3, kn.1, 22.

[147] Speech of G. D. Romm, 7 June 1915, in *S"ezdy i konferentsii konstitutsionno-demokraticheskoi partii*, t.3, kn. 1, 133.

[148] Speech of N. P. Vasilenko, 8 June 1915, in *S"ezdy i konferentsii konstitutsionno-demokraticheskoi partii*, t. 3, kn. 1, 155.

[149] Raymond Pearson, *The Russian Moderates and the Crisis of Tsarism, 1914–1917* (Basingstoke: Macmillan, 1977), 38.

[150] Lewis Siegelbaum, *The Politics of Industrial Mobilization in Russia, 1914–17: A Study of the War-Industries Committees* (New York: St Martin's, 1983), 42–50.

May/6 June, the newspaper *Utro Rossii* put forward a call for a "government of national defense" that included representation from these rapidly emerging social and political forces under the headline "Unity until the End!" During 26–28 May/ 8–10 June, the Ninth Congress of Industry and Trade Representatives picked up the thread, contemplating a call to reorganize the entire political system with the convocation of a Constituent Assembly, but eventually settling for a demand to immediately call the Duma back into session. They also called for a more comprehensive mobilization of industry through the creation of War Industrial Committees.[151] In early June, the congresses of the Union of Towns and the Union of Zemstvos met and echoed the demands of the industrialists, adding planks that included the demand for a more systematic and effective organization of the rear and of military support services more generally.

In sum, at the same time that the Moscow and Kostroma riots demonstrated the explosive effect of the military defeats upon social relationships in central Russia, the political system showed that it too could not bear up under the strain of the retreat. The public organizations responded to a clear need and promised a way past the bureaucratic inertia and parliamentary squabbling that defined the response of the government and Duma to the summer crisis. The threat these new organizations posed was thus significant both to ministers and the traditional opposition forces, and the government and leaders of the major parties reacted with alarm to the third force that had suddenly appeared on the political landscape.[152] As we shall see, the government had a range of options for dealing with the public organizations, but the Kadets, Octobrists, and Progressists faced a more limited set of choices. The public organizations put themselves forward as patriotic, non-political bodies devoted to organizing selfless public service for the good of the war effort and of the nation. Just as importantly, they did more than simply talk. While Duma members argued over the future of the country in the salons of Petrograd, the Union of Towns and Union of Zemstvos (Zemgor) and the War Industrial Committees were making bandages, sewing up wounds, manufacturing shells, and reaching out to Russians at the local level throughout the empire with pleas for people to volunteer their help. These activities made the public organizations much more difficult to attack politically. The only strategy that some Duma members adopted was to criticize participation in these new institutions on the basis that collaboration with the government was unwise or immoral. This was a problematic stance coming from people who had proclaimed total unity with the government in wartime just months earlier.

The more productive strategy, both politically and in terms of the war effort, was thus co-optation, an attempt to create a new center of Russian politics led (they hoped) by major party elites and committed to the goals espoused by the public organizations. This strategy had the added benefit of being consonant with the demands made by the public organizations to mobilize society in part by recalling and reinvigorating the Duma. In point of fact, the leaders of the public

---

[151] Gaida, 77.   [152] Pearson, 45.

organizations and the Duma centrists did share common goals and a common diagnosis of the ills of the country in general and the war effort in particular. Although their disagreements over strategy and leadership would remain significant, they shared much more in common than either did with the tsar's ministers.

Nicholas II faced a different array of options. In the face of growing opposition, he could fend off public participation by refusing to sanction the work of the public organizations and by keeping his government untainted by representatives of "society." He could disband the Duma and harass any members who protested. He could work cautiously to incorporate some individuals and ideas from society into the government and the war effort. Or he could embrace the idea of a partnership between throne and centrists and position himself as a popular and responsive monarch in days of terrible danger. Nicholas contemplated and tried all of these options save the last. Mass politics confused him, and he refused to acknowledge the political realities he faced, telling Stanley Washburn as late as October 1915, "You are always writing and talking about public opinion but we have no public opinion in Russia."[153]

With armies in flight and Poland crumbling, Nicholas at first heeded the advice of conservative centrists (especially Rodzianko and Krivoshein, the Minister of Agriculture and the most powerful voice in the cabinet). In June and early July, he fired the most objectionable ministers in his cabinet. Sukhomlinov was cashiered as Minister of War, and three influential arch-conservatives (N. A. Maklakov, V. K. Sabler, and I. G. Shcheglovitov) lost their portfolios at the Ministry of Internal Affairs, the Holy Synod, and the Ministry of Justice. As we have seen, he sanctioned the formation of the Special Commission for State Defense, and he soon allowed the formation of the War Industrial Committees as well. Over the course of the summer, the opposition pressed for more concessions, including the formation of bodies with more significant public participation that would bypass the Council of Ministers and report directly to the tsar. But Nicholas maintained the line of conservative co-optation right through mid-August, when the strategy was capped off by the formation of four "Special Councils" (of state defense, food supply, fuel, and transport). These councils incorporated many different political actors, including those from public organizations, but they remained directly under the control of government ministers. Key ministries such as the Ministry of Internal Affairs exercised significant independence and power in those areas where the councils and the ministries overlapped. As Peter Gatrell points out, these councils were as much a clever rebuff of the liberal challenge as they were a concession.[154]

The tsar also chose rapprochement rather than confrontation with the Duma, when he consented to a new Duma session, which opened on 19 July/1 August, the anniversary of the start of the war. There was tremendous pressure on center-left

---

[153] Stanley Washburn, *On the Russian Front in World War I: Memoirs of an American War Correspondent* (New York: Robert Speller and Sons, 1982 [1939]), 149. He was, apparently, equally mystified by American politics. When Washburn told him of his disappointment at Wilson's re-election, Nicholas "said very gently, 'I do not understand your politics, but I am sorry if you feel badly over the outcome'" (266).

[154] Gatrell, *Russia's First World War*, 90–2.

politicians to investigate the mistakes of the past year and to demand a greater role in governance going forward. Leaders such as Rodzianko, Guchkov, and Miliukov felt at the same time that they should grasp the hand the government was offering and not push the tsar too far or too fast. They toned down demands for a cabinet formally responsible to the Duma to a request to form a ministry that enjoyed public "confidence." Guchkov became the first non-governmental figure to attend a meeting of the Council of Ministers in nearly a decade when on 4/17 August he joined them to discuss the decree establishing the War Industrial Committees. In return, progressives hoped that the government would allow them a greater role in the war effort. They pushed for greater accountability from the ministries involved and demanded detailed information about military activities, supply problems, and other key issues.

These hopes were dashed. The purpose of recalling the Duma, from the government's perspective, was to deflect oppositionist sentiment rather than fully engage with it. The Council of Ministers repeatedly expressed frustration with the Duma in late July and early August. The ministers mainly wanted the Duma to pass the politically toxic measure of expanding the military draft to include second-tier reservists. These were men who, for reasons of health, age, or the fact that they were only sons in the family, had been exempt from military service and expected to remain exempt all their lives. The heavy losses of the first year of the war convinced the War Ministry that this manpower resource had to be tapped, and the generals and ministers went to the Duma in large part to seek political cover. That strategy quickly ran into problems. Instead of passing the bill and then adjourning quietly, as the ministers somewhat inexplicably hoped, the Duma balked. A. A. Polivanov, the Minister of War, explained the negotiations to his colleagues in the Council of Ministers in the following way:

> the committee demands from me, insistently, explanations about the situation at the front and about supplies. I dodge the first question – saying that one must direct such inquiries to Headquarters; and I say that the second question cannot be discussed publicly in wartime before the legislative bodies. But I think that without satisfying the demand we will not get the law on the soldiers.[155]

Despite the need for new soldiers, the ministers refused to make these concessions, sensing a political trap. Krivoshein urged his colleagues not to "grab the lure." Instead, they demanded further talks with political leaders such as Rodzianko who were, in Krivoshein's peevish words, "capable at all of conversing with representatives of the hated bureaucracy."[156]

Within the Duma itself, deputies were finding a lot of common ground across party lines. The far left continued to oppose cooperation with the government, and the far right continued to support the tsar's authority in relation to the parliament. Virtually everyone else agreed that the first year of the conflict had demonstrated governmental incompetence and that the Duma had a role to play in repairing the damaged war effort. A coalition did not emerge immediately, however, in part

---

[155] Cherniavsky, 47.   [156] Cherniavsky, 48, 50.

because there was a struggle over leadership of the newly enlarged opposition.[157] As we have seen, haggling over whether the Duma should demand a cabinet "responsible" to the Duma or one enjoying its "confidence" was soon concluded in favor of the latter position, and a large coalition, the "Progressive Bloc," formed to assert a role for the Duma in the midst of the war. The two core stances expressed in the Program of the Progressive Bloc were "1. The formation of a united government, composed of individuals who enjoy the confidence of the country and have agreed with the legislative institutions on the implementation of a definite programme at the earliest possible time. 2. Decisive changes in the methods of administration employed so far, which have been based on distrust of public initiative." They put forward concrete proposals to end persecution on political or religious grounds, to eliminate all restrictions on minority ethnic groups (including Jews), and to immediately draft a bill on Polish autonomy.[158]

This ambitious program had the support not only of the broad center of Russian politics, but also a majority within the more conservative State Council and within the Council of Ministers itself, where key figures such as Krivoshein had taken part in the discussions surrounding the formation and program of the Progressive Bloc. The plan was to submit the program to the government quietly, so as to allow the Bloc's supporters within the Council of Ministers to urge the government to support the plan willingly rather than under public pressure. A leak to the press foiled that strategy, but Krivoshein and others persisted in urging the Council of Ministers to work together with the Bloc. This lobbying succeeded. The Council accepted the program of the Bloc on 26 August with only one dissenting vote—that of I. L. Goremykin, the Council's chairman. The Bloc, in other words, was no longer a party of the opposition, but one in line with the relatively moderate ministers in place in the summer of 1915.

Thus, over the course of June and July, the tsar and his centrist ministers proved able to prevent a complete political implosion through the use of well-timed concessions that gave public figures some voice, but only in conditions and institutions controlled by the tsar's ministers. It was thus all the more surprising that Nicholas completely changed course on a dime in mid-August. On 22 August/ 4 September, he presided over the joint inaugural session of the new Special Councils and then left Petrograd at ten in the evening to assume command of all of Russia's armed forces. Grand Duke Nikolai Nikolaevich and his chief of staff General Ianushkevich were reassigned to the Caucasian Front. On 29 August/11 September, the Council of Ministers sent Goremykin to Stavka to inform the tsar that his government wished to work together with the Progressive Bloc. Instead, Goremykin expressed his minority opinion and persuaded the tsar to disband the Duma. The Duma was prorogued on 3/16 September.[159]

---

[157] On these political wranglings, see Gaida, 101–35; Pearson, 48–58.

[158] Cited in Pearson, 51.

[159] Pearson, 58. Members of the government had met with Bloc leaders at the home of State Controller P. A. Kharitonov on 27 August/10 September for an "informational meeting" at which Duma and State Council members presented their whole program and answered questions from the

The Council of Ministers exploded in anger. Polivanov attacked Goremykin at the next meeting of the council (on 2/15 September), asking him "*How* did you report our opinions to the Emperor?" Sazonov quickly piled on, asking "And *what*, specifically [did you report]?"[160] Goremykin huffed that it was inappropriate to grill him in this way, and Krivoshein glumly agreed, saying that the tsar had been informed of the wishes of his cabinet but had ignored the advice of his ministers. The ministers resigned themselves to their fates. Somewhat surprisingly, so too did the parliamentary members of the Progressive Bloc, which collapsed when the Duma, its institutional base, was sent home. The two major political institutions of the post-1905 era (the Duma and the Council of Ministers) had pushed hard for public involvement in the political sphere as part of a vibrant war effort. They had been firmly rebuffed by the autocrat, and took their defeat quietly, without open rebellion. It had been, as Joseph Stalin later acidly remarked, a "revolt on their knees."[161]

If Nicholas thought he had solved the political crisis of the summer of 1915 with an act of (uncharacteristic) decisiveness, however, he was terribly wrong. With the Duma now out of the picture, the government had to order the conscription of second-tier reservists. Polivanov did so, announcing on 4/17 September that the call-up would begin the following day.[162] This news, combined with the dispersal of the Duma earlier in the week, led to further unrest throughout the empire. For the first time since the outbreak of the war, massive strikes took place in the capital cities. Tens of thousands of strikers hit the streets in Petrograd and Moscow (mostly in Moscow).[163] Their demands were mainly economic, but they also pressed for the recall of the Duma.[164]

Meanwhile, revolts of reservists touched levels not seen since the initial mobilization in 1914 and which would not be seen again during the war. More than seventy different riots took place all across the empire, from Vladivostok to Pskov. Many of these riots, like the earlier ones, took the form of reservists looting local shops for foodstuffs and other goods. But some were explicitly political. In Tula on 8/21 September, reservists broke out of the courtyard of the draft office at noon throwing stones and shouting "we won't go until they draft policemen and reconvene the Duma." In Rostov-on-Don, a huge crowd of reservists marched out of the draft offices with red banners inscribed "Long Live the State Duma. Give us the Duma!" From time to time the Rostov reservists would stop to give speeches demanding the reconvening of the Duma and that policemen be sent to the war, and they then went to a local factory to urge workers to go on strike in support of

---

ministers. This meeting was reported in detail in *Russkie vedomosti* the following day: "Poslednie izvestiia," *Russkie vedomosti*, 28 August 1915: 3.

[160] Cherniavsky, 235.   [161] Cited in Pearson, 64.

[162] General Polivanov (Minister of War), Circular to district and city heads, 4 September 1915, RGIA, f. 1292, op. 1, d. 1775, l. 82. This had already been reported in the press a week earlier. See "Vazhneishie izvestiia," *Russkie vedomosti*, 28 August 1915: 1.

[163] Pearson, 60. Pearson cites the official figure of 20,500 strikers in the two capitals, but notes that Soviet historians have estimated the true number at closer to 70,000.

[164] Gaida, 129.

their revolt.[165] As the reservist demands made clear, many in the country were unhappy not only with the questions surrounding the Duma, but also with the continued draft exemption given to members of the police. In addition to highlighting a growing demand for fairness, the demand to draft the police revealed a fundamental conflict between the two armed branches of tsarist power—the police and the army. This conflict would be critical during the February Revolution in 1917, when soldiers would side with the crowd against the tsarist police.

At the same time, while the defanging of the Progressive Bloc and the subsequent decision by the major public organizations in early September to acquiesce to the tsar's maneuvers meant that revolution would not occur in 1915, political unhappiness increased significantly. On 7/20 September, in the midst of the mobilization riots and during the angry sessions of the Congress of the Union of Towns, A. I. Shingarev reminded his fellow oppositionists that the history of war and reform in Russia was on their side. "Now the decisive moment is beginning," he said. "For the sacred future we need just one more energetic push and we will achieve what the best Russians have dreamed."[166] Opposition leaders continued to meet and to maintain connections with one another. Even the most optimistic conservatives, the Kadet newspaper *Rech'* proclaimed, did not think that the dispersal of the Duma had solved the political crisis.[167]

Russian moderates found themselves in an awkward position as September ended and summer turned to fall. Convinced that the tsarist government was mismanaging the war effort, many also feared that if they raised the political temperature too high, the outcome would be anarchic revolution, not liberal technocracy. V. A. Maklakov, a sober and cautious Kadet, framed the issue in memorable terms in a famous article entitled "A Tragic Situation" in *Russkie vedomosti* on 27 September/10 October. Imagine, he wrote, that you were the passenger in a car on a narrow, bending road on which a single false move would result in death. In the car with you were your closest relatives, including your mother. "And suddenly you see that your driver is incapable of driving: either he doesn't know how to keep the car on the road or he's tired and no longer understands what he's doing, but he is leading you to destruction." Fortunately, Maklakov continued, there are people in the car who know how to drive. Obviously, they should take the wheel despite the danger of changing drivers at full speed. But what, he asked, if the driver was unwilling to relinquish his seat? "He is behind the wheel, he is driving the car, and one false turn or awkward movement of his hands and the car will crash. You know this, but he also knows it. And he laughs at your fear and your powerlessness: 'Don't dare touch me!' He's right, you don't dare touch him." What is worse, as you come to realize your tragic situation, you hear the voice of your mother pleading for help, and "not understanding your behavior, she blames you for your inaction and indifference. And who is to blame if she, having lost faith even in you, jumps out of the automobile along the

---

[165] "Perechen' 'besporiadkov', uchinennykh ratnikami 2-go razriada prizyva 5 sentiabria 1915 g., sostavlennyi v departmente politsii 2/XI/1915 g.," secret, RGIA f. 1292, op. 1, d. 1729, ll. 144, 146.
[166] Cited in Gatrell, *Russia's First World War*, 86.   [167] Gaida, 128.

way?"[168] Maklakov's painful description of the powerlessness and pessimism of Russian moderates struck a deep chord among many who could not bring themselves to foment revolution in the midst of a military crisis, but who could also not bear to watch events unfold.

CONCLUSION

The Russian armies operating in Poland had successfully avoided encirclement in August, though at the cost of surrendering all of the tsar's Polish provinces. The German offensive had not yet run its course, however. When the Germans learned of the sudden military shakeup occasioned by Nicholas' decision to assume command, Hindenburg ordered an immediate offensive near Vilnius that resulted in the so-called "Sventsiany Breakthrough."[169] The assault struck at the hinge of the Russian Northern and Western fronts on 27 August /9 September. By the following day, they had smashed through the lines, opening a path to Sventsiany (present-day Švenčiónys, Lithuania, near the current border with Belarus) and creating the possibility of turning the flank of the Fifth Army and encircling the Tenth Army. Virtually as soon as the new chief of staff at Stavka, General M. V. Alekseev, occupied his post, he was presented with a situation that Stavka had repeatedly botched over the previous year. He had to coordinate the activities of several armies and two fronts, rapidly deploy significant reserves to stop the breakthrough, and come up with a way to slow the German offensive in order to achieve these crucial goals. Otherwise, the path to the Russian heartland lay open.

Alekseev succeeded where his predecessors had failed. Indeed, he succeeded where he himself had failed as front commander just two months earlier at Przasnysz, where, as we have seen, armies fought over reserves and failed to coordinate their activities sufficiently. Rapidly seeing the merit in a suggestion of General Evert (the commander of the Western Front), he ordered the transfer of reserves up and down the line into a newly reformed Second Army that would plug the hole in the line. Meanwhile, he directed large cavalry groups and the newly arrived reservists to attack the advancing Germans in order to slow them down, built new fortified positions further to the east, and then directed an orderly retreat to those lines. The Sventsiany Breakthrough forced the abandonment of still further territory, bringing swathes of Lithuania and Belorussia (including Vilnius) under German occupational authorities, but it had not achieved any substantive strategic objectives. Russian armies bent without breaking elsewhere too, as German forces moved to the gates of Riga in the north but failed to take this important port city and the Russians retreated to defensible winter positions along the Styr River in the south. Finally, Falkenhayn gave up on the possibility of

[168] V. A. Maklakov, "Tragicheskoe polozhenie," originally published in *Russkie vedomosti* no. 221, 27 September 1915; reprinted in V. A. Maklakov, *Rechi: sudebnye, dumskie, i publichnye lektsii 1904–1926* (Paris: Izd. Iubileinogo komiteta, 1949), 198–200.
[169] Rostunov, 265.

encirclement. The German supply lines were increasingly stretched, and even if a great breakthrough were to occur again, it seemed unlikely that the German forces would be mobile enough to exploit it. Not wanting to repeat Napoleon's experience, Falkenhayn turned his focus westward to France instead. Ludendorff, Hindenburg, and Conrad remained convinced that they could win a big victory, and they tried to do so, but Falkenhayn had been right. Attacks bogged down and sputtered out as the Russians built stronger defenses and as the munitions situation began to improve. As of the end of September, the retreat could be declared over, with a new line that ran from Riga in the north through Daugavpils, Lake Naroch (presently Narach), Baranovichi, through the Pripet Marshes, and then south to Ternopil' and finally to the Romanian border.

The Great Retreat had lasted five long months. It had been an enormous success for German arms, as the Kaiser's troops cut deep swathes into Russian imperial territory, conquering Russian Poland, nearly all of present-day Lithuania, half of Latvia, and big chunks of modern-day Ukraine and Belarus. Huge Russian fortresses at Ivangorod, Novogeorgievsk, and Brest-Litovsk had been forced to surrender, and Russian casualties had been immense. And yet, at the end of the day, Russia remained in the war with its front intact and morale in the army steadily increasing.[170] The losses of the summer led some soldiers to despair, but once the front stabilized many more were filled with hatred for the German invaders. "There's a certain confidence," one wrote home, "that soon, soon we will move forward and no machine guns, poison gases and shells will slow our onslaught." "Yes," wrote another, "we'll have to fight with them a long time, but we'll slug it out until the very last soldier from the youngest to the oldest, but we won't remain under the oppression of the Germans." Part of this confidence (on the eve of the Duma's dissolution) was confidence in parliament. The "whole army was full of faith that the State Duma will fix all of the mistakes and will give the army all it needs for victory."[171] The Russian dagger that had been aimed at the heart of Austria-Hungary from the peaks of the Carpathians had been removed and the Polish salient had been overrun, but Russia had not been defeated militarily.

Much the same could be said in political terms. The retreat exposed all the inadequacies of the tsarist government and created unity among both Russian oppositionists and moderates, but what was there to show for the energization of the opposition? Despite intensifying ethnic antagonisms, there had been no nationalist uprisings. Despite the revival of labor activism, there had been no revolution. Party leaders, parliamentarians, and officials in public organizations had united to change the Russian political situation through the creation of the Progressive Bloc, but the tsar stemmed this tide of protest with a combination of clever co-optation in the Special Councils and the shutdown of the Duma. He then gradually purged his government of moderates as the fall and winter progressed.

[170] O. S. Porshneva, *Krest'iane, rabochie, i soldaty Rossii nakanune i v gody Pervoi mirovoi voiny* (Moscow: ROSSPEN, 2004), 193.
[171] "Obzor pisem iz deistvuiushchei armii," 24 August 1915, RGVIA f. 2067, op. 1, d. 3845, ll. 66–67.

At the same time, the supply crisis of the summer eased. Shells, bullets, and guns flowed with increased volume to the front, and as the military situation stabilized, it seemed that the worst might be behind the Russian autocrat and the Russian government.

But appearances were deceiving. Ironically, though the retreat began in the military realm, the events of the summer had the least lasting effects upon the armed forces, which grew stronger as 1915 turned to 1916. In contrast, the Russian society, political system, and economy had been fundamentally crippled by the events of the summer. The Sacred Union was destroyed for good, and politicians both inside government and outside acted warily and sullenly, keeping one eye on the war effort and one on their political opponents. Russian society had also been permanently transformed. Refugees, economic disaster, labor unrest, disease, and violence all spread into the Russian heartland. Social relationships broke under the strain, and people became harder, angrier, more suspicious, and more brutal. As we will see in Chapters 3 and 4, Russian citizens worked diligently to create a viable new system that could arrest this unfolding social, military, and political catastrophe, but their efforts at remobilization were unable to keep pace with the destructive forces that had been unleashed upon the empire in the summer of 1915.

3

Remobilizing the Military
Combat Innovation, POWs, and Forced Labor

Volodia O-v, a young volunteer officer, arrived in the 19th Artillery Brigade in late July 1915, in the midst of the Great Retreat. He wrote home to his mother that he knew that he might die in the war, but he felt it a small price to pay. "Risking one's head every second, you start to feel life in all its acuteness." Without that sharp sense of life, his existence was "empty vegetation." He asked his mother, in case of his passing, to "find consolation in the fact that your son wanted to be a citizen of his motherland by acting and that he died, not hiding behind someone else's back, but hiding others behind him." He called on her to remember Belgium, the "groans of the Polish border population," and the "heroes of Montenegro and Serbia." "Really," he concluded, "are these the same: to live until 50 or 60, to be sick your last ten years, and having recognized the baseness of life, to die in bed . . . or to die a 'beautiful death' at 21 with the consciousness of duty fulfilled?" On 6/19 January 1916, Volodia died from shrapnel wounds.[1]

The themes described by Volodia had inspired action among a significant number of Russian soldiers for much of the war: a strong sense that the war was just, a feeling that they were protecting the weak from the assaults of German militarism, and a solidarity with the Russian nation. As the war dragged into its third year, however, it became increasingly difficult for men to sustain their commitment to the conflict, and the army was running too quickly through fresh-faced idealists like Ensign O-v. Elsewhere, patience was evaporating, as one soldier song from 1916, sung with "a sad rhythm like a wave in the ocean," suggests:

> We marched across the Carpathians,
> We marched for victory.
> We got nothing,
> We had to retreat . . .
>
> Many of our brothers fell.
> A lot of blood was spilled
> For the German leaders
> Who prospered in Russia.

---

[1] Letter cited in Mikhail Lemke, *250 dnei v tsarskoi stavke: vospominaniia, memuary*, 2 vols. (Minsk: Kharvest, 2003) 2: 270–2.

When Warsaw was sold out
A German general
Stuffed his pockets with money
And ran off without apology.

Now Russia is dizzy with woe
The German has strongly attacked
Peaceful citizens have fearfully
Been driven deep into Russia.

What will happen, brothers, in the future?
The mothers and fathers groan
The wives and sisters groan
The soldiers are not coming home.[2]

The problems of combat motivation and soldier morale highlighted by these two very different responses to the European cataclysm were just part of larger questions of how Russia would and could wage war in the wake of the Great Retreat. As John Horne suggests in an influential edited collection, all of Europe faced a dilemma of mobilization in the middle of World War I. The initial burst of activity and of individual "self-mobilization" characteristic of the first months of the war were neither intended to sustain nor capable of sustaining a "novel experience of industrialized siege warfare." Fighting an extended conflict thus required a process of "remobilization," in which both the state and society developed new ways to organize themselves institutionally and psychologically in the face of this extreme emergency. The "radical heart of the First World War," he argues, "lay here, in the encounter between national mobilization and the industrialized killing fields of trench warfare."[3] Horne and his fellow scholars contend that this process of remobilization took place in different ways for each of the belligerent states, but that this basic dilemma of "remobilization" should be seen as the framework for such varied phenomena as the French mutinies of 1917 and the wartime debates over primary education in Italy.[4]

Most of the historians who contributed pieces to the Horne volume concurred that the peak period of European remobilization was in 1917 and 1918, after the grueling battles of attrition at Verdun, the Somme, and the Isonzo River. Scholars of Russia who have taken up Horne's suggestion to pay attention to wartime remobilization have also placed this period in 1917, right in the middle of the revolutionary events that promised to remake not only the war effort but the empire and nation as well.[5] Certainly, if we want to examine the wildest swings of

    [2] Vl. Paduchev, *Zapiski nizhnego china 1916 god* (Moscow: Moskovskoe tovarishchestvo pisatelei, 1931), 34–5.

    [3] John Horne, "Introduction: Mobilizing for Total War, 1914–1918," in *State, Society and Mobilization in Europe during the First World War*, ed. John Horne (Cambridge: Cambridge University Press, 1997), 3, 5.

    [4] Andrea Fava, "War, 'National Education' and the Italian Primary School, 1915–1918," in *State, Society and Mobilization*, ed. Horne, 53–70; Leonard V. Smith, "Remobilizing the Citizen-Soldier through the French Army Mutinies of 1917," in *State, Society and Mobilization*, ed. Horne, 144–59.

    [5] Peter Holquist, *Making War, Forging Revolution: Russia's Continuum of Crisis, 1914–1921* (Cambridge: Harvard University Press, 2002), 2.

soldier and civilian morale and the correspondingly volatile "balance between coercion and persuasion,"[6] then a focus on the period between March and October 1917 makes a great deal of sense.

We should not, however, neglect the important developments that occurred between the end of the Great Retreat in October 1915 and the fall of the monarchy in March 1917. I will argue in this chapter and the next that in fact the shock of defeat ushered in a period of "remobilization" that saw significant innovation and transformation in many different arenas: in combat tactics, in strategic goals, in the growth of forced labor, and in the expansion of social surveillance by "progressive" activists.[7] These remobilizing efforts were important in their own right, but they also established a very particular context both for the Russian Revolution and for the second phase of the war. At the same time, these new initiatives to strengthen the Russian army, the Russian state, and Russian society were undertaken at a moment when all of those entities were themselves in a state of crisis. The race between a "totalizing" program to build a functioning wartime system[8] and the powerful centrifugal forces that were tearing the empire apart was dramatic and close-run. As we will see, collapse won out over construction in the short run, but the efforts of social and political activists were not in vain. A totalizing, interventionist state dedicated to social mobilization and unification in a militant key would emerge from the rubble, perhaps not in the same form as that envisioned by the hard-working men and women of 1916, but one colored by their efforts nonetheless.

THE REJUVENATION OF THE RUSSIAN ARMY

One of the key arenas of remobilization was the military itself. The post-retreat period was a difficult one for officers committed to finding a way to turn the tide of the conflict. The army continued to develop new plans for ending the war militarily, and some of those plans showed promise. Russian troops won victories in Galicia, in Anatolia, and in Persia. But ultimately, the war had devolved into a strategic stalemate. Men killed each other, wallowed in the muck and cold, contracted diseases, and achieved precious little other than to put pressure on a minor position that might endanger a more significant strategic position, which could threaten a junior partner in the Central Powers' war effort. Russian soldiers continued to fight against their German, Austro-Hungarian, and Turkish enemies, but antipathy toward their own leadership grew too. Fedor Stepun recalled one

---

[6] John Horne, "Remobilizing for 'Total War': France and Britain, 1917–1918," in *State, Society and Mobilization*, ed. Horne, 195.

[7] There were other manifestations of this "progressive," interventionist urge at the same time, not only in the realm of food supply discussed by Holquist and Lih, but also in the introduction of a new income tax that reflected a European "drive for a comprehensive claim on citizens in conditions of total mobilization," while remaining a "political ambition that surpassed the administrative capacities of the state." Yanni Kotsonis, "'No Place to Go': Taxation and State Transformation in Late Imperial and Early Soviet Russia," *Journal of Modern History* 76, no. 3 (September 2004): 531–77, here at 557, 558.

[8] Horne, "Introduction," 3.

telling incident, when one of his friends, "not without pride," led him to the operational division of the army. The hour was late, but staff officers were still working hard. Telephones, reports, and large maps with blue and red lines marking the trench lines littered the room. "It was a valiant affair, behind which you didn't feel the despondency of autumn rains in washed-out trenches, chilling your soul with the fear of impending death." "The hatred toward staff officers," he observed, "is not because they live more cleanly, safely and sweetly, but because they believe they are the creators of history and the rulers of destiny."[9] The collision between the grand plans of high commanders and the morass of the actual lived experience of war became an ever greater source of tension within the army, within the corps of people who served it, and in the nation at large.

The Great Retreat ended in September. On 1/14 October 1915, General Alekseev began to suspect the truth: Falkenhayn had given up trying to achieve a strategic victory on the Russian Front. He sent telegrams to all his commanders on that day asking them to step up their intelligence activities and engage in more disciplined questioning of new prisoners of war to see whether German troops were being pulled off the front in order to bolster their reserves in France and prepare for new measures against Serbia.[10] The fighting had not stopped entirely. Indeed, artillery barrages continued to savage the Russian lines as the month continued. But the German attack had clearly slowed, and the Russians proved increasingly able to stop infantry attacks with coordinated machine-gun fire. Any hope of launching a counteroffensive in the near future ran into the problem of weapons shortages, however. On 10/23 October 1915, Alekseev received two telegrams, one from General Bonch-Bruevich at the Northern Front Headquarters, and the other from General Bolkhovitinov, the chief of staff of the Caucasian Army, each highlighting severe deficiencies. In the north, one entire corps lacked heavy artillery, while another had cannons but no shells. In the Caucasus, reserve Cossack units lacked guns. Another 3000 rifles would need to be sent before the army was battle ready. A week later, General Evert, the commander of the Western Front, reported that there were fewer men with rifles than without in two of his divisions.[11] By January 1916, the manpower shortage had eased, but the weapons shortages persisted. Fully 286,000 men lacked weapons on the Western Front alone.[12] Through the fall and winter, the German shift of focus and the Russian lack of supplies meant stalemate. "Trench warfare was our lot through the entire winter of 1915 and most of the next year," one soldier remembered. "Healing wounds, accumulating new strength, improving fortifications, rearranging positions, such was the business of the day."[13] With the exception of a bloody and inconclusive engagement on the Strypa River in Galicia from December 1915 to January 1916 that cost 70,000 men in

[9] Fedor Stepun, *Byvshee i nesbyvsheesia*, 2nd ed. (St. Petersburg: Aleteiia, 2000), 305.
[10] Lemke, *250 dnei*, 1: 98.   [11] Lemke, *250 dnei*, 1: 124–5, 157–9, 214.
[12] Lemke, *250 dnei*, 2: 162.
[13] Victor A. Yakhontoff, *Across the Divide: Impersonal Record of Personal Experiences* (New York: Coward-McCann, 1939), 129.

useless assaults across ground covered by enemy machine guns and artillery,[14] no major efforts were made to shift the balance of power.

As the winter progressed, more and more weapons began to flow into front-line units. This increased supply led to some uncertainty. There was no doubt that the extreme shortages of the previous year had been eliminated, but it was far from clear whether the amount of shell now in reserve would be sufficient to win battles. On the one hand, the vast caches of weaponry paid for and expected by the government as a result of foreign contracts and the work of the War Industrial Committees never fully materialized. Virtually all military units were understocked as a result.[15] On the other hand, no amount of shell would ever have satisfied certain cautious Russian commanders, who had grown accustomed to explaining all their failures by blaming supply problems.[16] Not every Russian commander remained recalcitrant in the winter of 1916, however. General Evert, for instance, correctly foresaw that Germany would launch a winter offensive in the west, and he pressed for an early offensive to hit the Germans hard once they did so.[17] Nevertheless, despite Evert's eagerness, Stavka planned to wait for a summer offensive, both to build up reserves of weapons and men and to allow the impassable mud of the Russian spring to harden enough to enable mobile operations.

Events soon conspired to wreck these plans of patience, however. The offensive that Evert had predicted began on 8/21 February 1916 at Verdun. General Joffre, the commander-in-chief of the French army, implored General Alekseev to launch an offensive to relieve the German pressure on their forces.[18] Even absent the French entreaties, however, the stripped down German lines would have been tempting for Stavka to attack. Alekseev, realizing that shortages were relative, took the decision to strike at several spots along the German front: on a southwestern vector from Dvinsk and northwestern vector from Lake Narach (see Map 6). The Russian command viewed the Narach front as particularly promising, and Alekseev devoted enormous resources to the Second Army, doubling its size and adding massive amounts of guns and shells. By March, the Russians had a manpower superiority of nearly five to one, and they had more guns, shells, and cavalrymen than their opponents as well.

The Battle of Lake Narach is one of the least known and yet most consequential of the war.[19] Russia had never had such numerical superiority over Germany on any portion of the front, and the key sector for the attack, a large hill that the Russians called "Ferdinand's Nose," for its similarity to the proboscis of Tsar Ferdinand of Bulgaria, was far from the nearest rail spur and thus difficult for the

---

[14] Timothy C. Dowling, *The Brusilov Offensive* (Bloomington: Indiana University Press, 2008), 50.

[15] O. R. Airapetov, "Narochskaia operatsiia i otstavka A. A. Polivanova," *Vestnik Moskovskogo Universiteta* ser. 8 (istoriia), no. 6 (2001): 80–97.

[16] Norman Stone, *The Eastern Front, 1914–1917* (New York: Penguin, 1999 [1975]), 226.

[17] On Evert's desire to launch an early offensive against German forces, see N. E. Podorozhnyi, *Narochskaia operatsiia v marte 1916 g. na Russkom fronte mirovoi voiny* (Moscow: Gosizdat, 1938), 9.

[18] Airapetov, 90.

[19] The basic texts from which nearly all accounts derive are Lemke and Podorozhnyi. There are short treatments in most of the general military histories of the Eastern Front based on these two sources, and one substantial scholarly article: Airapetov, "Narochskaia operatsiia."

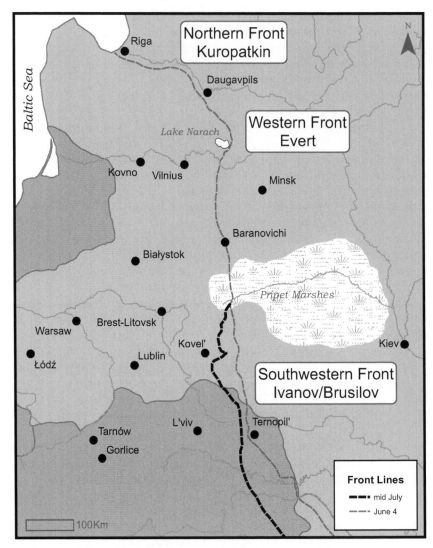

Map 6 Front Lines in Eastern Europe, 1916

Germans and Austrians to support with reinforcements.[20] The scale and location of the attack scared the German high command, which was expecting the blow to relieve Verdun to come from the British. The Germans saw the threat immediately and feared that the Russians were about to drive their forces backwards, out of Latvia, Lithuania, and Belarus.[21] At Stavka, the stakes were very high as well. The

[20] Airapetov, 95; Bernard Pares, *My Russian Memoirs* (London: Jonathan Cape, 1931), 372–3.
[21] Airapetov, 95.

army's top commanders believed that "if, having rested for nearly eight months and preparing as much as we could, we don't have success, it means that our cause is finally lost."[22]

The battle began on 5/18 March 1916, with a large artillery bombardment from the Russian side led by the army group of four corps (I Army Corps, XXVII Army Corps, I Siberian Corps, and VII Cavalry Corps) commanded by General Pleshkov. The artillery men did not consult with the infantry, and they fired largely on the basis of maps rather than reconnaissance and the proper registering of the guns. As a result, gunners wasted much of the precious shell, firing blindly into wooded areas with no enemy troops present. The Germans, on the other hand, had established both machine-gun and artillery positions that would allow them not only to put the approaches to their positions in a crossfire, but the first lines of their trenches as well. Pleshkov sent his men over the top in marshy ground that was covered in some places by up to a foot of slush.[23] They were strafed mercilessly. German guns covered one portion of the line so well that it became known as the "Valley of Death" and then the "Valley of Good and Evil."[24] The artillery barrage supporting the advance of the 22nd Infantry Division failed to destroy the German barbed wire and, as a result, the attempt just after noon to cut the wire "went slowly, since enemy rifle and machine gun fire took out hundreds of men."[25] An attempt later that afternoon by the 85th Infantry Regiment to take another section of wire was likewise fruitless thanks to "savage flanking fire from machine guns and batteries in the forest."[26] In places where survivors did reach the trenches, they found two surprises. The first was that the lines were abandoned. The second was that the Germans had pre-registered artillery on those positions and began blowing them apart. In Pleshkov's corps alone, 30,000 men died in the first four days of the battle. Attacks by other commanders had equally little success. The offensive sputtered to an icy, gory close.

Immediately, commanders began pointing fingers. General Evert blamed Pleshkov. Lemke blamed the tsar and the whole military administrative system. The tsar blamed the war minister, Polivanov, a man he had long distrusted and whom he dismissed on 15/28 March.[27] In all, the Russians took 100,000 casualties during the battle, including 12,000 who suffered from frostbite. The Germans lost 20,000 men and a few square miles that they won back with an offensive in April.[28] "Lake Narotch," Norman Stone concluded "was, despite appearances, one of the decisive battles of the First World War. It condemned most of the Russian army to passivity. Generals supposed that, if 350,000 men and a thousand guns, with 'mountains' of shell to use, had failed, then the task was impossible—unless there were extraordinary quantities of shell."[29] And in fact, with the Germans focused westward, and the Russian command paralyzed, no significant movement occurred on the front with the Germans for more than a year. As we shall see, Narach turned

---

[22] Lemke, *250 dnei*, 2: 356.   [23] Stone, 229.

[24] Airapetov, 95; Pares, 372.   [25] Podorozhnyi, 78.   [26] Podorozhnyi, 79.

[27] Lemke, *250 dnei*, 2: 381–6.   [28] Stone, 231.   [29] Stone, 231.

Evert's winter bluster into spring inaction. It also deeply affected Alekseev, who wrote in a letter to his wife on 21 March/3 April 1916:

> Once more it is necessary to live through tough times and a new period of unrealized expectations. Much was done to prepare: large forces were gathered, so too were sufficient material resources, despite the fact of our poverty, which we still can't escape. And all that was destroyed, not because of the staunchness or artfulness of the enemy, but because of our ignorance, incompetence, and tremendous light-mindedness, which was demonstrated both in large and small ways. The troops gave effort and courage, and the commanders paid them back with an incapability to use the qualities of our men. As a result, we didn't do what should have been done, which they had a right to count on. Losses are of course inevitable, but it's good when the losses are compensated for [by victory]. Losses in vain undermine faith. Even for me, they undermine faith in the possibility of doing something successfully in the face of this ignorance, and it's hard to fight this. They [officers] don't want to learn either from their own experience or the experience of others, in spite of the abundance and instructiveness [of that experience]. It's hard, shameful, and somehow hopeless.[30]

By the end of March, the soldiers and the high command had lost confidence in the capabilities of their field officers, at least in the Second Army.

This is not to say that the Russian military was dormant from 1916 onward. To the contrary, the year saw some of Russia's most notable successes in the war. The campaigns against the Ottoman Empire in the Transcaucasus had gone back and forth over the course of the summer of 1915, with the front line running right through the heart of Armenia and the region around Lake Van. At the same time, the Middle East became a much larger theater of action. The British began their Mesopotamian campaign in late 1914, taking Basra in December. They halted to fortify that position until a failed attack by the Ottomans in April 1915 convinced them that they could push further, perhaps even to Baghdad, and a column under General Charles Townshend began marching northward. The British-led assault on Gallipoli, which also began in April, lasted much of the year as well. This pressure on the Ottoman flanks troubled both the Ottoman leadership and their allies. When they looked to their eastern border, they saw a land, Persia, partially occupied by their enemies. The British and the Russians had partitioned Persia into spheres of influence in 1907, but then had settled down into a wary appraisal of one another, complaining when armed forces were used to affect Persian politics or when large new commercial enterprises were undertaken.[31] Great Britain and Russia were imperial rivals in the region, not friends.

In 1915, however, both Germany and the Ottoman Empire became increasingly involved in Persian affairs. In the second half of the year, German officials tried

---

[30] Vera Alekseeva-Borel', *Sorok let v riadakh russkoi imperatorskoi armii: M. V. Alekseev* (Sankt-Peterburg: Bel'veder, 2000), 421.
[31] Rose Louise Greaves, "Some Aspects of the Anglo-Russian Convention and Its Working in Persia, 1907–1914 – I," *Bulletin of the School of Oriental and African Studies, University of London* 31, no. 1 (1968): 69–91; A. V. Ignat'ev, "Politika soglashenii i balansirovaniia: vneshnepoliticheskii kurs Rossii v 1906–1914 gg.," *Otechestvennaia istoriia* no. 3 (1997): 31.

desperately to get Persia to formally join the Central Powers and to promise to attack Britain and Russia not only in Persian territory, but abroad in Afghanistan, Bukhara, and Khiva as well. Germany promised money and guns in return. When this ploy failed, German operatives under Count Georg von Kanitz and Wilhelm Wassmuss "used every possible means of influencing the government, parliament and press of the deeply divided country."[32] This finally drove Britain and Russia into each other's arms in regard to Persian policy. The British turned to Russia with a request early in 1915 to send military support to Persia in order to prevent a possible German/Ottoman blow to British India in the east.[33] The Russian Ministry of Foreign Affairs supported this position and requested the deployment of troops from the Caucasian theater. Both General Iudenich and Count Voront- sov-Dashkov (Viceroy of the Caucasus) rejected the idea, suggesting that it was a feint by the Germans intended to sap valuable Entente forces and resources from other fronts. In October, however, renewed pressure from the British and increased anxiety about Kanitz's activity led the new Viceroy of the Caucasus, the recently reassigned Grand Duke Nikolai Nikolaevich, to support the sending of an exped- itionary force to the region to undermine German activities and restore confidence in Russian power.[34]

The corps was led by General Baratov, and it formed gradually, first in Baku, and then in greater force in November, deep in the Russian zone in Qazvin, only 150 kilometers northwest of Tehran. Baratov's men split from there, quickly defeating Persian gendarmes and armed irregulars on their way to Hamadan and Qom, which they seized in December 1915 (see Map 7). German advisors fled in the direction of the Ottoman border, to the town of Kermanshah. The main goals of the expedition had been rapidly achieved.

In 1916, however, the situation grew more complicated. Townshend's exped- ition had run into serious trouble. Blocked by the new Ottoman Sixth Army, he had retreated in December 1915 to Kut-al-Amara, where the Ottomans promptly besieged his forces. By April 1916, it had become clear that the British would be unable to relieve him, and they pleaded with Russia to send Baratov's men to Mesopotamia to at least siphon men away from the siege. Again, Iudenich was the voice of reason, pointing to the near impossibility of organizing a successful march that would relieve Townshend in time. Again, the grand duke overruled him. Moving out of Kermanshah, the Russian forces ran into Ottoman troops detailed to stop them. The Russians won the first battle, in Kerind, but learned soon after that they were too late, since Townshend had surrendered on 13/26 April. In the meantime, disease was wasting the Russian forces. Lack of potable water led to large-scale dysentery and then cholera. Their horses starved to death. Heat caused a number of deaths as well, with 1.2 percent of Baratov's men perishing from

[32] Fritz Fischer, *Germany's Aims in the First World War* (New York: W. W. Norton, 1967), 127.
[33] Sean McMeekin, *The Russian Origins of the First World War* (Cambridge, MA: Harvard University Press, 2011), 180–1.
[34] E. V. Maslovskii, *Mirovaia voina na Kavkazskom fronte, 1914–1917g.: strategicheskii ocherk* (Paris: Vozrozhdenie, 1933), 216.

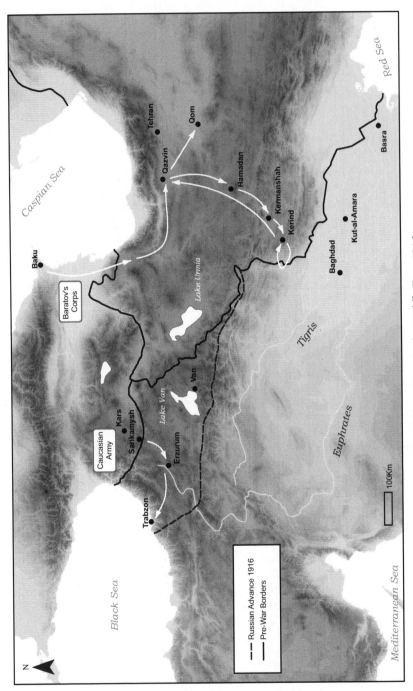

Map 7 Front Lines in the Middle East, 1916

sunstroke.[35] In the summer, malaria struck, killing soldiers and requiring the replacement of at least two commanders.[36] By August, Baratov had only 7,000 men in his corps facing a rejuvenated force of 25,000 Ottoman troops. They had to abandon all of the positions they had taken and retreat back to Qazvin. There, Baratov rallied his troops, recalling the heroism and suffering of the past ten months and exhorting them to remember that "the enemy wants to destroy the Great Power dignity of our Great Mother Russia in the eyes of the whole world by driving us out of Persia. That will not happen!"[37] It did not happen. The Russians and Ottomans fell back to a stalemate position in Persia for the remainder of the year. No matter what Baratov might claim in the heat of the moment, the Great War was not going to be decided in Qazvin or in Kut. As the fronts expanded, the war came down to a question of which side would break first.

Russian troops made more durable gains in Anatolia, but again they made very little difference in the overall strategic situation. At the end of 1915, with Entente troops evacuating Gallipoli, the Ottoman command began making plans to send their newly freed-up forces to the Caucasus for another assault on Russian positions. Catching wind of this, Iudenich began making preparations for battle. At the end of December he traveled to Tiflis to present the case for launching an offensive directly to the grand duke and Ianushkevich. After some "wavering," they agreed to attack.[38] On 28 December 1915/10 January 1916, Iudenich went into action.

After a few days of fighting back and forth, the Russians emerged victorious. Russian forces battered the Ottoman Third Army, inflicting serious casualties, taking thousands of prisoners, and moving to the town of Köprüköy, only 50 kilometers from the fortress of Erzurum, which guarded the entire region of Eastern Anatolia. Iudenich wanted to press the Russian advantage and to storm the fortress, but when he requested more shells, the grand duke balked. Worried that a failed assault after a rare military victory might turn into a public relations setback, and aware of the continuing shell shortages, Nikolai Nikolaevich wanted to err on the side of caution. As the interrogations of Turkish POWs continued, however, Iudenich became more and more convinced that the Ottoman forces were completely disorganized and demoralized. He phoned Nikolai Nikolaevich and asked him to change his mind. Over the course of a lengthy conversation, he proved able to do so, but the grand duke insisted that Iudenich take "complete responsibility in the case of failure." Undeterred, Iudenich agreed.[39] On 2/15 February 1916, Iudenich successfully stormed the fortress, taking it "like a toy" with relatively light casualties.[40] Immediately, the Russian press latched on to the first good news

[35] G. A. Melkumian, "Vrachi-Armiane na Kavkazskom fronte pervoi mirovoi voiny," *Patma-Banasirakan Handes. Istoriko-Filologicheskii Zhurnal* no. 3 (1975): 129.

[36] General Baratov, Telegram to General Prince Belosel'skii (in Kazvin), 19 August 1916, HIA, Nikolai N. Baratov papers, box 3, folder 1, n.p.

[37] General Baratov, Order to Corps, 21 August 1916, HIA, Nikolai N. Baratov papers, box 3, folder 1, n.p.

[38] Maslovskii, 232, 243.   [39] Maslovskii, 249–60.   [40] Lemke, *250 dnei*, 2: 239.

in months, turning the battle into a major public relations event. Within the military, Iudenich's stature rose. In society at large, the grand duke garnered the lion's share of the credit, a fact not lost on the suspicious tsar.[41] Two months later, Iudenich's forces moved north to the port of Trabzon, which they took with the assistance of an increasingly effective and disruptive Russian Black Sea Fleet on 5/18 April 1916. All of the militarily important points in Eastern Anatolia now lay in Russian hands. Still, as in Persia, nothing decisive had been won. The Russians had demonstrated a capacity to defeat Ottoman armies and clearly had the potential to do yet more damage, but the Ottomans remained in the war, and the fight continued.

The fight continued on Russia's European fronts as well, in part because of Russia's commitment to her allies. The Battle of Lake Narach in March had done nothing to draw significant numbers of German forces eastward, away from Verdun. It was left to a council of war in April at Stavka to decide how Russia would participate in the allied campaign against Germany. On paper, the decision was clear. The goal was to stretch Germany's capacity to fight a two-front war to its breaking point, and the locations of greatest superiority in terms of men and material were on the Russian lines facing those German positions on the Northern and Western Fronts. Unfortunately, the commanders of those armies were still smarting from the Narach debacle; indeed they were still fighting off the German counteroffensives in the area that restored the *status quo ante*. Rather than refuse outright, however, General Kuropatkin (Northern Front commander) and General Evert (Western Front commander) decided instead to demand impossible numbers of men and shells before they would move into action.

To everyone's surprise, however, the newly minted Southwestern Front commander, General Brusilov, indicated his willingness and desire to launch an offensive. Even when General Alekseev told him he would not be receiving massive new reinforcements or mountains of supplies, he stayed firm. The armies on his front, he maintained, would be prepared for the spring campaign. Brusilov had reason for some optimism. Prior to his promotion, he had commanded the Eighth Army, one of the few consistently effective groups in the Russian armed forces. In 1914, as the First and Second Armies were getting mauled in East Prussia, Brusilov's Eighth Army was successfully conquering large parts of Galicia and Bukovina. His men were among those perched in the Carpathians in 1915, ready to invade Hungary, and they were the ones who retreated when the collapse of the Third Army at Gorlice left them flanked and exposed. The Eighth Army fought respectably during the Great Retreat, even though it too had to retire on several occasions. In sum, though Brusilov's troops had not always been victorious, their record was far better than that of any others in the armed forces.

This success was not only due to the vagaries of fate. By all accounts, Brusilov ran a tight ship. In general, his men interacted with civilian populations on a more

---

[41] Lemke, *250 dnei*, 2: 320.

professional level, and he was respected both by those civilians and by leaders of public organizations as a result.[42] He was most noteworthy for his ability to manage the officers under his command, however. He insisted that officers know their men and their patches well, and troop morale was correspondingly high.[43] In addition, because he had a deserved reputation as a commander who sought out and rewarded competence rather than lineage, he attracted and promoted many of the army's top young officers, men who were "modest and sensible technicians" and formed the core of a "new Russian army."[44] Under Brusilov, these men worked hard as a "family" and achieved their goals. It was an atmosphere unlike any other in the Russian military.[45]

Still, competence alone could not overcome the fundamental dilemmas facing attacking forces on the Eastern Front. The most basic problem Russian command-ers faced was the same one faced by military men on all sides of the war, which was that the techniques needed to achieve a breakthrough were in conflict with the techniques needed to develop that initial success further.[46] In order to break through lines marked by deep and extensive trench networks guarded by three or more belts of barbed wire and carefully positioned machine-gun nests and artillery batteries, military planners believed that an extensive period of preparatory shelling was necessary. According to the studies by Brusilov's staff, it took either 400 heavy shells or 25,000 light shells to open a fifty-meter hole in just one belt of barbed wire.[47] In other words, 1,500,000 light shells would be necessary just to clear a one-kilometer sector of the front with three bands of barbed wire, even before attacking the enemy's troops or weapons. Such a furious wave of shelling was impossible. Russian munitions stocks had gradually improved, but not to this level, and, in any case, the Southwestern Front, as the "auxiliary" front, would not be getting massive shell reserves. When General Platon Lechitskii, the commander of the Ninth Army, wrote to Brusilov with an estimate of the shells he would need, based on Brusilov's staff's own calculations, he requested 78,000 heavy bombs and 300,000 lighter "grenades." Brusilov replied that the "accounting of shells is theoretically correct, but in practice it is beside the point." That quantity of shell was unavailable, and even if it were, the guns they had could not shoot them off at that scale. Thus, armies had to make plans based on the shells they had. "There is no other way out."[48]

In addition, even if the shells and guns had been sufficient, such a bombardment would indicate to even the dimmest enemy commander the exact location of the coming attack, allowing him to withdraw troops to a safer line of trenches and, above all, to prepare reserves to counterattack once the battle had finished its first

---

[42] S. An-sky, *The Enemy at His Pleasure: A Journey Through the Jewish Pale of Settlement during World War I* (New York: Henry Holt, 2002), 285.

[43] Lemke, *250 dnei*, 2: 399–408.   [44] Stone, 233.   [45] Lemke, *250 dnei*, 2: 509.

[46] Stone, 235.   [47] Dowling, 42.

[48] Secret report of General Lechitskii to General Brusilov (with Brusilov's marginal comments), 14 April 1916, in *Nastuplenie iugo-zapadnogo fronta v mae-iiune 1916 goda* (Moscow: Voenizdat, 1940), 165.

phase. Indeed, given German air superiority and the effectiveness of their intelligence arm more generally, German and Austrian commanders could often tell where Russian attacks were coming even before the battles had begun.

Such attacks were not always futile, as Russian commanders knew too well. In the spring and summer of 1915, Russian troops had been pummeled by just this sort of plan, and it had worked because the Russians' defensive fortifications were inferior, because the Russians lacked the shells to fire back at enemy artillery or to inflict serious damage on the invading waves of troops, and because the Russians used their reserves badly. The battles on the Strypa and at Lake Narach had demonstrated to the top generals that the Germans and Austrians were not vulnerable in the way the Russians had been the previous year, so most of them thought that only a colossal superiority in shells launched at a small sector of the front with a clearly defined strategic objective could possibly succeed.

Brusilov, however, understood that tactics pioneered by the French the previous September gave some reason for hope. The so-called "Joffre attacks" used in Champagne had called for moving trenches as close as possible to the enemy lines and using a brief artillery barrage to cover the advance of infantry. These attacks had achieved limited goals, but Brusilov and his staff saw the possibility for something larger. If they could attack across the entire front at once, they could at the very least disrupt the enemy's reserves. In addition, they understood that no line could be equally strong in every sector. This was easy enough to grasp. Harder to comprehend was that the weak spots in the line could not, even in principle, be determined "on a map in headquarters." Instead, as Brusilov directed his army commanders, the plan had to be developed "in the place of the attack, together with the infantry and artillery who would carry it out."[49] Thus, successful commanders had to trust the officers on the ground closest to the battle to make the key tactical decisions. Having witnessed German successes with decentralized storm troop units, Brusilov mimicked the enemy in this regard as well.[50]

This new direction was not just Brusilov's doing. Stavka itself, when planning for the summer campaign, decided not to indicate the goals the operation would seek to achieve. Alekseev tasked Russian forces with breaking the defense of the enemy and inflicting losses, but he did not indicate the means of developing the operation.[51] Brusilov was plainly aware of the change in attitude that was at the heart of his plan. When Lechitskii complained that Brusilov's orders had no concrete goal and thus no chance of strategic success, Brusilov replied: "It is undesirable to decide ahead of time whether a strike will be serious or not. Just let the strike be well

---

[49] General Brusilov, Directive no. 1039 to commanders of the Seventh, Eighth, Ninth, and Eleventh Armies (with copy to General Alekseev), 6 April 1916, in *Nastuplenie iugo-zapadnogo fronta*, 118. See also I. I. Rostunov, *Russkii front pervoi mirovoi voiny* (Moscow: Izd. Nauka, 1976), 296.

[50] Robert S. Feldman, "The Russian General Staff and the June 1917 Offensive," *Soviet Studies* 19, no. 4 (April 1968): 536.

[51] Rostunov, 292.

prepared and correctly executed . . . Superiority of numbers doesn't always decide the matter, skill and luck are serious elements."[52]

Brusilov's plan did not blindly rely upon luck, it simply acknowledged that luck would at some point play a role. It was just as important that the "strike be well prepared." Brusilov worked assiduously throughout April and May to ready his troops for his offensive, even building models of Austrian positions to use for training exercises just behind the lines.[53] His preparations became even more urgent in May, when a Habsburg attack on the Italian Front led Italian diplomats to plead desperately with their coalition partners to relieve the pressure on their forces. Russian leaders up to and including the tsar were sympathetic, and they urged military activity on the Southwestern Front as soon as possible. Brusilov was ready. Weeks earlier, he had delegated the responsibility of choosing promising sectors for attack to officers on the ground, and he had engaged in an intensive project of touring the lines to see for himself the choices and preparations they had made. Officers ordered trenches moved forward to 100 meters from the Austrian lines in many places, and they built dugouts for reserves close to the front as well. Brusilov's staff both desired surprise and realized that information was hard to fully control in these conditions of war. Thus, on the one hand, they prized secrecy to such an extent that Brusilov hid the planned starting date of the assault from the Empress, even under direct questioning when the royal family traveled to Odessa.[54] On the other hand, Brusilov's staff tried to deal with the inevitable leaks to enemy intelligence operations by seeking to plant so much information and misinformation that the enemy would freeze with indecision.[55] It is not clear whether disinformation or complacency affected the enemy more. Austro-Hungarian officers had a "wealth of information about enemy unit concentrations and feverish engineering projects," and deserters told them the exact time of the attack, but no serious countermeasures were taken. Habsburg commanders felt secure in their heavily fortified forward positions.[56]

One young twenty-year-old officer, the future Archimandrite Iov, was part of the preparations of the Eighth Army near the little town of Olyka in Ukraine, about thirty kilometers east of Luts'k. Olyka was home to the fantastic Radziwill Castle, which served as a convenient target for German artillery in the weeks leading up to the offensive. Still, the citizens of the town largely stayed put, rushing to cellars for protection during artillery barrages. Iov lived with a Jewish family, teaching their eleven-year-old daughter to play the balalaika in the relative calm before the

---

[52] Marginal comment of General Brusilov on secret report of General Lechitskii, 14 April 1916, in *Nastuplenie iugo-zapadnogo fronta*, 163. Cited also in Rostunov, 303.

[53] Dowling, 44–5.

[54] W. Bruce Lincoln, *Passage through Armageddon: The Russians in War and Revolution, 1914–1918* (New York: Simon and Schuster, 1986), 247.

[55] Dowling, 46.

[56] John Schindler, "Steamrollered in Galicia: The Austro-Hungarian Army and the Brusilov Offensive, 1916," *War in History* 10, no. 1 (2003): 40–1.

storm. After Easter, however, the pace of life picked up. He and others dug trenches closer and closer to enemy lines, building breastworks to protect themselves from rifle fire and carving out communications trenches to support the new lines ahead. As a scout officer, he was soon ordered to gain precise intelligence about the Austrian trenches and worked closely with a company commander in the forward lines to do so:

> The space between the trenches was covered with tall grass. May had come, with bright sunshine. The soldier weaved us caps of grass and flowers, and on the next day, talking in whispers, we approached the barbed wire barriers, looked where we needed to, and returned successfully to the trenches. I was given the task of destroying machine gun nests and creating two openings in the wire of about ten sazhens [twenty-one meters] each.

When the attack began a day or so later, he accomplished his task, using about 2000 light artillery grenades as he did so.[57] Iov was a perfect example of the way that Brusilov pushed the lines of authority downward, to the men who would have to achieve the goals set for them. Iov's experience also demonstrated the demand for precision in the initial tactical goals, a precision that had not previously been notable in most Russian offensives.

The seriousness of purpose and attention to detail shown by Brusilov's men was not matched by the Austrian troops on the other side of the line, a factor that certainly played into the success that Brusilov would achieve. The failure of the previous Russian offensives and the extensive defensive fortifications built by Austrian troops made Habsburg commanders not only confident enough to peel off units to support the Italian offensive but also secure enough to create semi-permanent structures in which to relax. They were quite sure that they would not be moving any time soon. Indeed, just two days before the opening of the offensive, Colonel Stoltzmann, the chief of staff for General Linsingen (the commander of troops facing the Russian Eighth Army), completely disregarded the possibility that the plainly forthcoming Russian offensive could succeed, citing the lack of over-whelming superiority of numbers, the "stupid" tactics normally employed by the enemy, and the "formidable positions" occupied by his own men. Not even "beginner's luck" could give the Russians a chance for success.[58] Russian reserves, another report scoffed, were no more than "weak momma's boys who immediately began to cry when attacked sharply."[59]

The start of the offensive was delayed several times as Brusilov attempted to coordinate with the recalcitrant front commanders to his north, but he finally lost patience and insisted to Alekseev that he be allowed to attack. Alekseev, like nearly

[57] Arkhimandrit Iov, "Vospominanie o moei zhizni do perekhoda na polozhenie emigranta, Okt. 1896- Dek. 1920," Biblioteka-fond "Russkoe zarubezh'e" (BFRZ) d. E-170, ll. 10–11. Unfortunately, Iov does not indicate how he successfully blew open gaps in the wire and destroyed machine-gun nests with 10 percent of the artillery firepower planners before the battle thought he would need for this task.
[58] Dowling, 57.   [59] Cited in Dowling, 51.

everyone else, thought Brusilov was wrong to abandon the idea of heavy concentrations of troops, and so he did his best to entreat and cajole Brusilov to change his mind. When that failed, Alekseev finally allowed the offensive to proceed, but only if Brusilov promised to attack towards Kovel' in order to link up with Evert's planned assault.[60] At 1 a.m. on 22 May/4 June 1916, Brusilov issued the order that began the offensive, placing the first goal as pinning down the enemy's troops and the second as taking Kovel'. "It is time to drive out the dishonorable enemy," he proclaimed. "All armies on our front are attacking at the same time. I am convinced that our iron armies will win the victory."[61]

Iov's unit saw action immediately. "On the morning of the attack," he remembered, "the trenches were full of soldiers with serious faces, dressed in clean shirts. After a short artillery preparation, there was a moment of silence, the order, and then everyone crossed themselves and jumped out of the trenches." The Austrians responded with "a hurricane of fire. My telephone connection was broken. Our lines lay under strong fire in front of the barbed wire. I remained in the trenches, with the earth flying in my pockets, behind my collar, in my ears. The shooting began to subside." After his men breached the wire and took the first line of trenches, the Austrians opened up with more machine-gun fire, but this time, in contrast to Narach, the Russians held their ground (though several had to be rotated to the rear for shattered nerves thereafter). By the evening, Iov saw the progress they had made and the cost it had incurred. "I remember one [dead] soldier about thirty years old, with dirt showered on his chest. His face was calm, his right hand, with its wedding band, lay on his breast. Someone would cry for him in a far off village."[62]

Almost immediately, the attacks began to produce results. On the southern sector of the front, Russian armies used poison gas as part of their assault on the battle-hardened troops of the Austrian Seventh Army under General Pflanzer-Baltin. After a day of spirited fighting, the Ninth Army under Lechitskii broke through on 23 May/5 June 1916. The following day, Shcherbachev's Seventh Army did the same just to the north. On 25 May/7 June the II Cavalry Corps rode in to capture 7,000 troops in Jazlovice, sending the Austrians reeling to the rear.[63] Contradictory orders led Austrian soldiers in two directions at once, and they confusedly came to a halt. By the middle of the month, the Habsburg forces "had almost disintegrated." In one engagement, on 4/17 June, the Russians took an Austrian bridgehead and 1500 prisoners while suffering just a single casualty (wounded) among their own men.[64]

The main offensive of the Eighth Army towards Luts'k was just as successful. A week after the bombardment started, that one army had taken roughly 76,000 prisoners.[65] Some of these were captured in large groups. Others, as Iov remembered, simply gave up individually. "Just ahead of us, a group of Austrians

[60] General A. A. Brusilov, *A Soldier's Notebook, 1914–1918* (Westport, CT: Greenwood Press, 1971 [1930]), 238.

[61] Cited in Dowling, 62. [62] Iov, "Vospominanie," BFRZ, d. E-170, l. 11.

[63] Dowling, 69–73. [64] Stone, 253. [65] Stone, 254.

was retreating. The distance between us closed to about twenty-five to thirty paces. Neither they nor we were shooting. On occasion, one of the Austrians would suddenly turn to face us and, raising his hands, would run to us. I would give him the sign with my hand to go to the rear."[66] In all, the Austrians lost a third of their forces as prisoners in the first week of the offensive. With all the casualties combined, they lost over half of their men. "The blow to Austrian morale," writes Stone, "was irreparable; from now on, Austrian troops fought with an ineradicable sense of inferiority, and the loss of positions which had universally been thought impregnable led to a deep disbelief in commanders and in fortifications of all kinds."[67]

After the first successful week, the Russians paused. In part this was due to the need to rest after the furious onslaught. Supplies were low in many of the units. Brusilov's men nearly ran out of bullets for their rifles and machine guns.[68] The human destruction was just as enormous. At about this time, Iov remembered, he crossed a bridge and found himself on a recent battlefield. "The field was red with poppies, the dead and wounded lay everywhere. The wounded begged for help and water. It was awful. I couldn't stop, as I had a task to perform; I told them that people would come soon for them, but I was far from sure that this was the case."[69] Russian casualties were high. The Eighth Army alone had lost 35,000 men.[70] In addition, the decision not to choose targets deep in the rear of the enemy meant that Brusilov's staff now had to define new objectives on the fly. Inevitably, there was disagreement and a pause to sort it out. The Eighth Army could take one of two paths. Either it could take advantage of the simultaneous breakthroughs in the north and south by pushing directly westward and then linking up with the Ninth and Seventh Armies to their south to encircle the Austrians completely, or it could stick to the original plan insisted on by Alekseev by moving north to the railway junction of Kovel' to seize that strategically important location and link up with Evert's troops on the Western Front to their north. The first plan was riskier but promised greater rewards, potentially even the long-dreamed-of goal of knocking the Austro-Hungarian Empire out of the war completely. Brusilov's replacement as the commander of the Eighth Army, General Kaledin, argued against taking the risk. He pointed out that the failure of Evert to start his attacks meant both that the Germans were sending reinforcements to his front and that even a successful drive westward would expose his flank to the idle German troops to his north. Evert's delays also compromised the possibility for the success of the more limited goal of taking Kovel'. On 30 May/12 June, Brusilov begged General Lesh, who had fought next to Brusilov's army for much of the war as the commander of the Third Army, to break free from Evert: "I am turning to you with a completely private and personal request on the basis of our old comradeship in battle; I need

---

[66] Iov, "Vospominanie," BFRZ, d. E-170, l.15.   [67] Stone, 254.

[68] "Dokladnaia zapiska generala Alekseeva Imperatoru Nikolaiu Vtoromu," 15 June 1916, HIA Mikhail V. Alekseev papers, box 1, folder 6, p. 1.

[69] Iov, "Vospominanie," BFRZ, d. E-170, l.14.   [70] Stone, 255.

the help of your army to conduct a very energetic offensive, especially the XXXI Corps, in order to move the right flank of the Eighth Army forward. I urgently and passionately beg you to fulfill this task quickly and strongly, because if you don't, I'll be tied down and will lose the fruits of the success that has been achieved."[71] Lesh did not respond. Two days later, Evert decided to delay his offensive once more. Brusilov was livid, and he appealed to Alekseev and the tsar to override the front commander. "By nature, I'm an optimist," he wrote, "but I can't help but note that our position is worse than bad. The troops don't understand—and of course I can't explain to them—why other fronts are quiet, and I have already received two anonymous letters with the warning that General Evert is a German and a traitor and that he abandoned us in order to lose the war. God forbid that this conviction take root in the troops."[72]

With the Russian commanders at each other's throats, the Austrians and Germans launched a counteroffensive on 3/16 June that went nowhere. However, the moment for potential success had passed for the Russians.[73] Evert finally moved two weeks later, on 19 June/2 July, sending his old Fourth Army under General Ragoza to conduct a traditional assault on a short front in the marshes north of Pinsk. A week later, nothing had been gained other than horrifying destruction— 80,000 Russian casualties compared with just 16,000 for the Germans.[74] Now Brusilov's only possible target could be Kovel', which itself lay amidst deep swamps. For the rest of the summer and into the fall, Russian forces reverted to their old practices, sending thousands of men to die in frontal assaults in poor territory, some of them even being strafed to death by German airplanes as they waded through waist-high muck. General Alfred Knox, the British military observer, witnessed this and gnashed his teeth: "The Russian Command for some unknown reason seems always to choose a bog to drown in."[75]

It has been easy, in retrospect, for historians to blame Evert (and the even more recalcitrant General Kuropatkin on the Northern Front) for the failure of the Brusilov Offensive. Contemporaries remained bitter for the rest of their lives. Colonel Sergeevskii wrote to Alekseev's relatives nearly fifty years later "The demonstration [Brusilov's attack] succeeded beyond expectations and without reserves—the whole Austrian army was nearly destroyed. And yet we refused to launch the main strike!!! Why? The cowardice of Evert and Kuropatkin? Intrigues against Alekseev? The actions of those who wanted a revolution?"[76] Yet, there were many good reasons why Evert and Kuropatkin should have been suspicious of Brusilov's tactics and strategy. The Joffre methods had achieved only localized success in the west. What good would a best-case scenario of limited gains be on the vast Eastern Front? To relieve some pressure from fronts in Italy, at Verdun, and on the Somme? Was this worth the sacrificial slaughter of yet more tens of thousands

[71] Telegram from General Brusilov to General Lesh, 30 May 1916, in *Nastuplenie iugo-zapadnogo fronta*, 275–6. See also Rostunov, 317–18.
[72] Letter from Brusilov to Alekseev, 5 June 1916, in *Nastuplenie iugo-zapadnogo fronta*, 345.
[73] Dowling, 92.   [74] Stone, 260.   [75] Knox, 2: 467.
[76] Letter from Colonel Sergeevskii, 14 June 1963, cited in Alekseeva-Borel', 435.

of men? Many commentators have excoriated the generals on the Western Front for their repeated, futile, and bloody assaults. But after Lake Narach, Evert and Kuropatkin essentially shared an equally pessimistic position. If a decisive military victory was unlikely to be won on the Eastern Front, caution was the logical reaction. Brusilov believed that Evert's foot-dragging robbed Russia of its best opportunity to knock one of its opponents out of the war. But perhaps he was wrong. Developing the breakthrough deep into the rear of an increasingly desperate force of now mixed Austro-Hungarian and German troops was hardly assured of success. Perhaps it was not Evert's dilatoriness but his eventual agreement to the disastrous attacks in July that should be blameworthy. In the end, Russia got the worst of both worlds—no chance for a coordinated knockout blow against the Austrians, while still enduring the pointless slaughter of Ragoza's men and those around what Russian officers came to call the "Kovel' pit."

General Alekseev took a different lesson from the sputtering offensive. Russian troops lost battles, he wrote to the tsar, because they lacked proper munitions. In his view, every front had serious shortages of shells and bullets. This was, as we have seen, rather too simple a claim. Supplies had increased, and Russia now frequently enjoyed material superiority during battle. Alekseev was now convinced that only eye-popping superiority could succeed, and in order to achieve that, he argued that the home front required an intensive process of remobilization. There was "not a single area of state and social life" as troubled as transportation, and as a result munitions factories lacked fuel and metals. "Criminal propaganda" infected industrial workers, and the strike movement grew daily. Foreign enterprises failed to meet their delivery schedules as well. As a result, Russia had to rely solely on its own resources. The current system of social and economic mobilization did not work. Therefore, he wrote, it was necessary to "unify power [at the front and in the rear] in one figure who could be called the Supreme Minister of State Defense." He would direct the activities of all the civilian ministries and of state and public organizations regardless of whether they were in the theater of military operations or not. He would answer to no one but the emperor himself. Alekseev begged Nicholas to adopt his scheme, using all capital letters in the final few lines of his report. Nicholas' only comment on the report was a note written in pencil in the margins making a slight correction to Alekseev's description of desirable worker exemptions.[77] The Council of Ministers quailed at the idea of military rule, and Alekseev's proposal was diluted into nothingness.[78] Nevertheless, it was now clear that progressive projects for social renovation and mobilization could be married to political demands for dictatorship. If nothing else, this was a concrete outcome of the offensives of 1916.

Brusilov himself doubted that he had produced much of anything through his initiative, mourning in his memoirs that his offensive had "brought no strategic

[77] Report from General Alekseev to Emperor Nicholas II, 15 June 1916, HIA, Mikhail V. Alekseev papers, box 1, folder 6, pp. 1–5.
[78] Michael T. Florinsky, *The End of the Russian Empire* (New Haven: Yale University Press, 1931), 93.

results."[79] In this case, Brusilov may have been too hard on himself. Russian troops did re-enter Galicia, this time chastened by their mistakes as occupiers the previous year. They now administered the region more soberly, and it is not difficult to imagine a postwar scenario whereby the region would have been annexed by the Romanov Empire.[80] In addition, the degradation of Austrian fighting capacity and the demonstration of Russian fighting mettle had other strategic consequences, among them the long-awaited entry of Romania into the war as an Entente partner. The Romanian campaign turned out, in the end, to be completely counterproductive, requiring Russian support to fight a disastrous losing battle. But Romania's decision to get off the fence is an indication of the importance of the offensive in the eyes of contemporaries. In this way, the Brusilov Offensive was similar to the Russian victories over the Ottomans in Persia and then, especially, in Eastern Anatolia. The year had been, on balance, militarily successful, but Brusilov was right that nothing strategically decisive had been gained. All of the Central Powers remained in the war with their armies in the field. Perhaps one more offensive, one more battle, one more railway station would have tipped the balance. That was the mirage that generals kept chasing throughout the war. But perhaps it was going to be the case that this war would not be won through the force of arms but through the strength of the societies at war. If so, defeat loomed all over the Eastern Front, as social bodies and political systems creaked and shuddered under the immense pressure of the conflict. In Russia the traditional society had been fundamentally transformed, as new groupings and political interests grew in the wartime atmosphere, affecting daily life and political fates alike.

PRISONERS OF WAR

As the war dragged on without a decisive moment on the battlefield, a new Russian society came into being. The main features of this wartime society and many of its key social groups had been formed or transformed in the war zone, had structured themselves around wartime needs, and had then insinuated themselves into imperial society as a whole. We have already had occasion to discuss two of these key groups—soldiers and migrants—but others existed as well. A whole catalog of these groups awaits further investigation: chaplains, aid workers, and new women workers in war industries to name just a few. My focus for this chapter and the next will be on three of these new social groupings: prisoners of war (POWs), conscript laborers, and military medical practitioners. I treat these in depth not only because of their practical and symbolic significance to wartime society, but also because they were intimately linked with two social "problems"—labor shortages and epidemic

---

[79] Dowling, 163.

[80] A. Iu. Bakhturina, *Politika rossiiskoi imperii v vostochnoi Galitsii v gody pervoi mirovoi voiny* (Moscow: AIRO-XX, 2000), 216; Mark von Hagen, *War in a European Borderland: Occupations and Occupation Plans in Galicia and Ukraine, 1914–1918* (Seattle: University of Washington Press, 2007), 72.

disease—that helped to transform the scope of state intervention and social remobilization as the war progressed. Contemporaries devoted much of their political
attention in 1916 to Grigorii Rasputin, the scandalous advisor to the empress, and
the chaotic roulette of ministerial appointments in Petrograd he inspired. But the
flowering of technocratic social policy amidst a rapidly changing society proved to
be a more durable and important transformation. Again, we see that a failing state
and a fractured society brought not only misery but also the scope for significant
creative innovation.

Over the course of the war, 3,343,900 Russian soldiers were taken prisoner. As
all big numbers, this one can be somewhat difficult to fully comprehend. It was 22
percent of all the men who served in the army during the war. Twice as many men
were taken prisoner as were in the army on the eve of the war, and the number
nearly equaled that of men mobilized in 1914. In return, Russian troops took
nearly 2,000,000 soldiers of the Central Powers into their own custody, most of
them from the Austro-Hungarian armies.[81] This scale of prisoner taking was
unprecedented, and POWs would come to play a very important role in postwar
politics and society throughout Eastern Europe. But even while they remained
incarcerated, POWs were crucial to the imagining and the practice of the war.
Captivity was, as the most comprehensive recent study of imprisoned Russians
proclaims in its title, "the other military experience."[82] It was also, both consciously
and unconsciously, a reciprocal and parallel experience, a comparative history even
as it was being lived, with the great imperial powers anxiously watching each other's
behavior and conditioning their treatment or use of POWs correspondingly.[83] As
with the issue of medical care, public organizations came to play a significant
political role. Those aid workers understood the aspect of reciprocity well, and
they urged each side to help their own soldiers by treating the foreign prisoners
under their care better, but it was of little use.[84]

Soldiers became prisoners in many different ways during the war. The great,
mobile, encircling battles that eluded the combatants on the Western Front after
the Battle of the Marne in 1914 were much more common in the East. Many of the
men in Samsonov's Second Army were rounded up and sent to the rear, as were the
victims of the Masurian battles early in 1915 and the straggling and covering units
of the Great Retreat. For their part, Russians swept up large numbers of Austrian
prisoners in the campaigns of 1914 and 1916. Daily reports from these battles
regularly recorded the taking of 8,000 or 10,000 men. Those numbers began to
add up after a while. But small-scale clashes also produced prisoners. Scouting
forays went bad, the brief taking of a trench by the enemy would see several men

[81] *Rossiia v mirovoi voine 1914–1918 goda (v tsifrakh)* (Moscow: TsSU, 1925), 4, 41.

[82] O. S. Nagornaia, *Drugoi voennyi opyt: rossiiskie voennoplennye Pervoi mirovoi voiny v Germanii
(1914–1922)* (Moscow: Novyi khronograf, 2010).

[83] See here Heather Jones, "Military Captivity and the Prisoner of War, 1914–1918," *Immigrants
and Minorities* 26, no. 1/2 (2008): 27.

[84] A. V. Romanova, "Doklad Imperatorskomu Rossiiskomu obshchestvu krasnago kresta Sestry
Miloserdiia A. V. Romanovoi o poseshchenii voennoplennykh v Avstro-Vengrii, 5 noiabria 1915–3
fevralia 1916 g.," 1916, RGVIA f. 12651, op. 11, d. 109, l. 73.

dragged back as the tide receded. If one were to believe the relatively small number of accounts produced by POWs, all of these occasions happened while the victim was immobilized by wounds, unconscious, or with his pistol out of bullets. As Peter Gatrell has remarked, POWs were "intent on creating a story of capture that enabled them to hold on to their honor and minimize their sense of shame."[85] A. A. Uspenskii, who wrote a very valuable account of his time in prison camp, recalled that though his unit was totally surrounded during the winter battles in Masuria, they still fought on, and he himself was taken only after being wounded in the head and rushed so quickly that he did not have time to draw his revolver.[86]

Lieutenant-Colonel K. P. Lisynov told a similar story. He commanded an artillery brigade defending the doomed Novogeorgievsk fortress in the summer of 1915. When the Germans attacked, he claimed, he and his men stood firm and refused to budge. In the midst of the artillery duel, however, his battery was hit hard. He was severely wounded in the left thigh and then took shrapnel to the face, which ripped out his left eye and left him mostly blind in his right eye. Before he was taken to the dressing station, yet another shell landed nearby, causing permanent near-deafness in his left ear and concussing him. The ensign to whom he transferred command would join him soon after at the dressing station, unconscious, and the next unlucky commander was killed outright. Blind, almost deaf, and crippled in the leg, he lay virtually untended in the fortress hospital until the Germans marched in to take the city. He was captured while helpless in bed.[87]

Of course, we ought not to believe that all men were taken in these extreme circumstances. Men in positions they considered hopeless frequently surrendered well before they had expended their last bullet, and they had good reason to do so. The summary execution of surrendering men on the field of battle was commonly practiced by all sides, and nothing prompted such murderousness quite so much as desperate and violent attempts by a cornered man against his captors. Soldiers quickly grasped this dynamic. After all, one of the dimensions of parallelism was that soldiers who became prisoners not infrequently had captured men in the past.

In addition, many Russians voluntarily surrendered. It was entirely reasonable for men fighting in the sickened, misled, and attrition-prone Russian army to calculate that their chances for survival were better in a POW camp than they were in the trenches, especially when they heard rumors that POWs were "living well" in the camps.[88] At least some of the tsar's army chose to believe these bright accounts rather than the atrocity propaganda spread by journalists such as Aleksei Ksiunin, who opened one of his dispatches with a tale of the murder of Russian POWs in a

[85] Peter Gatrell, "Prisoners of War on the Eastern Front during World War I," *Kritika: Explorations in Russian and Eurasian History* 6, no. 3 (Summer 2005): 562–3.

[86] Uspenskii, *Na voine: Vostochnaia Prussiia—Litva, 1914–1915 g.g., Vospominaniia* (Kaunas: n. p., 1932), 222.

[87] Lieutenant-Colonel K. Lisynov, "Russkie voenno-plennye v Germanii," 28 November 1916, RGVIA, f. 2000, op. 1, d. 2796, ll. 1–77.

[88] Lemke, *250 dnei*, 2: 275.

hospital by German nurses.[89] Many soldiers sought out opportunities to raise a white flag and march unsolicited to the enemy to turn themselves in. The scale of this practice is impossible to determine precisely, but we know that it consumed the attention of military commanders throughout the war. They ordered that the families of men suspected of voluntary surrender be deprived of their military rations, and several ordered their men to shoot at any of their comrades who gave themselves up.[90] This suspicion was present from the very beginning of the war. General Samsonov told his officers on the eve of the Tannenberg battle that news of men missing in action bothered him, because most of them had probably surrendered. "Being taken prisoner is shameful," he proclaimed. "Only the seriously wounded have a justification [for being captured]. Explain this to your units."[91] Days later, Samsonov himself faced the imminent shame of capture and escaped it only through suicide. Few chose to pursue this option. Ethnic concerns also played a role. After Germany had conquered Poland, there were reports that desertion (both to the enemy and to the rear) on the part of Poles and Jews had increased due to German propaganda promising them that they could simply go home if they surrendered. This led to unfulfilled schemes to transfer all Polish and Jewish soldiers to the Caucasian Front.[92]

As a result of these voluntary surrenders, a stigma hung over all POWs. In the military and civilian realms alike, POWs were more likely to be seen as shirkers than as heroes.[93] When Lisynov returned from the camps in 1916 to lobby for greater material assistance for POWs, he was told by the Grand Duchess Mariia Pavlovna that efforts to ease the lot of Russians imprisoned abroad were opposed by the General Staff, which looked suspiciously on POWs and did not want soldiers to think that life in the camps would be comfortable.[94] This sent Lisynov into a justifiable fury. He listed the string of botched operations—Samsonov's encirclement, the losses in the Augustow Forests, the fortresses, and Gorlice. "Is it really the fighting men who are guilty, the men who covered retreats, who were ordered not to retreat and to hold their ground no matter what?" No, it was "due to failed strategy that we have lost such a horrifying number of prisoners in this war."[95] But most of the men who could challenge the claims of the General Staff were far away behind barbed wire, so the huffing generals and politicians dominated the public discourse instead. On several occasions, activists from the public organizations lobbied for a new approach to the POW question, noting the significant difference between the conditions of British and French prisoners and Russian ones, and

---

[89] Aleksei Ksiunin, *Narod na voine: iz zapisok voennogo korrespondenta* (Petrograd: Izd. B. A. Suvorina, 1916), 3–19.

[90] Joshua Sanborn, *Drafting the Russian Nation: Military Conscription, Total War, and Mass Politics, 1905–1925* (DeKalb: Northern University Press, 2003), 108; M. N. Gerasimov, *Probuzhdenie* (Moscow: Voenizdat, 1965), 46–7.

[91] General Samsonov, Order no. 4 to the Second Army, 25 July 1914, in *Vostochno-Prusskaia operatsiia: sbornik dokumentov* (Moscow: Gosudarstvennoe voennoe izdatel'stvo Narodnogo Komissariata Oborony SSSR, 1939), 79.

[92] Lemke, *250 dnei*, 2: 19.   [93] Nagornaia, 36–46.

[94] Lisynov, "Russkie voenno-plennye v Germanii," RGVIA, f. 2000, op. 1, d. 2796, l. 4.

[95] Lisynov, "Russkie voenno-plennye v Germanii," RGVIA, f. 2000, op. 1, d. 2796, ll. 4–5.

reminding leaders of the importance of the morale of POW families. It was, they claimed, an issue of "great state importance," not only for humanitarian reasons but also for national dignity.[96] When Russian nurses visited camps as part of inspection teams, they quickly realized that the main benefit was the moral support they provided to prisoners. "Their happiness upon meeting sisters is indescribable: 'we've been waiting for you like our own mothers' are frequently repeated words. Greetings from their faraway motherland, like a ray of light, break through to these unhappy, fettered, gloomy men."[97] But the pleas of those who urged support of POWs were ignored, leaving prisoners virtually abandoned, bitter, and humiliated.

Humiliation, indeed, defined the lives of the prisoners of war. From the very first days of captivity, the enemy verbally abused and assaulted POWs for petty reasons.[98] Captors saw subjugation as necessary, and the proud among the captives felt the sting of their imprisonment on a daily basis. Conditions in the camps varied widely. In the first months of the war, Germany was not prepared for the number of prisoners they took, and men frequently had to sleep outside and to suffer from a lack of food and medical care. Cholera and typhus infected the camps, and many POWs died. It was only in the spring of 1915 that the Germans successfully constructed a camp system that would house the men and feed them regularly. Soon after that, they began to fine-tune the camp system for economic and political purposes. From this point forward, the camp experience increasingly depended on one's ethnicity and work assignment.[99]

Nevertheless, some commonalities remained. When not being overworked or humiliated, prisoners were bored, hungry, and irritable. Largely shut off from the world, they pined for female company, sexual and otherwise. They endured long stretches of monotonous routines and even more monotonous diets. Men recalled carefully planning their days so that they could sleep just before their meals to make the time pass faster and to calm their grumbling stomachs. When awake, they squabbled with each other, envying the British and French prisoners who received packages from home while they were forced to do without. Medical care was substandard, as women were not allowed into the barbed wire zones, and male doctors were indifferent, caring more about preventing diseases that could spread to the local population than the welfare of the prisoners. Mental health issues were, of course, acute. Traumatized men in these circumstances slipped into depression quite readily, and there was no treatment available for them.[100] All of these experiences were common not only for captured subjects of the Russian Empire, but also for the men the Russian army captured. Boredom, hunger, work,

[96] D. S. Navashin, "Neobkhodimost' oblegcheniia uchasti russkikh voennoplennykh," 17 July 1915, GARF f. 579, op. 1, d. 2112, l. 4.

[97] "Doklad sestry miloserdiia M. N. Gonetskoi," 1916, GARF f. 579, op. 1, d. 2190, l. 27.

[98] A. A. Uspenskii, *V plenu (prodolzhenie knigi Na voine): vospominaniia ofitsera v dvukh chastiakh* (Kaunas: n.p., 1933), 19; Lisynov, "Russkie voenno-plennye v Germanii," RGVIA, f. 2000, op. 1, d. 2796, l. 27.

[99] Nagornaia, 100.

[100] Nagornaia, *passim*. Much the same could be said about civilians living in internment camps during the war. On this, see Tammy M. Proctor, *Civilians in a World at War, 1914–1918* (New York: New York University Press, 2010), 203–38.

humiliation, and disease were well known to the men in Russian POW camps. Prisoners on both sides of the line attempted to create their own societies and cultures, with newspapers and theater, and they had some success, but the camp experience was deeply debilitating.[101]

For all the invisibility of actual prisoners, POWs were a major political issue during the war. Early on, the belligerents realized the political potential of their captive audiences. All the imperial powers in Eastern Europe were aware of nationalist movements of stateless peoples; indeed, as we have already seen, the front lines of the war lay astride those would-be nation-states, from Latvia to Armenia. Thus, each power wanted to stir up separatism in their enemy's lands while keeping their own national minorities quiescent. This was difficult. Collaborators of all stripes emerged to support the warring armies and the occupying forces, but imperial authorities were rightly anxious about empowering too many Poles or Ukrainians for fear of postwar complications. The situation with POWs was in a sense a bit easier. They could propagandize and agitate, but they could also have at least the illusion of control. They could use very concrete incentives to recruit national minorities and then be assured of access to those recruits throughout their entire military and ideological training. Unsurprisingly, all of the warring powers made efforts to isolate potential supporters and provide them with better living conditions. Ukrainian nationalists convinced the Austrian and German authorities to allow them to create separate Ukrainian camps in 1915.[102] Russia did this explicitly with the Slavs of the Austro-Hungarian Empire, and Germany did it with ethnic Germans, Poles, and Ukrainians.[103]

These attempts were only partially successful. Authorities did in fact build special camps with better treatment, and recruitment for various ethnic "legions" proceeded apace, but these groups did nothing of substance on the battlefield and just as little in terms of domestic politics in their homelands.[104] Russian observers noted with dismay that when they gave special privileges to Slavic prisoners, those privileges were abused. Slavic POWs would go out on the town to the theater or other amusements, shocking the local residents, or would simply take advantage of their greater freedom to flee.[105] Groups such as the Czech Legion and Piłsudski's Polish Legion had their real heyday after the great empires had collapsed, as they fought in the Eastern European civil wars and helped form a nucleus of nationalist

---

[101] On theater among Austrians and Germans in Russian captivity, see Alon Rachamimov, "The Disruptive Comforts of Drag: (Trans)Gender Performances among Prisoners of War in Russia, 1914–1920," *The American Historical Review* 111, no. 2 (April 2006): 362–82.

[102] Mark von Hagen, "The Great War and the Mobilization of Ethnicity in the Russian Empire," in *Post-Soviet Political Order: Conflict and State Building*, ed. Barnett R. Rubin and Jack Snyder (London and New York: Routledge, 1998), 39.

[103] Hakan Kirimli, "The Activities of the Union for the Liberation of Ukraine in the Ottoman Empire during the First World War," *Middle Eastern Studies* 34, no. 4 (1998): 177–200; Oleh S. Fedyshyn, *Germany's Drive to the East and the Ukrainian Revolution, 1917–1918* (New Brunswick: Rutgers University Press, 1971), 15; Nagornaia, 148.

[104] Ivo Banac, "South Slav Prisoners of War in Revolutionary Russia," in *Essays on World War I: Origins and Prisoners of War*, ed. Samuel R. Williamson Jr. and Peter Pastor (New York: Columbia University Press, 1983), 120.

[105] Colonel Mordvinov, Report to the tsar, 10 December 1915, GARF f. 601, op. 1, d. 626, l. 2.

activists. In part the failure of nationalist mobilization among prisoners of war was due to the nature of the Great War itself, in which legions of hundreds of men could not make a real difference in battles of hundreds of thousands of men. But in part too, these schemes faltered because there was a conflict in principle between the desire to retain or develop imperial control in the borderlands and the creation of modern nation-states across those borders.[106] This played out on the ground in many different ways. For POWs, the demands that these special ethnic groups continue to work in labor brigades and to willingly grit their teeth and smile in the face of ethnic condescension were incompatible with creating a truly "pro-German" or "pro-Russian" legion or group of political activists.

POWs also constituted an issue in international law. The Second Hague Convention of 1907 had made prisoners by definition an international political issue. The combatants were all signatories and, in principle, the rules for capturing and imprisoning men were set out in advance: surrendering soldiers could not be killed or abused; they were to be treated "humanely." They could be interned in specific towns or fortresses and required to live within those boundaries, but they were not supposed to be "confined" except in extreme and temporary circumstances. The government of the captors was required to maintain them (and to give officers the same salary they gave their own), and it could utilize the labor of the prisoners, but only if the tasks were "not excessive" and had "no connection with the operations of the war."[107] As we have already seen, none of the combatants observed these restrictions, and as a result, the claims of atrocity and other violations of international law were nearly daily currency. Accusations that the other side shot surrendering men proliferated, and newspapers and investigative commissions alike detailed the inhumanity and tight confinement experienced by many of the prisoners.

The most notable and widely violated article of the Hague Convention concerned the use of POW labor. Germany turned from a basic strategy of internment to a strategy of exploitation in 1915. The War Ministry issued instructions on 15/28 January 1915 regarding the assignment of POWs into work teams, and by April they were being used en masse in mines and other industrial enterprises. By the fall, labor shortages throughout Germany meant that economic planners used POW labor throughout the economy, in large and small concerns, in the cities and in the fields.[108] From the government perspective, the economic usefulness of forced labor began to overshadow all of the other aspects of the POW question. In Austria-Hungary, "nearly all" enlisted men served in work brigades that began at 6 a.m. and lasted until sunset.[109] Before long, they were being used not only in the

---

[106] Nagornaia, 152.

[107] International Committee of the Red Cross. "Convention (II) with Respect to the Laws and Customs of War on Land and its annex: Regulations concerning the Laws and Customs of War on Land. The Hague, 29 July 1899." <http://www.icrc.org/applic/ihl/ihl.nsf/ART/150-110010?OpenDocument> (accessed 5 June 2013).

[108] Iris Lentsen, "Ispol'zovanie truda russkikh voennoplennykh v Germanii (1914–1918 gg.)," *Voprosy istorii* no. 4 (1998): 130–1.

[109] Romanova, "Doklad," RGVIA f. 12651, op. 11, d. 109, l. 31.

"civilian" economy, but in the war economy as well, in direct contradiction to Article Six of the 1899 Hague Convention. They dug trenches, fixed bridges, and constructed dugouts, a fact that Russian observers could (and did) note through their binoculars.[110] The Austro-Hungarian Empire also used POW labor for military work. One inspector noted that nearly all of the hard infrastructure labor done on the Italian front was performed by Russian POWs. These men would be gone from the prison camp for months, only returning if they suffered from gunshot wounds or from disease.[111] Military work was, as A. V. Romanova observed, a "source of moral suffering" and the "worst aspect of imprisonment." Treatment was harsher, soldiers felt it violated their military oaths, and it was often dangerous, as when teams were ordered to string barbed wire on the Italian front.[112]

These miserable tasks were made even worse by heavy-handed control over the work teams. POWs had to work ten-hour days, even in circumstances when the private companies renting their labor did not require them to work all day. Employers who enjoyed the cheap labor were warned that they would lose their contracts if they treated their workers too well.[113] Discipline could be harsh. Guards were allowed to beat prisoners and even use guns on any prisoners who refused to work. Petty tyranny ruled everywhere. In Austria, guards used the punishment of "suspension" for even minor infractions of discipline in camps or on work teams. Prisoners had their legs bound and their hands tied behind their back, which were then attached to rings suspended in the air. The man was forced into a bent position, his arms tugged upwards all the while, for two hours at a time. The prisoners considered this use of "stress positions" to be a form of torture, and inspectors protested loudly against the practice after their tour of Austrian and Hungarian camps in 1916.[114]

There was one general exception to this rule of harsh treatment, which was for prisoners detailed to agricultural work. In addition to being more attractive to the many Russian soldiers who came from peasant backgrounds, the surveillance and discipline were milder, and the living conditions were much better. POWs in rural areas were close to a food source and suffered from hunger far less.[115] In the camps, hunger was a constant problem, both in terms of the quantity and the quality of the food. In Austria, POWs received between 333 and 500 grams of bread a day, and they were unable to buy additional food (or tobacco) because of the ration system in place in the country.[116] In contrast, many of the men working on the farms lived in villages with their employers, eating at the same table. A surprising number even moved into the empty beds of German farmer soldiers. In one unfortunately

[110] Lisynov, "Russkie voenno-plennye v Germanii," RGVIA, f. 2000, op. 1, d. 2796, l. 24.

[111] "Doklad sestry miloserdiia," GARF f. 579, op. 1, d. 2190, ll. 1–1ob.

[112] Romanova, "Doklad," RGVIA f. 12651, op. 11, d. 109, l. 35.

[113] Nagornaia, 137.

[114] "Doklad sestry miloserdiia," GARF f. 579, op. 1, d. 2190, ll. 4ob, 26; Romanova, "Doklad," RGVIA f. 12651, op. 11, d. 109, l. 22.

[115] It was indeed a political problem that many urban Germans ate less than Russian prisoners working on farms during the blockade-induced hungry years of the war. Lentsen, 132; see also Romanova, "Doklad," RGVIA f. 12651, op. 11, d. 109, l. 34.

[116] "Doklad sestry miloserdiia," GARF f. 579, op. 1, d. 2190, l. 7; Romanova, "Doklad," RGVIA f. 12651, op. 11, d. 109, ll.18–20.

unrepresentative sample (of men detained until 1921 in Kassel), 177 of the 500 men had married local women and an additional 32 had children outside of wedlock.[117] In Austria, fears of fraternization were so pronounced that women were punished even for talking to POWs.[118] This relatively more benign condition of rural imprisonment was the lot of the majority of soldiers. By the end of 1917, 54 percent of Russian POWs were working in agriculture and forestry, compared with only 19 percent in industry, 17 percent in the combat zones, and the 10 percent of prisoners (mostly officers) who were not assigned to work details.[119]

In Russia, the state moved to exploit the labor power of its prisoners as well. As early as August 1914, the Council of Ministers resolved to use POWs in labor brigades in a variety of locales.[120] Some enemy prisoners were sent to villages where they were employed and often accepted into village society. Agricultural work took more and more of the POWs as the war dragged on, as Russian authorities increased the number of detailed men from 295,000 to 460,000 between the fall of 1915 and the spring of 1916. Overall, twice as many POWs worked in villages than in industrial labor.[121] This caused justifiable anxiety on the part of absent husbands and fathers, as several thousand German and Austrian POWs took up with local Russian women. One anecdote from the time took a joking approach to the issue, telling of a Russian soldier who returned to find his farm in good shape and his wife with a new baby. The soldier, far from being angry, praised the German for the new piglets, calves, and for the human baby as well.[122] This response was fictional. Jealousy was far more common. Censors reported that letters home were filled with "serious concerns that POWs had been distributed to the homesteads of absent enlisted men and that living side by side would be dangerous for family morals."[123] The sexual integration of POWs into local communities demonstrated again the parallel experiences of imprisonment during the war.

LABOR SHORTAGE AND LABOR CONSCRIPTION

Even the vast supply of POWs did not meet the demands of fully mobilized war economies. When the commander of the Southwestern Front requested 120,000 POWs for work in the front zone in February 1916, he was told that they were already all being used in the domestic economy. Indeed, they were still 2,000,000 men short of what they estimated they would need in the fields the next year.[124] In addition, POWs were heavily used in road building and in the construction of the

---

[117] Nagornaia, 146.

[118] "Doklad sestry miloserdiia," GARF f. 579, op. 1, d. 2190, l. 7. Relations between Hungarian civilians and Russian POWs were substantially better and less regulated.

[119] Nagornaia, 129.   [120] Lemke, *250 dnei*, 2: 301–2.

[121] Alon Rachamimov, *POWs and the Great War: Captivity on the Eastern Front* (Oxford and New York: Berg, 2002), 108.

[122] Rachamimov, *POWs and the Great War*, 109.

[123] "Doklad o nastroenii voisk i naseleniia po dannym otchetov voennykh tsenzorov raiona 1-i armii za vtoruiu polovinu Iiunia 1916 g.," RGVIA f. 2106, op. 1, d. 1006 (part two), ll. 9–10.

[124] Lemke, *250 dnei*, 2: 301–2.

Petrograd–Murmansk railway, where 70,000 soldiers from the Central Powers worked in awful conditions from 1915 onwards.[125] In late 1915, the army also reversed its position on military work by POWs. Before this, they had only used Slavic prisoners in tasks such as trench digging, since they feared sabotage or espionage if they sent Germans or Austrians too close to the front. After complaints by their "favored" POWs, though, they began deploying Germans in the more dangerous conditions. "Hard, unpaid" labor would now be given to German prisoners, while "easy, paid" labor would be given to Slavs.[126]

Indeed, as in Germany, growing familiarity with POWs led to an increasingly relaxed regime in some places. In the Atkar district of Kazan' province, surveillance slipped to such a degree that one prisoner was able to open a lively trade in pornography, while another was found frolicking in the streets with a young woman at 1 a.m.[127] In 1916, reports that proper oversight was lacking toward POWs doing agricultural work led the Ministry of Internal Affairs to crack down. In no cases would prisoners get better supplies than free workers, and they would be required to work on holidays and on some Sundays as well. Rude or insubordinate workers would be put under arrest with only bread and water for up to a week.[128]

If one way of reacting to the growing integration of POWs into the imperial labor force was to insist on stricter treatment for enemy subjects, another was to start looking at Russian subjects as potential forced laborers. The army had conscripted local residents for urgent tasks on an ad hoc basis since the beginning of the war, but in late 1915 and 1916, the practice expanded. The wartime devastation and the mass flight of civilians from the war zone had left few workers in the region, and those who remained were not inclined to work for the military. As Stavka put it to the Ministry of Internal Affairs in January, "In view of the insufficient number of workers . . . willing to work for wages on different projects for military needs . . . military authorities have recently resorted very frequently to the requisition of labor from the local population."[129] With no additional POWs to use, and with tasks such as bridge construction on the Dnipro using 19,000 men, forced labor became a larger and larger feature of the front-line economic environment. As we will see in Chapter 5, this labor shortage would lead the government to the disastrous decision to conscript laborers from Central Asia in the summer of 1916, but in the meantime, tens of thousands of

---

[125] Reinhard Nachtigal, *Die Murmanbahn: Die Verkehrsanbindung eines kriegswichtigen Hafens und das Arbeitspotential der Kriegsgefangenen (1915 bis 1918)* (Grunbach: Verlag Bernhard Albert Greiner, 2001), 9.

[126] Mordvinov, Report to the tsar, GARF f. 601, op. 1, d. 626, l. 6.

[127] General Geisman, Order to Kazan' Military District no. 423, 12 May 1915, RGB f. D 156/8, op. Prikazy Kazanskomu voennomu okrugu, d. 1915, l. 423. Thanks to Paul Simmons for showing me this document.

[128] Boris Shtiurmer (Minister of Internal Affairs), Circular to all governors (6 April 1916), GARF f. 1791, op. 2, d. 544, l. 114.

[129] General Alekseev, Letter to B. V. Shtiurmer (Minister of Internal Affairs), 21 January 1916, RGVIA f. 2005, op. 1, d. 51, l. 2.

local civilians worked in conditions that closely approximated those of captured enemy soldiers.

We know very little about the experiences of these conscript workers or how they were drafted.[130] The legal situation was fairly clear: the army could basically requisition labor as it liked within the provinces under direct military rule. If early in the war this caused little problem, after the Great Retreat, the situation became dire. Not only had millions of civilians fled the zone, but the retreat itself had compressed the territory under military rule. Even on the Southwestern Front, where the retreat had been less significant than to the north, authorities had to return again and again to the Chernihiv and Poltava provinces for labor. Requests to expand the war zone were firmly rebuffed by a Council of Ministers that was still smarting from the loss of territorial authority it had suffered at the start of the war.[131] Nevertheless, orders for labor conscription were issued in "civilian" provinces such as Kaluga as early as November 1915. Roughly 5,000 workers from Kaluga were shipped off in teams in December, and more levies were conducted in 1916.[132] As for the selection itself, it apparently depended on the officer doing the requisitioning. In one locale in Novgorod province, the district police chief called up and sent away "the first ones he ran into, not considering whether the exiled workers were the only laborers in their families."[133] In a different district of the same province, they registered all the eligible workers and took one of every ten into a work brigade, this time taking into account whether they were fully able to work and the potential impact on families at home.[134] Women were frequently targeted as conscript laborers as well.[135] James Simpson, who visited the front near Ternopil' in August 1915, recalled seeing peasant women not only selling food and tobacco at railway stalls but also digging trenches "amidst a wealth of poppies and blue cornflowers, white umbellifers, thistles, and dandelions."[136] Conditions in these labor brigades were poor. Food and clothing were sometimes deficient,[137] and housing was often unspeakable. Epidemics spread through worker brigades like

---

[130] I am not aware, for instance, of any memoirs or recollections by any of these forced laborers. The evidence provided here is on the basis of scattered archival records.

[131] Letter from General Ivanov (Southwestern Front) to General Alekseev (Stavka), 8 January 1916, RGVIA f. 2005, op. 1, d. 51, l. 8; M. V. Rodzianko, Telegram to Emperor, 16 March 1916, RGVIA f. 2005, op. 1, d. 51, l. 15–15ob; "Osobyi zhurnal soveta ministrov," 13 September 1916, RGVIA f. 2005, op. 1, d. 51, l. 289.

[132] Irina Belova, *Pervaia mirovaia voina i rossiiskaia provintsiia, 1914-fevral' 1917 g.* (Moscow: AIRO-XXI, 2011), 45.

[133] Aleksandr M. (last name illegible, Novgorod province), untitled document, 12 February 1916, GARF f. 579, op. 1, d. 2193, l. 1ob.

[134] Pavel Vasil'evich Ramenskii (landowner in Novgorod province), Petition to Chair of the War Industrial Committee, 6 April 1916, GARF f. 579, op. 1, d. 2167, l. 1.

[135] Alfred G. Meyer, "The Impact of World War I on Russian Women's Lives," in *Russia's Women: Accommodation, Resistance, Transformation*, ed. Barbara Evans Clements, Barbara Alpern Engel, and Christine D. Worobec (Berkeley: University of California Press, 1991), 217.

[136] J. Y. Simpson, *The Self-Discovery of Russia* (New York: George H. Doran Company, 1916), 125.

[137] The caloric norm for trench workers was 2273 on normal days and 2060 on meatless days, which was above that provided for refugees but below a soldier's ration. *Otchet o deiatel'nosti meditsinskoi organizatsii komiteta zapadnago fronta Vserossiiskago Zemskago Soiuza za oktiabr', noiabr', i dekabr' 1915 g.* (Moscow: Vserossiiskii zemskii soiuz. Komitet Zapadnogo fronta, 1916), 20. These

wildfire. The crude dugouts made available to trench workers on the Ziabki–Dubrova line were so filthy at the end of December 1915 that visiting doctors called them "veritable quagmires." The quarters could not be disinfected, and they were so overrun with insects that the Zemgor officials simply ordered them burned to the ground.[138] When other doctors interceded with military engineers, pleading with them to exempt ill workers, they were routinely ignored.[139]

Commanders were aware of the acute labor shortage in the region and had to walk a fine line between building a needed military project and leaving the fields (and thus their future food supply) untended. They often released work brigades back home to work the fields in key seasons such as the sowing and the harvest, and even when the military tried raising wage scales for voluntary labor, it ran into trouble from the Ministry of Agriculture, which complained it would affect harvest totals.[140] Still, military needs got priority, as Alekseev reaffirmed to his main engineering commanders on 24 April 1916. At the same time, Alekseev and others recognized the agricultural labor crisis in provinces near the front, so they tallied up the labor needs for military projects and sent an urgent request to the Council of Ministers, asking them to find other labor sources, perhaps from men exempted from military service for health reasons or from refugees. They required 1,000,000 workers as soon as possible.[141]

As we shall see, the Council turned to draft-exempt ethnic groups instead, with painful results. But that process took time, and so through the summer campaigns of 1916, the military continued to scramble for labor. In the first year of the war, paranoia regarding espionage had led the military to deport large numbers of (neutral) Chinese and Korean immigrant laborers. A year later, they reconsidered. Many remained hostile to Asian workers because of continued spy mania, but the government split the difference by renewing the recruitment of foreign workers while imposing stringent new policing and surveillance requirements on employers and local authorities.[142] They occasionally drafted women, much to the horror of local society.[143] They looked greedily at 45,000 military age men in territories of northern Dobruja taken by Romanian and Russian troops.[144] But in the end, they kept taking local farmers away from their fields. In the midst of the Brusilov Offensive, Brusilov himself ruefully admitted that although he didn't want to take labor during harvest time, he was forced by military exigency to scoop up

norms, as inspectors such as Doctor Gonsiorovskii reported from the Second Army, were often not observed. Trench workers regularly received only one meal a day. *Otchet o deiatel'nosti meditsinskoi organizatsii*, 10.

138   *Otchet o deiatel'nosti meditsinskoi organizatsii*, 7.

139   *Otchet o deiatel'nosti meditsinskoi organizatsii*, 12.

140   Lemke, *250 dnei*, 2: 428–9, 451.

141   Report of 24 April 1916 meeting of Stavka (General Lodyzhenskii) to the Ministry of Internal Affairs, 1 May 1916, RGVIA, f. 2005, op. 1, d. 51, ll. 47–48ob.

142   Letter from General Aver'ianov (Quartermaster General of the General Staff) to General Alekseev (Stavka), 7 July 1916, RGVIA, f. 2005, op. 1, d. 51, ll. 168–169; Eric Lohr, *Russian Citizenship: From Empire to Soviet Union* (Cambridge: Harvard University Press, 2012), 127–8.

143   Excerpts from journal of a gathering of deputies of the nobility, Chernigov province, 9 May 1916, RGVIA, f. 2005, op. 1, d. 51, ll. 135–138.

144   Telegram from Commander of XLIV Corps (El'sner) to Stavka, 17 October 1916, RGVIA, f. 2005, op. 1, d. 51, l. 239.

35,000 workers and 5300 carts to build a rail line to his rear.[145] Any hesitation that might have existed about transforming the imperial economy into one heavily marked by forced labor had long since passed. Politicians and generals now took it as a matter of course that economic matters could and should include coercion, even on a mass, operational scale.

The labor crisis reached its peak in the final weeks of the old regime. The military movements of 1916 along the Romanian and Southwestern Fronts had driven many peasants away from the war zone as refugees. Those who stayed, as we have seen, were often dragooned into work brigades by army commanders. The rich fields of Ukraine, from Galicia and Bukovina down to Odessa, were now mainly empty. Army commanders estimated that in some regions, only 12 percent of the arable land would be tended in the coming growing season. Consensus was rapidly reached that the army (not to mention the local population) would go hungry the following year if something were not done. The chief supply officer of the Romanian Front asked for 40,000 workers and did not care much whether they were hired freely or coerced, "so long as they can arrive by 1 [/14]February in order to get busy sowing" in the Odessa district.[146] On the Western Front, commanders issued orders to draft "all the population capable of agricultural work of both sexes from fifteen to fifty years old" to work in the fields of Minsk province near the front.[147] Brusilov pleaded for a concerted effort to be made to return all refugees from Galicia and Bukovina back to their homes, calling on new funds to be assigned to the Ministry of Internal Affairs to accomplish this task.[148] Stavka quickly realized the seriousness of the situation as the spring sowing season loomed. Alekseev took the many reports warning of a food crisis to the tsar, who ordered a wide range of measures, including the deployment of new conscripts to farming squads, the cancellation of leave, and assigning reserve troops to agricultural work as well.[149] It was one of his last acts as monarch, issued only a couple of days before his abdication.

CONCLUSION

By appearances, the period between the Great Retreat and the revolutionary crisis of 1917 was marked by stasis. The army neither decisively defeated any of its enemies nor collapsed in the face of pressure from the Central Powers. With the

[145] Telegram from General Brusilov to Stavka, 11 July 1916, RGVIA, f. 2005, op. 1, d. 51, l. 271.

[146] Lieutenant-General Kiianovskii, "O naznachenii rabochikh dlia vypolneniia sel'sko-khoziaistvennykh i vesennykh rabot v Odesskom okruge," 21 January 1917, RGVIA f. 2003, op. 1, d. 39, l. 96.

[147] Telegram from Commander of Western Front to V. I. Gurko (Stavka), 29 January 1917, RGVIA f. 2003, op. 1, d. 39, ll. 108–109.

[148] Telegram from Brusilov (Commander of Southwestern Front) to Stavka, Ministry of Agriculture, and Ministry of Internal Affairs, 12 February 1917, RGVIA f. 2003, op. 1, d. 39, l. 118.

[149] Telegram from Alekseev (Stavka) to the Commander of the Southwestern Front and the Commander of the Romanian Front, 27 February 1917, RGVIA f. 2003, op. 1, d. 39, ll. 136–137ob.

emperor at the front, the government became consumed by intrigue and often seemed to care more about Rasputin than the war. The opposition fumed while the Duma largely stayed in recess. Soldiers grew increasingly tired and skeptical about the grand ideas that had framed the war from the outset. Civilians saw inflation and the looming specter of shortages. In retrospect, it seemed that the imperial music box was winding down, the dancers slowing before the machine finally stopped.

But behind this façade, major transformations were taking place. In the military, particularly in Brusilov's command, a "new army" took shape—technocratic, creative, decentralized, and purpose-driven. Socially, new groups such as POWs and conscripted laborers both reflected the changed world and gave scope for new forms of social, military, and political action. If the imperial state was failing, new forms of state-building were emerging. But could the pace of creation keep up with the scale of destruction? And if it could, what sort of state and society would be built by these "progressive" forces? These were questions that had to be addressed not only by politicians, by officers, and by those who tried to organize labor and food supply in the economy, but also by a much wider set of social groups. One of the most significant of these social forces were the men and women engaged in medicine during the war years.

4

Remobilizing Society
Nurses, Doctors, and Social Control

NURSES

In July 1914, Rimma Ivanova was only a year out of gymnasium in Stavropol', but she had already begun a career of social work as a zemstvo school teacher in nearby Petrovsk. Energetic and ambitious, she idolized active women, especially Nadezhda Durova, whose portrait hung on her bedroom wall. Durova was a famous Russian woman patriot who dressed as a man in order to enlist in the army during the Napoleonic Wars.[1] Thus, when the war began, Ivanova immediately declared to her parents that she intended to serve the soldiers on the front line as a nurse. Her parents reacted with horror. Ivanova's mother retorted that she was not letting her go anywhere, and her father threatened that if she snuck away he would get the police to bring her home. Events soon conspired in Ivanova's favor, however. Within days, the zemstvo organization for which she worked announced the formation of a provincial committee to assist wounded and sick soldiers and started equipping hospitals for that task. Together with the provincial Red Cross society, it also co-sponsored a short-term training course for nurses to staff the local facilities. Already, the wartime system of military medicine was in embryonic form, as the public organizations moved quickly to establish a network of trauma and infectious disease centers that would extend deep into Russia's hinterland and took responsibility for training and staffing those institutions.[2]

Ivanova now had the opportunity to participate in the war effort without violating her family's command to stay at home, and she took it immediately, as did many other women in Stavropol' society. In these early days of the war, the Red Cross had strict regulations regarding training programs for their nurses ("Sisters of Mercy"). Worried that lower-class women would be too dim-witted, insufficiently patriotic, and excessively lusty, they limited admission to nursing programs to the supposedly more charitable and restrained members of respectable society by instituting a literacy requirement.[3] In Stavropol', women had to have completed

<hr />

[1] Nadezhda Durova, *The Cavalry Maiden: Journals of a Russian Officer in the Napoleonic Wars*, trans. Mary Fleming Zirin (Bloomington: Indiana University Press, 1988).

[2] N. D. Sudavtsov, "Geroinia, protivopostavivshaia tevtonskoi zabronirovannoi sile svoiu velikuiu liubiashchuiu dushu russkoi zhenshchiny'," *Voenno-istoricheskii zhurnal* no. 3 (2002): 47.

[3] These restrictions weakened considerably as the war progressed. Zemgor did not have a literacy requirement for its nurses, and those organizations soon came to predominate.

at least four years of gymnasium to qualify for entry into nursing courses. What was limited to the women of the upper classes soon became a badge of honor among them. Ivanova, of a relatively modest background herself (she was the daughter of the treasurer of the Stavropol' consistory), was joined in her course by the daughters of local generals and dignitaries, including the daughter of the Stavropol' governor. Classes taught by the cream of Stavropol's medical establishment began less than two weeks after the outbreak of the war. The women rapidly passed through the course and took positions in the roughly forty newly opened hospitals across the province.[4]

At first, work was slow in Stavropol'. The first trainload of evacuated men arrived in late August with eighty-two men wounded on the Western Front, but then the influx slowed to a trickle, confusing medical staff and civilians alike. As we have seen, the summer and fall campaigns had been extensive and brutal. It soon turned out that the southern city of Stavropol' had been kept under full capacity because hostilities against the Ottomans seemed increasingly likely. After war with the Ottomans got under way in October, the wounded started coming in waves from that front. Ivanova developed a competency as a surgical nurse, which some of her fellow nurses avoided due to the high pressure and the extreme suffering of the patients. Some of those patients wrote to her later with thanks. "Dear little sister," one began, "I can't find the words to thank you for your care and kindness when I was lying in your hospital. I can't! I can't! . . . You are like a real sister to the sick."[5] Many of these letters contained reports from soldiers that medical care at the front suffered greatly from a lack of qualified personnel, and Ivanova resumed her entreaties to her parents to let her leave. At the end of 1914, they finally acquiesced.

Ivanova was soon attached to the 83rd Samurskii Infantry Regiment fighting in the Third Army. Unlike most nurses in this situation, she was familiar with some of the men and officers, since Stavropol' had been the location of the regiment's peacetime garrison. The regimental commander V. Stefanovich at first tried to keep her away from danger by locating her in a rear regimental infirmary (*lazaret*). He described the dangers of the front line to her, but she insisted that the more dangerous the work was, the more it was necessary. Ivanova must have been an especially persistent and persuasive young lady. Regulations prohibited women from service under fire.[6] Nearly all of the medics and stretcher-bearers who served during battle were male, while nurses were supposed to be stationed at some remove in field hospitals. Those hospitals were under constant danger from enemy artillery, airplane attacks, and cavalry raids, and nurses were part of "flying columns" that rendered aid in dangerous areas close to the front, but the army wanted to preserve the trenches as all-male spaces. Ivanova made herself an exception, even acquiring an army uniform and cutting her hair short to become nearly indistinguishable from the men around her. She was now more literally

---

[4] Sudavtsov, 47.   [5] Sudavtsov, 48.

[6] See, for instance, reaffirmation of prohibition of Sisters of Mercy in front-zone dressing stations in order of the commander of the Sanitary Division of the First Army, 2 April 1915, RGVIA f. 2106, op. 1, d. 890, l. 120.

fulfilling the Durova fantasy that inspired not only scores of nurses but Russia's unusual complement of female soldiers as well.[7] She wrote home shortly thereafter that she was happy and healthy and used to her new clothes and hairstyle. However, she needed more underwear, so she asked her increasingly anxious parents to send along four sets of men's underwear, "since it's inconvenient to wash women's underwear."[8]

In late February 1915, Ivanova found herself in the midst of fierce battles near the Vityne heights and the region of Kuche Male. She wrote her parents that the battles of 22–24 February/7–9 March had been so brutal that she fantasized about going home. Nevertheless, she was staying put, as she felt extremely satisfied in her work. "I can say without humility," she noted, "that I've accomplished more here over these three days than I did in the hospital over a much longer time. I feel great."[9] As she explained in a further letter, the first aid she performed on the field of battle was the same that she administered not far away in the dressing stations where most nurses stayed, but the impact was more significant. As a result, the "men don't look at me as a woman, but as a Sister of Mercy who deserves enormous respect." Commanders agreed, decorating her for bravery in the February battles.

Ivanova's suffering parents finally persuaded her to come home on leave in the summer of 1915. At that time no general directives had been published on whether, and for how long, nurses could take leave, but apparently her commander was sympathetic.[10] She brought with her both an attestation from her commander and medals on her breast. She was a changed woman in many ways. Friends and family noted that she had been transformed from a happy-go-lucky girl into a serious young woman. Her parents hoped, fruitlessly, that she would not want to go back to the front. Instead, like many soldiers on leave, the sweetness of the homecoming soon turned into a longing to return to the front. Ivanova wrote her brother at the front that "I won't be home long. Maybe a month. I'll satisfy the desire of our parents, but this time away from the regiment is costly. Soldiers were saddened and cried. The commanders were melancholy as well. And the main thing is that the soldiers were sure that the medics wouldn't work as conscientiously when I was gone . . . Maybe it will seem strange to you, but the regiment has become a second family for me."[11] Soldiers wrote her from the trenches, and each new casualty

---

[7] See Laurie Stoff, *They Fought for the Motherland: Russia's Women Soldiers in World War I and the Revolution* (Lawrence: University Press of Kansas, 2006); Joshua Sanborn, *Drafting the Russian Nation: Military Conscription, Total War, and Mass Politics, 1905–1925* (DeKalb: Northern Illinois University Press, 2003); Melissa K. Stockdale, "'My Death for the Motherland is Happiness': Women, Patriotism, and Soldiering in Russia's Great War," *American Historical Review* 109, no. 1 (February 2004): 78–116.

[8] Sudavtsov, 48.   [9] Sudavtsov, 49.

[10] Rules regarding nurses' leave were finally adopted in December 1915. They were allowed up to six weeks, had to have the leave approved by the head doctor, and continued to get paid. No more than 20 percent of a particular nursing staff could be on leave at the same time. "Proekt pravil ob uvol'nenii v otpuske sester milosediia sostoiashchikh v voenno-vrachebnykh zavedeniakh na teatre voennykh deistvii," 17 December 1915 (General Bonch-Bruevich), LVVA f. 3, op. 5, d. 25, l. 59ob. The tsar approved these regulations on 28 December 1915/10 January 1916.

[11] Sudavtsov, 50.

pained her. In the middle of August, despite the strong protestations of family and friends, she returned to the front.

On her way back to the 83rd Samurskii, she made the fateful decision to stop by the 105th Orenburgskii Infantry Regiment near Grodno, where her younger brother Volodya served. She arrived just in time for the beginning of the Sventsiany Offensive. Grodno fell to the Germans on 2/15 September, and on 9/22 September, the Orenburgskii Regiment found itself under heavy artillery fire. Infantry assaults soon followed, focused on the sector held by the 10th Company, where Ivanova was stationed. The casualties piled up quickly; soon no officers were left alive. She resolved to lead the men herself in a counterattack against enemy lines, rallied them over the top, and took the first line of German trenches before falling, mortally wounded. She was recognized both locally and nationwide for her battlefield exploits. In late 1915, a film about her was distributed, opening in Stavropol' on 26 November/9 December. The emperor himself, though hesitating, awarded her a posthumous 4th Degree St George's Cross, despite the fact that she was neither a man nor an officer.[12] Ivanova had transformed herself from schoolteacher to nurse to medic to war hero in the space of little more than a year.

Rimma Ivanova was unusual. Few Russian nurses engaged in combat; most of the women serving in the front-line zones did so in the ways envisioned by the regulations. But her story is also typical of the nursing experience in many ways. Educated women from across the empire volunteered in the first days of the war and passed through the same short-term courses Ivanova did. Others, such as nursing veterans of the Russo-Japanese War, enlisted to help in the new war as well.[13] Many of these women had husbands or loved ones at the front, and not a few had children as well. Some, like Lidiia Zakharova, had both. Zakharova recalled being surprised by the outbreak of the war, as she was vacationing with her family at the beach in present-day Estonia. The announcement of the war brought a flurry of activity. Her husband was called up, and tourists and local residents alike panicked and engaged in a "stampede" to move eastward. She packed herself and her children into an overloaded train car to her home in the capital.[14]

Her husband's departure left her depressed, however. It was, she recalled, "empty" both in her apartment and in her heart. Caring for the children only saddened her more, as her older son repeatedly asked where papa was, and her youngest reminded her of her spouse to a painful degree. "In a fit of powerlessness," she wrote, "I found salvation from my melancholy" by deciding to share the lot of her husband. She bustled about, overcoming hurdles and convincing her mother to take the children before ultimately succeeding in her goal. On the night before her departure, she felt calm, celebratory, and sad at the same time, but she felt, like Ivanova, as if she was about to be "baptized into a new life."[15]

---

[12] Sudavtsov, 51.

[13] See, for instance, the fragments of the manuscript memoirs of F. N. Slepchenko, who traveled to Petrograd from Iakutsk in 1916 to rejoin the brigade of nurses. N. I. Vladimirtseva, "Iz vospominanii sestry miloserdiia F. N. Slepchenko," *Otechestvennye arkhivy* no. 6 (1994): 58–72.

[14] Lidiia Zakharova, *Dnevnik sestry miloserdiia: na peredovykh pozitsiiakh* (Petrograd: Izd. Biblioteka "Velikoi voiny," 1915), 9–11.

[15] Zakharova, 11–12.

Zakharova was not disappointed. The war provided her not only with a new life but also with new meaning. She now felt herself a full part of the war effort that was the focus of all national attention. "From that moment forward, I was not that earlier woman...I was a sister, a new person with different interests, griefs, and joys."[16] Ivanova and Zakharova were not alone in this transformation of consciousness. Many nurses shared with male soldiers both the desire to have a new experience and the strong sense that it had been achieved. "Baptism" was the favored, and significant, word used to describe the shift. Soldiers universally used the term to describe the change that came over them after their first brush with death in battle. Nurses such as Zakharova had their baptism on seeing their first corpses or after their first experience with fresh battlefield casualties in their hospitals, dressing stations, and infirmaries. As a result of these experiences (and again just like the soldiers they served alongside), combat nurses also developed a strong sense of the separation between "front" and "rear." Late in her account, Zakharova became a patient herself. Having suffered from a debilitating fever and headaches for weeks, she was evacuated to rear hospitals in the cities of "L" (probably Łódź) and "R" (probably Riga). In "R," she commented benignly that "among the military, there are two categories, those who have been at war and those who have not yet tasted powder," as she observed in the rear hospitals those who were little more than "young girls in school uniforms" and were difficult to imagine in a field infirmary.[17] Khristina Semina was more blunt about herself and the women who went through nursing training with her: "Clean, young, happy-go-lucky girls left home, and after a year they were pale, nervous women."[18]

Similar to soldiers, nurses sought a deeper form of same-sex camaraderie, and they developed friendships and bonds amidst the suffering and privation. Zakharova's memoirs have many such tender moments, and outsiders also observed instances of solidarity. Violetta Thurstan, an intrepid English nursing volunteer, recalled a moment of fright on the eve of arriving at the front in Warsaw, wondering how English nurses would react if Russian women arrived without notice in their midst. Instead, she found not only hospitality but also a community marked by mutual commitment and self-sacrifice. The chief nurse set the tone, and the rest of the nurses followed her.

> The hospital was not "smart" or "up to date," the wards were not even tidy, the staff was inadequate, overworked, and villainously housed, the resources very scanty, but for sheer selflessness and utter devotion to their work the staff of that hospital from top to bottom could not have been surpassed.[19]

For Thurstan and Zakharova alike, Russian medical servitors were selfless and unified, not only amongst women, but also in the relationships between men and

---

[16] Zakharova, 23–4.   [17] Zakharova, 159.

[18] Christine D. Semine, *Tragediia russkoi armii Pervoi Velikoi Voiny 1914–1918 g.g.: zapiski sestri miloserdiia kavkazskogo fronta* (New Mexico: n. p., 1964), 1: 30.

[19] Violetta Thurstan, *Field Hospital and Flying Column, Being the Journal of an English Nursing Sister in Belgium and Russia* (London and New York: G. P. Putnam's Sons, 1915), 172–3.

women. Soldiers were reported to "love" all the sisters, and doctors and other male medical staff were all generally seen to be working harmoniously together with the women under their charge. Though we should not totally discount these reports of satisfied and friendly healers, we should note that both of these memoirists published their work while the war was still going on. Formal restrictions and self-censorship alike no doubt had an effect on their accounts.

Other observers saw a more varied set of experiences. S. An-sky, on visiting a Duma-sponsored hospital, wrote that the work was "endless and hard" for the "aristocratic volunteers" in the unit. "Relations among the volunteers were friendly, without petty friction," he noted. "This was unusual among the medical corps, which were always bristling with intrigue."[20] Leonid Andrusov, a male medic, confirmed that some units were indeed troubled. The head doctor at his dressing station, Tolmachev, established a poor tone. He "played at war," and most of the medical staff sought to stay far away from danger. The automobiles in the unit were used by Tolmachev to go touring the battle zone rather than to ferry wounded soldiers between medical facilities. Tolmachev hoarded supplies and looked out for his own interests.[21] Other sources also indicate that serious problems existed in some of the field hospitals. Hospital inspectors occasionally recommended firing or reassigning head doctors who treated subordinate doctors and nurses "rudely and tactlessly."[22] One soldier wrote to Kadet leader Pavel Miliukov complaining that his medical care had been a "humiliation," with a "horribly rude attitude to the patient on the part of the doctors and orderlies, with abuse, swearing, criminal neglect, scarcity, and a lack of medical supplies."[23] Semen Rozen'feld encountered an equally unpleasant atmosphere in his very first days in an infirmary. Senior medics abused junior ones who failed to show proper deference, doctors explained treatments to medics, nurses, and patients "at length and obscurely," and the doctor temporarily in charge was "cruel, rude, and always drunk, famous even among medics as a hopelessly illiterate and giftless healer."[24]

Doctors also had occasion to complain about the behavior of the nurses under their command. Not all of the early upper class volunteers were inclined to readily submit to the realities of army life. In the Polotsk Field Hospital #3, Doctor Bezpiatov had serious problems with Tatiana Osipova and Anna Sirenova, two of the nurses under his command. "My basic principle," he complained to Red Cross coordinators in Petrograd, "is that we're all soldiers here." But Osipova and Sirenova met his exhortations with "incomprehensible objections, which are

[20] S. An-sky, *The Enemy at His Pleasure: A Journey Through the Jewish Pale of Settlement during World War I* (New York: Henry Holt, 2002), 86–8.

[21] Leonid Nikolaevich Andrusov, manuscript of memoirs, BFRZ, d. E-134, l. 5.

[22] Report from hospital inspector to the commander of Sanitary Units of Armies of the Southwestern Front, 23 April 1915, RGVIA f. 2106, op. 4, d. 101, ll. 5–6.

[23] "A Soldier," Letter to P. N. Miliukov (n.d.), GARF f. 579, op. 1, d. 2100, l. 1.

[24] Semen Rozenfel'd, *Gibel'* (Leningrad: Izd-vo pisatelei v Leningrade, 1932), 78–9. Nurses and doctors at a different location later in the war were overwhelmed but not neglectful. See Rozenfel'd, 207–9.

intolerable from the point of view of military discipline." Finally, the affair reached a breaking point when they retorted that they were "free people" and ignored his direct orders. Bezpiatov sputtered that this was unacceptable: "At war there are neither men nor women, all are soldiers. These nurses demand some sort of special, exclusive treatment of some sort of salon character." He demanded that the two women be transferred out of his hospital and requested the return of two other nurses, Nadezhda Bogdanova and Vera Skulidas, who had been sent elsewhere.[25]

As this incident suggests, gender conflict was present in the medical units. Zakharova, having witnessed a proud young civilian woman carted away for spying, observed that while not condoning her actions, she could understand the logic behind committing espionage for one's country. She was immediately mocked for having a "female brain."[26] Sex was also a constant concern. Thurstan made sure to inform her English readers that the title Sister of Mercy did not mean that a nurse had taken vows, and sexual fears ran rampant among those in charge of medical units. One chief surgeon, a forty-year-old woman, policed her nurses quite "roughly, whenever she suspect[ed] a romance in the making," and she railed against both the "sexual instinct" and the "weakness of women."[27] Needless to say, not all of the sexual activity between medical workers was initiated by women. Nor was all of it legal. In 1916, when the front line had moved to Riga's gates, several teenage girls in the city started training to be nurses with field medical units. Aleksandr Kushinskii, an orderly in the 2nd Infirmary of the 109th Infantry Division, took advantage of the situation to sexually assault several of these girls, bribing them with candy and money to stay quiet.[28]

There is less variation in the sources regarding the relationship between soldiers and nurses. Nearly all of them attest to the veneration that soldiers had for the women who cared for them. Like Ivanova, many received letters from men they had healed. Others went further still. M. N. Gerasimov, writing decades later, recalled proposing marriage to the nurse who cared for him.[29] Unsurprisingly, Sisters of Mercy soon occupied an important place in the iconography of visual war propaganda.[30] Though petty tales of promiscuity attached themselves to the figure of the Sister, nurses were key figures in the wartime pantheon of heroes. In contrast, as we shall see in Chapter 6, the initiative of many women to assume combat roles as

[25] Doctor Bezpiatov (Head Doctor of the Polotsk Free Field Hospital #3), Letter to the George Community of the Red Cross in Petrograd, 22 December 1914, RGVIA f. 12651, op. 3, d. 360, ll. 365–365ob.

[26] Zakharova, 59.

[27] Tatiana Alexinsky [Aleksinskaia], *With the Russian Wounded* (London: T. F. Unwin, 1916), 10.

[28] Report from Head of the Riga Investigative Unit to Riga Police Chief, 29 August 1916, LVVA f. 51, op. 1, d. 13171, l. 234.

[29] She rejected him, saying "you don't love me, it only seems to you that you love me," a sharp observation on the complexity of feelings that developed between soldiers and caregivers at the front. M. N. Gerasimov, *Probuzhdenie* (Moscow: Voenizdat, 1965), 193–5.

[30] Hubertus Jahn, *Patriotic Culture in Russia during World War I* (Ithaca: Cornell University Press, 1995), 42.

soldiers was far more controversial. Though scattered cases of female soldiering existed prior to the February Revolution, the most significant developments on this front took place in the summer of 1917. Those later developments built on a substantial fact, however. No matter how strongly the front was gendered as "male" during the war, large numbers of women were present there, contributing to the war effort, suffering from privation, disease, and bombing raids, and providing aid to the combat soldiers under their care.

The situation with male medical workers was more mixed. Despite the fact that men had worked in military medicine as medics, nurses, and doctors throughout the history of the modern Russian army, most felt that men ought to be serving as combat fighters. Gerasimov reflected the view of many when he admitted that though the army "couldn't have made it" without the contributions of medical workers from Zemgor, many of the men working there were corrupt draft-dodgers. He used the mocking wartime neologism of "zemgusar" (zemstvo hussar) to describe the hale and hearty men walking around rear-zone areas in sharp uniforms and in no danger.[31] In a similar way, male medics had their masculinity questioned by soldiers and others in the wartime society.

Leonid Andrusov was one of many medical workers who found his way into a medical unit due to an aversion to fighting. In Andrusov's case, this was because he was a "principled antimilitarist" as well as an opponent of the tsarist regime. The war found him studying for his exams in the small settlement of Shirokaia, on the Black Sea coast just south of Novorossiisk. The declaration of war "agitated" the little town. As with Zakharova, he reported a "panic" in which tourists crammed trains to get home, and he too went to Petrograd soon after this initial rush. He immediately stopped studying for his exams, as graduation would have left him eligible for the draft, but he, like many of his compatriots, felt a duty to "take part in the global struggle." He retained his distaste for fighting, however, and tried to contribute through social work at the university. This was insufficient for him and many of his fellow students. Word that the student draft exemption would soon be lifted hit the university early in 1915, leading many to engage in patriotic demonstrations in a last ditch effort to preserve the exemptions by reassuring the government that student radicalism was overstated. This nearly led to blows at a demonstration, when one group sang "God Save the Tsar," while another faction sang "La Marseillaise." Andrusov, along with his fellow radicals, decided on the spot how to solve the gendered and political morass in which they found themselves: "We would all answer the draft with the consciousness of our duty to the motherland and would willingly lay down our lives, but we would die with 'La Marseillaise' on our lips. Eureka! The formula was found and students peacefully dispersed home."[32] The association between medical work and an unwillingness to fight was strengthened not only by students such as Andrusov, but also by the well-known fact that Russia's pacifist Mennonite population was exempted from the draft in return for non-military service in the medical corps.[33]

[31] Gerasimov, 72–4.   [32] Andrusov, BFRZ, d. E-134, ll. 1–4.
[33] Sanborn, *Drafting the Russian Nation*, 184.

DOCTORS

At the top of the hierarchy of hospital personnel, above the priests, supply clerks, nurses, and medics, stood the doctors. Most of the doctors were male, though some were women.[34] They were in charge not only of medical care, but also of the administration of these units, both in the stations that were formally part of the army's sanitary detachments and in the hospitals, dressing stations, and infirmaries established by Zemgor. Doctors came from all over the empire, leaving their city and village practices to help the war effort either as members of the reserves or as volunteers. Medical services on the home front suffered correspondingly.[35]

Because of their specialized medical training, few doctors were criticized for draft-dodging or unmanliness. All parties understood that they were more valuable with a scalpel than with a gun. Peacetime medical training did not necessarily ensure that doctors would be competent administrators, however. Some dealt uneasily with their elevated place in the military hierarchy, trying to become friendly and familiar with enlisted men working for them or under their care, and earning mockery from combat officers around them. Others became strict disciplinarians and abused their power, though at least one doctor commented that these cases were both "monstrous" and rare.[36] Nor did their pre-war training ensure that they would function effectively as medical practitioners. Massive trauma from shells, shrapnel, poisonous gases, and bullets was unfamiliar to them, and they also had a different array of diseases to deal with. In particular, the struggle against epidemics of infectious diseases was at the forefront of medical thinking throughout the war. Some doctors, such as Andrusov's boss Dr Tolmachev, were unfit for the responsibilities set before them. Many others, however, rose to the challenge. Soldiers and outside observers frequently came upon doctors and nurses doing lifesaving work in impossible circumstances. Fedor Stepun recalled that one of the most horrifying early experiences of the war for him was a visit to the field hospital in Krosno where his friend Rybakov had died. The wounded lay everywhere, with men still crumpled on stretchers waiting for cots and medical care, groaning and soaked through with rain and blood. In the midst of all of this, however, "several selfless doctors and nurses" made "heroic efforts."[37] Others, such as Count Dmitrii Heiden, made a distinction between "the indifference of the senior doctors in the rear" and the "selfless work on the front of regimental doctors."[38]

---

[34] Women comprised 10 percent of Russian doctors in 1913. The percentage of women near the combat front was probably lower than this, however. Sanborn, *Drafting the Russian Nation*, 147.

[35] Alfred G. Meyer, "The Impact of World War I on Russian Women's Lives," in *Russia's Women: Accommodation, Resistance, Transformation*, ed. Barbara Evans Clements, Barbara Alpern Engel, and Christine D. Worobec (Berkeley: University of California Press, 1991), 215.

[36] L. M. Vasilevskii, *Po sledam voiny: vpechatleniia voennago vracha* (Petrograd: Tip. Imp. Nik. voen. akad., 1916), 4–11.

[37] Fedor Stepun, *Byvshee i nesbyvsheesia*, 2nd ed. (St. Petersburg: Aleteiia, 2000), 284.

[38] Count Dmitrii Heiden, manuscript of unpublished memoirs (n.d.), HIA, Heiden papers, box 1, folder "Great War, 1914–1917," n.p.

Whatever the assessment of individual doctors or hospitals, everyone agreed that medical staffs in Russia's combat zone were overburdened with work. This shortage of front-line doctors and nurses is central to most of the accounts written by doctors in the war about their own service. Levon Oganesian remembered that his first medical experience in the fall of 1914 consisted of a handful of doctors treating scores of wounded soldiers at a dressing station. Crowds of lightly wounded men lay around a house with a Red Cross flag attached, while inside was an "unbelievably filthy and dark room without windows, with a hole in the roof through which the evening light pressed in, and which was overflowing with wounded . . . doctors worked on a few tables, bandaging the wounded."[39] Soldiers noted the same painful insufficiency of staff as well. In the first battles of the war, one recalled, medical assistance was "very weak, dressing stations were far away, [and] medics with stretchers for carrying away the wounded were absent."[40] Even the most whitewashed of wartime memoirs conceded the shortage, with men remarking on how one doctor would take care of 400 wounded men.[41]

Sergei Mirotvortsev had a similarly shocking first experience. He had served as a doctor in the Russo-Japanese War when only twenty-six years old. A decade later, newly arrived at a prestigious position at the university in Saratov, he nevertheless immediately petitioned for leave to serve at the front in 1914. His petition was granted, and he went to the main office of the Russian Red Cross in Petrograd to receive his assignment, running into many other prominent medical figures as he did so. They sent him to Vilnius, where the staff of the Western Front still had not given any consideration as to what experienced surgeon "consultants" like him should do. As with many other "famous Russian surgeons," he was sent to a rear hospital where, as yet, few casualties had arrived. Soon after that, he was sent to Warsaw, a bit closer to the front. But he still felt underutilized. Hearing of poor conditions in Lublin, he traveled there and found a horrific scene. The wounded were flooding in from the Battle of Krasnik (10–12/23–25 August), but there were no medical facilities and few professionals to tend to them. On his arrival, Mirotvortsev found nearly three thousand men lying wounded and untreated at the railway station. The superintendent of the city told him, "I can't do anything, I don't have any doctors, or medical personnel, or bandaging materials, or even resources with which to feed this mass of people, which completely unexpectedly fell into our laps. After all, Lublin was not among the cities to which wounded were supposed to be evacuated."[42]

Mirotvortsev began by trying to assist the masses of wounded men medically, but he soon realized that his labors were a small drop in a very big bucket, so he

[39] Cited in G. A. Melkumian, "Vrachi-Armiane na Kavkazskom fronte pervoi mirovoi voiny," *Patma-Banasirakan Handes. Istoriko-Filologicheskii Zhurnal* no. 3 (1975): 126.

[40] A. A. Uspenskii, *Na voine: Vostochnaia Prussiia-Litva, 1914–1915: vospominaniia* (Kaunas: n. p., 1932), 34.

[41] Vasilevskii, 27.

[42] S. R. Mirotvortsev, *Stranitsy zhizni* (Leningrad: Medgiz, 1956), 66. This episode is also analyzed in A. A. Budko, E.F. Selivanov, and N. G. Chigareva, "'Preodolevaia strakh i opasnost', Rossiiskie mediki s chest'iu vypolniali svoi dolg," *Voenno-istoricheskii zhurnal* no. 9 (2004): 42–8.

turned to the sphere of organizational work instead. He sent a telegram to Warsaw asking them to send medical workers and supplies, and he scoured the city of Lublin, recruiting whatever trained medical workers he could find and accepting civilian volunteers of all stripes willing to work at housing, feeding, and caring for the wounded men. Local craftsmen built stretchers for him, pharmacies gave supplies to him for free, and hundreds of women arrived to make coffee and to cook for the men.[43] Working non-stop for two weeks, they finally treated all the men abandoned at the railway station. Mirotvortsev learned several things from this experience. The first was that the war had created new conditions that required creativity and initiative to solve. He himself formed a new mobile surgical detachment with many of those with whom he had worked, "in view of the likelihood of a repeat of episodes like those which arose in Lublin." Almost immediately, they were proven right and had to rush to the city of Novaia Aleksandriia, where the Fourth Army was battling the Germans along the Vistula.[44] The second thing was that the very nature of the desperate, exhausting, but ultimately productive work provided significant solidarity for the medical staff. This was noted by nearly all of the accounts given by nurses, doctors, and medics. In Mirotvortsev's words, "The work went successfully and in a friendly fashion, as a result of which a strong, cohesive collective was formed. Later on, I frequently met with people who worked in that detachment, with whom I served at the beginning of World War One, and about whom I have the very best memories."[45]

Again, as with soldiers, this strenuous work provided the context not only for positive feelings of social solidarity but also for the emergence of traumatic mental illness. Though there appear to be no statistics on the level of mental illness amongst medical staff during the war, there is certainly testimony to the problems faced by nurses and doctors alike, ranging from depression and sleeplessness to suicide.[46] Khristina Semina's husband Ivan turned to alcohol early in the war. He was stationed in the Caucasus and dealt not only with the brutal fighting there, but also with the aftermath of the Armenian genocide. He treated frostbitten soldiers and "wild orphans" hiding in the mountains near Van after the murder of their families. Bouncing around from Tabriz to Baku to Urmia, he became more and more withdrawn. On Easter Eve 1916 Semina came back from a church service to find Ivan dead with a revolver in his hand.[47]

Russia's medical practitioners both lived with and had to treat the many forms of mental illness that flowered during the war. Russian nurses experienced most of the same ailments in this respect as Russian soldiers did, a fact that highlights how close to combat many nurses in aid stations were and how psychologically taxing their work was.[48] The subject of mental illness in the Russian army is as understudied as

---

[43] Mirotvortsev, 68.   [44] Mirotvortsev, 69.   [45] Mirotvortsev, 68.

[46] Z. G. Frenkel', "Zapiski o zhiznennom puti," *Voprosy istorii* no. 1 (2007): 89; see also some of the postwar Soviet literature on psychiatric illnesses during the war. S. P. Osipov, ed., *Psikhozy i psikhonervozy voiny: sbornik* (Leningrad and Moscow: OGIZ, 1934).

[47] Semine, 2: 32–57.

[48] This is an argument made explicitly in Laurie Stoff, *More than Binding Men's Wounds: Wartime Nursing Service in Russia during World War I* (Lawrence: University Press of Kansas, forthcoming). I thank Professor Stoff for allowing me to read portions of her manuscript prior to publication.

other medical topics in the war. The depressed prisoners of war and the nightmare-plagued soldiers mentioned previously are likely just the tip of the iceberg in this regard. The phenomenon of "shell shock," so familiar to students of the Western Front, also found expression in the Russian army. In contrast to many other military-medical establishments, however, Russian psychiatrists who handled what they called "traumatic neurosis" did not link this ailment with a highly gendered diagnosis of "hysteria." Nor did they press hard to return troubled soldiers to the front.[49] There was disagreement among doctors as to whether the condition resulted from a physical "contusion" produced by the air blast of a shell or from a psychological disability brought on by the exhaustion of the nerves, but most of them were far more sympathetic to the victims of this ailment than their compatriots on the Western Front were. Russian psychiatrists who warned of the danger of dissimulation and malingering were marginalized. They tried a variety of techniques to cure their patients, including rest, extended leave, better food, hot baths, "massage, 'direct suggestion,' (without hypnosis), and the 'general moral atmosphere' of the hospital." Some also tried electrotherapy, but apparently not with "strong currents with the intention of 'shocking the patients back into health.'" The problem with the treatment of mentally ill soldiers in Russia was not their overtreatment but the shortage of facilities and practitioners to deal with them.[50]

MEDICAL SHORTCOMINGS AND THE EMERGENCE OF "PROGRESSIVE" SOCIETY

The thin tissue of care for shell-shocked soldiers was just one manifestation of a more general problem. Russian forces had been involved in a modern war a decade earlier in Manchuria, and a cadre of experienced personnel had emerged able to train new practitioners in the methods of modern military medicine. But even that training could not prepare doctors and nurses fully for what they faced. For all of the devastation of the Russo-Japanese War, casualty rates were more than twice as high in World War I than they had been in Manchuria. In the first two years of the war, more than 2,800,000 men were wounded. Among enlisted men, this worked out to 85 percent of the average unit strength, as opposed to the 27 percent of average unit strength in the Russo-Japanese War (the numbers for officers were 78 percent and 39 percent respectively). Of those wounded, more than 2,500,000 required hospitalization.[51]

Russia's military authorities, however, had made medical preparations for a war on the scale of the Russo-Japanese War rather than the war they fought in 1914.

[49] Irina Sirotkina, "The Politics of Etiology: Shell Shock in the Russian Army, 1914–1918," in *Madness and the Mad in Russian Culture*, ed. Angela Brintlinger and Ilya Vinitsky (Toronto: University of Toronto Press, 2007), 118.

[50] Sirotkina, 122.

[51] "Sravnitel'nye dannye zabolevaemosti, smertnosti i nesposobnosti nizhnikh chinov v deistvuiushchikh armiiakh (krome Kavkazskoi armii) i v voennykh okrugakh za 2 goda voiny," Table 9, RGVIA f. 2018, op. 1, d. 64, l. 13.

Plans for the provision of medical services were outlined in the mobilization plan of 1910. They intended to create 251 infirmaries with 210 beds in each, in which to triage patients for further distribution to the rear. They also planned for 227 mobile field hospitals and 454 reserve mobile field hospitals (again with 210 beds each) for the severely and lightly wounded respectively. They planned for 79 hospitals in forts, another 100 evacuation hospitals with 420 beds each for extended care, and intended to appropriate permanent hospitals and clinics in the theater of military action to add yet more capacity. In all, they hoped to create and administer 309,610 hospital beds for their men, in addition to the 26,200 tagged for the Red Cross to develop. Offers by the Red Cross to expand its preparatory work for hospital provision were rebuffed by military authorities.[52]

Even if the military had been able to meet its targets, this planned capacity was insufficient. And the military did not come close to meeting its targets. Infighting within the army on new regulations for evacuating soldiers delayed acceptance of these figures until literally after the war started. Confusion was the result. As we saw in the case of Mirotvortsev, bewildered officials shuttled experienced military surgeons from city to city, while thousands of Russian soldiers languished without care near the battlefield. Already by 10/23 August 1914, the chief of the Evacuation Administration of the Main Administration of the General Staff admitted that medical establishments were "completely unprepared for the arrival and disbursement of patients; distribution and district points were not yet created; medical and supply personnel were neither assigned nor sent to units; there aren't any beds available for the wounded."[53] Stavka received panicked messages from up and down the front telling gruesome tales of trainloads of wounded and dying men rolling to no particular destination. Army commanders such as Brusilov were infuriated by the situation and blamed the Ministry of War for the catastrophe.[54] This news quickly reached those at home. The mother of the tsar demanded that the army immediately solve the problem, Sukhomlinov sent his highest sanitary official to the front to acquaint himself with the problems, and Chairman of the Duma Mikhail Rodzianko wrote to Grand Duke Nikolai Nikolaevich expressing the deep "anxiety" of society regarding these questions.[55]

It was in this context that "society" stepped into the gap left by the inability of the government and military to properly plan for wartime conditions. Once more, a failing state opened the door for a progressive and dynamic (if also fragile) social movement to emerge. The military high command turned to the leadership of the Union of Towns and Union of Zemstvos for help. They responded immediately, building, appropriating, and staffing hospitals and infirmaries from the front to deep in the rear of the country. The unions had come together "unbelievably quickly, almost by telegraph" within two weeks of the war, as civic activists joined

[52] A. B. Astashov, "Soiuzy zemstv i gorodov i pomoshch' ranenym v pervuiu mirovuiu voinu," *Otechestvennaia istoriia* no. 6 (1992): 170.

[53] Astashov, 170.

[54] General A. A. Brusilov, *A Soldier's Notebook, 1914–1918* (Westport, CT: Greenwood Press, 1971 [1930]), 51.

[55] Astashov, 170.

forces and resources to serve the war effort. The tsar sanctioned their efforts on 12/25 August 1914.[56] Hundreds of thousands of beds were in place by 1/14 December 1914, funded largely by the unions themselves. When the chief of the Sanitary and Evacuation Administration wrote his first yearly report in the summer of 1915, he outlined a situation in which the military maintained only 171,803 of soldier hospital beds in the country, 28.4 percent of the 597,229 present in the empire at large.[57] The inclusion of "society" into the provision of medical care doubled the capacity envisioned by military planners, even in conditions in which the military itself met only half of what it had originally planned to build. By October 1916, they had finally met demand, with the provision of 807,737 hospital spaces for soldiers, of which 542,744 were occupied.[58] By 1917, there were 967,221 beds in total.[59] The same story can be told in other spheres of military medicine as well. The mobilization plan called for 100 military sanitary trains. At the start of the war, however, there were only forty-six. By 12/25 September, there were fifty-seven, seventeen of them run by civic organizations. At the start of 1915, there were 300 trains to evacuate wounded men; by the end of 1916, there were 400.[60] The public organizations created all of this additional capacity. Still more capacity was created by the actions of individual citizens, many of whom took wounded men into their own homes for care, even in places well removed from the front.[61] Extensive efforts to mobilize volunteer services and to solicit donations to support hospitalized soldiers took place around the empire. Local committees collected gifts to send to the troops, held lotteries, sponsored benefit performances at local theaters, screened movies, and held lectures at which attendees were expected to contribute money for the well-being of the men.[62] There was no better example of an energized and mobilized society filling the vacuum of governance left by the failing state than the provision of medical care to men in uniform. As Prince L'vov, the head of the Union of Zemstvos, put it, "The Union's work has acquired all the significance of State work, for State work it really is."[63]

As the system solidified, the provision of medical services improved. Though the first battles saw many thousands of men literally left without medical care, as the war progressed there was a greater likelihood of being treated. Initial medical care normally happened in relatively small institutions. A typical infirmary just to the rear of the front lines had one doctor, one junior doctor, one supply chief, one

[56] V. M. Shevyrin, *Zemskii i gorodskoi soiuzy (1914–1917): analyticheskii obzor* (Moscow: INION RAN, 2000), 14.

[57] Shevyrin, 171.

[58] "Svedenie o kolichestve mest dlia ranenykh i bol'nykh voinov na 8 oktiabria 1916 g.," 8 October 1916, RGVIA f. 2018, op. 1, d. 73, l. 54.

[59] Budko et al., "'Preodolevaia strakh i opasnost'," 42.

[60] Budko et al., "'Preodolevaia strakh i opasnost'," 42.

[61] Irina Belova, *Pervaia mirovaia voina i rossiiskaia provintsiia, 1914-fevral' 1917 g.* (Moscow: AIRO-XXI, 2011), 133.

[62] Belova, 143.

[63] General Committee of the Russian Union of Zemstvos, *Russian Union of Zemstvos: A Brief Report of the Union's Activities during the War* (London: P. S. King & Son, 1917 [1916]), 2.

senior nurse and nine junior nurses.[64] Small units did not always deal efficiently with big influxes of patients, but they eventually got the job done. According to data gathered by the Russian Red Cross, of 2000 wounded men who arrived at one front-line regimental dressing station, 879 were treated within six hours, 395 after six to twelve hours, 383 after twelve to eighteen hours, and 243 after eighteen to twenty-four hours.[65] Lethality among hospitalized soldiers averaged about 2.4 percent for the sick and 2.6 percent for the wounded; 44 percent of sick soldiers returned to combat, while 46.5 percent of wounded soldiers returned. Overall, 5,812,935 sick and wounded officers and soldiers were evacuated from the front to rear medical institutions between August 1914 and November 1916.[66] Again, medical administrators worked hard to prevent the reoccurrence of the disasters of the first month of the war. Whereas early in the war, there were twice as many beds in the rear zones as there were in the front, by October 1916, the number had roughly equalized. More to the point, there was more spare capacity in front-zone hospitals (with the exception of the hospitals on the Caucasian Front, which were 94 percent full), than there was in the longer-term recuperation centers in the rear.[67]

TRAUMA AND DISEASE

Russian doctors and nurses, as their counterparts elsewhere in the war (and indeed in all wars), had two distinct sets of patients: those suffering from battle wounds and those afflicted with illnesses of various sorts. Both the trauma victims and the sick were considered casualties, and the struggle to deal with each consumed both doctors and those who planned medical services. Those suffering from combat-related injuries presented the most pressing and dramatic medical challenges. Part of the arms race prior to the start of the war had been not only in the numbers of weapons each state developed but also in the capacity of those weapons to create greater damage. The Hague Conventions had attempted to slow this trajectory of devastating weapons by banning things such as expanding bullets and poison gas, but those conventions were regularly violated during the war. Even weapons allowed by international law were fully capable of creating severe trauma:

> The shell had scooped out a huge pit some twenty-five feet deep and fifty-two feet around. In its flight, it had knocked off and dragged along a log from an unfinished house. A horse standing close by had been slashed in two; one half had zoomed over the roof and landed one hundred yards away. Next to the pit they found a bloodstained

[64] Spisok meditsinskago personala Evgeniinskago no. 3 etapnago lazareta (1916), GARF f. R-4094, op. 1, d. 8, l. 26.

[65] A. A. Budko, E. F. Selivanov, and N. G. Chigareva, "'V izvestnye momenty na voine ne meditsina, ne nauka, ne operatsiia igraiut samuiu vaznhuiu rol', a organizatsiia raboty': Voennaia meditsina Rossii v gody Pervoi mirovoi voiny," *Voenno-istoricheskkii zhurnal* no. 8 (2004): 61.

[66] Budko et al., "'V izvestnye momenty'," 61–2.

[67] Budko et al., "'V izvestnye momenty'," 58; "Svedenie o kolichestve mest," RGVIA f. 2018, op. 1, d. 73, l. 54.

vest with a military ID in its pocket; a bit farther on, human innards were dangling from a tree. Apparently, a soldier had been torn to smithereens, and all that remained of him were those bowels and that shred of clothing with his pass.[68]

Not all of those struck by new model shrapnel or bullets were killed, however. Those who survived often presented in ghoulish ways, not only because of the metal that tore their flesh but also because of the generally unsanitary conditions in which the men were wounded and then transported to hospitals. Microbes and larger creatures set upon the wounds almost immediately. "On one poor boy with a smashed leg," Thurstan recalled, "the insects could have only been counted by the million. About ten minutes after his dressing was done, his white bandage was quite grey with the army of invaders that had collected on it from his other garments."[69] The military had, of course, dealt with traumatic wounds and the need for field surgery in other wars. The scale of the war (and the high number of scientists enlisted into it either as doctors or as patriotic researchers) meant that there was a significant degree of experimentation and innovation within the medical community.

Prince A. P. Ol'denburgskii stimulated some of this work. Ol'denburgskii, one of the tsar's cousins, was a general and career military man who had demonstrated an interest in medical research as early as the 1890s and had founded the Imperial Institute of Experimental Medicine.[70] When the tsar agreed to create the position of supreme commander of sanitary and evacuation units in the wake of the public furor over poor medical care in the first month of the war, Ol'denburgskii was tabbed to clean up the mess. In some respects, he was poorly suited for the job. He was, according to Mirotvortsev (who worked with him as a medical consultant), an "unprincipled petty tyrant" and "undoubtedly a loathsome man."[71] Even war ministers and future war ministers thought that he was erratic and prone to "raving."[72] He occupied a high position at Stavka and got involved in military politics well beyond his charge.[73] But he was also energetic and highly mobile, conducting inspections throughout military sanitary units along the front and striking fear into the hearts of inefficient or sloppy doctors and supply clerks. He believed, rather unreasonably, that "with good will everything can be done in an hour."[74] In terms of innovation, he used his own personal wealth to jumpstart the production of iodine from seaweed and the collection of medicinal herbs in the Caucasus. Other entrepreneurs were also supported. B. I. Zbarskii, a doctor in the northern Urals, pioneered an improvement to the chloroform used to anaesthetize patients during surgery, and Ol'denburgskii brought him to Petrograd

---

[68] An-sky, 92.   [69] Thurstan, 166.

[70] John F. Hutchinson, *Politics and Public Health in Revolutionary Russia, 1890–1918* (Baltimore and London: Johns Hopkins University Press, 1990), 111.

[71] Mirotvortsev, 83.

[72] Michael T. Florinsky, *The End of the Russian Empire* (New Haven: Yale University Press, 1931), 72.

[73] Mikhail Konstantinovich Lemke, *250 dnei v tsarskoi stavke: vospominaniia, memuary*, 2 vols. (Minsk: Kharvest, 2003), 2: 180; Brusilov, 91.

[74] Florinsky, 72.

for a demonstration. When the new chloroform worked as promised, he fast-tracked its approval and adoption and tasked Zbarskii with immediately establishing a production center.[75] Not all of the innovation was successful, though. Surgeons at the front attempted to deal with the problem of large bullet wounds by trying to solve it "mechanically." "With great patience the entry hole was widened and by means of inserting a probe they tried to clear it through to the exit hole." Once finished, they plugged the hole with a wad of gauze. The widespread adoption of this procedure led to what Mirotvortsev called the "cult of the tampon," and the cult was damaging: many patients went into shock and many others developed sepsis in their wounds. Nevertheless, it was nearly impossible to get doctors to abandon this new and counterproductive strategy.[76]

Bullet wounds and surgery were hardly new in 1914. The introduction of poison gas as a weapon by the German army in Bolimów, Poland in January 1915, however, presented a special set of difficulties. Russian soldiers and front-line personnel were nearly helpless in the face of the first attacks, and they quickly became both frustrated and furious. Though the initial attack at Bolimów largely failed due to weather conditions, gas casualties soon became a regular fact of life. In all, during the war, 65,158 men and women attached to the Russian army became casualties of gas attacks, and in the twelve largest gas attacks, the general mortality reached 20.2 percent.[77] Stanley Washburn, an American correspondent working for *The Times* of London, later wrote:

> Though I had seen many people die, I never witnessed anything so terrible as the death of these gas victims. Nothing seemed to alleviate their suffering; morphine had no effect on them whatever. Most of them had choked and swallowed gas, getting it into their lungs and sometimes into their stomachs. When the gas united with the moisture of the mucous membrane it formed hydrochloric acid which was eating holes in their stomachs. There were whole wards of these miserable wretches. They had to be strapped to their beds, and in their last hours were given ether to ease their misery as they were passing out.[78]

Those who survived the attacks were far from unaffected. A. N. Zhiglinskii, an officer who gave his gas mask to a soldier during a December 1916 gas attack, was so badly poisoned that he had to go to a sanatorium in the Crimea, where he stayed for the next four years.[79] L. M. Vasilevskii visited a hospital in Warsaw where some of the victims were being treated: "Horror, disgust, and a hot pity for the victims— all of these swirled around in my soul. . . . It was after the first actual use of gas on our front, and therefore no one could successfully deal with this 'novelty.'" He felt, he said, the "fundamental nerve of militant Germanism. It was the breath of the

[75] Budko et al., "'V izvestnye momenty'," 59–60.   [76] Mirotvortsev, 72–3.

[77] Budko et al., "'Preodolevaia strakh i opasnost'," 45.

[78] Stanley Washburn, *On the Russian Front in World War I: Memoirs of an American War Correspondent* (New York: Robert Speller and Sons, 1982 [1939]), 113.

[79] A. N. Zhiglinskii, "'Ia gord tem, chto mogu byt' polezen Rossii': Pis'ma iz proshlogo, utrachennoe nasledie," *Istochnik* no. 3 (1996): 12–13.

devil himself which escaped from the balloons of chlorine."[80] In Fedor Stepun's unit, "after a gas attack everyone in the battery felt that war had crossed the final boundary, that from then on everything was allowed and nothing was sacred."[81] Russian troops "took as few prisoners as possible" in the battles following gas attacks.[82] The use of chemical weapons soon became a key factor in the press campaign against German atrocities. After an initial hesitance by Stavka, censors finally allowed news of German gas attacks to be published on 16/29 May 1915, and war correspondents like Aleksei Ksiunin filed stories that went to newspaper readers across the empire.[83]

Once more, wartime emergency prompted the further mobilization of society. The Russian scientific community stepped into the fray immediately. In the first place, they ramped up their own production of poison gas in major industrial centers such as Moscow, Petrograd, Kiev, and Minsk.[84] Though several types of gas were produced, Russian authorities decided not to escalate matters, refusing to use cyanide gas unless the Germans used it first, and apparently making only desultory efforts to send chlorine gas to the front. By the end of the war, only two tons of liquid chlorine had been sent, and it is unclear how much of it was used.[85]

Most importantly, though, work began on developing anti-gas technology and instructing soldiers how to use it properly. The first attempt at prevention, in Russia as elsewhere in Europe, was the distribution of "anti-gas bandages." In the spring of 1915, these bandages were proven ineffective. The Germans used gas several times near Gumin and Berzhimov on the Northwestern Front in May and June, culminating in an attack on 25 June/8 July 1915 that devastated several Siberian regiments, causing 4000 casualties and at least 100 immediate deaths. The command staff pointed to several reasons for the failure of the bandages, primarily that the gas was thicker and moved faster than in previous usages and that soldiers found it difficult to properly soak the bandages in the midst of fighting an intense battle. Enlisted men were more succinct: the bandages never fit correctly, so they let in the gas.[86]

The solution to this problem came from Moscow State University, where Nikolai Zelinskii worked. While his compatriots were developing new gases, Zelinskii worked on "passive chemical warfare." In the fall of 1915, he suggested using charcoal "activated" so as to maximize its capacity to absorb the poisons in the air. An engineer named Eduard Kummant then designed a rubber mask that could contain the charcoal filter and ensure that the seal around the soldier's head was

---

[80] Vasilevskii, 64.   [81] Stepun, *Byvshee*, 304.

[82] Washburn, *On the Russian Front*, 113.

[83] Lemke, *250 dnei*, 2:67; Aleksei Ksiunin, *Narod na voine: iz zapisok voennogo korrespondenta* (Petrograd: Izd. B. A. Suvorina, 1916), 91–7.

[84] Lemke, *250 dnei*, 2:186.

[85] Alexei B. Kojevnikov, *Stalin's Great Science: The Times and Adventures of Soviet Physicists* (London: Imperial College Press, 2004), 8.

[86] "O rasprostranenii germantsami udushlivykh gazov v raione Gumin-Berzhimov," 30 June 1915, RGVIA f. 12651, op. 1, d. 1152, ll. 95–96.

tight.[87] By 1916, the masks were in mass production, and though there were, inevitably, some problems, especially with the rubber breaking down under front-line conditions with a heavy gas presence, Russian soldiers and commanders praised the "Kummant-Zelinskii" masks as the best available means of anti-gas protection.[88] Soldiers were trained on how to deal with gas attacks and were told that their "mask is a type of weapon like any other." They were instructed to keep it from getting damp, to store it away from the sunlight and from fires. Soldiers inclined to run from the trenches when they saw the cloud approaching were reminded both that it was impossible to outrun a wave of gas and that they needed to remain in the trenches with weapon in hand to fend off the inevitable attack that would follow. After the attack, they were to wave the gas out of the trenches by billowing their sheets and by lighting large fires to burn the remnants of the poison away before cleaning everything from masks and rifles to telephones.[89]

As of August 1916, only 36,222 of the masks were available in the First Army, while medical authorities estimated that they needed 254,000 in that army alone to equip each soldier and maintain a healthy reserve.[90] Shortages persisted, not only because German gas attacks required all soldiers to own them if possible, but also because many of the masks were being unwittingly rendered useless by soldiers who discovered that activated charcoal worked as an excellent filter for moonshine. This made the masks "unsuitable for defense against gas," and led to suspicions among soldiers that the masks themselves were to blame.[91] By late 1916, though, the main weight of gas mask shortages was being felt by non-combatants. At first, they were not even distributed to doctors and nurses. The Red Cross had to repeatedly request masks for their workers at "front-line positions," but the army wanted to keep all of them for active soldiers. Mirotvortsev, who was by August 1916 the head of the Red Cross on the Western Front, asked the Second Army for 3000 masks for medical providers and 500 for patients, but the head of the sanitary services for the army denied his request.[92] Only the intervention of A. V. Krivoshein, the powerful Minister of Agriculture, forced the army to relent.[93]

The intervention was too late to save the members of the 13th Red Cross Detachment, which was gassed in the village of Tal'minovich on 21 August/3 September 1916. Only a handful of masks were available, and some of those

---

[87] Kojevnikov, 10.

[88] Telegram from Evstaf'ev to the commander of the First Army Sanitary Detachment, 12 August 1916, RGVIA, f. 2106, op. 4, d. 183, l. 8.

[89] "Ukazaniia na sluchai gazovoi trevogi" (n.d.), GARF f. R-4094, op. 1, d. 15, l. 175.

[90] Report from the commander of the First Army Sanitary Detachment to the commander of Sanitary Detachments for Armies on the Northern Front, 15 August 1916, RGVIA, f. 2106, op. 4, d. 183, l. 17.

[91] Colonel Daler (Administration of the Inspector of Artillery at Stavka), Telegram to the inspector of artillery for the Second Army, 10 January 1917, GARF f. R-4094, op. 1, d. 15, l. 146.

[92] Commander of the Second Army Sanitary Detachment, Secret military telegram to Mirotvortsev (Red Cross of Western Front in Minsk), 2 August 1916, GARF f. R-4094, op. 1, d. 15, l. 14.

[93] Head of Chancellery, Red Cross of Western Front, Telegram to commander of the Second Army Sanitary Detachment, 15 August 1916, GARF f. R-4094, op. 1, d. 15, l. 16; commander of the Second Army Sanitary Detachment, Telegram to Special Plenipotentiary of the Red Cross with the Second Army, 20 August 1916, GARF f. R-4094, op. 1, d. 15, l. 18.

lacked eye protection. In all, 31 medical workers became casualties.[94] Local civilians were left completely without protection, and the Red Cross also begged authorities to send aid to them, if only in the form of previous, outdated gas masks. It turned out that there was no great supply of old masks, and that reserves remained sufficiently low that there was not nearly enough to help the local population.[95] Russia had adapted to the new age of chemical warfare, but its soldiers, nurses, and civilian populations still remained vulnerable.

In addition to treating battle wounds, medical workers had to devote a great deal of time to dealing with illnesses among soldiers. The conditions of life at the front meant that soldiers suffered from the full range of sicknesses that plagued the Russian population at an even more intensive level. In the first two years of the war alone, doctors treated 2,241,338 soldiers of the active army for sickness, an additional 620,440 soldiers in military districts in the theater of war fell ill, and 1,227,456 men in internal districts required hospitalization, making a total of more than four million men.[96] Some of these illnesses were non-infectious, such as frostbite, sunstroke, or scurvy, which afflicted 362,256 soldiers during the war, more than any other non-infectious disease. Infectious disease posed the greatest threat to Russia's military establishment, however. Dysentery, smallpox, and scarlet fever each claimed the lives of thousands of Russian soldiers, but the main targets of health officials were cholera and the range of illnesses classified as a variety of "typhus"—typhoid fever *(briushnii tif)*, relapsing fever *(vozvratnii tif)*, and spotted fever *(sypnoi tif)*. Between August 1914 and September 1917, hundreds of thousands of Russian soldiers were treated for these diseases in various medical establishments.[97]

Disease	Number of soldiers treated	Mortality rate
Typhoid fever	97,522	21.9%
Relapsing fever	75,429	2.4%
Dysentery	64,264	6.7%
Cholera	30,810	33.1%
Spotted fever (typhus)	21,093	23.8%
Smallpox	2,708	n/a

Venereal diseases also plagued the active armed forces. Between August 1914 and August 1916, 56,993 Russian soldiers on European fronts contracted syphilis (45 of them dying), and 120,162 suffered from other venereal diseases.[98] Again,

---

[94] N. Svobodin (Senior Doctor of 13th Red Cross Detachment), Telegram to Special Plenipotentiary of the Red Cross with the Second Army, 22 August 1916, GARF f. R-4094, op. 1, d. 15, ll. 80–81.

[95] Special Plenipotentiary of the Red Cross with the Second Army, Telegram to the Anti-Gas Division of the Red Cross of the Western Front, 23 February 1917, GARF f. R-4094, op. 1, d. 15, l. 155.

[96] "Sravnitel'nye dannye zabolevaemosti, smertnosti i nesposobnosti nizhnikh chinov v deistvuiushchikh armiiakh (krome Kavkazskoi armii) i v voennykh okrugakh za 2 goda voiny," Table 7, RGVIA f. 2018, op. 1, d. 64, l. 10.

[97] Budko et al., "'Preodolevaia strakh i opasnost'," 46.

[98] "Sravnitel'nye dannye zabolevaemosti, smertnosti i nesposobnosti nizhnikh chinov v deistvuiushchikh armiiakh (krome Kavkazskoi armii) i v voennykh okrugakh za 2 goda voiny," Table 8, RGVIA f. 2018, op. 1, d. 64, l. 12.

sources detailing the sexual activities that resulted in venereal disease are relatively difficult to come by, but one of the factors clearly was prostitution. One case that did make it into the archives concerned El'za Vimba, a thirty-two-year-old peasant whose husband was called up during the general mobilization in 1914. Vimba was found and arrested when seven members of the 567th Orenburg Infantry Detachment stationed in Riga became infected with an unspecified venereal disease. All of them admitted getting it from a woman named El'za who plied her trade in the park near the Apollo Theater. The military authorities put the guilty soldiers under increased surveillance and canceled their leave. They forcibly hospitalized Vimba and then deported her from the zone of military activity for the remainder of the war.[99]

Illness constantly drained the fighting power of the army. A more fine-grained set of statistics than the general ones presented in the table are available for a weekly report in February 1915 on sickness in the Eighth Army, which had a little over 200,000 men. Soldiers contracted 112 new cases of cholera or suspected cholera, nearly all of them coming from just two regiments, 168 cases of suspected or confirmed spotted fever, 1193 cases of relapsing fever, 1003 of dysentery, and 2288 of frostbite.[100]

The Russian military understood the danger of disease for the proper functioning of the army. Historically, far more men had died from sickness during Russian military campaigns than had died from combat. As a result, officers developed preventative measures from the very start of the war. During mobilization, Dmitrii Heiden recalled joining Aleksei Brusilov's staff at the XII Army Corps in Vinnytsia. As men gathered there, typhus raged in at least five villages in the district. Heiden quarantined all the soldiers arriving from those villages and had them sent to their units later, after their health had been cleared by doctors. None of their troops contracted typhus in the first few weeks of the war.[101] Even before the first battles in East Prussia, military hospitals set aside separate rooms for contagious soldiers.[102] Indeed, only isolated cases of infectious disease struck the army as a whole at the very outset of hostilities. Still, medical experts began ringing warning bells as early as September 1914, saying that signs of possible epidemics were already visible.[103] Nearly all of their recommendations focused on measures to prevent the spread of disease into either the army or deep into the interior of the empire. Heiden's instinct to quarantine was largely shared.

Isolating those who presented symptoms of epidemic diseases took two major new directions. The first was an effort to create an entire parallel structure of medical units dedicated solely to treating infectious disease, strictly separated from

---

[99] Documents related to court case of El'za Vimba, August–November 1915, LVVA f. 3, op. 1, d. 18744, ll. 1–10ob.

[100] "Svedeniia o chisle vnov' zabolevshikh nizhikh chinam 8 armii ostro-zaraznymi boleznami za 7 fevralia 1915," 7 February 1915, RGVIA f. 2134, op. 1, d. 402, ll. 1–4.

[101] Count Dmitrii Heiden, manuscript of unpublished memoirs, n.d., HIA Heiden papers, box 1, folder "Great War, 1914–1917," n. p.

[102] Frenkel', 82.

[103] "Protokol soveshchaniia g.g. Upolnomochennykh Rossiiskago Obshchestva Krasnago Kresta v deistvuiushchikh armiiakh severo-zapadnago fronta pod predsedatel'stvom Osoboupolnomochennago A. I. Guchkova 18-go sentibria 1914 goda v gor. Belostoke," 18 September 1914, RGVIA f. 12651 op. 7, d. 130, l. 26ob.

the hospitals and infirmaries that treated combat wounds or non-infectious diseases. This network of quarantined health care facilities expanded greatly over the course of the war; orders to create additional space for those with infectious disease can be found throughout the time period.[104] Public organizations enthusiastically supported these efforts. The Union of Zemstvos established isolation hospitals along major train routes, and the Union of Towns advised the military on where to put urban isolation hospitals in the rear.[105] Not all of these hospitals functioned well. Many were short on staff, and some practitioners simply avoided contact with their infectious patients.[106]

The second initiative focused on controlling vectors of human movement, especially along railway lines. Some of the first cases of typhus along the Northwestern Front appeared on the Warsaw rail line, and this understandably worried medical authorities. Though they knew they had to evacuate infectious soldiers from the front, they also understood that this would create the potential for the further spread of these diseases. The first plan to deal with epidemics suggested dedicating not only special train cars for infected soldiers, but even entire trains and train lines serviced by special "disinfection detachments." Soldiers and civilians alike were to be closely observed for signs of disease before being allowed to travel by train, and the ill were to be formally "sorted" by doctors to ensure that infections did not spread.[107]

These processes of surveillance and sorting became more institutionalized as the war proceeded.[108] Indeed, the more that "progressive" society replaced old regime governmental structures during the war, the more intrusive these "state" practices became. Civilians in particular found their access to transportation and medical care curtailed due to fears of disease. Some sympathetic doctors had to petition their superiors in order to be allowed to treat ill civilians in separate buildings,[109] while others proudly reported treating soldiers and local residents in the same quarantine hospitals.[110] Surveillance extended to everyone. All wounded and ill soldiers traveling through Warsaw in January 1915 had to stay in the city for five days. During that time they were closely watched by doctors for any sign of stomach ailments. Those whose stomachs stayed strong were allowed to be evacuated further to the rear. Those who developed intestinal problems were placed in isolation wards and had their clothes and linen disinfected. Further, all hospitals were to keep close

---

[104] See, for instance, General Alekseev, "Prikaz nachal'nika shtaba verkhovnago glavnokomanduiushchago no. 291," 27 November 1915, RGB f. D 36/340, op. Prikazy Kievskomu voennomu okrugu, d. 1915, l. no. 291.

[105] Tikhon J. Polner, *Russian Local Government during the War and the Union of Zemstvos* (New Haven: Yale University Press, 1930), 114–15; Frenkel', 88.

[106] Order of commander of the Sanitary Detachment of the First Army, 17 April 1915, RGVIA f. 2106, op. 1, d. 890, ll. 272ob.–273.

[107] "Protokol soveshchaniia," RGVIA f. 12651 op. 7, d. 130, ll. 26ob–27.

[108] See, for instance, "Soveshchanie raionnykh vrachei i raionnykh zaveduiushchikh khoziaistvom s predstavitelem medico-sanitarnago otdela," 27 December 1915, TsDIAK f. 715, op. 1, d. 269, ll. 3–4.

[109] Senior Doctor of the Echelon Infirmary (Red Cross) of the Ekaterinburg Community of Sisters of Mercy, Letter to the Head Plenipotentiary (Red Cross) to the Southwestern Front, 10 July 1915, GARF f. R-4094, op. 1, d. 9, l. 33.

[110] See "Doklad no. 8 ob epidemicheskikh otriadakh," TsDIAK f. 715, op. 1, d. 269, ll. 5–6.

account of the water they had purified by coloring all "safe" water with either red wine or cranberry extract.[111] Every significant railway station along track running to or from the front established "medical surveillance."[112] Authorities made clear that preventing the spread of disease through mobile carriers could not be accomplished by forbidding human movement, but only through strict observation. "The whole task," one argued, "is surveillance."[113]

It was not exactly the whole task. Authorities also focused on hygienic measures such as water purification to prevent or slow the emergence of diseases. They repeatedly ordered army units to pay close attention to food safety by ensuring that meat was of high quality and properly cooked, by storing other foodstuffs in clean locations, and by boiling water and keeping water sources clean. Inspectors made sure to investigate these issues whenever they visited military units or hospitals, and they undertook broad education measures by posting flyers with titles such as "Rules for protecting yourself against cholera" in buildings.[114] Travelers in front-line zones observed that the army had posted signs everywhere warning "do not drink fresh water" and "do not eat fresh fruit."[115] Commanders soon turned to even more heavy-handed tactics, such as posting sentries near river crossings downstream of settlements with cholera cases.[116] Officers in civilian areas soon issued safety directives as well.[117] Dealing with bacteria and parasites addressed the factors associated with cholera and dysentery, but more general hygiene was necessary to deal with the diseases on the typhus spectrum, which were contracted and spread through insects such as fleas and lice. Controlling bugs proved even more difficult in the grime of the front zone than ensuring food safety. Commanders could, and did, order soldiers to "strictly observe cleanliness of body, underwear, and clothes,"[118] but these orders did little to clean up the men or the trenches. Again, it was Zemgor that stepped in to address these issues. They established 372 bath houses (with a smaller number of attached laundries) across the front. By the second half of 1916, those bath houses had the capacity to serve 200,000 men per day, and actually averaged somewhere close to 100,000 men per day.[119] While this was a substantial number, it did not meet the hygiene needs of millions of soldiers living in mud and cold in the open air.

---

[111] "Instruktsiia gospitaliam, lazaretam i pereviazochno-pitatel'nym punktam gor. Varshavy o meropriatiakh protiv rasprostraneniia ostro-zheludochnykh zabolevanii," 2 January 1915, GARF f. R-4094, op. 1, d. 1, l. 28.

[112] "Mery po bor'be s zaraznymi zabolevaniiami," n.d., but 1915, RGVIA f. 2018, op. 1, d. 66, l. 46.

[113] "Soveshchanie pod predsedatel'stvom kniazia Borisa Aleksandrovicha Vasil'chikova po voprosu o bor'be s zaraznymi zabolevaniiami," 14 July 1915, RGVIA f. 2018, op. 1, d. 66, l. 49.

[114] Order to the Supply Detachments of the First Army, 14 April 1915, RGVIA f. 2106, op. 1, d. 890, ll. 221ob.–222; Protocol of Sanitary Subcommission of the Red Cross of the Western Front, 17 January 1916, GARF f. R-4094, op. 1, d. 6, l. 10.

[115] J. Y. Simpson, *The Self-Discovery of Russia* (New York: George H. Doran Company, 1916), 125.

[116] "Mery po bor'be," RGVIA f. 2018, op. 1, d. 66, l. 44.

[117] Mandatory directive to the Kiev Military District, 8 June 1915, TsDIAK f. 1439, op. 1, d. 1667, l. 67.

[118] Order of commander of Sanitary Units of First Army, 2 April 1915, RGVIA f. 2106, op. 1, d. 890, ll. 119–120.

[119] Polner, 219–22.

Zemgor also successfully lobbied for large-scale inoculations of troops against cholera, typhus, and smallpox. This was first urged by a conference of the Pirogov Society of Russian Physicians in late December 1914, but resistance to the plans of progressive medical authorities on the part of the Ministry of Internal Affairs and by General A. Ia. Evdokimov, the chief military sanitary inspector, meant a significant delay in implementation. Pressure both from combat commanders and from the public organizations finally succeeded in forcing Evdokimov to accede in late summer 1915,[120] and the inoculation campaign successfully began in the autumn of 1915 on a massive scale. On the Western Front alone, the Zemstvo Union gave 19,097 anti-cholera vaccines, and 228,060 anti-typhus vaccines.[121] A year later, a conference of military doctors and zemstvo doctors agreed that the campaign was working,[122] and combat commanders such as Aleksei Brusilov were so convinced of the efficacy of the vaccines that they ordered every one of their soldiers to get either a first inoculation or a booster shot.[123] These measures were not always popular with the troops, as the process and recovery were painful, often led to fever, and required rest afterwards.[124] Evidence from later campaigns also suggests that soldiers and civilians in Russia, as in other places faced with the strange and counterintuitive process of inoculation, doubted the efficacy of the program.[125] Letters from individual soldiers confirm the scale of this suspicion, as men wrote home that there were many fatalities in units in which typhus inoculations were taking place.[126]

Though medical authorities were well aware that epidemic diseases spread easily between soldiers and civilians, they made far fewer provisions for civilian populations than for military men. This was true, as we have seen, for populations who attempted to live through the war in front-line zones. It also rapidly became true for people living on the home front. Soldiers evacuated in the first chaotic period of the war and the political deportees described in Chapter 2 both carried disease back to central Russia. At the end of 1914, a typhus epidemic blazed through provinces such as Kaluga, Voronezh, Riazan, and those near the Volga River.[127] It was also true for refugees, though the clear danger of these tired, sick, and mobile individuals to public health in interior regions of the empire was immediately understood. Near the front, refugee camps sprang up, and these soon became deadly quarantined zones. As An-sky remembered, refugees from both Austrian Galicia and Russian territory gathered in a camp near Rovno, where they died, helpless, of

---

[120] Hutchinson, 131.

[121] *Otchet o deiatel'nosti meditsinskoi organizatsii komiteta zapadnago fronta Vserossiiskago Zemskago Soiuza za oktiabr', noiabr', i dekabr' 1915 g.* (Moscow: Vserossiiskii zemskii soiuz. Komitet Zapadnogo fronta, 1916), 18.

[122] Polner, 213.

[123] General Brusilov, Order no. 1706 to the armies of the Southwestern Front, 15 October 1916, TsDIAK f. 715, op. 1, d. 448, l. 1.

[124] Lemke, *250 dnei*, 2: 549–50.

[125] Letter from the Medical Section of the Zemstvo Union to the commander of Sanitary Units for Armies of the Southwestern Front (April 1917), TsDIAK f. 715, op. 1, d. 343, l. 129; untitled newspaper clipping, n.d. but probably 1918, GARF f. R-4094, op. 1, d. 56, l. 40.

[126] Report from the military censor of the First Army, February 1916, RGVIA f. 2106, op. 1, d. 1006 (part one), ll. 500–501ob.

[127] Hutchinson, 117.

both hunger and cholera. Many of these refugees were Jews. Synagogues in the area soon became refugee dwellings where children perished from cholera en masse.[128] Aid organizations on the Caucasian Front also noticed the spike in disease among refugees in 1915 and proposed building special hospitals for them.[129] As the social crisis from the Great Retreat deepened, government figures debated the question of refugees and disease at the highest levels. In late July, Prince Shcherbatov, the Minister of Internal Affairs, pleaded with General Ianushkevich to contain the refugee problem near the front, writing to him that "in view of the spread of typhus and cholera among [Galician refugees], it is impossible to allow them to move to the interior of Russia."[130] As we have seen, Stavka was both unwilling and unable to slow the flow of refugees in the midst of the military retreat.

Peter Gatrell has rightly argued that the fevered nightmares about refugees serving as a vector of disease were fed by various strong cultural currents that made "wandering" people a potential danger and did not always correspond to the scale of the problem.[131] However, as Gatrell also notes, illness was a real issue, and refugees suffered from infectious diseases disproportionately.[132] Officials on the ground reported both the scale of the problem and the reasons for it. Iosif Feliksovich Ban'kovskii, a landowner in Kobrin district, described the situation at hand in July 1915. Ten thousand refugees lived in a camp near Kobrin, where they lacked sufficient bakeries and food. Understaffed kitchen workers served what food they had in vats, and refugees lined up to grab their share, spreading germs and leaving the weak to fend for themselves. Cholera and hunger spread further. Roads and squares where refugees squatted became "dumps of trash and filth" which would require tons of lime to disinfect, though of course there was no lime to be had. With no ambulances, those sick with cholera and smallpox remained living and eating alongside healthy members of the community. These ill and hungry people had taken to foraging and stealing, leading to increased contact, even fist fights, with the local population. And all of this slowly moved eastward.[133] When refugees finally made it onto trains, those boxcars became deadly as well. Officials at the highest levels of the armed forces discussed the problem of refugees and disease, and they urged that trains be equipped with hospital cars staffed by the Union of Zemstvos in order to quarantine the sick.[134] The government responded with yet more attempts at surveillance. At a cost of 100,000 rubles a day, Zemgor officials on the Southwestern Front set up "filtration points" to prevent the spread of cholera and other infectious diseases.[135]

---

[128] An-sky, 184, 206.

[129] "Doklad kavkazskogo komiteta pomoshchi postravadvshim ot voiny o ego deiatelnosti," 1915, GARF f. 579, op. 1, d. 2077, l. 2.

[130] Telegram from Shcherbatov to Ianushkevich, 20 July 1915, RGVIA f. 2005, op. 1, d. 42, l. 74.

[131] Peter Gatrell, *A Whole Empire Walking: Refugees in Russia during World War I* (Bloomington: Indiana University Press, 1999), 8, 81.

[132] Gatrell, *Whole Empire Walking*, 58.

[133] Excerpts of letter from Iosif Feliksovich Ban'kovskii (landowner in Kobrin district) to K. G. Skirmunt (member of State Council), 17 July 1915, RGVIA f. 2005, op. 1, d. 42, l. 78.

[134] Telegram from General Alekseev to General Danilov, 19 September 1915, RGVIA f. 2005, op. 1, d. 42, l. 272.

[135] "Moskva i voina: bezhentsy," *Russkie vedomosti*, 29 July 1915: 4.

CONCLUSION

Throughout 1915 and 1916, participation in the non-governmental sphere took on increasing importance. The aid workers who looked out for the interests of war victims such as local civilians or POWs increasingly claimed competence in wide-ranging matters and demanded resources.[136] Progressives in the military and in society respected one another. Brusilov was well liked by both aid workers and leaders of public organizations.[137] We should note the dual thrust of technocratic progressivism espoused by these enlivened activists. On the one hand, to be sure, they were deeply critical of the existing order. They saw themselves as the force that would fix what the tsar and his courtiers in the military and government had so badly broken. On the other hand, they were impassioned supporters of the practices of filtration, surveillance, inspection, and labor maximalization that emerged from the intersection of the new social problems and the emerging new political groups.[138] Indeed, it was through their aid efforts that many activists became consciously and explicitly involved with political questions on multiple levels.

At the very end of 1915, a particularly revealing exchange took place at a conference of district doctors and district economic chiefs employed by Zemgor in Ukraine. Much of the meeting had to do with the daily work these doctors did in implementing progressive programs such as mandatory vaccinations. Some noted a difficulty in doing their work due to coordination problems between different zemstvo agencies and between the zemstvo workers, the military, and the local governors. The activists proceeded cautiously, however, because they were aware that Zemgor was coming under increasing assault from the government. Conservatives had been deeply suspicious of the public organizations from the beginning. As early as November 1914, the Ministry of Internal Affairs was warning the Council of Ministers and the tsar that the energized unions were engaged in political intrigues and recommended clipping their wings.[139] The centerpiece of the government's attack by late 1915 was the question of corruption among Zemgor officials. Increasingly, critics called aid workers to account for their activities and their expenditures. As one delegate observed:

> We have to fulfill two very large tasks: we have to give an account not only to our consciences, but also to Russian society. The urgency which is now displayed in the demand for accountability is not accidental. . . . Our organization is in great danger, which is apparent to us. They are launching a systematic assault on us, and that assault

---

[136] Lemke, *250 dnei*, 2: 164.   [137] An-sky, 285; Lemke, *250 dnei*, 2: 455.

[138] For more on the rise of this "revolutionary" transformation of politics, see Peter Holquist, "What's so Revolutionary about the Russian Revolution? State Practices and the New-Style Politics, 1914–1921," in *Russian Modernity: Politics, Knowledge, Practices*, ed. David L. Hoffmann and Yanni Kotsonis (New York: St. Martin's Press, 2000), 87–111; Peter Holquist, *Making War, Forging Revolution: Russia's Continuum of Crisis, 1914–1921* (Cambridge, MA: Harvard University Press, 2002).

[139] Shevyrin, 22.

has only one weapon, which is that we have no accountability. Under the term accountability they mean more than how much has been done, how many people have been fed or given medical treatment and so forth, they also mean how it was done and how much it cost. I just read in the last issue of *Moskovskie vedomosti* that when it appeared that the attacks on our account books had failed, they then said: it's all in perfect order, but did you buy things well, sufficiently cheaply, with sufficient attention to society's donations? There's no doubt that corruption exists, but it's so insignificant in scale.... Unfortunately, not everyone relates to the Union like we do, we have serious enemies.... There is a powerful battle between bureaucratic authority and the public organizations.[140]

The struggle was already under way by the time these doctors met. An attempt by the Moscow Central Cooperative Committee to petition the government for greater political freedoms in November had been shut down quickly by gendarmes.[141]

In 1916, this "battle" between the public organizations and the tsar's bureaucracy intensified. A wave of congresses held by these various organizations in the first months of the year testified to the fact that the center of the political opposition had been transferred from the Duma to the non-governmental organizations (NGOs). In February, there was a congress of representatives of War Industrial Committees. In March, delegates from Zemgor convened. The War Industrial Committees met again that month, as did the worker sections from those committees. Regional congresses in Kiev, Tula, Khar'kov, and Omsk soon followed. In April, a conference of statisticians gathered. So too did a congress of medics (*fel'dshers*). Plans were in the works for an agricultural congress and a congress of refugee assistance organizations, as well as the creation of an All-Russian Central Supply Committee and a Union of Cooperatives. This wave culminated with a congress of the Pirogov Society on 14–16/27–29 April, at which doctors were very outspoken about the issues facing the country. A worried police section reported that all of these groups had moved from technical questions to political ones. Calls for a new administration were made at nearly all of them, and the spirit of these meetings was captured by a speech on 13/26 March 1916 at the congress of the Union of Towns: "In order to pull the country out of the present ever-deepening economic crisis, we need a system of state organs that unite all of the active and capable forces of the nation (*vse deesposobnye sily natsii*) in the form of the public organizations, which embrace all the parts of the population, and transfer power into the hands of their responsible leaders."[142]

---

[140] "Soveshchanie raionnykh vrachei i raionnykh zavedushchikh khoziaistvom," 28 December 1915, TsDIAK f. 715, op. 1, d. 269, l. 15–15ob.

[141] Department of Police (Ministry of Internal Affairs), Completely Secret Circular to the chiefs of Provincial Gendarme Administrations, 3 November 1915, GARF f. 217, op. 1, d. 437, l. 145.

[142] "Obzor politicheskoi deiatel'nosti obshchestvennykh organizatsii za period s 1 marta po 16 aprelia 1916 goda," (1916), HIA B. Nikolaevsky Collection, box 802, folder 7, p. 31. Description of activities, *passim*. For more context regarding the public organizations, see Polner, *Russian Local Government*; Thomas Fallows, "Politics and the War Effort in Russia: The Union of Zemstvos and the Organization of the Food Supply, 1914–1916," *Slavic Review* 37, no. 1 (March 1978): 70–90; and Thomas Earl Porter, "The Emergence of Civil Society in Late Imperial Russia: The Impact of the

The response of the tsar's administration was uncompromising. The police report cited here did not call for nuance. Instead, the police concluded that the leaders of those organizations "under the rubric of the defense and salvation of Russia from destruction" were instead directing their attentions "toward changing the existing order, which has taken on threatening dimensions for the state order." They recommended further persecutions of the public organizations.[143] In April, orders were issued forbidding free and open exchanges between enlisted men and aid workers unless specifically allowed by the military leadership.[144] The police also found a receptive audience in the tsar, who had earlier rebuffed Alekseev's plea to send congratulations to the Zemgor Congress with the comment: "What for? All that work systematically undermines me and all my leadership. I very well understand those types. It would be better to arrest them than thank them." The tsar relented when Alekseev persisted, but he did so only while muttering "Well, ok, ok, send them. The time will come when we'll reckon with them."[145] But the opposition of the tsar and his government did not reduce the influence of progressive public activists. To the contrary, the public organizations had successfully framed the issues of the war as discrete problems (such as disease or refugee housing) that could be solved if specialists were allowed to deploy their expertise.

Still, this collision between conservative defensiveness and progressive technocracy did not lead either to a resolution of the larger political conflict or of the many "questions" that progressives sought to solve. To the contrary, the outcome was tension, uncertainty, and foreboding about the future, as *Russkie vedomosti* divined in its New Year's edition in 1916:

> There's no aspect of life which isn't a question... Will this city or that locale be supplied with produce in a timely fashion—is a question; will there be enough fuel—is a question... There's a "supply question," a "fuel question," a "relief question," a "transportation question," an "inflation question." There's no movement without an obstacle, no occurrence without complicating questions. Russian life resembles those small billiard games called "Chinese" for some reason, where the ball rolls along an inclined plane, running every second into a multitude of little studs which deflect it away from its goal, stopping it for several moments, as if it had suddenly gotten past all the difficulties, but only at the last moment to be thrown somewhere unexpected and to land someplace completely different than where it was expected to land.[146]

The situation in Russia was thus far from stagnant, no matter what was happening with the armies. The social and political transformation of Russia in 1915 and 1916 had thrown Russian citizens around like pinballs, and as 1916 drew to a close, they were looking for a place to land.

Russo-Japanese and First World Wars on Russian Social and Political Life, 1904–1917," *War & Society* 23, no. 1 (May 2005): 41–60.

[143] "Obzor politicheskoi deiatel'nosti"; See also Lemke, *250 dnei*, 2: 615.

[144] Lieutenant General Kvetsinskii and Quartermaster-General Major General Lebedev, Completely secret letter to chiefs of staff of armies on the Western Front, 27 April 1916, GARF f. 579, op. 1, d. 2168, l. 1.

[145] Lemke, *250 dnei*, 2: 392–3.

[146] "Moskva 1 ianvaria," *Russkie vedomosti*, 1 January 1916: 2.

5

Revolution

VIOLENCE AND CRIME

Just as the Great Retreat drew to a close, General Ivanov noticed a disturbing trend in the areas controlled by his troops on the Southwestern Front. Violent crimes in the civilian population were increasing sharply at the same time that civilian judicial institutions were collapsing due to the evacuation of personnel. Ivanov was concerned enough that he appropriated even more judicial power for his rickety military justice system. He enumerated a set of crimes—intentional homicide, rape, robbery, banditry, arson, among them—for which civilians would immediately be sent to military courts for judgment.[1] In a separate order, he instructed his men to increase the severity of punishments for these crimes.[2] Ivanov was right. The scale of criminality was growing, fed not only by increasing civilian thuggery, but also by men in uniform who roamed deep into the rear fomenting unrest and fear.[3]

Take, for instance, the sleepy Ukrainian district of Kaniv, roughly 100 kilometers south of Kiev on the Dnipro River and almost 500 kilometers from the fighting (see Map 8). In April 1916, residents and police were disturbed by the discovery of an unidentified corpse along the road between Kyp'yachka and Potik. The mysterious man had died a violent death, but the police could not identify either the victim or the perpetrator.[4] On 9/22 June, in Malyi Rzhavets, three armed intruders with rifles and revolvers broke into the home of the prosperous peasant Vasilii Stepanenko, beating him and firing a shot before disappearing into the dark. All of the men were young and in military uniform; one of them was barefoot. Police swept the woods and settlements in the area without result. On 28 July/10 August, Aleksandra Rudenko, the wife of a soldier at the front, was attacked in her village of Hrushiv. Two armed men took more than ten rubles before slipping away. These men were unwise enough to board a riverboat soon afterwards, witnessed by a suspicious local who did not know them, and they were arrested when the police called ahead to officials at the next

---

[1] General Ivanov, Order no. 1198 to Armies of the Southwestern Front, 18 September 1915, TsDIAK f. 1439, op. 1, d. 1667, l. 181.

[2] General Ivanov, Order no. 1220 to Armies of the Southwestern Front, 18 September 1915, TsDIAK f. 1439, op. 1, d. 1667, l. 291.

[3] Communication from the governor of Chernigov to district police, November 1915, TsDIAK f. 1439, op. 1, d. 1667, l. 258.

[4] Letter from the Kanev district police chief to the chief of the Kiev Gendarme Administration, 8 April 1916, TsDIAK f. 274, op. 1, d. 3732, l. 6.

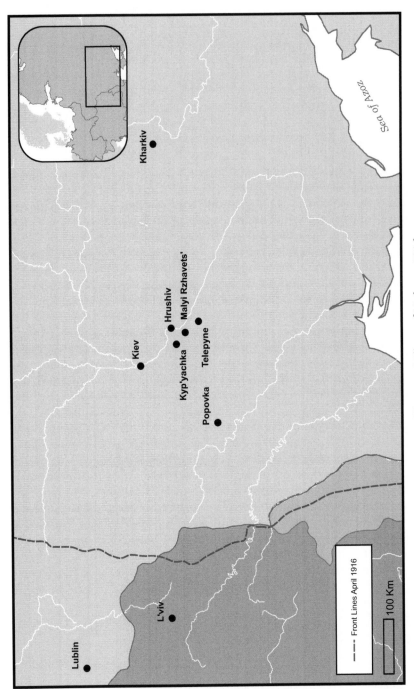

Map 8 Ukrainian Villages of Violence, 1916

stop. The felons were both young deserters.[5] In October, a woman going to buy cows was robbed and killed on the road. It was little relief to the police to discover that the murderer was a civilian, in fact the grandson of her sibling.[6] In January 1917, a report that deserters were hiding in the home of Ivan Solov'ev in the village of Popovka led the local policeman, Ignatii Panasiuk, to call upon the services of two local peasants and to attempt an arrest. When his small posse arrived, a battle erupted. The former soldiers quickly got the upper hand, grabbed Panasiuk's revolver and saber and cut off his left arm before fleeing.[7] These were not unusual developments in Central Ukraine. A similar set of files exist for neighboring districts as well.[8]

Growing violence also led to episodes of ethnic conflict. On 16/29 May 1916, in Telepyne, Ukraine a group of young men, most of them eighteen or nineteen years old and due to be drafted soon, showed up on the market square between eight and nine in the morning. They immediately began making mischief, pinching goods from the stalls and refusing to pay when caught. At around eleven, a large group of these teenagers gathered near the candy merchants and converged on Rukhlia Goldschmidt. Some grabbed candy, and others grabbed dried fish from her stall. Goldschmidt protested the thievery and was clubbed on the arm with a stick by one of the young men involved. This first act of physical violence served as a trigger for more. Soon the boys were going up and down the whole row of stalls, taking goods and beating the Jewish merchants. According to the indictment, members of the crowd yelled "Hurray! Beat the Yids! Give 'em what they deserve!" One of the young men, Efim Movchan, hopped up on to the table of Goldschmidt's stall and began to dance. The crowd grew quickly, and other parts of the marketplace were soon robbed as well. It was half an hour before the police arrived and the crowd dispersed.[9] Nine of the ten men arrested were literate, as were three of the five women. One of them was an enlisted man on sick leave. They all denied taking part in the violence, though they were forced to admit being part of the crowd and of having looted goods in their possession.[10]

A similar dynamic took place in Riga. The Great Retreat of 1915 had ended virtually at the gates of the city, and as a result the region swarmed with uniformed men. Soldiers and civilians lived cheek by jowl from 1915 to 1917, providing a laboratory for soldier–civilian relationships. One of the most notable phenomena

[5] Letter from the Kanev district police chief to the chief of the Kiev Gendarme Administration, 8 August 1916, TsDIAK f. 274, op. 1, d. 3732, l. 32.
[6] Letter from the Kanev district police chief to the chief of the Kiev Gendarme Administration, October 1916, TsDIAK f. 274, op. 1, d. 3732, l. 39-39ob.
[7] Report of the Kanev district police chief to the gendarme chief of Cherkassk, Chigirin, and Kanev districts, 11 January 1917, TsDIAK f. 274, op. 1, d. 3732, l. 59ob.
[8] See, for instance, the report from the chief of the second subdistrict of Chigirin district to the gendarme chief of Cherkassk, Chigirin, and Kanev districts, 11 October 1916, TsDIAK f. 274, op. 1, d. 3756, l. 12ob.
[9] Indictment in the Case of Anti-Jewish Disorders on 16 May 1916 in the settlement of Telepino (Chigirin district), n.d., TSDIAK f. 315, op. 2, d. 718, l. 223.
[10] Report of the Prosecutor of the Cherkassk District Court for Important Cases in the settlement of Kamenka, 27 May 1916, TsDIAK f. 315, op. 2, d. 718, l. 158.

was a sharp rise in crime and increasing hostility between policemen and soldiers. On 15/28 October 1915, a police officer named Belokopytov entered an apartment on Tula Street after receiving a complaint. Upon entering he found one soldier in bed with a woman and another sitting at the table with two ladies drinking homemade beer. One soldier grabbed his rifle but, seeing Belokopytov's military decorations, said "I won't shoot you now, since you used to be at the front yourself." When Belokopytov refused to show similar consideration to the soldiers and demanded that they come with him, however, the soldiers attacked him with the stocks of their rifles and fled.[11] Other soldiers showed similar disregard for civilian authority and civilian norms, as reports flowed in throughout the year recording thefts, vandalism, mass takeovers of public transportation, rapes, murders, and other manifestations of disorder.

Nor was the problem limited to enlisted men, as the commander of the Riga Fortified Region had occasion to complain in an order of the day issued only to officers on 13/26 April 1916:

> There have been incidents recently in Riga when officers . . . have been drunk and have acted in a disorderly fashion, insulting police officers and private citizens–frequently women, including the wives of officers. . . . In normal life, everyone was used to considering an officer as the model of orderliness, no one would have entertained the thought that an officer who had committed some sort of misdemeanor would hide himself like a coward in a crowd and thereby avoid responsibility for his mistake, as the elementary rules of orderliness demand from every morally educated individual.[12]

Officials, thus, were clear that the problems in Riga were part of a more general breakdown of civilized, orderly behavior. The crime would only worsen and become more violent as 1916 progressed, as the chief of detectives would report to the Riga police chief in October: "In the last two months, the number of felonies has noticeably increased: robberies and especially thefts, and also incidents of murder. The work of the detective unit shows that the overwhelming majority of these crimes are committed by enlisted men." The chief also pointed to the significant role in the crime wave played by deserters from the newly formed Latvian units, several of whom had criminal records and knew the city and its underworld well.[13] As the crime wave continued to rise in the winter, the Lifliand governor reproached the police chief for his "inaction."[14] The chief, in his response, had several excuses, nearly all of which pointed to the decline of restraining individuals and institutions on the Riga streets. Not only had the number of policemen declined but the draft had also taken away the young

[11] Report of the Riga police chief to the governor of Lifliand, 20 October 1915, LVVA f. 3, op. 1, d. 18730, l. 6.

[12] Order to officers of the Riga Fortified Region, 13 April 1916, LVVA f. 3, op. 5, d. 24, l. 10.

[13] Report from the head of the Riga Investigative Unit to Riga police chief, 9 October 1916, LVVA f. 51, op. 1, d. 13171, l. 415.

[14] Letter from the Lifliand governor to the Riga police chief, 1 December 1916, LVVA f. 51, op. 1, d. 13541, l. 15.

doormen and nightwatchmen, leaving behind only the elderly to observe and protect property and civilians throughout the city.[15]

Criminal violence increased over the course of the war as models of proper behavior and restraining institutions and individuals weakened. As conditions changed, ever more anti-social behavior developed among soldiers and spread to others. Officers forgot what it meant to be an officer. Soldiers mocked and beat first Jews, then other civilians, and then even policemen. Civilian miscreants also pushed the limits of orderly behavior beyond the breaking point. As 1916 drew to a close, this atmosphere of violence and disorder was visible and pronounced. The failure of the state to provide sufficient security to its citizens and the social pathologies that emerged over the course of 1915 and 1916 are critical for an understanding of the Russian Revolution. Anger at the tsarist regime and frustration regarding goods shortages were necessary but not sufficient conditions for the great, violent social upheaval that would destroy both the autocracy and the empire. The pangs of fear and the visceral sense of chaos and impending doom felt by citizens across the country provided the radical edginess needed to transform disgust and protest into the violent acts of mutiny and rebellion that would characterize imperial life throughout 1917 and beyond.

ANTI-COLONIAL REBELLION: CENTRAL ASIA IN 1916

That violent mutiny began in the imperial borderlands, indeed in the most colonial of all the Russian Empire's territories, the lands of Central Asia. These regions were among the last to be annexed to the empire. Tashkent was conquered in 1865, and repeated military victories over the next twenty years brought several decaying khanates under Russian control. By the time Russia and Great Britain fixed the lines of their respective imperial holdings in 1887, the empire had acquired vast tracts of land between the Caspian Sea and the Tien-Shan mountains. From the start, tsarist officials combined old forms of Russian imperial control with new techniques of colonial governance borrowed from their western neighbors. On the one hand, elite co-optation and the delegation of local governance to native "chiefs" remained the linchpin of the colonial system. Local elders were given the opportunity to profit both economically and politically from their positions, and as a result "a sort of *modus vivendi* between nomads and colonial rulers" emerged.[16] On the other hand, intensive resource extraction in the form of cotton plantations in the Fergana Valley and several waves of European settler colonization made the heavy hand of the European metropole very evident. Unhappiness with Russian colonial oppression was manifest in big ways and small, from assaults on colonists and collaborators to an attempt to spark a rebellion through a surprise attack on a

---

[15] Report from the Riga police chief to the Lifliand governor, 20 December 1916, LVVA f. 51, op. 1, d. 13541, ll. 16–17ob.

[16] Daniel Brower, *Turkestan and the Fate of the Russian Empire* (London and New York: Routledge Curzon, 2003), 129.

Russian military garrison in Andijan in 1898. That uprising failed, however. As elsewhere in the empire, the Russian army proved up to the task of militarily defeating anti-colonial insurgents.[17]

When the war began in 1914, the region remained calm. Imperial conscription law made distinctions between different sorts of ethnic minorities in the realm. Those who were fully "civilized" were liable for conscription, unless, like the Finns, struggles over conscription posed serious political risks.[18] Other minorities, especially those who had not fully embraced a sedentary lifestyle, were exempted from the draft, as planners doubted their military usefulness and believed that the recruits would perish from sickness in harsh new climates. Finally, the tsarist regime had used draft deferments and exemptions as social incentives to induce young men to engage not only in such favored pursuits as teaching or policing, but also in colonization.[19] First-generation Slavic settlers in the Central Asian lands were granted an exemption from the draft. As a result, only those men born in Turkestan of European extraction went west to war in 1914.

Despite being thousands of kilometers from the front, Central Asia began experiencing the social and economic pathologies discussed in Chapters 3 and 4 soon after the Great Retreat. The first steps down the path of colonial (and anti-colonial) violence began in February 1916. The cause, as usual, was the combination of inflation, price controls, and a deficit of goods. Local administrators, faced with greater than normal food shortages (and associated higher prices) at the end of the winter, took the now standard wartime response of imposing the *taksa* on key items. At this announcement, tensions arose in the bazaar on Starogospital'naia Street in the European quarter of Tashkent. One Muslim woman had a stall with mounds of potatoes for sale prior to the imposition of the new prices, but she warned her (European) customers that she could not sell at reduced prices. The following day, with the rules in effect, she was no longer open for business. Rumors spread that the potatoes were being stockpiled elsewhere. Meanwhile, at other stalls, shopkeepers ignored the *taksa* and sold potatoes at two to three times the fixed price. A crowd of angry colonist women soon formed as the local police stood by passively. At 10 a.m., they launched themselves at the stalls, destroying them in a pogrom that soon spread to six other bazaars in the city. The police did little to stop them. When they did arrest a couple of women, the crowd quickly forced their release. This was not only an economic conflict but also an ethnic one. Pogroms did not occur in bazaars in the largely Muslim Old City; only Europeans took to

---

[17] Edward Dennis Sokol, *The Revolt of 1916 in Russian Central Asia* (Baltimore: The Johns Hopkins Press, 1954), 56–8.

[18] The imperial government had abolished the special status of Finns in the conscription law of 1901 as part of its larger Russification program, but widespread protests and disturbances forced an unusual retreat. From 1904 onward, Finns paid a special tax instead of serving in the military. Tuomo Polvinen, *Imperial Borderland: Bobrikov and the Attempted Russification of Finland, 1898–1904*, trans. Steven Huxley (Durham, NC: Duke University Press, 1995), 126–9; Pertti Luntinen, *The Imperial Russian Army and Navy in Finland, 1808–1918* (Helsinki: SHS, 1997), 155–83.

[19] Joshua Sanborn, *Drafting the Russian Nation: Military Conscription, Total War, and Mass Politics, 1905–1925* (DeKalb: Northern Illinois University Press, 2003), 20–5.

beating their local tradespeople.[20] Thus, the same triggers for social and economic unrest that we witnessed in the western borderlands in 1914 and in central Russia in 1915 were spreading to the east by early 1916. But in Tashkent, the more explicitly colonial context made the problems more acute. A larger ethnic conflict was barely avoided in February. During the pogrom itself, Slavic factory workers considered joining the women on the streets before backing off. In the days that followed, when police investigators arrested some of the ringleaders, armed workers threatened not only a strike but also violence, bringing grenades to their demonstrations. Nor was the Tashkent pogrom an isolated incident. Market violence occurred in several cities across the region.[21]

If the economic questions of inflation and shortages stimulated the violence of the Slavic colonists, it was the labor shortage described in Chapter 3 that sparked the uprising of the local Muslim populations. In the spring of 1916, tsarist military planners faced a desperate situation. They needed a million men to work in the front zones on infrastructure projects, but they had bled the local populations and POW camps dry. They also knew that they had exhausted the draft-eligible population. In September 1915, they drafted the only sons and physically weak men in the second-tier reserve, and they had already dropped the minimum draft age by two years. Though they considered a military draft of the exempt ethnic minorities, they kept returning to the conviction that nomads from the steppe could not fight a modern war. The solution seemed obvious. In May 1916, the Council of Ministers resolved to draft the ethnic minorities into labor battalions. Other groups considered, such as men who failed their medical exams (a possible 120,000 recruits) or refugees (a possible 800,000 recruits) were much smaller than the more than three million men they could expect to draft in Russian Asia. Notes of caution from the two ministries most aware of the technical and political challenges involved with such a draft—the ministries of war and internal affairs—were brushed aside.[22] So too did ministers ignore warnings from Duma members who found out about the scheme.[23] All of these discussions took place without any consultation with colonial governors or local elites, much less with local populations.

As a result, the announcement on 25 June/8 July 1916 that previously exempt populations in Central Asia would be drafted as conscript laborers struck local Muslims like "thunder out of a clear blue sky."[24] There was, not surprisingly,

---

[20] Marco Buttino, *Revoliutsiia naoborot: Sredniaia Aziia mezhdu padeniem tsarskoi imperii i obrazovaniem SSSR*, trans. Nikolai Okhotin (Moscow: Zven'ia, 2007 [2003]), 60.

[21] Buttino, 60–2.

[22] Joshua Sanborn, "Unsettling the Empire: Violent Migrations and Social Disaster in Russia during World War I," *Journal of Modern History* 77, no. 2 (June 2005): 318.

[23] Speech of Deputy Dzhafarov at session of State Duma, 13 December 1916, in Manash Kozybaev, ed., *Groznyi 1916-i god (sbornik dokumentov i materialov)*, 2 vols. (Almaty: "Kazakstan," 1998), 1: 191.

[24] "Protokol chastnogo soveshchaniia predstavitelei kazakhskogo naseleniia Turgaiskoi, Ural'skoi, Akmolinskoi, Semipalatinskoi i Semirechenskoi oblastei o vystupleniiakh naseleniia protiv mobilizatsiia i provedenii neobkhodimykh meropriatii po osushchestvleniiu prizyva na tylovye raboty," 7 August 1916, in Kozybaev, ed., 1: 31. Central Asian populations were not the only ones newly liable under this

widespread confusion and a proliferation of different responses to the edict, not only on the part of the local and imperial officials assigned to implement it,[25] but also on the part of the people being drafted. In some respects the initial response to conscription echoed the various ways that Russians had responded to the draft since its implementation in 1874: proclamations of loyalty, requests for deferments and exemptions, evasion, corruption, and protest. But the peculiar nature of this draft soon made itself felt. In the first place, it was for labor rather than combat, a distinction that insulted some of the men in the region, one group of whom proudly sent a telegram to the authorities stating they were ready "to go where we are ordered, not only with hatchets and spades for work in the rear, but also armed on our horses for the defense of our common mother Russia."[26] Secondly, and more importantly, the labor draft was conducted without the extensive technical and ideological preparation necessary to make it run smoothly. As one Duma deputy put it, "the native population had no idea what was being asked of them, they didn't understand either the goals or the character of the new responsibility that had been unexpectedly placed on them."[27]

Some bits of ideological preparation were in place. Many officials and native correspondents with officialdom knew to stress themes such as loyalty and duty. Other tsarist administrators rapidly attempted to explain the nature and purpose of the draft once the decree was issued.[28] But much of this ideological training ran at cross purposes with the fact that this was a labor draft that excluded them from "honorable" military service. Again, the idea that military service was not only a duty but also a badge of civic belonging was present, at least among the educated elite. Among modernizing Jadids, there was "enthusiasm for recruitment and . . . dismay at the uprising" because they had (correctly) viewed the draft exemption as a symbol of exclusion from mainstream imperial life.[29] One group of Kazakh elites met the edict with "satisfaction, seeing in it the beginning of their equalization in responsibilities and rights with the core population of the empire."[30] The biggest

---

law—the Muslim population of the Transcaucasus (with the exception of Turks and Kurds) and indigenous peoples in many areas of Siberia were also made liable, but the unrest was largely in Central Asia.

[25] Colonial officials on the ground, such as the governor of the Turgai region, were also unaware that a labor draft was imminent. Telegram from commander of Kazan' Military District (General A. G. Sandetskii) to the chief of the Main Staff, 3 January 1917, RGVIA f. 1720, op. 2, d. 194, l. 2 [cited hereafter as "Sandetskii telegram"]. General Kuropatkin, sent to put down the rebellion, agreed, writing in his diary on 23 July 1916 that the "unbelievably rushed measures . . . were the reason for the unrest." In I. Galuzo ed., "Vosstanie 1916 g. v Srednei Azii," *Krasnyi arkhiv* 3, no. 34 (1929): 45.

[26] "Telegramma aksakalov Poludenskoi volosti Petropavlovskogo uezda General-gubernatoru Stepnogo kraia N. A. Sukhomlinovu," 9 July 1916, in Galuzo ed., "Vosstanie 1916 g. v Srednei Azii," 16.

[27] Speech of Deputy Dzhafarov at session of State Duma, 13 December 1916, in Kozybaev, ed., 1: 194.

[28] Sandetskii telegram, l. 2ob.

[29] Adeeb Khalid, *The Politics of Muslim Cultural Reform: Jadidism in Central Asia* (Berkeley: University of California Press, 1998), 241.

[30] "Postanovlenie sobraniia predstavitelei Kazakhskogo naseleniia i mestnoi administratsii Cherniaevskogo uezda ob organizatsii mobilizatsii rabochikh na tylovye raboty," in Kozybaev, ed., 1: 21.

technical problem was that there had been no process of registration prior to the edict. In Orthodox parts of the realm, draft authorities had relied heavily on parish records to establish the age of their recruits (and even then had to judge a young man's age by sight quite frequently). Compiling registration lists was a time-consuming process that began well before each draft cadre came to the induction point. Authorities in central Russia had been registering and drafting men for more than forty years and still ran into problems there. None of that registration work had occurred amongst the Muslim populations of Central Asia. The state simply ordered native local officials to draw up the draft lists on their own.

Thus, in one fell swoop, and in the context of deteriorating social and ethnic relations in the borderlands, Petrograd introduced a deeply unpopular and danger-ous decree while fatally compromising the thin strata of co-opted elites through which they governed their Central Asian possessions. State authority splintered as the process "destroyed the last remnants of lawfulness in the relationship between the administration and the natives (*inorodtsy*)."[31] As the decree was slowly revealed (governors were given discretion as to the timing of its announcement in their territories), resistance began. Violent clashes started in Khojent on 4/17 July, sparked in Samarkand district on 7/20 July, and spread from Ural'sk to Fergana in the following days before culminating in a large demonstration in Tashkent on 11/24 July (see Map 9). If some chose to fight, others chose flight. In the Turgai region, "the Kirgiz [Kazakhs] were gripped by panic: they quit their jobs, decamped to the depths of the steppe, began gathering in large crowds and stopped listening to officials and even their own chiefs, whom they didn't trust. The Kirgiz, according to the governor [of Turgai], decided not to submit to the draft and that it was better to die at home in the steppe than in the trenches."[32]

As this testimony suggests, hostility to the decree crystallized quite quickly, and it manifested itself as resistance in several directions: against the colonial regime, against co-opted elites, and against the European settlers in their midst—in other words, this was a classic anti-colonial rebellion. From the start, Russian colonists and officials, used to friendly interactions when visiting villages for trade or other purposes, experienced a "sharp change in the relationship between Kirgiz and Russian; the previous joy and hospitality was transformed into indifferent or even plainly hostile attitudes."[33] Local Kazakh officials, used to acting as intermediaries between their communities and the imperial state, found their position even more precarious. One hapless official, N. Saganaev, was sent from the city of Akmolinsk (present day Astana) back to his home in the Karabulakskaia district to "explain the goal of the draft" and to threaten punishment in the case of evasion. The residents of his hometown told him in no uncertain terms that "they would all die in the place where they were born and that they would not go into the work brigades, that

---

[31] "Zaprosy grupp deputatov gosudarstvennoi dumy pravitel'stvu po povodu sobytii v oblastiakh turkestanskogo i stepnogo general-gubernatorstv pri vypolnenii tsarskogo ukaza o mobilizatsii korennogo naseleniia na tylovye raboty," no earlier than 12 December 1916, in Kozybaev, ed., 1: 154.

[32] Sandetskii telegram, l. 2ob. The ethnic group that Russians referred to as Kirgiz in this time period are now called Kazakhs.

[33] Sandetskii telegram, l. 10ob.

Map 9 Central Asia in Revolt, 1916

they considered him [Saganaev], as an emissary of the government, to be a traitor to the Kirgiz revolt, and that it would be best to kill him." Saganaev managed to escape, but not before some of his compatriots were beaten in the ensuing scrum.[34] Saganaev was fortunate. Many such officials were lynched, and some of the Kazakh rebel groups began attacking and punishing not only open collaborators but also those who were inclined to obey the orders of the state in any way. Kazakh society thus divided along the lines of rebels and law-abiding subjects, along generational lines (young men took the lead in the rebellion, while the older men were more prone to preach patience and obedience), and along the lines of class. The elites and well-to-do bribed themselves off the draft lists and acquired legal exemptions, while the poor were disproportionately burdened with the demands of the draft. Some were even arrested for failing to offer bribes.[35]

It is of course no contradiction to note that an uprising against colonialism should include serious conflicts within the colonized groups themselves. Indeed, this is the normal pattern of events in situations of decolonization. It does not lessen the fact that the core of the rebellion was a struggle against Russian rule. After the initial flare-ups of violence, rebel groups organized more methodically, building strength in the wide-open spaces of the steppe. European settlement and power remained more concentrated in the cities and, to a lesser extent, in the Russian villages that were built in the areas of agricultural colonization (especially in the eastern Issyk-Kul region). From the steppe, Kazakh insurgents launched attacks on the core instruments of Russian power. They cut telegraph lines, attacked railways, and launched offensives against Russian garrisons and Russian-dominated towns. In some areas, they attempted to exterminate the Russian settlers. In all areas, they challenged the right of immigrant Russians to rule. As General Sandetskii, the commander of the Kazan' Military District responsible for sending both the initial detachments of Cossacks and the later expeditionary force to the region, explained: "Gathered together in large crowds numbering in the thousands of people, having elected khans for themselves, having earlier secured reserves of food for themselves, having concerned themselves with the organization of the crowd and having armed it, the Kirgiz began a mutinous movement against the Russian People's right to rule and in general against Russian culture."[36] In November, one general in the Turgai region ruefully reported that virtually the entire population was aligned against the relatively modest Russian forces in the region. "There is no doubt," he wrote, "that it will take at least one or two years to pacify the region."[37]

Thus, though the rebellion began with a confusion of declarations of loyalty, sullen acquiescence, flight to the steppe, and uncoordinated revolts, it coalesced

---

[34] "Protokol nachal'nika Akmolinskogo uezda A. S. Veretennikova s pokazaniiami 'pochetnogo' kazakha N. Saganaeva o bezuspeshnosti ego popytok sklonit' naselenie Karabulakskoi volosti vypolnit' ukaz o mobilizatsii na tylovye raboty," 7 August 1916, in Kozybaev, ed., 1: 30.

[35] Kuropatkin diary, 8 September 1916, in Galuzo ed., "Vosstanie 1916 g. v Srednei Azii," 53.

[36] Sandetskii telegram, l. 5ob. Capitalization in original.

[37] Telegram of General Lavrent'ev attached in report of the combat division of the Kazan' Military District to the chief of the General Staff in Petrograd, November 1916, RGVIA f. 1720, op. 2, d. 195, l. 10.

into something much larger by August. At this stage, Russian expeditionary forces marched in and engaged in a typical colonial war, with small numbers of well-armed European troops able to hold key positions and to disperse rebel formations at important moments. Take, for instance, the battle for Kozhekul', a village about seventy kilometers from the town of Irgiz. The residents of Kozhekul' had begun threatening the wealthy and powerful Kazakhs in their midst, and a Kazakh militia had coalesced to give weight to those threats. A unit of fifty Cossacks under the leadership of Captain Urzhuntsev arrived in the village on 19 October/1 November 1916, where they found a crowd of 2500 people fronted by 600 men armed with pikes, sabers, guns, axes, and bludgeons. The Cossacks withdrew, while fighting, to the top of the nearest hill where, despite being surrounded, they fought for more than two hours from a strong position. The Kazakhs eventually retreated after taking heavy casualties. Cossack officers gleefully recounted tales of bloody valor in which men, shot off their horses, charged their enemies on foot, steel flashing, until they "cut the head off of a fanatic with a single strong blow of their saber."[38]

Throughout Central Asia, Russian troops successfully suppressed the rebellion, finishing the job with an orgy of destruction in the Issyk-Kul region. There, Kyrgyz cavalry detachments had launched a series of devastating attacks on Russian settlements beginning in August. The Kyrgyz offensive was not only intended to prevent conscription in the area but was also "in a real sense a settling of accounts with colonists at whose hands they and their clans had suffered."[39] The Kyrgyz murdered the Russian inhabitants and put their villages to the torch, reinforcing the Orientalist preconceptions of Russian military commanders that these were Asian barbarians and Islamic fanatics, preconceptions that were only strengthened by the demonstrative and grisly treatment of Russians who had fallen into rebel hands throughout the summer.[40] The Russian expeditionary forces, however, engaged in the very same practices.[41] In August, commanders reported with satisfaction that one rebellious region had been subdued: "Cornet Aleksandrov with his [Cossack] hundred entered the steppe on 10 [/23]August . . . all the people in three villages (*aula*) were destroyed, the nomad camp was burned, the livestock was driven away, on the twelfth the remaining people in the district surrendered and gave us hostages."[42] Similar scenes played out throughout Central Asia, as troops burned villages, executed suspected rebels, drove encampments across barren mountains into China, and then armed Russian settlers, who took their full measure of revenge for the events of the preceding months. Internal military documents make clear that the goal was to "punish the rebels" and to "terrorize the population."[43] Those goals

---

[38] Report from the Ataman of the Orenburg Cossack Host to the commander of the Kazan' Military District, 29 October 1916, f. 1720, op. 2, d. 194, ll. 97–98.

[39] Brower, 161.   [40] Sandetskii telegram, l. 8.

[41] On these measures see G. Sapargaliev, *Karatel'naia politika tsarizma v Kazakhstane, 1905–1917 gg.* (Alma-Ata: Nauka, 1966), 297–372.

[42] Cited in Sapargaliev, 298.

[43] Draft report in files of commander of Kazan' Military District, n.d., RGVIA, f. 1720, op. 2, d. 195, l. 19.

were met, as later investigations revealed that "in the end, Russian cruelty was equal to that of the Kirgiz."[44] General Kuropatkin, who led the army's response, admitted in his diary that many complaints about Russian atrocities were "justified," though he hoped that the brutal attacks were "exceptions."[45] Unfortunately, they were not, as he had occasion to learn during his further travels, when he arrived in villages with hundreds of "unarmed, innocent Kirgiz" corpses.[46] This had become both an ethnic war and a war about the possibility of continuing imperial rule. The tsarist state had won the initial battle, but at huge cost and with little benefit. Only about 100,000 workers were successfully mobilized, far less than the army had requested or needed. Those workers, as predicted, fell victim to disease at a high rate, leading many to be hospitalized and permanently demobilized as a result.[47] After the February Revolution, the Provisional Government quietly admitted failure, rescinding martial law in the Turgai region on 26 April/9 May 1917 and ordering the return of requisitioned workers to their homeland on 5/18 May.[48]

EMPIRE AND THE FINAL CRISIS OF THE STATE DUMA

The effects of the rebellion were not limited to Central Asia, where violent decolonization continued despite the success of Russian punitive expeditions. The snapping of the imperial threads became an important political issue in the metropole as well. As early as August, outraged legislators led by the socialist Aleksandr Kerenskii went on a fact-finding mission to Tashkent, Bukhara, Samarkand, and Andijan. The rebellion grabbed Kerenskii's interest for a number of reasons. He had grown up in Tashkent, living there from the time he was eight years old until he left for university. His brother worked as a prosecutor in the city.[49] Just as importantly, Kerenskii had a well-deserved reputation as a scold to the military hierarchy. When soldiers had complaints, they frequently addressed their letters to Kerenskii, and he took to reading them aloud on the floor of the Duma.[50]

The State Duma had been licking its wounds ever since its summary dispersal in September 1915. It reconvened in February 1916 and worked continuously through to 20 June/3 July 1916 before taking a recess. The summer and fall of 1916 were difficult for Petrograd politicians. This was the era of "ministerial leapfrog," when the government churned constantly under the pressures of war

---

[44] Cited in Brower, 162.

[45] Kuropatkin diary, 3 September 1916, in Galuzo ed., "Vosstanie 1916 g. v Srednei Azii," 50.

[46] Kuropatkin diary, 12 October 1916, in Galuzo ed., "Vosstanie 1916 g. v Srednei Azii," 59.

[47] Order of the chief of the Sanitary Division of Armies on the Northern Front, 28 December 1916, LVVA f. 3, op. 5, d. 22, l. 71–71ob.

[48] Journal of the meeting of the Provisional Government, 26 April 1917, in V. A. Kozlov and S. V. Mironenko, eds., *Arkhiv noveishei istorii Rossii* (Moscow: Rosspen, 2001), 7: 355; Journal of the meeting of the Provisional Government, 5 May 1917, in Kozlov and Mironenko, eds., *Arkhiv noveishei istorii Rossii*, 8: 21.

[49] Vladimir Fediuk, *Kerenskii* (Moscow: Molodaia gvardiia, 2009), 69.

[50] Speech of Deputy Kerenskii (Saratov) at closed meeting of State Duma, 19 August 1915, RGIA f. 1278, op. 5, d. 216, l. 24.

and of the bad advice of Grigorii Rasputin and the empress.[51] As the country suffered under the impact of the military, economic, social, and ethnic struggles described earlier, the incompetence and arrogance of the tsar's ministers became increasingly unbearable. In October, the budget commission of the Duma met and unanimously agreed that the food supply situation was reaching a crisis point. They asked the prime minister, Boris Shtiurmer, to come before them to explain his position and the steps he intended to take to resolve the economic malaise. He refused. On 23 October/5 November 1916, Germany and Austria issued the "Two Emperors' Manifesto," which promised the creation of a self-governing Polish Kingdom out of the former Russian lands, with borders and mechanisms of rule to be determined after the war. Shtiurmer's government was silent on the matter in the final week of October.[52]

Thus all of the issues that were tearing Russia apart came together in early November on the floor of the Duma. On the very first day of the session, the Kadet leader Pavel Miliukov delivered a shocking speech in which he listed the failures of the government. Miliukov then leveled the incendiary charge that Shtiurmer and his recently arrested private secretary Ivan Manasevich-Manuilov had taken bribes, and he linked that dirty money darkly to the German government. At the end of the speech, Miliukov asked acidly, "Is this stupidity, or is this treason?" Newspapers rushed to cover the scandal, only to be censored overnight, leaving large white blanks on the front pages of their issues. Word of Miliukov's speech nevertheless spread quickly, with copies of the text making the rounds in the provinces in an early version of *samizdat*.[53] Vasilii Maklakov soon followed with an even more revolutionary oration on 3/16 November. Miliukov had hedged his bets, leaving the door open for the possibility that the problem with the government was stupidity, not treason, and limiting his call for action to the dismissal of the hated Shtiurmer. Maklakov went much further. He was, we should recall, the cautious Kadet who had written so poignantly about the "tragic situation" faced by the opposition when the tsar had disbanded the Duma in 1915. At that time, a year earlier, Maklakov had argued that it was too dangerous for oppositionists to try to run the country. Now, in November 1916, he believed that the country was on the verge of a demoralizing panic produced by the catastrophic leadership of the country. Everyone had to choose between their loyalty to the monarch and their love of Russia. It was now as impossible to do both as it was to choose both "God and Mammon." The "Stupidity or Treason" and "God or Mammon" speeches galvanized the political class in Petrograd and focused the attention of

---

[51] W. Bruce Lincoln, *Passage Through Armageddon: The Russians in War and Revolution, 1914–1918* (New York: Simon and Schuster, 1986), 286–90.

[52] Piotr S. Wandycz, *The Lands of Partitioned Poland, 1795–1918* (Seattle: University of Washington Press, 1974), 351–2. The government officially protested on 2/15 November, a day after the Duma opened.

[53] Irina Belova, *Pervaia mirovaia voina i rossiiskaia provintsiia, 1914-fevral' 1917 g.* (Moscow: AIRO-XXI, 2011), 170. "Samizdat" or "self-publishing" was a key practice of the oppositional intelligentsia in the Soviet period. They evaded censorship by creating a limited number of manuscripts of their works and having them passed hand to hand between members of their intellectual and political circles.

contemporaries and later historians on the "crisis of the elites" that would develop further with the assassination of Rasputin on the night of 16–17/29–30 December 1916 and would culminate with the February Revolution.[54]

Lost amidst these dramatic events was the rising tide of indictments of imperialism. Indeed, the first speech at the first session of the reconvened Duma on 1/14 November 1916 was delivered not by Miliukov, but by Jan Harusewicz, one of the few remaining Polish nationalists left in the Fourth Duma. Harusewicz urged his colleagues not to accept the new partition of Polish lands produced by the German occupation regime and called on them to fulfill the promise made by Grand Duke Nikolai Nikolaevich in 1914 to use Russian power to establish an independent Polish state. He was outraged by the "fateful silence of the government" on the issue and worried that it would tip sentiment in Poland even closer to Germany. Instead, he urged the government and his colleagues to work towards the "unification of all Polish lands and the restoration of a free Poland."[55] Deputies from Russian areas soon seconded his call, saying that they could not ignore the fate of the Polish people in these trying times.[56] Kerenskii, for his part, also noted the shame of Shtiurmer's Polish policy, the string of broken promises to Finland, and the failure of the government to support small nationalities. What, he asked, should the "masses of Armenians, Lithuanians, and Ukrainians" think, other than that the Russian Empire would continue to be a state run by the Russian people, the Russian government, and the Russian nation?[57]

Despite the sharply reduced representation from non-Russian areas in the Fourth Duma, others joined Harusewicz in his outrage. Later on the first day, well before Miliukov's speech, Nikolai Chkheidze, a Menshevik from Georgia, made imperial questions central to a critique leveled as much at liberals in the Duma as at the government itself. "You believed, gentlemen," he intoned, "and still believe that the basic idea of this war is its liberationist character. But you well know, gentlemen, what this liberation has brought to Belgium, Montenegro, and Serbia, what it is now bringing to Romania and what it will bring to Greece." Miliukov, he recalled, wanted to blame all this on the conscience of Germany, "but what liberation did you gentlemen bring to Galicia, when you were the victors? . . . And what did the liberation of Armenia bring? How many Turkish Armenians remain among the living?" Chkheidze went on to list more offenses: the closing of Ukrainian enlightenment organizations that had existed since Stolypin's time, the repression of Metropolitan Andrey Sheptytsky, the de facto abolition of the Finnish parliament (Sejm), and the artful sidestepping of the question of whether

---

[54] I discuss some of these issues further in Joshua Sanborn, "Liberals and Bureaucrats at War," *Kritika: Explorations in Russian and Eurasian History* 8, no. 1 (Winter 2007): 141–62.

[55] Speech of Deputy Garusevich (Lomzha) in meeting of State Duma, 1 November 1916, in V. D. Karpovich, ed., *Gosudarstvennaia Duma, 1906–1917: stenograficheskie otchety*, 4 vols. (Moscow: Pravovaia kul'tura, 1995), 4: 31–2.

[56] Speech of Deputy Shidlovskii-1 (Voronezh) in meeting of State Duma, 1 November 1916, in Karpovich, ed., 33.

[57] Speech of Deputy Kerenskii (Saratov), in meeting of State Duma, 1 November 1916, in Karpovich, ed., 41.

a future Poland would be autonomous or independent. "You, gentlemen, must have the civic courage to say that for all this time the Poles have been humiliated and that you supported this humiliation."[58] After highlighting the abuses taken by Russian peasants and workers as well, he warned that "the war, as it developed, raised all the elements of future conflicts, in comparison to which, perhaps, the most evil and horrible conflicts of today will seem like idylls."[59] As the Duma sessions proceeded, they grew increasingly raucous, with multiple deputies, including Kerenskii, being excluded from future sessions for violation of internal order. Many of these sanctioned deputies, such as Chkheidze (Georgia), Chkhenkeli (Georgia), Dziubinskii (Siberia), and Keinis (Lithuania), were from the periphery of the empire.

The Kadet deputy Mamed Iusif Dzhafarov (the only Muslim representative from the South Caucasus in the Fourth Duma) was the first to link imperial questions, the political questions related to the incompetence and hostility of the autocracy, and the Central Asian uprising. On 3/16 November, Dzhafarov, speaking in the name of the Muslim fraction, reminded his fellow deputies that the best example of the utter failure of the "bureaucratic mechanism" was the tragic and foolish decision to requisition *inorodtsy* for trench work. Only a state utterly unaware of realities on the ground and the social contract that existed in these regions could have taken this step so heedlessly. It was one of many reasons that the political system needed to be expanded, so that at the end of the day, "through the bloody fog of military hatred, we can open our eyes to the light of a fraternal life of many peoples." All minority ethnic groups, including Muslims, had to be given the right to live their own lives in freedom.[60]

At the very end of these dynamic sessions, Kerenskii and Dzhafarov presented their reports on the Central Asian uprising. Kerenskii started his speech by noting that the uprising did not only touch "far-off borderlands," but also the difficult disagreements that deputies were dealing with on "all questions of state life in Russia."[61] He then quickly moved to the question of the legality of the order. Given the scale of the rebellion, it was perhaps surprising that he would spend many minutes discussing fine-grained details about the legal status of the edict that called *inorodtsy* to labor service. He had many complaints: new state burdens were not legally supposed to be implemented by emergency decree, wartime exemptions to this rule were supposed to be limited to the front zones, the Ministry of Internal Affairs and the Ministry of War promised in point two of the edict to issue guidelines for the draft but never did, and so forth. At core, however, these legal complaints were essentially constitutional. Kerenskii was perturbed by the wanton violation of the Fundamental Laws, which he clearly took to be a constitutional constraint upon the actions of the tsar and his bureaucracy, even if the

---

[58] Speech of Deputy Chkheidze (Tiflis) in meeting of State Duma, 1 November 1916, in Karpovich, ed., 35.

[59] Karpovich, ed., 36.

[60] Speech of Deputy Dzhafarov (Baku) in meeting of State Duma, 3 November 1916, in Karpovich, ed., 56.

[61] Speech of Deputy Kerenskii (Saratov) to closed session of State Duma, 13 December 1916, in Kozybaev, ed., 164.

tsar himself gave no evidence of having considered these legal questions before issuing the decree.

His critique of the bureaucracy developed further due to the particular setting of the revolt. "After all, gentlemen," he argued, "Turkestan and the Kazakh steppe regions—they are not Tula or Tambov province. We need to look at them as the English or the French look at their colonies. This is a large world with its own particular cultural, economic, and political content."[62] The failure of the metropole to come to terms with the differences between Tula and Turgai meant that politicians were stumbling about violently, blindly, and illegally, with highly destructive results. "The reason for everything that occurred in Turkestan lies exclusively with the central government, which issued and implemented an illegal order in an illegal way while violating all the elementary demands of law and justice."[63]

Nor did Kerenskii stop with the violations of domestic law. He then moved, tellingly, to the questions of atrocity and civilization. The actions of the administration, he charged, had "thrown our [Russian] culture into the filth in the eyes of the masses, the local native masses," largely through a campaign of "planned and systematic terror unacceptable not only in a cultured European state, but also in any sort of eastern despotism." It would be very difficult for Russians "to speak now about Turkish atrocities in Armenia, very difficult to talk about German atrocities in Belgium, given that what happened in the mountains of Semirechie has never been seen before."[64] He returned to the theme of atrocity and civilization several more times in his speech before concluding, in a startling but logical fashion, with a call to fundamentally re-envision imperial rule. "At present, gentlemen, a great responsibility lies on us, on Russian society (*obshchestvennost'*), not only toward our own people, but also toward the mass of foreign peoples and nationalities that the heavy chain of Russian statehood has welded together with us." The revolt "places before us new colossal questions, questions of a new form of governing our borderlands, in particular Turkestan."[65] In this way, the questions of atrocity and civilization, deployed to strong effect as a mobilizing theme of the war against the Central Powers, were now turned against the Russian state itself in its moment of crisis. Tsarist power was under attack not only because of the way it treated Russian social elites, but also because its strategies of imperial governance disqualified it as a truly civilized state. The empire was reaching that critical moment in the process of decolonization when the metropole cracks along the same fissures that divide the periphery.

THE END OF THE DYNASTY

On New Year's Day 1916, journalists had despaired of the set of wartime "problems" that the empire faced and likened the position of the Russian people to

[62] Kozybaev, ed., 167. [63] Kozybaev, ed., 170.

[64] Kozybaev, ed., 177–8. [65] Kozybaev, ed., 187.

pinballs bouncing around a table. The crises of 1916 had turned this disorientation into principled fury. By New Year's Day 1917, the talk was of regime change. Soldiers at the front eagerly read newspapers describing the political crisis in the capital, citing phrases from Duma deputies and latching on to rumors of peace with special attention.[66] General Brusilov noted at the time that enlisted men and commanders alike were focused on Petrograd rather than on the Germans, and he turned his own attention back to the capital, connecting with important Petrograd politicians and making clear his sympathy for drastic action.[67] Ominously, a string of soldier mutinies that had begun late in 1916 continued into January the next year, as enlisted men, deprived of leave and freezing in the trenches, refused to move to the forward lines in several locations.[68] The political elite, for its part, was consumed with the idea of a palace rebellion. A blizzard of rumors and plans swirled around the winter capital. Liberals anxiously plotted with generals and spoke openly to foreign military attachés of the prospect of a coup.[69] Conspiracies at Stavka had been bubbling since the Lake Narach disaster in 1916, when the Quartermaster General M. S. Pustovoitenko confided to his assistants that General Alekseev was being considered as a possible military dictator.[70] In December, Prince L'vov convinced A. I. Khatisov, the mayor of Tiflis, to invite Grand Duke Nikolai Nikolaevich, the former supreme commander, to take power from his nephew.[71] The royal family itself, upset that Nicholas had sent Grand Duke Dmitrii Pavlovich into exile in Persia for his role in the murder of Rasputin, discussed revenge at the imperial yacht club. At the front, a group of well-heeled officers sat down to toast the new year, when one of them raised his glass and exclaimed "To a free Russia, gentlemen!" Then, Fedor Stepun recalled, "something strange happened, something which would have been impossible a year before: the revolutionary words of a volunteer officer were drowned out by the loud applause of all the assembled officers."[72]

Yet none of these patriots got very far in his plans. Whatever others were saying about Alekseev, he remained cautious in both his counsel and his actions. He had suggested the possibility of a military dictator subordinate to the tsar in June, but

---

[66] "Doklad o nastroenii voisk i naseleniia po dannym otchetov voennykh tsenzorov raiona 1-i armii za Noiabr' mesiats 1916 goda," RGVIA f. 2106, op. 1, d. 1006 (part two), ll. 1009–1010ob.

[67] Semion Lyandres, *The Fall of Tsarism: Untold Stories of the February 1917 Revolution* (Oxford: Oxford University Press, 2013), 251.

[68] Pol Simmons [Paul Simmons], "Anatomiia bunta: volneniia v 223-m pekhotnom Odoevskom polku nakanune Fevral'skoi revoliutsii," *Russkii sbornik* 11 (2012): 232–54.

[69] V. V. Galin, *Voina i revoliutsiia* (Moscow: Algoritm, 2004), 80. An extensive selection of these rumors of conspiracy can be found in the outraged collection of a diehard monarchist written around 1950 and published in 1970 in New York. Viktor Kobylin, *Imperator Nikolai II i zagovor generalov* (Moscow: Veche, 2008 [1970]).

[70] Mikhail Konstantinovich Lemke, *250 dnei v tsarskoi stavke: vospominaniia, memuary,* 2 vols. (Minsk: Kharvest, 2003), 2: 485–7.

[71] Iu. N. Danilov, *Velikii kniaz' Nikolai Nikolaevich* (Paris: Navarre, 1930), 314–18. This story has been repeated many times, normally using Danilov as a source. Danilov notes that the news first came to light in an article in the newspaper *Poslednie novosti,* but insists on its accuracy, saying that "before including it in my book, I carefully verified the facts presented in the story by questioning people involved in it, people who deserve full trust" (316).

[72] Fedor Stepun, *Byvshee i nesbyvsheesia,* 2nd ed. (St. Petersburg: Aleteiia, 2000), 306.

there is no clear evidence that he ever actively participated in serious discussions about supplanting the tsar prior to the February Revolution. Grand Duke Nikolai Nikolaevich thought for a couple of days before refusing to join L'vov's coup plans, citing the inability of soldiers, as representatives of the Russian people, to understand complex political machinations at the top of the imperial system.[73] Liberals got little traction, though a large coup plot led by A. I. Guchkov was supposed to be executed the next time the tsar was in the capital, in early March, 1917.[74] Soldiers and officers continued to man the trenches, squabbling with each other on occasion.[75] If they had all been pushed into sympathy with regime change, none were bold or desperate enough to act decisively. As the revolutionary Lev Trotskii put it dismissively, the coup planners never got much beyond "patriotic sighs over wine and cigars."[76]

The same was not true of women activists in Petrograd, who planned and executed several marches in the capital city on International Women's Day (23 February/8 March). Goods shortages provided the necessary catalyst for the demonstrations. As elsewhere in the empire, the spread of the war to the interior of the country during the Great Retreat significantly disrupted consumption in Petrograd. The question of how and why scarcity and high prices developed to dangerous degrees in 1916 and 1917 is a fairly complicated one. Harvests were weaker in 1916 than in the previous war years, but not catastrophically so. The larger problem was the huge wartime shift of food producers to food consumers, most notably in the form of millions of peasant soldiers and peasant men and women who moved to work in urban factories, but also in the millions of farmers from the western borderlands who fled as refugees to northern parts of the empire where good soil was scarce. Another issue was the intense pressure on the transportation system that real or imagined military needs produced. At the end of the day, these were serious but manageable problems. Much larger food crises in recent memory had been survived by the regime (in 1891 and 1902, for instance). But the tsarist government and military high command were not up to the task of dealing effectively with economic problems over the course of the war. As we have seen, scapegoating merchants as "speculators" served political purposes but only made the underlying issues worse. An attempt late in the day, in November 1916, to institute noncoercive requisitions of grain by the Ministry of Agriculture was supposed to bear fruit by the summer of 1917, but it was already plainly failing by February. In sum, as Peter Gatrell argues, "tsarist food supply policies were inept and contributed to a growing perception of official incompetence."[77]

---

[73] Danilov, 318.   [74] Lyandres, 252.

[75] See, for instance, the complaint of some enlisted men that their officers did not deserve the better rations they received. Enlisted men of the 39th Infantry Division of the I Army Corps, Petition to Grand Duke Nikolai Nikolaevich, 29 January 1917, RGVIA f. 2294, op. 1, d. 140, l. 6. The response of the corps commander—that soldiers were wrong because his officers sometimes didn't get fresh meat!—foreshadowed the conflicts of the year to come (l. 9–9ob).

[76] Leon Trotsky, *History of the Russian Revolution*, trans. Max Eastman, 3 vols. (London: Sphere, 1967 [1932–1933]), 1: 84.

[77] The best short analysis of this topic is Peter Gatrell's chapter on food supply in his *Russia's First World War: A Social and Economic History* (Harlow: Pearson Longman, 2005), 154–75, here at 170. See his chapter bibliography for the key monographs on the subject.

At the ground level, this incompetence was evident and devastating. One landowner in Saratov province wrote a terse telegram in February 1917 that encapsulated the problems succinctly: "The livestock are dying, there is no one transporting food, there are no workers and few POWs, they are working badly, coercive measures are not being taken, the situation is critical."[78] Bread lines began appearing in northern cities in the autumn of 1915, when half of the cities in Russia experienced bread shortages and 75 percent had deficits of produce.[79] The situation dramatically worsened over time. In late 1916, some had to sleep in those lines overnight. In early 1917, women spent nearly forty hours per week standing in queues for various types of goods.[80] Those goods were rising rapidly in price, as the political police (the Okhrana) noted in a report in early February. Bread cost 15 percent more than it had even in mid-December of the previous year, potatoes cost 25 percent more, milk cost 40 percent more, and shoes 30 percent more.[81] Over the course of the war, price increases had been crippling. In a three-year period from April 1914 to April 1917 in Kaluga, sugar had increased in price by more than 150 percent, firewood by nearly 300 percent, and meat by more than 500 percent. The increase in the price of wood, combined with the influx of refugees and economic migrants, led to an increase in housing prices, which also jumped up by more than 300 percent.[82] Since women in the urban working class fully experienced the "double burden" of full-time wage labor combined with full-time household chores that their Soviet sisters would later lament, this added pressure on their time was at first heavily taxing and then completely unbearable. Male workers and socialist leaders consistently underestimated their dire situation. The final straw came in mid-February 1917, when city authorities, alarmed by a sudden reduction in rye deliveries to the city, decided to implement rationing in early March. This decision quickly hit the newspapers and led to panic and hoarding. Women across the capital, in different settings and in different social classes, began planning their protest. Some women factory workers in the Vyborg district called for strikes.[83] Larger groups of women in the more bourgeois districts of town led a large march on the city's main Nevskii Prospekt, with few women workers present.[84]

For the most part, the citizens who organized these protests did not do so under the direction of any of the major socialist parties. Written accounts of their activism are apparently absent. They were also women. As a result, some contemporaries

[78] Doctor Romanov (landowner in Novouzensk uezd [Saratov province]), Telegram to Minister of Agriculture, copy to Duma member Aleksandr Novikov, 25 February 1917, GARF f. 1791, op. 2, d. 544, l. 4. The telegram in Russian is even more clipped and urgent: "скот гибнет корме возить никому рабочих нет пленных мало работают плохо принудительных мер не принимается положение критическое."

[79] Belova, 68.

[80] Orlando Figes, *A People's Tragedy: The Russian Revolution, 1891–1924* (London: Pimlico, 1996), 299–300.

[81] Tsuyoshi Hasegawa, *The February Revolution: Petrograd, 1917* (Seattle and London: University of Washington Press, 1981), 200.

[82] Belova, 66, 76.

[83] Michael Melancon, "Rethinking Russia's February Revolution: Anonymous Spontaneity or Socialist Agency?" *Carl Beck Papers in Russian and East European Studies*, no. 1408 (2000): 17.

[84] Figes, 308.

(especially socialist party members) declared that the marches on 23 February/8 March were "spontaneous" rather than "conscious," economic rather than political, riotous rather than revolutionary. Generations of historians both in the Soviet Union and abroad followed their lead.[85] The idea that food protests were non-political would have confounded many tsarist officials at the time, who knew only too well that food was the top political issue of the day in February 1917. The police had issued a devastating report early in the month that made clear the relationship between hunger and revolution, with one agent commenting:

> Resentment is felt worse in large families, where children are starving in the most literal sense of the word, and where no other words are heard except, "Peace, immediate peace, peace at all costs." And these mothers, exhausted from standing endlessly at the tail of queues, and having suffered so much in watching their half-starving and sick children, are perhaps much closer to a revolution than Messrs. Miliukov, Rodichev and Co., and of course, they are much more dangerous . . . [86]

Miliukov, Rodichev, and other liberals in the Duma were also aware of this fact. Indeed, as late as the second day of the revolution, on 24 February/9 March, the Duma spent nearly its entire time in session debating food distribution and food supply issues.[87] By the time they stopped debating the revolutionary threat posed by shortages, the revolution was an accomplished fact, right under their noses. Around the empire, officials made clear that they feared a revolution of consumers as much as a revolution of producers.[88]

The initial marches led by women on 23 February/8 March in Petrograd were supported by significant numbers of sympathizers. On the first day, several factories came out (or were called out) on strike. The number of people in the street grew on the second day, even as scattered acts of violence and repression took place. On 25 February/10 March, a general strike crippled the city and unleashed torrents of people into public spaces. Ominously, Cossacks and garrison soldiers sometimes refused to obey the instructions of civilian police and even fought skirmishes with them. Authorities resolved on the evening of 25 February/10 March to take a more aggressive stance by shooting protestors and restoring order to the capital. General S. S. Khabalov, the military commander of the city, assured the Council of Ministers and the tsar at Stavka that 30,000 soldiers would launch an offensive the next day against any rebels who ignored his orders to clear the streets and return to work.[89]

This would be the moment of truth for the revolution. "There is no doubt," Trotskii wrote in reference to the events of 26 February/11 March and 27 February/

---

[85] A brief historiography of this discussion can be found in Melancon, 1–9.

[86] Cited in Hasegawa, *The February Revolution*, 201.

[87] Hasegawa, *The February Revolution*, 242.

[88] See, for instance, the instructions by the Kiev province governor to Kiev police to carefully watch all spots where "any type of food products are sold" for possible "expression of unhappiness by the population." Secret addendum to order of Kiev City Police, 1 March 1917, TsDIAK f. 274, op. 4, d. 639, l. 1.

[89] Hasegawa, *The February Revolution*, 265.

12 March, "that the fate of every revolution at a certain point is decided by a break in the disposition of the army."[90] For most of 26 February/11 March, the army's disposition remained the same. The police implemented Khabalov's orders, and army units assisted them. Soldiers fired into the crowd, killing dozens and sending demonstrators fleeing down side streets. Still, all was not well in the barracks. Over the previous three days, soldiers had frequently (though not always) stood to the side during the protests and police actions. On 26 February/11 March, commanders simultaneously sought to isolate them from the revolutionary infection and to use them more aggressively to intervene. The first unit to crack under this contradiction was the Pavlovskii Regiment. The training detachment of the Pavlovskiis took part in shooting demonstrators on Nevskii Prospekt that day, but when the remainder of the unit learned that their compatriots had taken the side of the police, they stormed the munitions stores and hit the streets to confront their fellow men. Loyal troops stopped and arrested the mutineers. The next day, however, repeated entreaties from the crowds and the new leaders of the revolution convinced soldiers in several city garrisons to revolt. By the end of the day, the tsar's writ was no longer valid in his own capital.

The armed forces played the central role in the revolution beyond the street battles in Petrograd. The initial response of the tsar and Stavka was to send troops from the front to put down the rebellion. General Ivanov, the commander of the Northern Front, was assigned two infantry regiments and two cavalry regiments from the "strongest and most reliable units" on his front to accomplish the task on the evening of 27 February/12 March, and he decamped immediately with three loyal companies of men to accompany his train. Alekseev ordered a similar number of men to be detached from the Western Front at the same time.[91] The tsar, against advice, also boarded a train to the capital, both to be with his increasingly isolated family at Tsarskoe Selo and to be closer to the unfolding events.[92] As these trains rolled toward Petrograd, new reports made clear to Alekseev for the first time the scale and seriousness of the events in the capital. He opened tentative negotiations regarding possible political solutions with members of the liberal political elite, but events always outstripped the plans. At first, Alekseev pledged to lobby the tsar to allow a "responsible" ministry. By the time these garbled discussions had concluded, it was already clear that abdication in favor of Tsarevich Aleksei was necessary. By the time abdication was accepted, the monarchy itself had been rendered untenable by events. To its credit, the high command came to realize that a military invasion of Petrograd would only make things worse. Ivanov, who had been forced to withdraw his small contingent of men from Tsarskoe Selo in haste under pressure from mutinous soldiers, quietly began ordering the larger group of reinforcements to return to the front on the evening of 1/14 March. General Ruzskii soon made the same decision regarding the troops from the

[90] Trotsky, 1: 126.   [91] Hasegawa, *The February Revolution*, 461–2.
[92] Vera Alekseeva-Borel', *Sorok let v riadakh russkoi imperatorskoi armii: M. V. Alekseev* (St. Petersburg: Bel'veder, 2000), 475–6.

Western Front.[93] By the morning of 2/15 March, the end was evident to Alekseev as well. He worked quickly over the course of a single morning to acquire the support of all his front commanders in requesting Nicholas to step down. Nicholas agreed at 3 p.m. and signed the abdication decree at 11 p.m. that evening. Urban women had begun the revolution, and socialist activists had maintained and extended it, but the decisive moments came with the revolt of the garrisons on the streets of Petrograd and the quiet coup at Stavka. The Romanov dynasty had survived three centuries thanks in part to its ability to effectively control its armed forces. The war destroyed the bond between army and monarch. When revolution came, the withdrawal of military support for the throne brought the whole system crashing down.

REVOLUTION IN THE STATE,
REVOLUTION IN THE ARMY

Imperial state power, authority, and legitimacy had been declining rapidly over the course of the war. On 2/15 March 1917, this decline crossed the point of no return. The failing state looked on the verge of turning into a failed state. Elites at the top were aware of this danger and moved quickly to fill the center of the imperial order with a governmental structure. The Temporary Committee of the Duma gave way to a new "Provisional Government" headed by Prince L'vov, the head of the Union of Zemstvos. New ministers were appointed, including Aleksandr Guchkov as the Minister of War. Continuity in the army was assured by appointing General Alekseev as commander-in-chief. But a state on paper and a functioning state were two different things. Notably, the Provisional Government lacked two core attributes of a state: a monopoly on legitimate violence and legitimacy as such.[94] Some of this legitimacy (over violence and more broadly) was captured by the Petrograd Soviet, a council of worker (and eventually soldier) delegates that first appeared in the Revolution of 1905 and re-emerged with vigor in the revolutionary days of 1917. Thus, there was institutional "dual power" at the top from the moment that Nicholas abdicated. But this duality obscured a deeper duality of power: "[t]he essential nature of dual power was not the conflict between the Duma Committee and the Executive Committee of the Petrograd Soviet, as it has been hitherto argued, but rather the conflict between the authority emanating from the Duma Committee and the self-government established by the insurgents in the form of the workers' militia and the soldiers committees."[95] At the most basic level, the connection between central power and local authority had been severed. First Petrograd, and then the country at large, both decentralized and became more democratic, as local actors grappled with local problems using local institutions and resources. "Something fundamental took place during the February Revolution,"

---

[93] Hasegawa, *The February Revolution*, 478–9.
[94] Max Weber, *Sociological Writings*, ed. Wolf Heydebrand (New York: Continuum, 1994), 24.
[95] Hasegawa, *The February Revolution*, 408.

observes Tsuyoshi Hasegawa, "the locus of power had filtered down to the lowest level of administrative organizations."[96]

Nowhere was this pattern of radical decentralization more evident and startling than in the institutions of "legitimate violence" themselves. Liberal elites and military officials, of course, tried from the very moment the revolution began to keep the forces of order functioning as usual. This strategy failed miserably. Soldiers rebelled, sailors mutinied, and the police fled quickly, frequently in disguise. The Soviet was significantly more enthusiastic about the collapse of the government's monopoly on legitimate violence, welcoming the military revolt and cheering the end of the police. Nevertheless, Soviet leaders also wanted to reharness the mobs of men with guns in the capital's streets, and they worked together with the Provisional Government to do so in the early flush of revolutionary success. But the crowds in Petrograd, and then at the front in the empire at large, were not inclined to shoulder the yoke again quite so soon. Political forces long submerged, repressed, and ignored suddenly asserted themselves in dramatic ways. Much of the early story of the revolution consists of the shock and missteps of the elite oppositionists in the face of these surprising and unwelcome challenges.

The restoration of public order was the first and most pressing task of the new authorities. By 28 February/13 March, order in the capital had completely broken down. Police were on the run, which meant good things for the revolution, but it also meant good things for felons. New criminal elements emerged at the same time that convicts were freed from city jails along with political prisoners. These men then took the lead in sacking and burning courts and police stations. Several of them, when arrested for new crimes later in the summer, were found to have kept the case files they had pinched the previous winter.[97] Violent crimes and crimes against property soared. Efforts by various parties to discipline violence in these critical days would have lasting effects. The new leadership in both the Soviet and the new Provisional Government wanted to regain control of the streets in order to end the armed uprising and to contain criminality. Proposals to have citizens surrender their arms to the city government went nowhere. Soldiers, workers, and many other Petrograders besides preferred to prevent a counterrevolution by starving the authorities of guns and by organizing local brigades to patrol the streets and dispense summary justice where necessary. The idea of a grass-roots militia struck a chord with many socialists and democrats for ideological reasons, but there is little doubt that the impetus for creating them came from worried citizens in the chaos of the revolution. On 27 February/12 March, organizations began to form in some Petrograd districts to provide public order, and many more would follow on 28 February/13 March. While some of these militias aligned with the Soviet and readied themselves to fight counterrevolution as well as crime, the majority of these

[96] Tsuyoshi Hasegawa, "*Gosudarstvennost', Obshchestvennost',* and *Klassovost'*: Crime, Police, and the State in the Russian Revolution in Petrograd," *Canadian-American Slavic Studies* 35, nos 2–3 (2001): 162.

[97] V. B. Aksenov, "Militsiia i gorodskie sloi v period revoliutsionnogo krizisa 1917 goda: problemy legitimnosti," *Voprosy istorii* no. 8 (2001): 38.

groups simply wanted to establish order. There were three basic types of militia in Petrograd after the revolution: town militias formed by the City Duma, worker militias sanctioned by the Soviet, and student militias created by the Committee of Military-Technical Assistance.[98] They not only intended to deter law-breaking, but they also hoped to stem the epidemic of self-authorized arrests that began in those revolutionary days.[99] Popular pressure quickly led to the replacement of police with militia in other cities as well.[100]

It is possible for power to devolve and for local authorities to exercise state power more effectively than central bureaucracies. There is no logical reason, as a result, why rapid decentralization would necessarily have to lead to state collapse. In Russia in 1917, however, local power was weak and ineffective. The new militias assumed police power, but they were civilian volunteers, most of them with day jobs, and none of them with training in police work. Many of them came from criminal backgrounds, enticed by the promise of a free gun and a claim to authority.[101] If militias helped prevent complete anarchy, they did not effectively provide security for residents. Here again, phenomena first experienced by civilians living in military zones emerged in the metropole in 1917. As Rex Wade remarks, "Forming a central government was relatively easy, whatever its effectiveness; but establishing new norms of local government among a citizenry unaccustomed to participation in the public life of the state was much more arduous."[102] Over the course of the year, these urban militias aligned themselves more and more closely with the Soviets, as "Red Guards" formed across the empire and came to play an important role in the events surrounding the October Revolution. As a result, the impromptu moves to restore order to a chaotic city became fixed as an essential feature of the revolution.

Revolution from below also marked the genesis of the dramatic changes within the army. Once more, elites began with the hope that the empire's structure of power could be transferred intact into their own hands. On 28 February/13 March, Duma leaders, spooked by the insurrection, ordered soldiers back to the barracks and to obey their officers.[103] Rebellious soldiers had no intention of giving up the fruits of their efforts just because some politician signed an order, however. Instead, they began arresting their own officers, fearful that they would be disarmed and disciplined if they let their old bosses back into the driver's seat. At the same time, they turned politically to the Petrograd Soviet in the left wing of the Tauride Palace. As socialist leaders debated the prospect of dual power amongst themselves on 1/14 March, a group of soldiers suddenly burst through the door and hijacked the proceedings, demanding that the Soviet address soldier demands and protect those soldiers from the attempts of the Duma Committee in the right wing of the Tauride Palace to reharness them. They dominated the proceedings for the rest of the day, forwarding resolutions, doing most of the speaking, and arranging

[98] Aksenov, 36.

[99] Aksenov, 41; Rex A. Wade, *Red Guards and Workers' Militias in the Russian Revolution* (Stanford: Stanford University Press, 1984), 38–52.

[100] Minutes of Riga City Duma meeting, 4 March 1917, LVVA f. 2736, op. 1, d. 40, l. 10ob.

[101] Aksenov, 39–40.   [102] Wade, 58.   [103] Hasegawa, *The February Revolution*, 376.

negotiations with the military commission of the Duma, before finally dictating Order No. 1 to stunned revolutionaries in less than thirty minutes.[104]

Order No. 1 was a response to the particular circumstances that the Petrograd garrison found itself in, and it was explicitly issued only to those soldiers of the garrison. It had seven points, but the most important one was the first, which established "committees from the elected representatives of the lower ranks" in every military unit in the city. Other key features were that weapons were to be controlled by the new committees rather than by individual soldiers or officers, and that officers and soldiers would enjoy equal levels of civic and interpersonal respect when off duty.[105]

The fact that Order No. 1 was technically limited only to troops in Petrograd was rendered virtually meaningless as soon as news of it spread to troops around the country and up and down the front. Angry troops demanded an end to humiliating disciplinary practices, deposed unpopular officers, and formed committees of their own at every level. Bitter émigrés and conservative historians have regularly pointed to Order No. 1 as the precipitating factor in the collapse of the armed forces in 1917, an act cunningly devised by socialist intellectuals to destroy military discipline, lead soldiers to chatter on endlessly rather than to fight, and to undermine the sacred bond between motherland, officer, and soldier.[106] But Allan Wildman is no doubt closer to the truth when he argues that the order probably prevented real chaos rather than generated it. It was the revolution, not the Order, that fundamentally transformed the nature of social and political relations in the army.[107] This was certainly true for troops in the Petrograd garrison, but there is reason to think that officers throughout the army were going to have tough sledding after the February events regardless of which decrees were issued from the capital.

Initially, officers warned that while a strong enemy faced them, army reforms should proceed with caution or not at all. The majority were dismayed by the changes that had occurred as a result of the revolution. Early in March, the Eighth Army polled its officers to learn their views of proposed changes in army disciplinary structures. Only 6 percent of them thought it "possible for the army to immediately introduce new relations [between officers and enlisted men]," while only 7 percent thought that the military should take part in political activities. Higher positive responses were given on questions relating to whether officers should begin addressing their soldiers more formally using "you" (*vy*) rather than "thou" (*ty*). Thirty-eight percent thought more formality would be appropriate, 40 percent were opposed, and 22 percent gave no answer. Some officers felt that changes were necessary but had to be deferred: "first, we'll fight the war to a successful victory and save the motherland from destruction, and then, in

---

[104] Hasegawa, *The February Revolution*, 400.

[105] For text in English, see Allan K. Wildman, *The End of the Russian Imperial Army: The Old Army and the Soldiers' Revolt (March–April 1917)* (Princeton: Princeton University Press, 1980), 187. For text in Russian, see V. E. Poletaev et al., eds., *Revoliutsionnoe dvizhenie v Rossii posle sverzheniia samoderzhaviia*, 10 vols. (Moscow: Izd. Akademii nauk SSSR, 1957), 1: 189–90.

[106] Richard Pipes, *The Russian Revolution* (New York: Alfred Knopf, 1990), 302–7.

[107] Wildman, 193.

peacetime, we'll deal with the rest."[108] Others reacted more violently, claiming that all the changes were sponsored by the Social Democrats in order to destroy the army. "The internal way of life of the army must remain inviolable, not allowing politics or the agitation of political parties."[109] Still others devised rationales for existing practices such as the requirement to salute superiors even when off duty.[110] One complained mournfully that soldiers should be told that "allowing them to smoke on the streets does not give them the right to blow smoke in the face of passing officers."[111] Nevertheless, despite their distaste for the revolution in the army, many commanders tried to come to terms with their men soon after the revolution developed. Even General Alekseev eventually reconciled himself to the new reality.[112] By the start of May, officers knew that the revolution was an accomplished fact. Officers from the Special Army, on the eve of the First All-Union Congress of Officers, declared that they trusted and fully subordinated themselves to the Provisional Government as the "only legal holder of state power," that they recognized the Petrograd Soviet as an organ that exercised great authority in the army, and that they welcomed the broadest democratic reforms.[113] The revolution shook the officer corps but did not destroy it. As Wildman suggests, Order No. 1 in general, and soldier committees in particular, helped to channel the negotiations over power and allowed officers to take part in decision-making, at least in the early months of the revolution.

Still, if Order No. 1 helped to focus the revolutionary energy in the armed forces, it did not provide a mechanism to replace the traditional bonds of authority and legitimacy that had been destroyed in recent weeks. As in the case of the militia, it represented a move toward radical decentralization. Soldier committees were hardly under the political direction of the Petrograd Soviet, which involved itself very little with those committees in the first period of the revolution. Indeed, the Provisional Government proselytized more actively at the front and among soldiers than the Soviet did in this period.[114] There was real diversity within these soldier committees on many of the key political issues of the day. Some supported the position of the Soviet, which called for peace with "no annexations or indemnities," but a surprising number in March and early April supported a continuation of the war and criticized the Soviet's role in the dual power system.[115] Soldiers representing these "pro-war" committees were not eager to continue fighting, but they were convinced of the defensist position that a failure to prosecute the war effort would lead to German conquest and the suffocation of the revolution by German hands rather than Romanov ones. Regardless of their political leanings, however, the

---

[108] Poll responses to the questions provided by the War Ministry in its Order No. 144 and telegram 9215, n.d., RGVIA f. 2134, op. 1, d. 1003, ll. 1–2.

[109] Commander of 32nd Infantry Division, Report to the commander of Eighth Army, 9 March 1917, RGVIA f. 2134, op. 1, d. 1003, ll. 7–9ob.

[110] Colonel Godlevskii (commander of the 86th Reserve Infantry Regiment), Report to the War Minister, 10 March 1917, RGVIA f. 2134, op. 1, d. 1003, l. 10.

[111] Poll responses, RGVIA f. 2134, op. 1, d. 1003, l. 2.   [112] Wildman, 261.

[113] Circular to all armies from the union section of the Special Army, 1 May 1917, RGVIA f. 2067, op. 1, d., 3797, l. 80.

[114] Wildman, 253.   [115] Wildman, 292–3.

committees ended the monopoly on military power that Stavka had previously enjoyed. Military authorities struggled mightily with this fact, but the army had, in practice, been democratized.

REVOLUTION AND EMPIRE

The relatively inchoate swarming of political ideas in the army in March began to coalesce in April, and it coalesced around anti-imperial positions. The Russian Revolution exposed in stark form the internal contradiction in Allied war aims: on the one hand, a moral call for the "liberation" of oppressed people, on the other an effort on the part of the world's largest empires to benefit in tangible ways from victory in this terrible conflict. No figure better embodied this contradiction than the new Foreign Minister, Pavel Miliukov. During his years in opposition, he was sympathetic and attentive to issues of nationalist striving, and he consistently argued for a solution in which minorities enjoyed cultural autonomy within the bounds of an all-Russian sovereign state.[116] His papers are filled with letters from distressed ethnic minorities in Russia and abroad. But he was also a dedicated patriot, and this left him unable to imagine a Russian state shorn of its ethnically diverse borderlands and incapable of projecting power on the international stage. On 4/17 March, in his first note to Russian diplomats in foreign countries, he stressed that the new Provisional Government would "strictly observe the international obligations contracted by the fallen regime," while also following the "democratic principles of consideration toward the small and the great nations, of freedom of their development, and of a good understanding among peoples."[117] Miliukov's sentiments were sincere, and he believed that they made him a friend of oppressed nationalities. "At that time," he wrote in his memoirs, "I completely shared the ideological aim of the war of 'liberation' but I considered it impossible to influence the official policy of the Allies."[118]

But he was also aware that socialists viewed him as a liberal imperialist. Chkheidze had called out Miliukov by name in his lacerating speech of 1/14 November 1916 on the Duma's complicity in imperialist oppression. After the revolution, Chkheidze departed from his former Duma colleagues, refusing to participate in the Provisional Government and becoming chairman of the Petrograd Soviet. Within days, he took his more expansive idea of nationalist liberation to the world stage. On 14/27 March 1917, the Soviet issued an "Appeal to the Peoples of All the World." After asserting that the new "Russian democracy" had

[116] Melissa K. Stockdale, "Miliukov, Nationality, and National Identity," in *P. N. Miliukov: istorik, politik, diplomat,* ed. V. V. Shelokhaev (Moscow: ROSSPEN, 2000), 275–87; Melissa K. Stockdale, *Paul Miliukov and the Quest for a Liberal Russia, 1880–1918* (Ithaca: Cornell University Press, 1996).

[117] P. N. Miliukov, note to Russian diplomatic representatives abroad, 4 March 1917, in Robert Paul Browder and Alexander F. Kerensky, eds., *The Russian Provisional Government, 1917: Documents,* 3 vols. (Stanford: Stanford University Press, 1961), 2: 1042–3.

[118] Paul Miliukov, *Political Memoirs, 1905–1917,* ed. Arthur P. Mendel, trans. Carl Goldberg (Ann Arbor: University of Michigan Press, 1967), 434.

now entered the family of nations as an "equal" member, the Soviet went on to proclaim: "Conscious of its revolutionary power, the Russian democracy announces that it will oppose the policy of conquest of its ruling classes by every means, and it summons the peoples of Europe to common, decisive action in favor of peace."[119] At the same time, Chkheidze reaffirmed that "in addressing the Germans, we do not let the rifles out of our hands."[120] This became the firm Soviet policy on war aims: Russia ought not to follow acquisitive policies, but it must prevent Germany from imposing its will on the new democracy. This line was expressed in the slogan "Peace without Annexations or Indemnities."

The Soviet's declaration did not sway Miliukov, who retorted that "peace without annexations" was a "German formula that they endeavor to pass off as an international socialist one." He maintained that Allied policy was to liberate the peoples of Austria-Hungary, to return "Italians to Italy" and "Rumanians to Rumania," to advance the "natural unification of the Serbian people," and to free "Armenians from the Turkish yoke."[121] These fine phrases were political cover for expansionism, not a rejection of imperialism. Promising the "unification" of Italy or Serbia meant in practice the annexation of new territories by those states. Miliukov also equivocated on the question of Arab nationalism, saying that the fate of Arab peoples "should be decided in a favorable manner." Closer to home, he argued for a "union of the Ukrainian population of the Austrian regions with the population of our own Ukrainian regions"—in other words, for the incorporation of Galicia into the Russian Empire through the rhetorical device of Ukrainian nationalism. As early as 1915, Miliukov had come out in support of territorial annexation. Russia had not started the war, he argued, but once it began, it was only right that the "Russian nationalities" under foreign rule (i.e. Ukrainians in Eastern Galicia) would come under Russian control. A "reunited" Poland, in line with the grand duke's 1/14 August 1914 Manifesto, would get autonomy under the Russian scepter, and its territories would include Western Galicia and those parts of Prussia in which Poles predominated. A Greater Armenia would also be expanded and included within the empire.[122] Now, in 1917, he added the Straits to the list, saying that they were not really Turkish ("the Turkish nation, in spite of five hundred years' domination, has not spread its roots deeply there") and that the "transfer of the Straits to us would in no way contradict the principles advanced by Woodrow Wilson when he spoke of the possibility of transferring their ownership. The possession of the Straits is the protection of 'the doors to our home,' and it is understandable that this protection should belong to us."[123]

[119] "Soviet Appeal to the Peoples of All the World," 14 March 1917, in Browder and Kerensky, eds, 2: 1077–8.

[120] Report in *Izvestiia* on the debate in the Soviet regarding the Appeal, 16 March 1917, in Browder and Kerensky, eds., 2: 1077.

[121] Miliukov interview in *Rech'*, 23 March 1917, in Browder and Kerensky, eds., 2: 1044–5.

[122] P. N. Miliukov, "Territorial'nye priobreteniia Rossii," in *Chego zhdet Rossiia ot voiny: sbornik statei*, ed. M. I. Tugan-Baranovskii (n.p: Prometei, 1915), 49–62.

[123] Miliukov interview in *Rech'*, 23 March 1917, in Browder and Kerensky, eds., 2: 1044–5.

This was the death knell of Russian liberalism. The Kadets as a group and Miliukov individually had fought in principled ways throughout their long years in opposition for the ideals of ethnic and civic equality. They had emerged from the February Revolution as a dominant force in the Provisional Government and had become the face of that government to the world. In the borderlands, some Kadet leaders even joined other public figures in calling for a new federated republic.[124] But in the space of two months from late April to late June, the insistence of Kadet leaders in Petrograd on maintaining Russia as an imperial Great Power would doom the party. The tentative proposals of non-Russian Kadets to re-examine the party's position on federalism were literally laughed at during the Seventh Party Congress in late March, and things only got worse from there.[125] Leaders of the Soviet, genuinely disturbed by Miliukov's pronouncements but also aware of the political gain to be made on the issue, pressed the Provisional Government to renounce Miliukov's stance and to adopt a position of revolutionary defensism. Ministers to the left of Miliukov (such as Kerenskii and Tereshchenko) successfully forced a compromise declaration on 27 March/9 April. This statement deferred "to the will of the people, in close union with our Allies, the final solution of all problems connected with the World War," while asserting that "the aim of Free Russia is not domination over other nations, or seizure of their national possessions, or forcible occupation of foreign territories, but the establishment of a stable peace on the basis of the self-determination of peoples."[126] At the same time, the Provisional Government, which had removed all formal ethnic discrimination within the empire in the first days of the revolution, now moved to recognize some limited political rights for nationalities within the empire. On 27 March/9 April, Estonia requested "local self-government," and the government responded quickly with a set of regulations on 30 March/12 April that demarcated the boundary between Estonia and Latvia while allowing for extensive elected self-government on the local level, including the use of local languages in local government documents. However, the region was still run by a commissar appointed by the Provisional Government and all communications between the center and the locales had to be conducted in Russian.[127] On 1/14 April, the Riga City Duma discussed a new composition of local authority that would guarantee proportional representation to minority ethnic groups in the city: eleven slots to Germans, nine to Russians, eight to Jews, seven to Lithuanians, and two to Poles, plus one special soldier representative from the Latvian Riflemen.[128]

---

[124] William G. Rosenberg, *Liberals in the Russian Revolution: The Constitutional Democratic Party, 1917–1921* (Princeton: Princeton University Press, 1974), 63.

[125] Rosenberg, 87.

[126] Provisional Government's Declaration of War Aims, 27 March 1917, in Browder and Kerensky, eds., 2: 1045–6.

[127] Journal of the meeting of the Provisional Government, 27 March 1917, and Journal of the meeting of the Provisional Government, 30 March 1917, in Kozlov and Mironenko, eds., 7: 179, 199–200.

[128] Minutes of Riga City Duma meeting, 1 April 1917, LVVA f. 2736, op. 1, d. 40, l. 17.

Miliukov, engaged in a complicated diplomatic dance with the other Allied powers, unwisely decided to buck this growing trend towards anti-imperialism. The Provisional Government's 27 March/9 April statement had purposely not been a diplomatic note but a domestic declaration, and Allied diplomats played along by noting that they had not received any revision of the new government's war aims. This only increased pressure on Miliukov to issue a formal note to clarify the situation, which he did on 18 April/1 May with a document that mostly consisted of a paean to Wilson, "the President of our new ally, the great transatlantic republic." He did not mention the Straits or any other potential foreign acquisitions, and he repeated his desire for the "self-determination of the oppressed nationalities." But he also clearly and firmly rejected the possibility of a separate peace and asserted that it was the "general aspiration of the whole people to bring the World War to a decisive victory."[129] The insistence on honoring alliance obligations and fighting the war to full victory was a declaration of sympathy with imperialism, as members of the Soviet immediately understood. If Russia were to stay in the war until Britain and France decided that victory had been achieved, then, at the very least, it would be fighting for *their* imperialist ambitions, since no one expected British or French leaders to adopt the slogan of "peace without annexations or indemnities."[130] Miliukov was betting his career and the fate of Russian liberalism that it was the "general aspiration of the whole people" to continue the war on the basis of Allied war aims.

He lost the bet. The strong consensus in the army, as we have seen, was on the basis of revolutionary defensism. As Brusilov mournfully noted, "I never succeeded in getting them [enlisted men] to advance or to attack the enemy positions. I was always met by the words 'No annexations and no reparations,' and one could get no further."[131] Even a group of enthusiastic volunteers seeking to create special shock detachments on 2/15 June promising to "throw themselves on German barricades" did so to ensure a "peace without annexations or reparations, on the principles of national self-determination."[132] In contrast to Miliukov's claim of a desire for complete victory, soldiers in the 47th Ukrainian Regiment on the Southwestern Front had refused days before to occupy the line, declaring that "we don't need hilltop 1064" and protesting that only officers talked about "smashing the Germans." They eagerly awaited the news that the Soviet had concluded a peace.[133]

[129] Telegram from P. N. Miliukov (Minister of Foreign Affairs) to Russian representatives attached to Allied powers, 18 April 1917, in Browder and Kerensky, eds., 2: 1098.

[130] The British military attaché, Alfred Knox, was horrified even by the suggestion: "A long article in to-day's *Pravda*, by Kamenev, whose real name is Rosenfeldt, points out that the adoption by the Provisional Government of the formula 'Peace without annexations' is a pretence unless accompanied by action leading to the withdrawal of all troops from occupied territory by all the powers at war. England must withdraw her forces from India, Egypt, and Ireland!" Major-General Sir Alfred Knox, *With the Russian Army, 1914–1917: Being Chiefly Extracts from the Diary of a Military Attaché*, 2 vols. (London: Hutchinson & Co., 1921), 2: 623.

[131] General A. A. Brusilov, *A Soldier's Notebook, 1914–1918* (Westport, CT: Greenwood Press, 1971 [1930]), 290.

[132] Cited in Svetlana A. Solntseva, "Udarnye formirovaniia russkoi armii v 1917 godu," *Otechestvennaia istoriia* no. 2 (2007): 52.

[133] Wildman, 333.

If the Central Powers were to offer a separate peace based on no annexations or indemnities, Russian soldiers would want to accept it.

This tension between popular opinions on the war and Miliukov's statement came to the fore when the contents of the note were published. Vladimir Lenin, recently arrived from Switzerland, helped author resolutions of the Bolshevik Central Committee that attacked the "naked imperialist character" of the Provisional Government, which, "bound hands and feet to Anglo-French and Russian capital," had showed that all of its promises of peace were deceptions.[134] On the same day, soldiers in the Petrograd garrison showed that they agreed. Led by members of the Finland Guards Regiment, soldiers of the Keksgol'msk Guard Regiment, and the famous Pavlovskiis, 25,000 soldiers gathered on the square in front of the Mariinskii Palace with placards saying "Down with the Policy of Miliukov," and "We Cheer Peace Without Annexations or Indemnities."[135] The demonstration turned into a meeting filled with angry words and slogans, and smaller meetings among citizens and soldiers grew across the city (and indeed across the country) on the same day. Counter-demonstrations also grew, as groups supportive of Miliukov and the Provisional Government hit the streets with signs saying "Long Live the Provisional Government" and "Down With Lenin!"[136] General Lavr Kornilov, recently brought from the front to command the Petrograd garrisons as head of the Petrograd Military District, asked for permission to use his troops to suppress the rebels. The government denied his request, saying that their strength lay "in moral influence."[137] A disappointed Kornilov asked for and received permission to rotate back to the front lines. Late that night, a delegation from the Soviet, led again by ethnic minorities from the borderland (Chkheidze and Tsereteli) met with the Provisional Government and urged them to revoke the note.[138] Once more, Miliukov took a hard line, saying that it would be impermissible to introduce such confusion into his diplomacy. The next day, however, demonstrations on the street turned violent, and several people were wounded in a gun battle near Nevskii Prospekt. Leaders in the Soviet and the Provisional Government, spooked by the specter of further revolution, came to a compromise on 22 April/5 May. Miliukov issued a clarification that nothing in his note contradicted the sentiments against imperialist aims expressed in the government's 27 March/9 April declaration. The Soviet accepted the explanation and urged workers and soldiers to cease their armed demonstrations.[139]

But the damage had been done. Throughout the army, the jumble of ideas about war and revolution now crystallized into a critique of imperialism and demands for peace. On Easter Sunday, Fedor Stepun recalled, the soldier meetings resounded with anti-imperial slogans: "For Land and Freedom!" "For Peace Without Annexations and Indemnities!" "For the Self-Determination of Peoples!"[140] In late

---

[134] Resolutions of Central Committee of Bolshevik Party, 20 April 1917, cited in G. N. Golikov and Iu. S. Tokarev, "Aprel'skii krizis 1917 g.," *Istoricheskie zapiski* 57 (1956): 41.
[135] Golikov and Tokarev, 42.   [136] Golikov and Tokarev, 45.
[137] Browder and Kerensky, eds., 3: 1241.   [138] Golikov and Tokarev, 48.
[139] Brower and Kerensky, eds., 2: 1100–1; 3: 1241–2.
[140] Stepun, *Byvshee i nesbyvsheesia*, 316.

March, the resolutions of army committees took a variety of positions on the question of continuing the war. Over the course of April, however, socialists embarked on a concerted effort to convince soldiers of the righteousness of the Soviet's position on peace. Even before the publication of Miliukov's note, soldier committees "became fully cognizant of the issues at stake and came down four-square in support of the Soviet's positions," in no small part because "they could not but be struck with the similarity between Kadet pronouncements and those of their senior officers."[141] After the April Crisis, this sense was confirmed, and the "Soviet mode of politics, particularly on the question of war and peace, had come to sway the front committeemen and could even overcome the reservations of apolitical officers and militantly defensist intellectuals."[142] The April Crisis represented a definitive defeat for Miliukov's positions and the Kadet party.

Once more, the Bolsheviks took the opportunity to publicize their consistent platform of supporting national self-determination. At the Seventh All-Russian Conference of the Social Democratic Party, Lenin reiterated his support for a right to secede. On the same day (29 April/12 May), Stalin delivered a report that called anew for autonomy for those peoples who did wish to remain a part of a multi-national state.[143] These initiatives bore immediate fruit. Left-wing nationalism was strong in Eastern Europe. The Bolsheviks attracted many followers as a result of their leadership on this issue. Władysław Solskii, a radical student who fled Łodz in the first days of the war, recalled that

> the fact that the Bolsheviks—and only the Bolsheviks—forwarded the slogan of self-determination for Poles played a large role in increasing support for the Bolsheviks among the Polish refugee masses in Russia. This support was important for the Bolsheviks not only in the western provinces. Hundreds of thousands of Poles lived in Petrograd at that time, no less than one hundred thousand in Kiev, just as many in Khar'kov, about fifty thousand in Odessa and so forth. In addition, there were no less than a half a million Poles in the Russian army, and probably many more.[144]

Days after the end of the street disturbances, Kerenskii called for a new coalition government with greater socialist participation. Miliukov and Guchkov resigned their posts, and the new Provisional Government, which was formed on 5/18 May, swung even further to the left, though several Kadets remained. Kerenskii took the portfolio of Minister of War, and Tereshchenko replaced Miliukov as Minister of Foreign Affairs.

CONCLUSION

In the midst of all of this conflict on the issues of war and peace, the independent socialist tribune Maksim Gor'kii wrote an essay in his newspaper *Novaia zhizn'*

---

[141] Wildman, 293, 324.   [142] Wildman, 329.

[143] Francine Hirsch, *Empire of Nations: Ethnographic Knowledge and the Making of the Soviet Union* (Ithaca: Cornell University Press, 2005), 55–6.

[144] Vatslav Solskii, *1917 god v zapadnoi oblasti i na zapadnom fronte* (Minsk: Tesei, 2004), 63.

(New Life). Published on 21 April/4 May, the same day that the street clashes turned deadly, the article began with the observation that speaking the truth, even in conditions of free speech, "is the most difficult of all arts." Surprisingly, Gor'kii was concerned on this day not with Miliukov and the Straits, but with telling the truth about German atrocities. "I hope," he wrote, "that we can quite accurately establish the facts concerning the brutal treatment by the German soldiers of the soldiers of Russia, France, and England, as well of the peaceful populations of Belgium, Serbia, Rumania and Poland. I have the right to hope that these facts are beyond doubt and as indisputable as the facts of Russian atrocities in Smorgon, in the towns of Galicia, etc."[145] His piece serves as a reminder that no matter how deeply certain events (such as the April Crisis) in 1917 became enshrined in the revolutionary narrative, at the time they were mostly understood within the narrative of the war, even by committed socialists. But Gor'kii had another purpose in writing this essay. It was a warning. War was brutality, and if the new revolutionary democracy could not support the pacifist inclinations of the men currently fraternizing with the enemy on the front, then the dark forces lurking in the breast of every man would return. "Just think, reader," he concluded, "what will happen to you if the truth of a mad beast overpowers the sane truth of man?"[146]

---

[145] Maxim Gorky, *Untimely Thoughts: Essays on Revolution, Culture and the Bolsheviks, 1917–1918*, intro. Mark D. Steinberg, trans. Herman Ermolaev (New Haven: Yale University Press, 1995), 9–10.
[146] Gorky, *Untimely Thoughts*, 12.

6

Decolonization

While Russia convulsed with revolution, the war continued in all its fury. In January 1917, Germany resumed unrestricted submarine warfare, which pushed the United States into the conflict. Congress voted to declare war in April, though substantial military forces would not arrive until 1918. In the meantime, the Entente continued to seek victory through coordinated attacks on several fronts at once. Discussions had been taking place throughout the winter months regarding the proper location for these attacks, but all the Allies were agreed on the necessity for joint action. The Russians specifically agreed to join in at the Second Chantilly Conference in November 1916, though they grumbled, again, that Britain and France seemed to want to ensure the protection and comfort of their troops while expecting the Eastern Allies to bear a heavier burden.[1] The revolution obviously changed the calculus in Petrograd. Alekseev was forced to admit to his government and to his allies on 13/26 March that Russia could not launch any serious efforts until July at the earliest, and perhaps not even then.[2] The changing balance of forces confused the situation further. The British planned for a summer offensive in Flanders, while the French, under their new commander-in-chief, Robert Nivelle, launched an offensive on 3/16 April 1917 between Reims and Soissons. This offensive failed catastrophically. Nivelle had predicted a breakthrough in forty-eight hours at the cost of 10,000 men. Instead, victory never came, and the casualties totaled 134,000. Mutiny erupted in more than half of the French divisions, and Nivelle was cashiered on 2/15 May. A campaign on two fronts seemed all the more necessary as spring began to turn into summer.

In the meantime, both combat officers and Kerenskii as the new War Minister cast about for ways to preserve the Russian army intact. The Germans had launched a successful but brief battle on the Stokhod River in March, but fighting was only sporadic through the spring. The Central Powers welcomed the breathing space that the revolution provided and began focusing more on unraveling the Russian army politically and socially than on defeating it militarily.[3] They dropped

---

[1] I. I. Rostunov, *Russkii front pervoi mirovoi voiny* (Moscow: Izd. Nauka, 1976), 332–3.

[2] Rostunov, 353; Allan K. Wildman, *The End of the Russian Imperial Army: The Road to Soviet Power and Peace* (Princeton: Princeton University Press, 1987), 5.

[3] Erich von Ludendorff, *Ludendorff's Own Story, August 1914–November 1918*, 2 vols (New York and London: Harper and Brothers, 1919), 2: 14.

propaganda leaflets, encouraged fraternization, and generally avoided strengthening the defensism of the Russian soldiers.[4] The Russian army, mostly freed from combat, focused on other issues. Meetings of all sorts proliferated, soldiers began to think more and more about their hometowns, and desertion intensified. The authority of officers declined dramatically.[5] With a separate peace still anathema to a large sector of the political elite and to all of the military brass, and with the army succumbing to indiscipline and political rumblings while stationary, the logical decision was taken to refocus soldier attention on the war by means of a new military offensive. Brusilov and other commanders reached this conclusion in late March 1917, and they persuaded Alekseev of its merits as well. On 30 March/12 April, Alekseev signed a directive ordering commanders to prepare for a new offensive in early May.[6]

Growing concerns about morale, especially during the April Crisis, led to postponements so that spirits could be raised. Kerenskii, now the Minister of War, traveled up and down the line giving stirring speeches, trying to build cohesion, and devoting a great deal of his new political capital to the cause of the new offensive. Further confusion ensued in May, when Alekseev addressed the All-Union Congress of Officers with a speech that both attacked the "utopian phrase" of "peace without annexations or indemnities" and argued that a strong state capable of "forcing every citizen to honorably fulfill his duty to the motherland" was needed.[7] In the wake of the furor in the previous month, this was unacceptable. Kerenskii fired Alekseev as commander-in-chief, replacing him with Brusilov on 22 May/4 June. Two other generals deemed hostile to the revolution—Gurko and Dragomirov—were also cashiered.[8] Thus Brusilov was able to take command of the operation he had been among the first to champion. In many respects, the June Offensive should be called the Second Brusilov Offensive. It was planned and fought largely on the territory of the first offensive and had a similar strategic goal: the taking of L'viv and knocking Austria-Hungary out of the war. The June Offensive lacked the surprise elements of the first Brusilov Offensive, but Brusilov enjoyed superiority in terms of men and ammunition, with nearly three times as many men and twice as many artillery pieces as his enemies possessed.[9]

In addition, Brusilov hoped that he had found internal resources to raise morale by combining a novel tactical approach with a new method for recruiting and organizing military units. In 1915, the German army had created special "storm" and "shock" units to accomplish particularly important and dangerous goals on the battlefield. These tactically decentralized squads worked independently, creeping

---

[4] The Stokhod assault, indeed, had soured some soldiers on both fraternization and prospects for peace with the Germans. Wildman, *Road to Soviet Power and Peace*, 25.

[5] V. P. Buldakov, *Krasnaia smuta: priroda i posledstviia revoliutsionnogo nasiliia* (Moscow: ROSSPEN, 1997), 124.

[6] Rostunov, 354.

[7] General Alekseev, Speech to All-Union Congress of Officers, 7 May 1915, RGVIA f. 2067, op. 1, d. 3797, ll. 100–107.

[8] Robert S. Feldman, "The Russian General Staff and the June 1917 Offensive," *Soviet Studies* 19, no. 4 (April 1968): 535.

[9] Rostunov, 359.

forward from crater to crater, raiding trenches, and leading larger attacks. Storm units therefore required soldiers with high morale and a capacity for independent action toward a common goal. Entrance into these units was voluntary, and the shock and storm troopers enjoyed their distinctive status.[10] As we have seen, Brusilov had formed shock troops of his own for use in the 1916 offensive, and he felt that shock units could be used to good tactical effect in the summer of 1917 as well.[11] At the same time, the revolution had inspired a wave of civic virtue in the country, and many individuals urged the army to make use of this new passion for voluntarism, honor, and self-sacrifice on behalf of the motherland by organizing new units of enthusiasts. Prince S. V. Kudashev, for instance, lobbied the Minister of War (Guchkov) in April to "create special 'shock' groups in all the armies of the front, which will be for the most part doomed to extermination and should consist exclusively of volunteers, since a heroic deed can be such only if it results from free will."[12] In May, Kornilov approved the formation of shock units in the Eighth Army, and soon thereafter Brusilov authorized them throughout the armed forces in response to a request from Captain M. A. Murav'ev, a prominent member of the Socialist Revolutionary Party who would become an important figure in the Civil War in the summer of 1918. These units were formed quickly and wore special insignia to distinguish themselves as shock, or occasionally even as "death," units. As in the German Army, these men were paid better, treated better, and took on the most dangerous assignments. By October there were more than 600,000 men enlisted in 313 "death" units, and the army's top brass was considering creating an entire "death army."[13]

The most interesting of these fighting forces, however, were the sixteen new volunteer military formations composed exclusively of women. Women volunteered as soldiers for many reasons in 1917. Dozens, perhaps hundreds, of them had done so prior to the revolution either by hiding their identities or by petitioning the tsar for approval to join the army. Some wanted to participate in the war effort in a direct and tangible way, as nurses were doing. Others sought escape from abusive conditions at home. Nearly all were deeply patriotic.[14] In 1917, there were two other good reasons: revolutionary feminism and horror at the disintegration of the army at the front. A desire for equality was especially visible in a handful of grass-roots militia units sponsored by feminist organizations. Matriona Zalesskaia, for instance, created a unit among Kuban Cossacks in Ekaterinodar on behalf of the

---

[10] Bruce I. Gudmundsson, *Stormtroop Tactics: Innovation in the German Army, 1914–1918* (Westport, CT: Praeger, 1989), 49, 81–2.

[11] Robert S. Feldman, "The Russian General Staff and the June 1917 Offensive," *Soviet Studies* 19, no. 4 (April 1968): 536.

[12] Cited in Svetlana A. Solntseva, "Udarnye formirovaniia russkoi armii v 1917 godu," *techestvennaia istoriia* no. 2 (2007): 48; for English translation see Svetlana A. Solntseva, "The Russian Army's Shock Formations in 1917," trans. Liv Bliss, *Russian Studies in History* 51, no. 4 (Spring 2013): 51.

[13] Solntseva, "The Russian Army's Shock Formations," 57.

[14] On patriotism and women soldiering, see Melissa K. Stockdale, " 'My Death for the Motherland is Happiness': Women, Patriotism, and Soldiering in Russia's Great War," *American Historical Review* 109, no. 1 (February 2004).

"Organization of Women-Volunteers," both to raise soldier spirits and to "restore the equality and equal rights of women in electoral reform and political life lost under absolutism."[15] The main reason for the proliferation of female formations in 1917, however, was a desire on the part of many women and many top military officials to "shame" Russian men into fulfilling their military duties by showing that even women were willing to fight for the country's cause in the war. This propaganda goal predominated among the most visible supporters of the women's military units, especially the most prominent commander, Mariia Bochkareva, and the Minister of War, Kerenskii. These battalions had a negligible impact on the fighting (only one of them saw combat) and angered more men than they inspired, but they did establish a precedent for much larger female participation in combat during the Civil War and, especially, World War II.[16]

As these varied, even desperate, schemes suggest, top politicians and military officials were deeply anxious about morale on the eve of the June Offensive, and they asked for updates on this topic constantly. General Kornilov, the new commander of the Eighth Army, reassured his bosses at the headquarters of the Southwestern Front that the mood among his men was satisfactory, even "firm, conscious, and healthy."[17] Others, even those in the Eighth Army, took a more measured tone. General Cheremisov reported that discipline varied from regiment to regiment. Some refused orders, some obeyed willingly. Among all of them, gambling at cards was flourishing.[18] Pessimists were easy to find as well. Major General Bolkhovitinov, the artillery inspector for the XVI Army Corps (Eighth Army) warned that

> if we sometimes hear about the so-called start of the rejuvenation of the army, then it is the result of an insufficiently thoughtful approach to affairs.... Ever-wider circles of soldiers are gripped by a wild unruliness. The war has been forgotten. In the villages closest to the front, the sounds of harmonicas, wild screams, and foul cursing ring out all night long. Unrestrained card games are present everywhere. The soldiers, tired from their nighttime gambling and debauchery, can't perform their service or work productively the next day. Everything is becoming unraveled at the seams, and after six months, if things go as they are, the army will completely cease to exist.[19]

If this was the situation in the most battle-ready army in the revolutionary armed forces, it was a bad omen for the success of Brusilov's campaign. Socialist activists among the troops also noted a souring of the mood on the eve of the attack. "What

---

[15] Cited in Laurie Stoff, *They Fought for the Motherland: Russia's Women Soldiers in World War I and the Revolution* (Lawrence: University Press of Kansas, 2006), 94.

[16] Stoff's book is the main resource for understanding this movement, but see also Stockdale, "My Death for the Motherland is Happiness," and Joshua Sanborn, *Drafting the Russian Nation: Military Conscription, Total War, and Mass Politics, 1905–1925* (DeKalb: Northern Illinois University Press, 2003).

[17] Report from commander of the Eighth Army to the commander-in-chief of the Southwestern Front, 10 June 1917, RGVIA f. 2134, op. 1, d. 1306, l. 44.

[18] Telegram from General Cheremisov (Staff of Eighth Army) to commander of Eighth Army, 8 June 1917, RGVIA f. 2134, op. 1, d. 1306, l. 44.

[19] Report from inspector of artillery of the XVI Army Corps to the commander of the XVI Army Corps, 20 June 1917, RGVIA f. 2134, op. 1, d. 1306, ll. 106–107.

sort of revolution is it," soldiers repeatedly asked, "if we have to fight, just like before, and we don't get enough to eat, just like before?"[20]

The June Offensive began on 16/29 June. Three Russian armies were engaged, the Eleventh at the northern end near Brody, the Seventh in the center just south of Ternopil', and the Eighth on the southern flank from Halych to the Romanian border. The first two days of the battle consisted of an intensive artillery barrage supported in new and effective ways by artillery observers gauging light, sound, and topography and by airplane reconnaissance. On 18 June/1 July, the infantry of the Seventh and Eleventh Armies moved forward. They advanced successfully into the ruined enemy lines, taking two to three lines of enemy trenches in the first day, and then pausing. Unmoved by the exhortations of their officers, they began questioning orders to advance further and held meetings to decide the next course of the offensive. In the majority of regiments, they decided to cease the attack. On 23 June/6 July, Kornilov's Eighth Army moved forward. Within ten days they had advanced past the city of Kalush, more than thirty kilometers from their launching point (see Map 10).

Abandoned by neighboring armies, the soldiers in the Eighth Army now began to mutiny. On 4/17 July, one corps commander reported that "the mood of units in the 21st Division has changed sharply. The majority of the mass of soldiers openly come out for a defensive form of action. . . . Every attempt by officers and soldiers to point to the necessity of achieving peace through an offensive is met with sharp protests." In the 162nd Division, a desertion crisis grew as agitators rallied troops behind the idea of an immediate peace.[21] On 5/18 July the commander of the XVI Army Corps confirmed that the mood had improved during the early success of the offensive, but that it collapsed over the course of a twelve-day battle filled with bad weather, hunger, and defeat. Nearly all regiments now refused orders to go on the offensive.[22]

The following day, on 6/19 July, the Germans launched a counteroffensive on the northern part of the sector, driving the Eleventh and Seventh Armies backwards. The Eighth Army now joined the headlong retreat. By the time the retreat stopped, nearly three weeks later, they were at the Zbruch River, nearly 200 kilometers away from Kalush. They had given back not only all of the gains of the June Offensive, but all of the territory gained by the Brusilov Offensive in 1916 and more besides. Cities that had stayed under Russian control since early in the war, such as Ternopil', fell without serious fighting. In the midst of the retreat, as Russian troops put everything to sword and flame, an ammunition dump exploded, sending shockwaves with a radius of several kilometers and an ominous plume rising into the Galician sky.[23] Chernivtsi, the hinge between the Southwestern and Romanian Fronts, was surrendered on 21 July/3 August.[24] On the Northern and

---

[20] Vatslav Solskii, *1917 god v zapadnoi oblasti i na zapadnom fronte* (Minsk: Tesei, 2004), 68.

[21] Telegram from the chief of staff of the III Caucasian Army Corps to the Quartermaster General of the Eighth Army, 4 July 1917, RGVIA f. 2134, op. 1, d. 1306, l. 168.

[22] Report from the commander of the XVI Army Corps to the chief of staff of the Eighth Army, 5 July 1917, RGVIA f. 2134, op. 1, d. 1306, l. 169.

[23] Wildman, *Road to Soviet Power and Peace*, 117.   [24] Rostunov, 359–61.

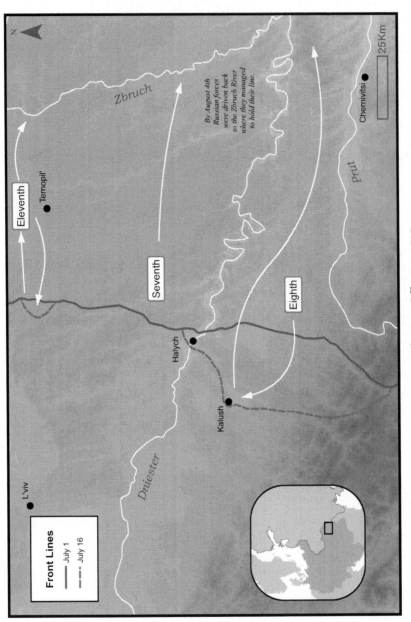

Front Lines

—— July 1
—·—·— July 16

By August 4th
Russian forces
were driven back
to the Zbruch River
where they managed
to hold their line.

Eleventh

Seventh

Eighth

Zbruch

Prut

Dniester

L'viv

Ternopil'

Halych

Kalush

Chernivitsi

N

25Km

Map 10 The June Offensive, 1917

Western Fronts, the Russian offensive launched a bit later, on 9/22 July, and it disintegrated even as it began. Units of the Fifth and Tenth Armies mutinied at the prospect of moving forward, attacked their officers, and disobeyed orders.[25]

Less than a month later, the Germans pressed their advantage in the north. Riga had long been a target for German military planners, not only because the port was important to the Gulf of Riga and the Baltic coast more generally, but also because they knew that the seizure of Riga would strike fear in the hearts of the citizens of Petrograd. In mid-August, the Germans struck. Troops (and later Soviet historians) were suspicious that the weak link in the Russian military on this occasion was not jabbering soldier committees but the high command, which might have welcomed the Germans taking Riga and Petrograd and thereby taking care of their growing Bolshevik problem in the northern zone of the empire. Whatever the reason, the commanders of the Northern Front did not defend the city effectively. They ignored intelligence reports on the upcoming offensive, withdrew men from defensible areas to vulnerable ones, and proved incapable of fending off the German assault. The attack began with an artillery barrage (including chemical weapons) on the morning of 19 August/1 September, and the infantry assaults began later in the morning. Almost immediately, the Germans forced the Dvina River south of Riga, and repeated counter-assaults by Russian troops failed to dislodge them. To the west of the city, two corps of Siberians were nearly surrounded and escaped only because of the fierce fighting of two Latvian rifle brigades. The Russian command-ers gave up quickly, abandoning the city center on the third day of the battle and retiring to secondary positions. They were pushed back further over the next three days, but dug in successfully on 24 August/5 September roughly forty kilometers to the east of Riga. German officials withdrew troops for use on other fronts in the midst of this pursuit, deciding to reap the benefits of the city capture rather than press on towards Petrograd.[26]

IMPERIAL PROBLEMS, NATIONAL SOLUTIONS

If the abdication of the tsar had provided the watershed moment in the process of state failure, the crisis surrounding the June Offensive proved critical for the growing assertiveness of nationalist movements. Nationalists across the borderlands had moved cautiously early in the revolution. As we have seen, the Provisional Government granted requests for limited autonomy in places such as Estonia, and it sanctioned the formation of nationalist military units in Ukraine (though, as we shall see, it resisted the reshuffling of existing units on an ethnic basis). At first, the region with the clearest case for autonomy (and later independence) was Finland. Finland had entered the empire in 1809 on a special basis. Finns swore loyalty to the tsar, but they retained significant local powers separate from the main imperial bureaucracies. The increasingly aggressive imperial state had begun to erode that

---

[25] Wildman, *Road to Soviet Power and Peace*, 103–11.   [26] Rostunov, 367–71.

autonomy in the final decades before the Great War, but Finland's legal position was unique in the empire. Finnish nationalists seized upon the abdication of the royal family as a legal release from their political dependence on Russia. Members of the Provisional Government argued unpersuasively that sovereignty had passed unaltered to them and that Finns owed fealty as a result, at least until the formation of the Constituent Assembly. Some nationalist Finns resisted, saying that "we have had to defend ourselves against Russian tsarism already; in regard to a Russian federation strengthened by national sentiment, our situation would be precarious. Under these circumstances we can only envisage the final solution of the Finnish question in the shape of absolute sovereignty."[27]

Kerenskii warned the Finns against extreme solutions, reminding them that the proximity of Finland to Petrograd and the fear of establishing a precedent for other ethnic groups made Russian hostility to Finnish independence likely. Given that Finns themselves were divided on the major political questions, nationalists did not press the conflict with the Provisional Government to the logical conclusion of declaring independence, at least at first. Instead, they worked up a bill that asserted substantial autonomy, leaving only defense and foreign affairs in the hands of politicians in Petrograd. This bill was tabled in May, but in the midst of the summer crisis it came back on the agenda. On 20 June/3 July, Finnish Social Democrats appeared at the All-Russian Congress of the Soviets and told delegates that they were supporting "the right to complete self-determination ... in other words, the recognition by the Russian Government of Finnish independence."[28] The Finnish Parliament (Sejm) did not press matters this far. As noted previously, it argued for Russian control of defense and foreign policy matters, but the claims for local law-making were absolute, and the bill passed on 5/18 July.[29] The reaction of Russian newspapers was intense. *Russkie vedomosti* growled that though Russia was weak, Finland was mistaken if it thought that the army could not "show her will." *Den'* opined that "The Finnish Sejm has passed a bill inspired by distrust toward the revolution, a project permeated with narrow-minded national egotism." Even *Izvestiia*, the organ of the Soviet, called for the Finns to recognize the authority of the Provisional Government until the Constituent Assembly gathered.[30] Kerenskii reacted grandiosely and peevishly to Carl Enckell, the Finnish State Secretary: "So there you are, the representative of Finland, which has declared itself independent and wants to break off relations with Russia. ... Will you force it so far that Russia begins taking military measures against you and closes the frontier between the two countries?"[31]

[27] Student memorandum on the Finnish Question presented to A. F. Kerenskii, 15 April 1917, in *Finland and Russia, 1808–1920, From Autonomy to Independence: A Selection of Documents*, ed. D. G. Kirby (London and Basingstoke: Macmillan, 1975), 159.

[28] Speech of Finnish Social Democrat Party Representative Khuttunen at Congress of Soviets, 20 June 1917, in Robert Paul Browder and Alexander F. Kensky, eds., *The Russian Provisional Government, 1917: Documents*, 3 vols. (Stanford: Stanford University Press, 1961), 1: 341.

[29] Richard Abraham, *Alexander Kerensky: The First Love of the Revolution* (New York: Columbia University Press, 1987), 205, 222.

[30] Press selections in Browder and Kerensky, eds., 1: 347–51.   [31] Abraham, 231.

Despite the threats, the Provisional Government turned first not to violence but to the political step of dissolving the Sejm and calling for new elections.[32] This was not quite such an undemocratic maneuver as it appeared at first. Finnish citizens in fact disagreed on the question of present and future relations with Russia. Not only was the country currently dependent on shipments from Russia for basic foodstuffs, but it was also far from clear to everyone that a complete divorce from Russia was necessary or desirable, as the violent conflicts of the impending Finnish Civil War would demonstrate. Indeed, two efforts to convene the Sejm in defiance of the Provisional Government's order failed when less than half of the delegates agreed to attend. The new Sejm was duly elected on 18–19 September/1–2 October.[33] Finland had clearly moved into the phase of decolonization in which conflict between indigenous political groupings over the future of the nation overlapped with the period of formal imperial control. Russian resources were now increasingly deployed in what was shaping up as an internal battle, most notably in the form of Red Guards who supported the Finnish communists, but in other ways as well.[34]

Finland was an extreme example of what was happening across the empire. Nationalist groups seized the revolutionary opportunity to form committees, congresses, and representative bodies, which uniformly called for a new democratic federation that preserved the borders of the Russian state at the same time that it guaranteed significant cultural rights and local autonomy for non-Russians.[35] The only exception to this rule was Poland, which the Germans continued to occupy. Now, the Polish politicians who remained in Petrograd demanded recognition of full independence as a means of countering the Two Emperors' Manifesto. The Provisional Government and the Petrograd Soviet both did so by 16/29 March. Elsewhere, from Crimea to Turkestan and from Chechnia to Estonia, the message from these self-appointed nationalist groups was the same: no more empire, but federation rather than independence.[36] Many of these groups continued to forward these limited goals throughout 1917, but those that turned to more radical positions began to do so in the midst of the military and political conflict that peaked during the June Offensive and the July Crisis.

Ukraine was the largest and most significant of these radicalizing areas. As with other regions, the first response to the revolution was to form a nationalist body— in this case the Ukrainian Central Rada (parliament), which was convened on 4/17 March—and to promote the idea of cultural and territorial autonomy within a Russian federation.[37] The moves toward a more expansive vision of autonomy came earlier than in many places, thanks in large part to the deliberations of the

---

[32] "Manifesto on the Dissolution of the Sejm and on the Holding of New Elections," in Browder and Kerensky, eds., 1: 351–2.

[33] Browder and Kerensky, eds., 1: 359–61.

[34] C. Jay Smith, Jr., *Finland and the Russian Revolution, 1917–1922* (Athens: University of Georgia Press, 1958), 22–3.

[35] On the question of federalism in 1917, see the excellent article I. A. Zhdanova, "Problema federativnogo ustroistva v Fevral'skoi revoliutsii 1917 g.," *Voprosy istorii* no. 7 (2007): 17–29.

[36] An extensive sampling of these documents is in Browder and Kerensky, eds., 1: 317–433.

[37] Browder and Kerensky, eds., 1: 370–1.

First Ukrainian Military Congress (5–8/18–21 May). As was the case more generally, soldiers in Ukraine had radicalized more quickly than other sectors of the population, and these men, already gearing up for the new planned offensive, did not disappoint. They demanded the appointment of a special minister for Ukrainian affairs who would become part of the Provisional Government, and, more consequentially, they demanded the "immediate consolidation of all Ukrainians [now serving] in the armies into one national army."[38] As we have seen, the Provisional Government had consented to certain measures of national autonomy: it tried to clarify borders, it sanctioned the use of local languages in local institutions, and it continued the wartime trend to allow volunteer military formations composed of a particular ethnicity. But anything beyond these limited measures spooked Petrograd politicians virtually across the political spectrum. Only the Bolsheviks remained adamant that the Provisional Government's policy was an unacceptable recapitulation of tsarist imperialism and that independence was a legitimate choice. For all others, including moderate socialists, demands to change the composition of the Provisional Government or to forcibly segregate existing military units were seen as encroachments upon sovereignty and military efficiency that were unacceptable in the period of war and revolution the country was living through.[39] As was the case with Finland, Russians either reacted angrily to the Ukrainian demands or tried to deflect the radical thrust with cool and empty phrases.

Ambiguity laced with spite did not appease the Ukrainian soldiers and nationalists. The Rada complained that "all remains as of old in this sphere [of Russian attitudes toward the Ukrainian movement], and the Russian public circles for the most part assume the old, vague positions."[40] For their part, soldiers tried to convene a second congress, which Kerenskii, citing the need for soldiers to remain at the front, prohibited. Over the first days of June, tensions rose considerably, and on 10/23 June the Rada issued its "First Universal" on the question of imperial relations. At this stage, it was still a demand for autonomy rather than independence: "Let there be a free Ukraine. Without separating from all of Russia, without breaking away from the Russian State, let the Ukrainian people on their own territory have the right to manage their own life."[41] Nevertheless, Russian politicians and opinion-makers flew into a fury. The Kadet newspaper *Rech'* called it "another link in the German plan to dismember Russia" because it challenged the authority of the Provisional Government and proposed collecting new taxes for the use of a Ukrainian government. Another Kadet paper, *Volia naroda*, called it "illegal, mistaken, and dangerous." Prince L'vov begged them not to "take the perilous course of splitting up the course of emancipated Russia." Even the socialist

---

[38] Resolutions of the First Ukrainian Military Congress, 5–8 May 1917, in Browder and Kerensky, eds., 1: 373–4.

[39] Zhdanova, 23.

[40] Memorandum of the Delegation of the Ukrainian Rada to the Provisional Government and the Executive Committee of the Soviets (n.d.—late May or early June), in Browder and Kerensky, eds., 1: 374.

[41] First Universal of the Central Rada, 10 June 1917, in Browder and Kerensky, eds., 1: 383.

newspaper *Izvestiia* reaffirmed that "the revolutionary democracy of Russia stands for the indivisibility of the state."[42]

Realizing the depth of the crisis, the Provisional Government sent a delegation to Kiev to negotiate with the Rada. Tereshchenko and Tsereteli were joined by Kerenskii, who was at the front attempting to inspire soldiers just as the offensive got underway. The Provisional Government saved face and its most important principles with a compromise. It confirmed the role of the Rada in helping to select a new General Secretariat that would govern Ukraine, deferred resolution of the land question and of the general political questions to the Constituent Assembly, and gave military commanders the right to stop the Ukrainization of existing troops. New recruits could be formed into ethnic units.[43] Even this was too much for the Kadet Party. Angered that Kerenskii, Tereshchenko, and Tsereteli had signed an agreement on their behalf without their consent, and also categorically opposed to any concessions to substantial local self-government prior to the convening of the Constituent Assembly, the Kadet ministers in Petrograd resigned en masse.[44] If imperialism abroad had crippled the power of the Kadets in April, imperialism at home destroyed it in July.

As events would prove, however, the Kadet blind spot on imperialism was widely shared. Petrograd politicians, both left and right, were ignorant and dismissive of representatives from the borderlands.[45] "If you want to bring any meeting of the Russian government to an end," complained V. I. Nutsubidze, "just bring up the national question, and everyone will disperse." Ethnic minorities gave speeches to empty rooms both in soviets and in meetings of the Provisional Government.[46] Though part of the compromise agreement, Kerenskii was also adamantly against making substantive changes in the political structure of the Russian state in such unsettled conditions. He showed his intransigence to the Finns with his hostility toward their declarations of autonomy and the disbanding of the Sejm. He would soon do the same with the Ukrainians. The General Secretariat had forwarded its interpretation of the 3 July agreement, but Kerenskii pushed it away and issued his own set of new regulations for Ukraine on 4/17 August that gave the vague compromise of July more specific content. The Rada was outraged because they thought them too favorable to Russians. It claimed that the regulations violated the July agreement, that they were "dictated by distrust toward the aspirations of the entire democracy of the Ukraine" and "imbued with the imperialist tendencies of the Russian bourgeoisie toward the Ukraine."[47] Ukrainian nationalists had already issued a barely veiled threat of civil war when they warned that Ukrainian soldiers had offered to defend the Rada from its abusers, and they now threatened to cease

[42] Browder and Kerensky, eds., 1: 386–8.   [43] Browder and Kerensky, eds., 1: 389–90.
[44] Rosenberg, 172–5.
[45] Mark von Hagen, "The Great War and the Mobilization of Ethnicity in the Russian Empire," in *Post-Soviet Political Order: Conflict and State Building*, ed. Barnett R. Rubin and Jack Snyder (London and New York: Routledge, 1998), 34–5.
[46] Zhdanova, 22.   [47] Browder and Kerensky, eds., 1: 398.

fighting the Germans.[48] Kerenskii made his views on nationality issues well known at the same time, when he opened the Moscow State Conference in August with references to the "impossible" and "ruinous" demands of the Finns and Ukrainians.[49]

It was reasonable for nationalists to wonder, in the late summer of 1917, what possible sort of acceptable framework could emerge from a Constituent Assembly made up of Russians completely tone-deaf to their concerns. Even Kerenskii, the man who, as we have seen, had argued on the floor of the Duma just months earlier that Russian society had a duty to question its moral authority to govern the borderlands, now appeared to be a Russian imperialist after all. Still, nationalists also knew that there were many other political parties and ideas within their "own" territories and that their support was limited. Political weakness and principled intransigence by all parties helped freeze the situation in place as the country continued to unravel over the course of the year. An increasing number of politicians mouthed the slogan of "national self-determination," but they meant much different things by these words. Instead of "federalism," a term which many wary politicians avoided, liberals and moderate socialists spoke enthusiastically of "decentralization" and the creation of a state system that would allow local governments to deal with strictly local issues so as to ease the burdens on lawmakers in the capital. This stance represented the "continuation of the imperial tradition."[50]

RISE OF THE WARLORDS

Questions over state and national sovereignty were much less pressing than the questions over local sovereignty that were exposed by the failure of the imperial state, however. The June Offensive had been a desperate attempt to discipline the army and end the war, and it had failed. Two phenomena that had existed in embryo since the beginning of the war now rose to the fore and would define the character not only of the remainder of 1917 but of the entire Russian Civil War. The first was the unleashing of undisciplined men with guns upon the civilian population of the empire. It had happened, as we have seen in earlier chapters, in front-line areas in Poland in 1914, and it had expanded significantly across the front-line zone and deeper in 1915 and 1916. We will see shortly that 1917 exacerbated the problem of wild soldiers significantly.

The second phenomenon was the development of warlordism.[51] In certain ways, the wartime experience had conditioned Russian officers and soldiers for this possibility. The assertion of military authority over civilian life in front-line zones created a precedent, developed experience, and convinced officers that they could

---

[48] D. Ia. Bondarenko, "Vremennoe pravitel'stvo i problema avtonomii ukrainy (iiul'-oktiabr' 1917 g.), *Otechestvennaia istoriia* no. 1 (2006): 60.

[49] Abraham, 259.   [50] Zhdanova, 22–4.

[51] Some material from this discussion on warlordism was originally published in Joshua Sanborn, "The Genesis of Russian Warlordism: Violence and Governance during the First World War and the Civil War," *Contemporary European History* 19, no. 3 (August 2010): 202–7.

not afford to concede governance over their territories to non-military men. General Ianushkevich's grand plans for ethnic cleansing (conducted despite the sharp protest of the Council of Ministers) were just the most obvious manifestation of this inclination in the early years of the war. Ianushkevich essentially controlled both military and political life in the territories where Russian armies stood, and he saw little distinction between his military and political ambitions. Just as importantly, many of the restraining forces that might have served to retard the development of warlordism were weakening or had failed already. Well-dressed ministerial bureaucrats and the fancy salons of Petrograd were far away, and men in uniform were becoming accustomed to making decisions on a much wider range of issues than they had done before the war. But Ianushkevich was not a warlord. Indeed, he was well known as a lively and entertaining guest, one "gentle to the core," at those very salons whose importance was fading away.[52] He was, in Alfred Knox's estimation, a "courtier rather than a soldier."[53] He killed people with his pen, not his sword. Just as importantly, he still fully embraced the discipline and chain of command that linked him to the rest of the military organism and that linked that organism to the rest of the Russian political and social system. He remained subordinate to his boss, Grand Duke Nikolai Nikolaevich, and both of them followed the orders of the tsar. When Nicholas abruptly sacked the grand duke and Ianushkevich from their positions after the disasters of 1915 and reassigned them to the Caucasus, they left quietly and without open recrimination. Ianushkevich's farewell speech to his staff consisted of him telling them "I am to blame for all that has occurred."[54] As the later lack of a coup demonstrated, there were no lone wolves in the army pack in early 1917.

The revolution changed that situation by initiating a sharp decline in the legitimacy of the officer corps and a noticeable increase in insubordination. One might have expected that the crippling of the social group most likely to become warlords would have retarded the growth of warlordism, but in fact it served to accelerate the process. As the army broke apart, opportunities arose for ambitious leaders to take command of parts of it on their own authority. As it turned out, the process of vetting, lynching, dismissing, or reaffirming one's commander served to bolster the personal power of particular commanders, even as it weakened the centralized army structure as a whole. Officers too could experiment with insubordination. It had become possible to gather groups of armed men loyal to their commander more than to the high command or indeed to fellow soldiers from other units. These commanders, precisely to the extent that they challenged central authority, required support from their soldiers and the means to supply those soldiers with civilian goods. If for no other reason than survival, nascent warlords

---

[52] Mikhail Lemke, *250 dnei v tsarskoi stavke: vospominaniia, memuary*, 2 vols. (Minsk: Kharvest, 2003), 1: 182–8.

[53] Major-General Sir Alfred Knox, *With the Russian Army, 1914–1917: Being Chiefly Extracts from the Diary of a Military Attaché*, 2 vols. (London: Hutchinson & Co., 1921), 1: 42.

[54] Knox, 1: 192.

would have to engage in civilian affairs, though most had political desires that
would have led them to the path of civilian rule in any case.

The first person to combine all of these features and ambitions—the first true
warlord of the period—was Lavr Kornilov. Kornilov's talent for command and his
extreme intolerance of military indiscipline were well known. Those who loved
him, loved him. Those who hated him did so with a passion. He apparently
recognized the dangers and possibilities of his situation quite quickly, and he
began forming cadres of his men loyal to him rather than to his military or political
superiors, most notably an elite corps of Tekke Turkmen called the "Tekintsy."
These men served him personally and well. So did several other trusted units. But
the polarization produced by the revolution and by Kornilov's personality also led
many men under his command to resist.

The June Offensive brought this conflict to the fore. As we have seen, despite
early successes, the Eighth Army rebelled against authority in the first days of July
and refused to attack further. When the German counteroffensive came, morale
collapsed. Soldiers fled to the rear, looting and pillaging as they went. Kornilov
reacted violently and independently. There is no indication that Kornilov had
harbored either a desire or a plan for striking out on his own prior to July 1917, but
he made three fateful choices over the ensuing month. First, he began using terror
as a command strategy. Second, he began to assert his independence from central
authorities. Finally, he began to envision combining military and political authority
in his own person.

As soon as the troops began to break, Kornilov turned to drastic measures.
Soldiers evacuating Galicia turned the region into a platform for atrocities. The so-
called "Savage Division" of troops from the Caucasus was particularly active. The
division had been detailed to the front for explicitly political work. On the eve of
the offensive Colonel Chavachadze began his briefing by saying: "Gentlemen, I am
sorry indeed that the young officers who joined our colours recently will have to
start their fighting career by doing a rather repulsive sort of police work."[55] That
work was to attack any soldiers or units engaged in mutiny or desertion, and it was
welcomed by many members of the unit. One of the officers in the division, Sergei
Kurnakov, admitted that he "hoped to be able to avenge some of the insults the
mutineers had inflicted on my brother-officers."[56] Instead, when the offensive
collapsed, Kurnakov reported undertaking a much different kind of police work.
Entering the town of Kalush, he encountered a monstrous scene. Driving down the
main street, Kurnakov thought he saw snow in July. Instead, it was the down of
feather beds floating through the air. He saw looting soldiers, "the body of an old
Jew . . . hanging out of one of the windows, his arms nailed to the window sill," and
finally the gang rape of a pregnant woman, which he dispersed with machine-gun
fire from his car.[57]

---

[55] Sergei Kournakoff, *Savage Squadrons* (Boston and New York: Hale, Cushman, and Flint, 1935),
321.
[56] Kournakoff, *Savage Squadrons.*   [57] Kournakoff, 338–41.

Other reports confirm the brutality of the retreating Russian army in Galicia that July, but most indicate that far from acting to stop the carnage, Kornilov's favorite division was one of the main instigators of atrocity, not only in Kalush, but in towns such as Ternopil' and Brody as well. As one official reported as late as August, "we are continually receiving petitions regarding robbery and violence" by members of the Savage Division.[58] One such petition from landowners complained that the Caucasian troops stole vegetables, robbed men of their money, and killed several people. "The local people," they wrote, "are in a state of panic."[59] While Kornilov did not officially condone this behavior, he did exacerbate it by issuing a scorched earth policy similar to that which was implemented in 1915. He ordered mass deportations once more, targeting all military-age men for removal along with their goods and horses.[60] He also pursued a terror campaign against his own soldiers by summarily executing deserters and others whom he blamed for the military defeat, despite the prohibition of the death penalty in place in the Revolutionary Army.[61]

Far from recognizing that ordering his troops to conduct campaigns against civilians and shirkers was contributing to indiscipline, he came to believe that only further terror could end the problem of military collapse. He, as most former officers, was outraged by the insubordination, the desertion, and above all the soldier committees and political commissars that had ruined his beloved army. In his opinion, the only way to reverse the collapse of the Russian military was to strengthen and unify the authority of officers that had been destroyed by the revolution. This was a non-negotiable issue for Kornilov. Furious that enlisted men would issue demands and ultimatums to their officers, he nevertheless became the first general to demonstrate insubordination to the political leaders above him in the chain of command. The pattern of conflict with the Provisional Government began early. As we have seen, Kornilov fumed in April when Kerenskii refused his offer to use military force to put down the anti-Miliukov disorders in Petrograd. When Kerenskii offered him the position of commander-in-chief in July, Kornilov responded with a set of demands that included the controversial measure of reinstituting the death penalty for soldiers and an insistence on complete autonomy in choosing military commanders. Kerenskii urged his colleagues to rescind the offer because Kornilov had demonstrated an unwillingness to subordinate himself to civilian authority, but he was rebuffed.[62] Other battles soon followed. Kornilov was head of the Southwestern Front when promoted, and the Provisional

---

[58] Report to the commander of the Eighth Army (author unknown), 28 August 1917, RGVIA f. 2067, op. 1, d. 1198, l. 5.

[59] Petition from landowners of Edinets volost, Khotinskii uezd to General Kul'zhinskii (Staff of Eighth Army), n.d., RGVIA f. 2067, op. 1, d. 1198, ll. 38–39. This file is filled with similar reports and runs to 471 pages.

[60] Mark von Hagen, *War in a European Borderland: Occupations and Occupation Plans in Galicia and Ukraine, 1914–1918* (Seattle: University of Washington Press, 2007), 84–5.

[61] The death penalty was not reinstated by the Provisional Government until 12/25 July, five days after Kornilov began the practice during the retreat.

[62] A. F. Kerensky, *The Prelude to Bolshevism: The Kornilov Rising* (New York: Dodd, Mead, and Company, 1919), 27.

Government had appointed General Cheremisov to command the front at the same time it moved Kornilov up the chain of command. Kornilov took this as a violation of his ultimatum that politicians must not interfere with command decisions, and he named his own favorite, General Baluev, instead. Cheremisov did not yield willingly, and it took all the wiles of the Provisional Government's commissar M. M. Filonenko to resolve the situation without a major conflict in the high command erupting into the open.[63]

By August, Kornilov was convinced that saving the army required not only the restoration of "harsh measures" in the army, [64] but also dictatorial methods in the rest of Russian government. Other top generals worked together with the Union of Officers to insist that the Provisional Government admit its mistake in distrusting military commanders, stop sticking its nose in army affairs, render the Declaration of Soldier Rights as "null and void," and, again, legalize the death penalty.[65] Kerenskii and other political leaders attempted over the course of July and August to calm the generals down by explaining the lengthy period necessary for legislation and by suggesting how suicidal such a legislative program would be for the Provisional Government itself. These conversations led to a simple logical conclusion for Kornilov: the army could not succeed without discipline, discipline could not be restored without firing squads, and firing squads could not be implemented by a weak Provisional Government in tandem with a seditious Petrograd Soviet. Hence "Dual Power" had to be eliminated to save the army. Dictatorship was necessary.

Kornilov and his later supporters claimed that though he had desired a dictatorship, he had not insisted that he himself be the dictator. Although Kornilov never openly avowed a desire to overthrow Kerenskii's government, the general was of course far too experienced to issue such openly treasonous proclamations. His actions suggest that he sought the mantle of the dictatorial savior. He soaked up the adulation of the political elite at the State Conference in Moscow in August, where he gave a speech that displayed political ambition as well as a strong military presence. More importantly, he began moving troops loyal to him close to Petrograd, most notably the "Savage Division," and began emptying the revolutionary Kronstadt fortress and naval base. His own chief of staff, General Lukomskii, threatened resignation on hearing of these moves before being reassured with the explanation that the repositioning was to defend the Provisional Government in the event of a Bolshevik coup. Kerenskii was hardly Kornilov's friend, however; a fact highlighted during Kornilov's visits to the Winter Palace, visits always taken with the Tekintsy by his side.

---

[63] George Katkov, *The Kornilov Affair: Kerensky and the Break-up of the Russian Army* (London: Longman, 1980), 45.

[64] These were Kornilov's words immediately after taking up his role as commander in chief. Katkov, 51.

[65] Katkov, 53. The Declaration of Soldier Rights, which was issued at Kerenskii's urging on 11/25 May 1915, extended the provisions of the more hasty and limited Order No. 1 to the whole army and included additional provisions such as freedom of conscience and religion in the armed forces. See a copy of this declaration in Browder and Kerensky, eds., 2: 880–3.

In late August, Kornilov made his move. He sent troops under the command of General Krymov from the front to Petrograd with the intention of disbanding the Soviet, arresting the Bolsheviks, and instituting a military dictatorship with himself at the head. These troops, shunted onto sidings by railway workers, were literally derailed. Similarly, Kornilov's expectation (fed by an extremely high level of miscommunication) that Kerenskii would support the coup was dashed when Kerenskii ordered him dismissed and arrested. The historical controversy that has swirled around the "Kornilov Affair" ever since has focused on Kerenskii's intentions, on whether Kornilov planned to allow civilian ministers into his circle of leadership, on how long he intended this state of emergency to last, and whether the aim of this coup was to destroy the Provisional Government or simply to "save" it from the Bolsheviks. All parties agree that Kornilov intended to intervene politically to create a dictatorial regime in which he would play a leading role.[66]

Thus, though the Kornilov Revolt in August is normally understood as the major counterrevolutionary moment in 1917, in a certain respect it was also the moment when revolution (in the form of insubordination to the established hierarchy of authority) reached its apogee. The coup failed. Kornilov's bid to become Russia's supreme warlord was stopped not as most such attempts had been in the past with defeat by the modern state and its army, but by the opposite phenomenon. Power had fractured to such a significant degree that military commanders could no longer expect to have their rule accepted over large territories. The army was divided amongst itself, as was the country as a whole. Kornilov had unwittingly discovered an important truth about warlordism—it works better on small regional scales than it does over large territories.

The coup failure itself helped to bring about the final disintegration of the army and the country. A new explosion of hostility between officers and enlisted men erupted. As General Gromyko of the Southwestern Front admitted in mid-September, the Kornilov uprising had destroyed whatever trust remained between the ranks. "The general mood is satisfactory," he reported, "but in connection with recent events it is angry with the command staff."[67] Another warned that defeatist propaganda was taking root and that a "wave of irresponsible Bolshevism" was washing through the army.[68] So too did ethnic tension tick up, this time between Cossacks and those who equated Cossacks with right-wing reaction. Peasants began refusing to sell grain or forage to Cossack units, and fellow soldiers began to ostracize Cossack units. "The mass of soldiers," one officer morosely reported, "hate Cossacks."[69]

---

[66] This is the view even of Kornilov's most ardent defenders, such as Richard Pipes. Richard Pipes, *The Russian Revolution* (New York: Alfred Knopf, 1990), 453–64.

[67] Telegram from General Gromyko (Southwestern Front), to the Quartermaster General (Stavka), 12 September 1917, RGVIA f. 2067, op. 3, d. 31, l. 107.

[68] Telegram from Tsvetkov (Temporary Commissar of the Eleventh Army) to Verkhovskii (War Minister), 16 September 1917, in M. B. Keirim-Markus, "O polozhenii armii nakanune oktiabria (Doneseniia komissarov Vremennogo pravitel'stva i komandirov voinskikh chastei Deistvuiushchei armii)," *Istoricheskii arkhiv* no. 6 (November 1957): 38.

[69] Telegram from the Commissariat of Cossack Troops at Stavka (Shapkin) to the Military Revolutionary Committees of the Northwestern, Southwestern, and Romanian Fronts, 24 November 1917, RGVIA f. 2067, op. 3, d. 31, l. 18.

The disintegration of the army went well beyond the mistrust towards officers and Cossacks. The wild destruction of Kalush described earlier in the chapter was repeated many times as soldiers and deserters moved bloodily eastward. As the future Hetman Pavel Skoropadskii would comment, the soldiers became animals. "Robbery, murder, violence and all kinds of other disorder became commonplace occurrences. Neither women nor small children were spared. And this was amongst a population which was sympathetic to them."[70] Two major centers of this violence were Ukraine and the Baltic littoral. The disorders described at the start of Chapter 5 increased many times over. In Podol'sk, soldiers attacked manor houses and Jews with equal relish in early July.[71] On 5/18 July, 5000 men refused to go to the front, deserted, ransacked a weapons cache, named themselves the Hetman Polubat'ko Regiment, and marched on Kiev. They quickly took the city fortress, seized the police and military district headquarters, and even arrested the chief of the city and the head of the police. Only a joint effort by the Ukrainian Hetman Bogdan Khmelnitskii Regiment, the leaders of public organizations, the Rada, the Soviet, and the new General Secretariat was able to defuse the situation and restore public order.[72] A month later, in Chernihiv, an angry crowd of women formed around the city food administration building, where the local militia succeeded initially in pacifying them. The arrival of reinforcements from the army resulted not in the establishment of order but the opposite. The soldiers joined the women in revolt, demanding the arrest and near lynching of Iankevich, the militia commander. The soldiers then dispersed around the city conducting searches of stores and apartments in a mood of "pogrom agitation." Only the arrival of a reliable artillery unit and the promise by local authorities to dismiss the entire local food administration prevented further violence.[73] Ukrainian leaders quickly, firmly, and correctly linked this explosion of violence not only to the collapse of the front but also to the collapse of the state. One of the reasons for Ukrainian urgency in establishing the General Secretariat as the decisive executive power in the land was to deal with anarchy. Symon Petliura, the future Ukrainian warlord, warned Petrograd in late July that "counter-revolutionary agitation is already developing in Kiev. We have to take power quickly in the region in order to paralyze this movement and also to deal in a timely fashion, with firm power, with the results of the retreat: deserters and bands of runaways. In general, it's necessary to tell them [Kerenskii and Tsereteli] that the situation is precarious."[74]

---

[70] Cited in Buldakov, 129.

[71] "Postupivshiia v Glavnoe Upravlenie po delam militsii 8 Iiulia s. g. svedeniia o vydaiushchisia proisshestviiakh pravonarusheniiakh i obshchem polozhenie del na mestakh," GARF f. 1791, op. 1, d. 49, l. 72.

[72] "Postupivshiia v Glavnoe Upravlenie po delam militsii 14 Iiulia s. g. svedeniia o vydaiushchisia proisshestviiakh pravonarusheniiakh i obshchem polozhenie del na mestakh," GARF f. 1791, op. 1, d. 49, l. 117.

[73] "Postupivshiia v Glavnoe Upravlenie po delam militsii 12 Avgusta s. g. svedeniia o vydaiushchisia proisshestviiakh pravonarusheniiakh i obshchem polozhenie del na mestakh," GARF f. 1791, op. 5, d. 51, ll. 67–68.

[74] Cited in Bondarenko, 56.

In the Baltic region, violence and decentralization also flourished. Soldiers joined locals in ransacking estates while also supporting the replacement of Russian bureaucrats with Estonians and Latvians.[75] In Rūjiena and its suburbs, "armed bands calling themselves Bolsheviks...terrorized the population," arresting citizens and confiscating money. The Provisional Government's commissar and the local militia stood by helplessly.[76] In July, the Valmiera district commissar complained that the behavior of the First Baltic Cavalry Regiment had taken on a "threatening character," as drunken soldiers abused persons and property in the region, "terrorized local citizens," and beat up militiamen.[77] In September, the same official was desperate:

> We request you to immediately take measures against the destructive requisitions of horses and livestock in the front regions of Lifliand Province: prohibit soldiers from seizing food and other property on their own volition, establish military patrols in Venden and Vol'mar [Valmiera] districts to protect the lives and property of the citizens, apply quick demonstrative punishments to marauders in the rear and to deserters and robbers who terrorize the population, publicize these measures widely among the population, use transport drivers appropriately for military needs and don't let them eat and live on the backs of the labouring people. Prevent the ignorant soldier masses from thoughtlessly destroying local welfare, for the population is threatened with famine, introduce flying military police units for the immediate investigation of all of this growing crime, return judicial authorities.[78]

Neither the Lifliand province commissar nor the military commanders in the region had the capacity to institute any one of these measures, of course, much less all of them. The conditions continued to deteriorate as the summer turned to fall. In Belarus, a sharp rise in crime was noted starting in late June. The state had "lost authority not only among the peaceful population, but also among bandits and thieves." Local militias were helpless, courts were swamped, and felonious behavior mushroomed.[79]

If this expansion of violence was concentrated near the front, it was not absent elsewhere. Deep in Siberia, a group of soldiers assisted a local peasant gathering in attacking the local military chief and a group of Roma suspected of theft. Eight of the Roma were shot on the spot.[80] In Penza province, on 5/18 July, a crowd of

---

[75] "Postupivshiia v Glavnoe Upravlenie po delam militsii 3 Iiulia s. g. svedeniia o vydaiushchisia proisshestviiakh pravonarusheniiakh i obshchem polozhenie del na mestakh," GARF f. 1791, op. 1, d. 49, l. 40.

[76] "Postupivshiia v Glavnoe Upravlenie po delam militsii 21 Iiulia s. g. svedeniia o vydaiushchisia proisshestviiakh pravonarusheniiakh i obshchem polozhenie del na mestakh," GARF f. 1791, op. 1, d. 49, l. 162.

[77] Telegram from the Vol'mar district commissar to the Lifliand province commissar, 27 July 1917, LVVA f. 7233, op. 1, d. 20, l. 12.

[78] Telegram from the Vol'mar district commissar to the Lifliand province commissar, 4 September 1917, LVVA f. 7233, op. 1, d. 20, l. 30.

[79] Solskii, 89.

[80] "Postupivshiia v Glavnoe Upravlenie po delam militsii 20 Iiulia s. g. svedeniia o vydaiushchisia proisshestviiakh pravonarusheniiakh i obshchem polozhenie del na mestakh," GARF f. 1791, op. 1, d. 49, l. 155.

1000 people lynched another suspected thief and his parents. In Nizhegorod province, the local authorities ruefully noted that "all of the lawbreaking and anarchy was linked with the arrival of deserters, soldiers on leave, or delegates from regimental committees. Under the influence of the agitation of these delegates and soldiers, the local peasantry has strengthened in its conviction that all civil laws have lost their force and that all legality must now be regulated by peasant organizations."[81] This decentralization of legitimate violence was also apparent in borderland areas. The Provisional Government soon heard rumors of negotiations between Kazakhs living in China and Turkestan to create autonomous military units.[82] As refugees and demobilized trench workers returned to Central Asia, tensions intensified. Russian settlers successfully pleaded for weapons, in case ethnic violence were to explode once more.[83]

It was in this context of a strong anti-imperial mood, radicalized and anarchic soldiers, and rapid decentralization that the Bolsheviks quickly grew in influence. For most of 1917, the party experienced wild swings of fortune. Lenin and his compatriots had two very serious political liabilities in wartime Russia. First, they did not play nicely with others. They elicited sharp hostility, of course, from those on the right and center of the political spectrum, who saw in them the embodiment of all that was wrong with the revolution. But the antipathy among fellow socialists, even their fellow Social Democratic Mensheviks, was nearly as great. There is no mistaking the special venom that socialists displayed when attacking their purported comrades, and this led to increasingly violent all-or-nothing struggles amongst the revolutionary leadership. It quickly became clear, for instance, that the political contest between Kerenskii and Lenin could only end with the utter defeat of one or the other. Second, and more importantly, the Bolsheviks were tied in the popular mind to pro-Germanism. The Bolsheviks had staked out a radical defeatist position at the outset of the war, a position that isolated them from nearly all other parties, socialist or otherwise, across the continent. If defeatism made logical sense from a revolutionary perspective, it made no sense at all to the Russian public and the Russian army. Most wondered how the Bolsheviks could support a Russian defeat that would allow militaristic Germans to rampage across the motherland. Even in 1917, when soldiers and citizens lobbied for peace, they did so on the condition that Germany stayed on its own side of the pre-war border.

Bolshevik ties to Germany nearly undid them. Lenin made it back to revolutionary Russia in April only through the good graces of the German high command and the famous "sealed train" that whisked him from Switzerland to the Finland Station. In addition, the Bolsheviks had willingly taken huge payments from a

---

[81] "Postupivshiia v Glavnoe Upravlenie po delam militsii 2 Avgusta s. g. svedeniia o vydaiushchisia proisshestviiakh pravonarusheniiakh i obshchem polozhenie del na mestakh," GARF f. 1791, op. 5, d. 51, l. 10.

[82] "Postupivshiia v Glavnoe Upravlenie po delam militsii 4 Avgusta s. g. svedeniia o vydaiushchisia proisshestviiakh pravonarusheniiakh i obshchem polozhenie del na mestakh," GARF f. 1791, op. 5, d. 51, l. 27.

[83] Marco Buttino, *Revoliutsiia naoborot: Sredniaia Aziia mezhdu padeniem tsarskoi imperii i obrazovaniem SSSR*, trans. Nikolai Okhotin (Moscow: Zven'ia, 2007 [2003]), 151.

German government that had come to see revolution as a far more feasible option for knocking Russia out of the war than military campaigns had proven to be. Though German agents spread money around to a number of groups, including Ukrainian nationalist ones, they gave far more to the Bolsheviks.[84] As the summer offensive faltered, mass protests erupted across the revolutionary state, most notably in Petrograd, where crowds threatened to unseat the government once again. The Bolshevik leadership wavered on the question of whether to take power during the so-called "July Days," and their indecision proved costly. Kerenskii unleashed a furious denunciation of Lenin and his comrades, accusing them of trying to hijack the revolution on behalf of their German paymasters. The charges rang true, even to many workers and soldiers, and top party officials had to flee the capital to avoid arrest. At the front, soldier committees angrily denounced the Bolsheviks as traitors working with counterrevolutionaries and German spies.[85]

At the same time, however, many soldiers also had dark suspicions regarding the ties of the military high command to Germany. Their concern, as we have seen, was present from the beginning of the war, and the war had allowed it to metastasize. Already by late 1915 censors reported that "rumors about the treason [of 'German' generals] were persistent and that ever-worsening commentary by enlisted men was taking fantastic forms and colossal dimensions."[86] Though most of the generals with German names and the "German" empress had disappeared by the middle of 1917, a new fear emerged: that their own authoritarian elite would welcome a German invasion and suppression of the revolution. These conspiratorial thoughts were strengthened as a result of the fall of Riga, as many soldiers believed that the inexplicably bad troop maneuverings prior to and during the battle were intentional.[87] Thus, there were credible claims to be made by both sides, each of which claimed that the other was in cahoots with the Germans. If soldiers were more persuaded of Bolshevik perfidy in July, that situation began changing in early August, when front committees learned of the counterrevolutionary speeches at the Moscow State Conference. In the final days of August, Kornilov's failed coup sealed the deal. Soldiers were now set in "the attitudes that carried both the masses and the revolutionary institutions toward the October denouement."[88]

With their liabilities neutralized, the Bolsheviks were able to take advantage of their significant political strengths in September and October. They had consistently maintained an anti-imperial line, attacking Russian chauvinism and even supporting independence movements when no one else would. They had never compromised with the now discredited Provisional Government and army high command. They maintained organizational capacity both in factories and in the armed forces. Finally, and most importantly, they had no compunctions about

[84] Oleh S. Fedyshyn, *Germany's Drive to the East and the Ukrainian Revolution, 1917–1918* (New Brunswick: Rutgers University Press, 1971), 47.

[85] Wildman, *Road to Soviet Power and Peace*, 113.

[86] Lieutenant Lashkevich (Military-Censor Bureau), untitled, undated document, RGVIA f. 2006, op. 1, d. 1006/21, l. 120.

[87] Wildman, *Road to Soviet Power and Peace*, 189.

[88] Wildman, *Road to Soviet Power and Peace*, 223.

bourgeois or aristocratic "honor" or "duty" when it came to signing a rapid, separate peace and allowing the soldiers to go home. No other party could claim these advantages, and the Bolsheviks wisely exploited them to their advantage, repeatedly contrasting their own positions with those of their political opponents. They believed, and acted upon the belief, that power would be won or lost among soldiers and among the urban soviet constituencies. They more or less ignored the vast ocean of rural Russia and its peasants.

Once the Bolsheviks had seized control of the executive committees of the biggest soviets, they suddenly became strident proponents of the slogan "All Power to the Soviets." A device that had been a "taunt" to timid moderate socialists from April to August now became a real platform once the Bolsheviks had gained majorities in the Petrograd (31 August/13 September) and Moscow (5/18 September) soviets.[89] Forwarding the cause of the soviets was still a cynical maneuver. Lenin stood steadfast in his demand for one-party rule. He thus remained ambivalent about using the soviets, which were still very much multi-party at this stage of the revolution, even if they did offer the potential to eventually extend the writ of the Central Committee across the country through the organizational network that had developed over the course of 1917.

We might also add that the call for all power to be transferred to the soviets corresponded to and resonated with those who had benefitted from the rapid decentralization occasioned by the collapse of the imperial state. At the front, in the national borderlands, even well into the interior of the country, power had moved downwards into local hands, and local politicians seized the moment both practically and conceptually. One Siberian activist, writing in July 1917, asked "what should Siberian regionalist-autonomists be seeking?" and gave a one-word answer: "decentralization."[90] Just as the slogan of "Peace" served to recognize and ratify the core decisions already made by soldiers deserting the front en masse, so too did the slogan of "All Power to the Soviets" recognize and ratify the power of local authorities. Or, more accurately, it staked out a position in the thousands of local battles that were yet to come in the Civil War. It also served as a justification for the events of 25 October/7 November, when the Bolsheviks launched their October Revolution. Led by Lenin and Trotskii, they seized power in Petrograd on the eve of the Second Congress of Soviets, occupied the main military installations in the city, took control of the means of communication, and arrested the Provisional Government (minus Kerenskii, who had fled the scene just in time). When the Congress of Soviets blanched at this unilateral assertion of sovereignty and blasted the Bolsheviks for adventurism, Bolshevik soldiers dispersed the meeting. "All Power to the Soviets" appeared to really mean "All Power to the Bolsheviks."

---

[89] Sheila Fitzpatrick, *The Russian Revolution*, 2nd ed. (Oxford: Oxford University Press, 1994), 61.

[90] David Rainbow, "Saving the Russian Body: Siberian States in the Russian Civil War," paper delivered at the Jordan Center for the Advanced Study of Russia, New York, 28 September 2012. Many thanks to the author for providing me with a copy of this paper and allowing me to cite it.

We should not imagine, however, that the Bolsheviks actually had all of the power after the October Revolution. To the contrary, as the Civil War would demonstrate, their hold on national and local power alike was quite tenuous. They certainly knew that they could not allow the army to turn against them, and this conditioned their actions soon after the coup in Petrograd. The Bolsheviks were strong in the army, but not so strong that they could ignore other political affiliations. They held firm control only in the Second Army. In all of the others, they had to work together with other groups.[91] Above all, they had to satisfy the main soldier demand of peace right away.

CEASE-FIRE. ARMISTICE. PEACE?

On 8/21 November, Lenin ordered General Dukhonin at Stavka to offer a ceasefire and peace negotiations to the Germans. This put Stavka in an impossible spot: either it had to recognize the legitimacy of Bolshevik rule and obey the order, or it publicly had to thwart the soldier desire for the end of the war. It chose the only possible path by temporizing, but Lenin had none of it. The new Council of People's Commissars (Sovnarkom) bypassed the high command entirely, informing committees up and down the fronts that their generals had refused to make peace offers and instructing them to immediately make contact with their counterparts across the lines.[92] This was yet another instance of radical decentralization: the end of fighting on most of the front was accomplished not by central edict or by diplomats in a chandelier-filled hall, but by repeated instances of mud-caked Russian soldiers coming to terms with relieved German officers under a flag of truce. Many such deals were concluded within two weeks of the appeal. As the lower-level negotiations spread, army and front committees joined in the process. On 19 November/2 December, the Western Front (comprising the Second, Third, and Tenth Armies) signed an armistice, and by 4/17 December, the groundwork had been laid for a general ceasefire between Soviet Russia and the Central Powers.[93] Bolshevik forces moved on Stavka's position in Mogilev, at which point General Dukhonin released the leaders of the Kornilov Coup from prison before being lynched by an angry mob of soldiers for resisting the tide of peace.

The cease-fire seemed to be the end of the war, as few believed that the old Russian army would ever fight again. General Mikhail Bonch-Bruevich, the former commander of the Northern Front and the brother of Lenin's close confidant Vladimir Bonch-Bruevich, was appointed to replace Dukhonin at Stavka and given the task of organizing the demobilization of the army. The scale of the proposed effort was sobering. It would take more than two months to ship all the soldiers away from the front, even if they ran eighty trains per day at peak capacity.[94] It

---

[91] Wildman, *Road to Soviet Power and Peace*, 379.

[92] Wildman, *Road to Soviet Power and Peace*, 380–5.

[93] Wildman, *Road to Soviet Power and Peace*, 393.

[94] "Zhurnal no. 102-i chastnago zasedaniia Soveshchaniia po demobilizatsii pri Shtabe Verkhovnago Glavnokomanduiushchago," signed by M. D. Bonch-Bruevich, 23 November 1917, RGVA f. 79, op. 1, d. 5, l. 67ob.

would take even longer to transport the wounded and the ill.[95] Even so, the process got underway only slowly. The failure to rapidly sign a permanent peace put the whole situation in limbo. As General Shcherbachev worriedly reminded his army commanders on the Romanian Front in mid-December, the agitators who referred to a general demobilization were wrong, as neither Sovnarkom nor the Ukrainian government had given such an order. With no peace treaty, an attack could be imminent. "Woe to them," he wrote, "who throw themselves on the mercy of the enemy."[96] The Germans were not the only threat. In Belarus, Polish armed forces had become active, leading to armed clashes between Russian and Polish forces and the threat of a Belorussian uprising against the occupying Poles.[97] These clashes became serious enough that Krylenko had to delay the disbanding of Stavka because of the "large battles with the Poles near Mogilev," in which old army troops were needed to support the 1500 new Red Army volunteers currently facing a Polish force of 14,000.[98] But the troops that Krylenko hoped to transfer to the sector had largely disappeared of their own volition. No one was guarding large stretches of the line, and the "masses await peace no matter what . . . the soldiers are completely inert and their only thought is to go home as quickly as possible. Desertion is taking the character of mass flight. . . . On 9/22 January in Radoshko-vichi soldiers and residents destroyed Jewish shops as the result of a sharp rise in prices."[99] Elsewhere, observers reported soldiers swarming the railways and over-filling the wagons headed east.[100] The Germans scouted the lines vigorously and took "measures to ensure a quick offensive in case of a breakdown in peace negotiations. There are no armed forces at the front able to offer any sort of resistance to the enemy."[101]

The October Revolution also introduced a new shock into the nationalist politics of the borderlands. It was not at all obvious that local dumas, radas, and sejms would or should recognize the Bolsheviks' seizure of power. In any case, the Provisional Government that had so tenuously maintained the legal continuity of the Russian Empire had now been deposed. The Ukrainian Rada, forced by circumstances to act, issued its Third Universal less than two weeks after the revolution on 7/20 November. "A heavy and difficult hour has fallen upon the

---

[95] "Zhurnal no. 103-i chastnago zasedaniia Soveshchaniia po demobilizatsii pri Shtabe Verkhovnago Glavnokomanduiushchago," signed by M. D. Bonch-Bruevich, 24 November 1917, RGVA f. 79, op. 1, d. 5, ll. 81ob–82.

[96] General Shcherbachev, Order to all army commanders, 15 December 1917, RGVIA f. 2134, op. 1, d. 1310, l. 4–4ob.

[97] "Razgovor po priamomu provodu mezhdu Pol'skii komissariat i tov. Stalin (Petrograd) i delegatsii pol'skogo komissariata (Stavka)," 18 January 1918, Russian State Military Archive (RGVA) f. 1, op. 4, d. 3, l. 51.

[98] "Razgovor po priamomu provodu mezhdu Balandinym (Petrograd) i Krylenko (Stavka)," 24 January 1918, RGVA f. 1, op. 4, d. 3, ll. 66–67.

[99] Sologub (Minsk), Secret Telegram to Podvoiskii (Commissariat of Military Affairs) and Miasnikov (Western Front Command), 12 January 1918, RGVA f. 1, op. 4, d. 6, ll. 41–42.

[100] "Rasporiazhenie no. 68 Upravlenie Krasnago Kresta 2-i d. armii," 22 December 1917, GARF f. R-3341, op. 1, d. 124, l. 13ob.

[101] Sologub (Minsk), Secret Telegram to Podvoiskii (Commissariat of Military Affairs), 15 January 1918, RGVA f. 1, op. 4, d. 6, ll. 86–87.

land of the Russian Republic," it noted. "The Central Government has collapsed, and anarchy, lawlessness, and ruin are spreading throughout the state. Our land is also in danger." To fend off this threat, the Rada proclaimed the creation of a new Ukrainian People's Republic. "Although not separating from the Russian Republic and therefore maintaining its unity, we nonetheless shall stand firmly on our own land."[102] If the Rada, through this statement and later actions, proved itself hostile to the Petrograd Bolsheviks, it worked earnestly to gain the support of soviets throughout Ukraine. In large part, it was successful, gaining statements of allegiance from the Kiev Soviet and several others throughout the country.[103]

As a result, the struggle for power in Ukraine now focused on the struggle for power within the soviets themselves. An important snapshot of the political sympathies of the citizens of Ukraine was provided by the returns of the elections to the Constituent Assembly, which were finally held beginning on 12/25 November. Nationwide, the Bolsheviks did fairly well, especially among their core constituencies of workers and soldiers. They took about 25 percent of the total vote, winning outright majorities in the major cities of Petrograd, Moscow, and Minsk. They earned the majority of votes among soldiers on the Northern Front and Western Front and among the sailors of the Baltic Fleet.[104] In Ukraine, however, the Bolsheviks fared miserably. They took just 4 percent of the votes in Kiev province. A list of candidates provided by the Ukrainian bloc took 77 percent in the same locale. In Poltava, where several Ukrainian parties ran separately, and where voter turnout was over 70 percent, the Bolsheviks were swamped too, getting only 64,460 votes out of more than a million cast. The Ukrainian Socialist Revolutionaries (SRs), a party that appealed to the peasant base of the SRs and also took strong nationalist positions, got 727,427 votes in Poltava.[105] These results do not suggest that a majority favored Ukrainian independence, something not even the Rada had proposed yet, but they do strongly suggest that a massive majority supported autonomy and wanted Ukrainian parties to represent their interests at the Assembly. Had the Bolsheviks been the keen supporters of national self-determination that they represented themselves to be in the summer of 1917, Ukraine would have established an autonomous socialist state as the year ended.

Lenin and the Bolsheviks instead sought to impose their own idea of democratic legitimacy—that only politically "conscious" workers should properly determine the fate of the nation and that one proved one's "consciousness" by supporting the Bolshevik Party. Implementing this ideal varied tremendously depending on the political and military circumstances in the regions in question. The Bolsheviks everywhere tried to leverage whatever "indigenous" support they enjoyed into local seizures of power. In Finland, Lenin continued to support communists in the largely Russian garrisons and among the Red Guards, and he would continue to do

---

[102] Text of preamble to the Third Universal, 7 November 1917, in Paul R. Magocsi, *A History of Ukraine: The Land and Its Peoples*, 2nd ed. (Toronto: University of Toronto Press, 2010), 510.

[103] Magosci, 510.

[104] Oliver H. Radkey, *Russia Goes to the Polls: The Election to the All-Russian Constituent Assembly, 1917* (Ithaca and London: Cornell University Press, 1990), 150.

[105] Radkey, 150, 160.

so during the brief Finnish Civil War from January to May 1918.[106] But tactically the Bolsheviks thought it prudent to allow Finland to separate, with Sovnarkom making a late-night decision over the New Year's holiday to formally acknowledge Finnish independence.

Ukraine was a different situation. When Bolshevik efforts to sway the Kiev Soviet to their side failed, they changed strategies. The only soviet in Ukraine to pledge support to the Bolsheviks rather than the Rada in the wake of the October Revolution had been in Kharkiv, located in the more industrial and more ethnically Russian eastern portion of Ukraine. The Bolsheviks set up shop there, convening the First All-Ukrainian Congress of Soviets of Workers', Soldiers', and Peasants' Deputies and establishing a government. On 17/30 December, they issued an ultimatum to the Rada, ordering it to close within forty-eight hours or consider itself at war "against the Soviet government in Russia and Ukraine."[107] The Rada turned immediately for outside help, sending a delegation to the ongoing peace negotiations between the Bolsheviks and the Central Powers at Brest-Litovsk on 22 December/4 January and requesting recognition as a partner in those negotiations.[108] Ukraine was now plainly in the midst of its own decolonizing moment, with rival political groupings making claims for their own legitimacy at the same time that the neighboring imperial powers tried to put their thumbs on the scales.

Events developed dramatically over the next six weeks. The Bolsheviks made good on their threat of war. Vladimir Antonov-Ovseenko, the son of an officer and a native of Chernihiv (in Ukraine) amassed volunteer Red Army troops (most of them ethnically Ukrainian) and marched on Kiev from his Kharkiv base. Despite these forces only numbering 8,000 at first, they quickly got the upper hand on the scattered formations loyal to the Rada led by Symon Petliura. The Rada's base of support proved very thin, as civilian support swung toward the Kharkiv army and Petliura's men transferred their allegiances.[109] Although Antonov-Ovseenko had personally departed the army to lead forces fending off counterrevolution on the Don, his chief of staff, the left Socialist Revolutionary Mikhail Murav'ev, reached Kiev on 27 January/9 February. The Rada fled to Zhytomyr, while the "centralist" Murav'ev occupied the capital and immediately implemented a reign of terror, executing several thousand people deemed anti-Bolshevik in the city.[110]

At the same time that the Rada's military collapsed, its young diplomatic corps scored a notable success. At first, the Ukrainian delegation sought recognition by noting that Sovnarkom did not represent either Ukraine or the Southwestern

---

[106] See, for instance, his insistence at the 7th Party Congress that "we have not betrayed Finland any more than the Ukraine. No worker can accuse us of that," in *Finland and Russia, 1808–1920*, ed. Kirby, 233.

[107] Magosci, 511.

[108] See here Irina Mikhutina, *Ukrainskii Brestskii mir: put' vykhoda Rossii iz pervoi mirovoi voiny i anatomiia konflikta mezhdu Sovnarkomom RSFSR i pravitel'stvom Ukrainskoi Tsentral'noi Rady* (Moscow: Evropa, 2007).

[109] Serhy Yekelchyk, *Ukraine: Birth of a Modern Nation* (Oxford: Oxford University Press, 2007), 71–2.

[110] Yekelchyk, 73; Geoffrey Swain, "Russia's Garibaldi: The Revolutionary Life of Mikhail Artemevich Muraviev," *Revolutionary Russia* 11, no. 2 (December 1998): 61–2.

Front, but it did not request recognition as an independent state. That position changed once the Central Powers made clear that a separate peace was possible if the Ukrainian People's Republic declared itself independent. The Rada met on 27 December/9 January and resolved to make the final break. On the next day, Vsevolod Holubovych, one of the Rada's negotiators, demanded official recognition at the talks. Trotskii quickly declared that he recognized them as an "independent delegation,"[111] though he made no comment on whether they represented an independent state. Observers and later historians remain divided as to Trotskii's motives. The Ukrainian delegation believed that he did so in the expectation that the Ukrainians would ultimately side with the Bolsheviks to fend off the annexationist pressure of the German imperialists.[112] John Wheeler-Bennett, the author of the standard English-language work on the treaty, believes that the Germans basically trapped Trotskii in his own rhetoric of national self-determination.[113] More recently, P. V. Makarenko has argued that Trotskii did so because he believed that Germany would sign a separate peace with Ukraine if the Bolsheviks refused to bring them into the discussions.[114] On 9/22 January 1918, the Rada pressed its advantage by releasing its Fourth Universal. That document declared that the Ukrainian People's Republic had become "an independent, subordinated to none, free, sovereign state of the Ukrainian Nation" and proclaimed a desire to live in peace and friendship with all of its neighbors.[115] It was now clear that Soviet Russia and the Ukrainian People's Republic would pursue very different goals at the Brest-Litovsk parleys. As Bolshevik forces raced towards Kiev, the Ukrainian diplomats sealed their deal with the Central Powers, obtaining an agreement that Kholm province would be part of Ukraine (not Poland) after the war, promising to deliver food to the hungry cities of Central Europe, and obtaining assurances of military support from the German army. The two processes culminated on the same day, 27 January/9 February 1918, when Ukraine and the Central Powers signed the first peace treaty of World War I and when Bolshevik troops took the Ukrainian capital into their hands.

Trotskii immediately insisted that the treaty was invalid and reiterated a claim he had first made on 19 January/1 February that the Ukrainian delegation should be sent packing, since they represented a government that no longer controlled events in Ukraine.[116] His protest was ignored. The peace with Ukraine, combined with increasing anger over Bolshevik appeals to German troops to mutiny, had made the German and Austrian delegations even more intransigent. There had been

---

[111] Stephan M. Horak, *The First Treaty of World War I: Ukraine's Treaty with the Central Powers of February 9, 1918* (Boulder, CO: East European Monographs, 1988), 34.

[112] Horak, 35.

[113] John W. Wheeler-Bennett, *The Forgotten Peace: Brest-Litovsk, March 1918* (New York: William Morrow & Company, 1939), 158.

[114] P. V. Makarenko, "Bol'sheviki i Brestskii mir," *Voprosy istorii* no. 3 (2010): 8.

[115] Translated text of the Fourth Universal (9/22 January 1918), in Horak, 160. The document was released on 11/24 January 1918 but was backdated two days to the time when the Rada meeting had occurred.

[116] Aleksandr Shubin, "The Treaty of Brest-Litovsk: Russia and Ukraine," *Lithuanian Historical Studies* 13 (2008): 92.

significant pressure from the Austrians early in the process to sign a quick peace, since they were threatened with a revolutionary situation brought on by food shortages in January 1918. The deal with Ukraine promised to ease those shortages, however, and this made peace with the Bolsheviks a less urgent matter.[117] In turn, the Ukrainian peace allowed the Central Powers to forward their war aims more aggressively. From the start, the German military had insisted on severing all the territories occupied by their troops from the Russian state. On 5/18 January, General Hoffmann had produced a map with a blue line that left all of Poland, all of Lithuania, half of Latvia (including Riga), and the (Estonian) Moon Sound Islands on the German side of the line. Now, on 27 January/9 February, the Germans extended their claims to include the rest of Latvia and Estonia. There was probably room for a final negotiation here if the Bolsheviks agreed to sign a peace on the basis of Hoffman's original map, but Trotskii decided not to play the diplomatic game that way. Instead, with the backing of Lenin, he took the risk of walking out of the peace negotiations. He announced that he refused to sign an annexationist peace but that he was declaring an end to the war and demobilizing the Russian army. The declaration of the "no war, no peace" strategy left the room breathless. "Unheard of!" protested General Hoffmann, as Trotskii and his delegation left the room.[118]

In many ways, this was a brilliant maneuver. If the Germans invaded further, it placed all the onus for continuing the war on them and made plain the purely annexationist character of the conflict. If they did not, the Bolsheviks got the benefits of peace without having to dirty their hands with imperialist diplomats. The risk was twofold. First, and most urgently, there was a danger that a renewed and determined German offensive could take Petrograd quickly and perhaps destroy the revolution. Second, as Lenin quickly realized, the cost of any German pushback on their ploy would be the loss of Estonia and Latvia. "It has been said here," he told the Central Committee, "that they will take Livonia [eastern Latvia] and Estonia, but we can give them up for the sake of the revolution . . . If we cede Finland, Livonia, and Estonia—the revolution is not lost."[119] The gamble almost paid off, as the professional German and Austrian diplomatic corps argued that they should accept the peace and move along to the intensifying conflict on the Western Front. The Bolsheviks too thought at first that the ploy had succeeded. Over the next several days, however, imperialist voices in the German government and high command gained the upper hand, and the Germans declared an end to the armistice effective from 18 February.[120]

With their bluff called, the Bolsheviks grew desperate even as the Germans suddenly found a new patience for letting military events develop. There were no

---

[117] Borislav Chernev, "'The Future Depends on Brest-Litovsk': War, Peace, and Revolution in Central and Eastern Europe, 1917–1918," (Ph.D. diss., American University, 2013).

[118] Wheeler-Bennett, 227–8.

[119] Cited in Olavi Arens, "The Estonian Question at Brest-Litovsk," *Journal of Baltic Studies* 25, no. 4 (1994): 319.

[120] Wheeler-Bennett, 238. On 1/14 February 1918, the Bolsheviks moved to the Gregorian calendar. All dates after this one are rendered in one form only.

real forces between the German army and the hearth of the revolution. On 19 February, Lenin sued for peace, but the Germans took their time in recognizing the surrender. On 21 February, the Bolshevik leadership, fearing for their existence, appealed to both patriotic and revolutionary sentiments across the country with a call to arms under the slogan "The Socialist Fatherland is in Danger!"[121] Germany, unfazed, issued new demands on 23 February, by which time they had moved forward nearly 250 kilometers. The Bolsheviks immediately accepted, but the Germans moved on, demanding the presence of a Soviet delegation at Brest-Litovsk before signing a peace. German planes bombed Petrograd for the first and only time in the war on 27 February from airfields in Pskov.[122] The Soviet delegation, now without Trotskii, arrived at German headquarters on 28 February and were presented with yet harsher terms, including the cession of the provinces of Ardahan, Kars, and Batum to the Ottoman Empire. The Germans wished to set up a sub-commission to negotiate the details, but the Soviets once more refused to act diplomatically. They would sign anything put before them, but they would not negotiate a clearly dictated peace. The Germans finally gave up trying, and the document was signed on 3 March 1918.[123]

The Treaty of Brest-Litovsk was the culmination of a year of revolution and a key moment in the decolonization of the Russian Empire. Many issues agitated the political consciousness of the peoples of the Romanov lands over that year, but two of the most significant were the war and the status of the empire. The treaty seemed to bring both of these to a close. Revolutionary Russia and the Central Powers declared in Article I that "the state of war between them has ceased" and that they were "resolved to live henceforth in peace and amity with one another." Articles III–VII, at the same time, brought an end to the Russian Empire in Eastern Europe. The Soviet delegation agreed that all territories west of the "line agreed upon by the contracting parties which formerly belonged to Russia, will no longer be subject to Russian sovereignty." Russian political and military forces, already driven from Poland, Lithuania, and parts of Belarus, were required to evacuate Finland, Estonia, Latvia, Ukraine, Eastern Anatolia, Kars, Ardahan, and Batum. Both sides agreed to "respect the political and economic independence and the territorial integrity" of Persia and Afghanistan.[124] Russia's Great War, entered into in order to protect the empire, thus concluded with imperial destruction.

Despite the promises in the text, the Treaty of Brest-Litovsk ended neither warfare nor the political engagement of Great Russians with the elites and societies of the imperial borderlands. Within days, German and Austrian troops were fighting against Bolshevik forces in Ukraine, as the delegates from the Central Powers had promised, and as all the signatories to both Brest treaties knew they would. Within weeks, they had driven Red forces out of Ukraine, culminating with the seizure of Kharkiv on 8 April. On 5 March, German troops arrived in Finland at the reluctant invitation of Karl Mannerheim in order to fight Red Guards modeled after and supported by their Russian counterparts. Russian involvement

---

[121] Sanborn, *Drafting the Russian Nation*, 42.   [122] Wheeler-Bennett, 265.
[123] Wheeler-Bennett, 265–9.   [124] Wheeler-Bennett, 405–7.

withered over the course of March, in part because Finnish communists began to see Lenin's help as a liability.[125] The Finnish Whites soon won the war. There was precious little "peace and amity" to be had between the contracting parties of the agreement, and the German military continued its relentless movement forward, reaching as far as Rostov on the Don River.

As for the Bolsheviks, the treaty was clearly linked not with demobilization, which had already happened, but with an urgent call for the rapid growth of the Red Army. The Central Committee, in a series of letters to local officials, explained the reasons for signing the peace, but always stressed the need for Red Army recruitment at the same time. As Elena Stasova wrote from the Secretariat of the Central Committee to a district soviet in Ufa province on the day the treaty was signed, "the question of war and peace has now become very urgent, and in connection with this question arises the question of the Red Army. What are you doing in this regard? You must understand that in order to fight with worldwide imperialism, we need a well-disciplined and trained socialist army."[126] On 15 March, General Bonch-Bruevich wrote a detailed memo to Lenin urging that conscription be reimplemented in order to fight hostile German forces. Lenin agreed at the end of the month, setting in motion the train of events that would result in the mass Red Army.[127] A month later, Trotskii would reiterate in a speech to the Soviet leadership that the main threat to the Bolshevik regime was not domestic counterrevolution but Imperial Germany.[128] The Treaty of Brest-Litovsk had brought many changes to Eastern Europe. Peace was not among them, either on the ground or in the minds of politicians.

CONCLUSION

What explains the odd circumstance of a peace treaty that does not end hostilities but rather ensures further warfare? The answer lies in the intimate relationship between self-determination and civil war, a process that accelerated beginning with the steppe rebellion of 1916. That uprising was really the start of the final revolutionary crisis, as it brought several developing processes to the fore. Grounded in the economic and social tensions of the war (especially labor shortages and consumer unrest), it quickly became something bigger and more dangerous than the previous strikes and pogroms of the wartime period had been. First of all, it shone a spotlight on imperial issues. Initial unhappiness with a wide range of political institutions, including indigenous ones, soon coalesced into an

[125] Smith, 48–63.

[126] Letter from E. D. Stasova (Secretariat of Central Committee) to the Executive Committee of the Zainsk Soviet of Soldier and Peasant Deputies of Menzelinsk District, Ufa Province, 3 March 1918, in A. N. Sokolova, "Iz pisem Sekretariata TsK RSDRP(b) na mesta v dni bor'by za Brestskii mir," *Voprosy istorii KPSS* no. 6 (1958): 72.

[127] Sanborn, *Drafting the Russian Nation*, 43.

[128] L. D. Trotskii, "Krasnaia armiia (Rech' na zasedanii VTsIK 22 aprelia 1918 g.)," in *Kak vooruzhalas' revoliutsiia*, 3 vols. (Moscow: Vysshii voennyi redaktsionnyi sovet, 1923–1925), 1: 113.

anti-colonial mutiny. The savage response of the tsarist state and of the Russian settlers in the region turned the mutiny into a civil war. This, in turn, prompted political observers both on the ground and in the metropole to reflect upon the future viability of the Russian Empire. The inclusion of the issues surrounding civil war in Turkestan in the great political crisis of November 1916 was no accident. Among the most significant criticisms of the imperial regime at the end of 1916 was thus precisely that it was imperial. Unable to understand indigenous peoples on the periphery, it oppressed and exploited them. A revolution would have to end Russian ignorance and chauvinism and grant a measure of self-determination to non-Russians across the country.

The revolution did not end either Russian ignorance or chauvinism, but it did end up granting first autonomy and then independence to many colonized societies. As with the rest of the revolutionary progression, this process of decolonization was the result of dynamic wartime developments. The Russian Revolution as a whole was a product of the war and was decisively influenced by soldiers at every key stage. The revolt of the garrisons in February 1917, the pressure to abdicate from the generals in March, the soldier-led protests against Miliukov in April, the political explosion surrounding the summer offensive in June and July, the Kornilov Revolt and its suppression in September, the October Revolution itself—all of them not only included soldiers but were virtually unthinkable without them. So too were soldiers integral to the disarticulation of the empire, in particular in the development of the ideology and practice of the "self-determination of nations."

The slogan of national self-determination has generally been associated with a particular "Wilsonian Moment" at the end of the war and through the peace process. As Ezra Manela, one of the most recent students of that moment notes, however, neither the idea of self-determination nor the linkage of that idea with the peace process originated with Wilson. Instead, he argues, the strongest founders of the movement were Lenin and Trotskii.[129] Manela is right to look to the Russian Empire as the heartland and birthplace of the Wilsonian Moment, but the association between national self-determination and peace pre-dated the arrival of Lenin and Trotskii on the scene in 1917. It is true that Lenin had addressed the question of self-determination both prior to and in the middle of the war, writing "The Revolutionary Proletariat and the Right of Nations to Self-Determination" in late 1915 and "The Socialist Revolution and the Rights of Nations to Self-Determination" in April 1916. But these were theoretical skirmishes with Austro-Marxists (the first, indeed, was written in German) written in Switzerland, not broad appeals to wartime publics in any nation.[130]

The concept of national self-determination as a political force really emerged in the enthusiasm of the February Revolution, which was understood to be the assertion of the "Russian" people of their own sovereignty and a transformational

---

[129] Erez Manela, *The Wilsonian Moment: Self-Determination and the International Origins of Anticolonial Nationalism* (Oxford: Oxford University Press, 2007), 6.
[130] Borislav Chernev, "The Brest-Litovsk Moment: Self-Determination Discourse in Eastern Europe before Wilsonianism," *Diplomacy & Statecraft* 22, no. 3 (2011): 370–1.

moment for peace at the same time. As the Petrograd Soviet put it in its "Appeal to the Peoples of All the World," the Russian people had seized "full political freedom," and would

> assert their mighty power in the internal self-government of the country and in its foreign policy. And, appealing to all people destroyed and ruined in the monstrous war, we say that the time has come to begin a decisive struggle against the acquisitive ambitions of the governments of all countries; the time has come for the peoples to take into their own hands the decision of the question of war and peace.[131]

Already, in early March, while Lenin and Trotskii were still in exile, the Soviet had linked self-determination, anti-imperialism, and peace. The chairman of the session that authored the appeal was Nikolai Chkheidze, the Georgian Menshevik who had insisted on the importance of the theme of imperialism during the political crisis of November 1916.

The Provisional Government had to clarify its own war aims as a result. It was only then, on 27 March/13 April, that Prince L'vov and Miliukov declared that "the aim of free Russia is not domination over other nations, or seizure of their national possessions, or forcible occupation of foreign territories, but the establishment of a stable peace on the basis of the self-determination of peoples."[132] In the minds of many denizens of the empire, including most of its soldiers, the April Crisis solidified the idea that peace should come "without annexations or indemnities." This was explicitly understood to mean that peace had to be anti-imperial and that national self-determination would resolve any lingering questions of proper political sovereignty. Given his earlier writings, it was not surprising that Lenin latched on to this revolutionary theme with special relish, taking the idea to its logical conclusion and lambasting his enemies for their hesitance and hypocrisy on imperial issues. First Miliukov, and then Kerenskii, gave plenty of fodder for these attacks, and the Bolsheviks emerged at the end of the year as the purest party on the issues of anti-imperialism and peace. National self-determination had become one of the defining themes of the Russian Revolution, and the Bolshevik Party issued a "Decree on Peace" through the Congress of Soviets in the very first session after their coup which devoted much of its space to the idea that the war was about national oppression and that peace could only come through self-determination.[133]

In early 1918, this discursive construction became one of the revolution's major exports. Diplomats from the Central Powers cynically seized upon it as a way to use the Bolsheviks' own slogan to cement their wartime gains, resolving to do so even before the peace negotiations had begun.[134] On 12/25 December 1917, the Austrian Foreign Minister Count Ottokar Czernin made this commitment public

---

[131] Soviet Appeal to the Peoples of All the World, 14 March 1917, in Browder and Kerensky, eds., 2: 1077.

[132] Provisional Government's Declaration of War Aims, 27 March 1917, in Browder and Kerensky, eds., 2: 1046.

[133] "Dekret o mire," 26 October 1917, in *Dekrety sovetskoi vlasti*, 18 vols. (Moscow: Gosizdat, 1957), 1: 12–16.

[134] Chernev, "Brest-Litovsk Moment," 372.

on behalf of the Central Powers, granting "validity" to the right of self-determination "everywhere in so far as it is practically realizable."[135] More broadly, the Brest-Litovsk talks impelled other belligerents to state their aims too. Lloyd George announced on 23 December 1917/5 January 1918 that self-determination was one of Britain's war aims, and Wilson openly supported the Bolshevik negotiating stance in the speech of 26 December 1917/8 January 1918 that announced his Fourteen Points.[136] At Brest-Litovsk itself, the rhetoric of self-determination dominated the negotiations. Even at the moment of greatest German frustration, General Hoffmann attacked Trotskii and the Soviet delegation by using the trope of self-determination, accusing them of "relentlessly suppressing all who think differently," not only in Russia but in Belarus and Ukraine as well. He also whined that the spread of Bolshevik propaganda amidst German workers and soldiers amounted to a violation of Germany's right to operate without foreign interference.[137] When the Ukrainian delegation arrived, it was indeed very difficult for Trotskii to protest their inclusion, and he accepted them in the meetings up until the time that the Rada lost control of the country. When Grigorii Sokol'nikov signed the final treaty, Trotskii fumed that it was a peace "which Russia, grinding its teeth, is forced to accept. This is a peace which, whilst pretending to free Russian border provinces, really transforms them into German States and deprives them of their right of self-determination."[138] Across Europe, this Carthaginian peace became another exhibit in the indictment of German militarism, and the defense of the concept of self-determination became a major part of the discussion of war aims and peace for the remainder of the war.[139]

As we have seen in this chapter, however, the marriage of the ideals of national self-determination and peace never made much sense, certainly not in the volatile and violent conditions of wartime Eastern Europe. Another of Lenin's writings from 1915 made plain that he expected the end of the imperialist war to come only with the onset of a civil war.[140] This is what the device of national self-determination logically suggests—not peace emerging from war, but the shift from an interstate war to an intrastate war. These civil wars, especially those in periods of decolonization, are hardly parochial or limited. Instead, outside forces affect both the political struggles to define the "nation" and the military conflicts that surround those struggles. Already in November 1917, the Central Powers had prepared the ground for pro-German declarations of "self-determination" in places like Estonia, where they launched a propaganda campaign and a petition drive to support the idea that Estonia wished to be annexed by the Reich.[141] In the military realm, the Germans fought the Bolsheviks in an open proxy war for Ukraine for much of 1918. The Petrograd Bolsheviks had signed the peace, but the Kharkiv Bolsheviks

---

[135] James Brown Scott, *Official Statements of War Aims and Peace Proposals, December 1916 to November 1918* (Washington DC: Carnegie Endowment for International Peace, 1921), 222.
[136] Scott, 233, 234.   [137] Wheeler-Bennett, 162.   [138] Wheeler-Bennett, 268.
[139] Chernev, "Brest-Litovsk Moment," 383.
[140] V. I. Lenin "Sotsializm i voina (otnoshenie RSDRP k voine)," in *Sochineniia*, 4th ed., v. 21 (Moscow, 1951), 286.
[141] Arens, 312–17.

fought on. The Ukrainian People's Republic that had inked a deal with the Central Powers was then unceremoniously cashiered by those same powers in April, when the Germans installed Pavlo Skoropadsky as Hetman.[142] The transition from Great War to Civil War was seamless in these areas. Not even the uniforms changed. Indeed, as the uprising in Turkestan described in Chapter 5 showed, the line between the two wars had been blurred throughout the revolutionary period.

[142] Yekelchyk, 73–6.

Conclusion: Imperial Apocalypse

CIVIL WAR

The signing of the Treaty of Brest-Litovsk was the most tangible moment of decolonization in 1918, but it certainly did not stop the process of imperial collapse. Civil war continued across the territory of the former empire, as violent local struggles for power popped up nearly everywhere in the wake of the Bolshevik coup. Much of this fighting was done by soldiers who had been demobilized or who had fled from the war zone on their own. These men had lost their appetite for fighting the Great War, but they had left neither their weapons nor their taste for violence at the front. Many of these men initially supported the Bolsheviks, as they had during the crises of late 1917, and Soviet power expanded in the wake of demobilization as they made it home. The connection between former soldiers and the party was strong in other ways too. Local residents often associated them with the party and hence associated the party with the return of violent men and disorder to their towns and villages.[1] As time went on, veterans took more and more positions in the party, especially in rural areas where Bolshevik influence had traditionally been modest.[2] Still, it would be incorrect to assume that war veterans constituted a unified or organized pro-Bolshevik bloc. When the Red Army launched a campaign of voluntary recruitment in the winter and early spring of 1918, it tried to make it easy for veterans to re-enlist. Few enlisted men chose to do so.[3] The officers who volunteered largely preferred the anti-Bolshevik (White) armies, and many fled south to the Cossack lands after the imperial capitals were lost to the Reds. The White "Volunteer Army" was composed almost entirely of officers at first, with few enlisted men to command.[4]

---

[1] See Sarah Badcock, *Politics and the People in Revolutionary Russia: A Provincial History* (Cambridge: Cambridge University Press, 2007); Aaron B. Retish, *Russia's Peasants in Revolution and Civil War: Citizenship, Identity, and the Creation of the Soviet State, 1914–1922* (Cambridge: Cambridge University Press, 2008); Liudmila Novikova, *Provintsial'naia 'kontrrevoliutsiia': beloe dvizhenie i Grazhdanskaia voina na russkom Severe, 1917–1920* (Moscow: Novoe literaturnoe obozrenie, 2011).

[2] On this, see also Marco Buttino, *Revoliutsiia naoborot: Sredniaia Aziia mezhdu padeniem tsarskoi imperii i obrazovaniem SSSR*, trans. Nikolai Okhotin (Moscow: Zven'ia, 2007 [2003]), 151.

[3] Joshua Sanborn, *Drafting the Russian Nation: Military Conscription, Total War, and Mass Politics, 1905–1925* (DeKalb: Northern Illinois University Press, 2003), 44–5.

[4] Peter Kenez, *Civil War in South Russia, 1918: The First Year of the Volunteer Army* (Berkeley: University of California Press, 1971), 72.

Would-be civil war commanders in the first half of 1918 had plenty of political will and hostility, but they lacked the soldiers required to fight a large-scale war. Small-scale skirmishes between committed bands of Reds and Whites were intense and deadly, as the veterans of the Ice March (February–May 1918) and the first leader of the White forces, General Kornilov (who died in battle on 13 April 1918), could attest. In the midst of these early conflicts, the Bolsheviks appeared ascendant. Soviets asserted power in most urban locales of the empire in late 1917 and early 1918. Anti-soviet towns and villages that resisted faced revolutionary train caravans full of activists, as the Bolsheviks fought what they called an "echelon" war not just in the South but in Siberia and Ukraine as well.[5] Throughout the country, though, soviet authority was thin in the towns and even shakier in the countryside. In Siberia, for instance, the Bolsheviks took power in the major cities along the Trans-Siberian Railway, but that rule was "rudimentary." Whatever good will the Bolsheviks had generated among Siberian peasants through the Decree on Land had been destroyed by brutal grain requisitions in Western Siberia in early 1918.[6] In Arkhangel'sk province, the heavy-handed throttling of the new, revolutionary forms of local self-government led all social strata to join forces to defeat the alien forces from the capital. Even the regional soviet rejected Sovnarkom's claim to authority in the area.[7]

In the spring of 1918, however, both sides turned to more expansive political and military mobilization. Conscription was reintroduced in both White and Red areas, and each side sought allies amongst the variety of domestic and foreign actors whose participation in the conflict had not yet been secured. At first, the key alliances seemed to be foreign ones. Germany occupied Ukraine with relative ease soon after Brest-Litovsk was signed in March and, as we have seen, installed Skoropadskii as Hetman in April. On 8 April, the Bolshevik redoubt of Kharkiv fell to the Central Powers. On 8 May, the Germans made it all the way to Rostov-on-the-Don. They played a large role in the struggle for Ukraine and South Russia. In the north, the German move towards Petrograd in February and their support for Finnish Whites in March spooked the Allies enough to warrant the expansion of British forces in Murmansk by several hundred men. In the east, Japanese and British marines moved into Vladivostok in April. It was easy enough to see that these forces might eventually link up with the anti-Bolshevik opposition. For foreign armies and politicians, the mixture of nationalists, monarchists, and liberals was far more congenial than the Red threat that Lenin and his comrades represented.

Nevertheless, the most important foreign ally for the Whites in 1918 was not a member of the Great Powers. Instead, it was a collection of 35,000 Czech and Slovak POWs trying to make their way home to fight for independence. As we saw

    [5] Evan Mawdsley, *The Russian Civil War* (Boston: Allen & Unwin, 1987), 17.
    [6] Jonathan Smele, *Civil War in Siberia: The Anti-Bolshevik Government of Admiral Kolchak* (Cambridge: Cambridge University Press, 1996), 13–14.
    [7] Liudmila G. Novikova, "A Province of a Non-Existent State: The White Government in the Russian North and Political Power in the Russian Civil War, 1918–1920," *Revolutionary Russia* 18, no. 2 (2005): 126; Yanni Kotsonis, "Arkhangel'sk 1918: Regionalism and Populism in the Russian Civil War," *Russian Review* 51, no. 4 (October 1992): 534, 538.

in Chapter 3, Russia (along with other belligerents) had recruited ethnic legions among disaffected minorities in their POW camps, hoping both to augment the military forces at their disposal and to exploit the national fissures in the imperial structures of their enemies. The Czech Legion was one of the most successful of these enterprises. It had fought on the Russian side on the Eastern Front ably and in relatively large numbers, especially after the Provisional Government had allowed Czech recruiting agents to proselytize in the camps in the spring of 1917. Delicate negotiations resulted in the Bolsheviks agreeing to allow them safe passage eastward to Vladivostok and thence by boat to the United States and eventually Europe, but only if they surrendered their weapons. Germany understandably put significant pressure on the Bolsheviks to enforce this last provision, especially in the wake of the Brest-Litovsk Treaty. The Czechs, just as understandably, trusted no one in Revolutionary Russia, and they boarded their trains both armed and wary. When they caught wind of an order by Trotskii to enforce the disarmament decree, they resisted violently, fearing that they would be arrested and shot. On 25 May 1918, fighting broke out all along the Trans-Siberian Railway, where their trains were traveling. The legionnaires defeated their Red opponents easily and soon found themselves the dominant military force in most major cities along the railway.[8]

The rebellion provided an opportunity for anti-Bolshevik politicians to reassert themselves and latch on to the possibilities of this new army. Just a few days earlier, General Petr Krasnov had been chosen ataman by the Don Cossack Host and was energetically strengthening his army and defeating Red detachments in his territory. With the Germans and Skoropadskii in Ukraine and Denikin's Volunteer Army still decamped in the south as well, much of the southwestern corner of the empire was now hostile to the Bolsheviks. The seizure of the Trans-Siberian now put Bolshevik rule in the east in jeopardy. Russian worker soviets continued to control major cities in Central Asia such as Tashkent, but they were now cut off from the Red heartland by a White Siberia (see Map 11). Liberals and moderate socialists quickly flocked to the banner of counterrevolution and formed a Committee of Members of the Constituent Assembly (or Komuch) which set up a headquarters and new government in Omsk, complete with a green and white flag that represented an autonomous Siberia. These Siberian autonomists were not separatists, however. They sought a new federal state, but they also wanted federalism to strengthen, not weaken, Russia as a whole. When raising their new flag, they also declared that they were rallying in the "defense of free Siberia, through whom we will save also our native mother Russia!"[9]

In July, the opposition struck at the heart of Russia. A major rebellion by the Left Socialist Revolutionaries, who had maintained a queasy alliance with the Bolsheviks

---

[8] W. Bruce Lincoln, *Red Victory: A History of the Russian Civil War* (New York: Simon and Schuster, 1989), 93–4.

[9] David Rainbow, "Saving the Russian Body: Siberian States in the Russian Civil War," paper delivered at the Jordan Center for the Advanced Study of Russia, New York, 28 September 2012, 19. See Rainbow for more on the story of Siberian autonomy and Russian state power.

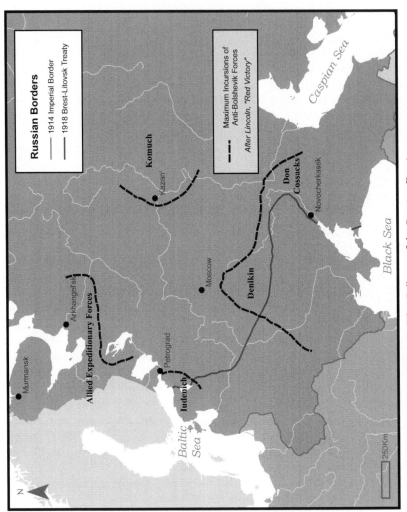

Russian Borders

1914 Imperial Border
1918 Brest-Litovsk Treaty

Maximum Incursions of
Anti-Bolshevik Forces
After Lincoln, "Red Victory"

N

Baltic
Sea

Murmansk

Arkhangel'sk

Allied Expeditionary Forces

Petrograd

Iudenich

Moscow

Komuch

Kazan'

Denikin

Don
Cossacks

Novocherkassk

Caspian Sea

Black Sea

250Km

Map 11 The Collapse of the Russian Empire

since October, led to street fighting and the assassination of the German ambassador in Moscow, to a major uprising in Iaroslavl, and finally, on 10 July 1918, to a significant defection. Mikhail Murav'ev, the commander-in-chief of the Red Eastern Army Group and the man responsible for the Red conquest and purging of Kiev earlier in the year, abandoned the Bolshevik cause and took his troops to Simbirsk, Lenin's birthplace. He was killed there by the Bolsheviks, but much of the damage had been done.[10] Within weeks, Komuch forces seized the cities of Ufa and Simbirsk. On 7 August 1918, they successfully conquered Kazan' with only three battalions of Czechoslovaks and Komuch troops numbering 2500 men. With the exception of a unit of Latvian Riflemen and the Latvian commander Ioakhim Vatsetis (the new head of the Eastern Front), the Red forces broke. They were, said Vatsetis, "completely useless as a result of their poor training and indiscipline."[11] The communist forces fled so quickly that they abandoned a huge gold reserve of 650,000,000 rubles, a stash that would keep the Whites financed for some time to come. The Russian Empire had really begun with Ivan the Terrible's seizure of the Khanate of Kazan' in 1552, which represented Moscow's first expansion beyond its Central Russian and Novgorodian homelands. For the first time in more than 365 years, Moscow no longer ruled non-Russian territories. The Russian Empire had completely collapsed.

IMPERIAL CHALLENGE

I suggested in the introduction that we should see the end of the Russian Empire as part of a process of decolonization that occurred over the course of the Great War and culminated in the apocalyptic death spiral of the Russian Civil War. That process consisted of three phases: (1) imperial challenge, (2) state failure, and (3) social disaster. The succeeding chapters made clear that these stages were not strictly sequential, but instead overlapped. The imperial challenge phase lasted well into the Civil War, by which time both state failure and social disaster had already reached their peaks. But the imperial challenge stage started first. As we saw in the introduction, anti-imperial sentiment developed in many of the empire's borderlands over the course of the 19th century. For the most part, however, this early history of imperial challenge belonged only to educated national elites. Mass politics was slow to develop in the Russian Empire, and the development of nationalist anti-imperialism therefore lagged as well. A combination of events at the end of the century began changing the political dynamic. Large social changes occurred as industrialization, urbanization, and the expansion of education and military conscription heralded the onset of modernity. As part of this larger process, political activism blossomed as well, starting with the development of political parties (including nationalist parties) across the empire in the 1890s and culminating in the Revolution of 1905. Finally, the ill-considered program of forced

[10] Mawdsley, *Russian Civil War*, 56–7; Swain, *Civil War in Siberia*, 75.
[11] Mawdsley, *Russian Civil War*, 58–9; Lincoln, *Red Victory*, 100–1.

Russification imposed by the state beginning in the 1880s strengthened ethnic awareness and hostility to the Russian metropole among wide swathes of subjects who had previously identified more closely with their respective social estates than they had with their ethnic belonging.

Nevertheless, the imperial challenge was relatively weak. Uprisings in Finland in 1901 and in Poland and the Transcaucasus in 1905–1906 frightened imperial bureaucrats, but they never posed as serious a problem to the tsar as the urban unrest, soldier mutinies, and peasant rebellions of that revolutionary period did. There was never a moment when an agenda for autonomy, much less independence, became viable. Nationalists who got too ambitious in their dreaming were quickly reined in by more realistic members of the nationalist movement. Just as importantly, there was no serious anti-imperial movement developing among the metropolitan elite in these pre-war years. There were, to be sure, liberals and moderate socialists who wanted to see an end to ethnic discrimination, a full program of equal civil rights, and other measures that would ameliorate the nastiest features of the colonial project, but they continued to see the Russian element as a progressive force for modernity in benighted colonial regions. None of them contemplated support for autonomy or independence for the many peoples living along the imperial borderlands. Poland and Finland were really the only exceptions to this rule, and even they were exceptions only for a segment of the imperial elite.

The last decade before the war was nevertheless important for the development of the imperial challenge. In the wake of the Revolution of 1905, political mobilization became more possible. The establishment of the Duma allowed nationally minded politicians to run for office. Even though borderland nationalists occupied only a small number of parliamentary seats, the very fact of campaigning, articulating party programs, and developing political organizations built an infrastructure for future efforts and allowed them to proselytize more widely than had ever been possible before. At the same time, the metropolitan elite found itself in the final pre-war years in a conceptually difficult situation. Still hostile to the aspirations of nationalists at home, officials and important public thinkers became increasingly enamored with the prospect of decolonization in the Austro-Hungarian and Ottoman Empires. Visions of a Russian Galicia danced through their heads, and the struggle of the brave Slavs on the Balkan Peninsula appealed to their romantic political proclivities. This enthusiasm would peak between 1908 and 1913. The annexation of Bosnia by the Austro-Hungarian Empire in 1908 infuriated Russia's political class, and the Ministry of Foreign Affairs worked assiduously to support what it considered its Balkan clients in the succeeding years. At the last moment, when it was too late to turn back, it began to dawn on Russian officials that these states might not really be "clients" at all and might be pursuing a dangerous agenda of their own. At the same time, radicals in the Russian Empire also watched the events in the Balkans with extreme interest. The Balkan Wars prompted the Social Democrats to engage with questions of decolonization with vigor, with some Mensheviks pushing for extraterritorial cultural autonomy on the floor of the Duma. In theoretical debates, Lenin and Stalin responded by asserting once again their support for the ideal of national self-determination and the rights of oppressed colonies to secede. It was in this context that Stalin wrote his seminal 1913 essay on "Marxism and the National Question."[12]

The Balkan Wars of 1912 and 1913 thus marked the real start of the intensive phase of East European decolonization that occurred in the period of the Great War. The members of the new Balkan League—Serbia, Bulgaria, Montenegro, and Greece—all fought not for their own independence (which had already been secured) but for the elimination of other empires in the region and the expansion of their own political ambitions in Macedonia, Bosnia, and Albania. The Balkan League fought not just against the Ottomans and Habsburgs but against the idea of empire as such, and it was marked by extreme levels of international and domestic violence. In this context, the outbreak of war in 1914 can be seen as a Third Balkan War. Albania and Macedonia had been torn from the Ottoman Empire in the First Balkan War, but Bosnia remained under imperial control, and this rankled the decolonizing forces in the region. The Habsburgs, moreover, were dead set on doing what the Ottomans could not: destroying the threat of Balkan nationalism. For all the reasons discussed in the introduction, Russia cast its lot in with the Serbian anti-colonial movement and quickly moved to dampen nationalist fervor in its own empire by pre-emptively promising some form of autonomy to Poles and Armenians in the very first weeks of the war.

Ideas about empire ran in different directions during World War I. On the one hand, the failure of the imperial state led some anti-colonial actors to nurture dreams about the future and to work quietly to set the stage for fulfilling them. Mayors in towns abandoned by the imperial bureaucracy during the war began exercising de facto self-rule. Activists recruited ethnic legions both from undrafted volunteers and from prisoner-of-war camps. Some of the more ambitious collaborated with one of the belligerent powers, but most tried to keep their heads down amid brutal conditions of combat and widespread fears of espionage. This was no time to be developing openly separatist movements, and few did so. On the other hand, imperial dreams in the metropole were, if anything, strengthened. War with the Central Powers opened the possibility for a decisive resolution of lingering imperial conflicts. Perhaps Russia could re-establish its role as patron in the Balkans with a grateful Serbia and a chastened Bulgaria. Galicia could be annexed to the empire, bringing more Slavs to the empire and fulfilling the dewy dream of reuniting the lands of medieval Kievan Rus'. Persia could be placed under a Russian sphere of influence, and the ever shifting border in Eastern Anatolia might be pushed a bit further to the west. Finally, the Straits could be put under Russian control, ensuring Russian dominance in the Black Sea and the Balkans, and allowing Russia to aspire to a truly global empire. Ironically, these imperial dreams crested at the very moment when the imperial state entered its final crisis. In 1916,

---

[12] Lenin contributed several pieces of his own to this debate from 1912 to 1914, including "The Balkan War and Bourgeois Chauvinism" and "On the Right of Nations to Self-Determination." Francine Hirsch, *Empire of Nations: Ethnographic Knowledge and the Making of the Soviet Union* (Ithaca: Cornell University Press, 2005), 26–8.

as Russian troops moved into Galicia, occupied Northern Persia, and conquered the major fortresses of Eastern Anatolia, the vast steppe rebellion in Central Asia demonstrated the weakness of the imperial edifice. The tsarist state was failing in many respects: failing to preserve territorial integrity, failing to manage the wartime economy, and failing to provide justice, order, and security for its subjects. The steppe rebellion clearly demonstrated all of these failures, not only to the people living in Central Asia, but also to those in the metropole, where these questions of empire and governance became central to the "crisis of elites" that rocked Petrograd in November 1916.

In 1917 and 1918, state collapse accelerated and consistently ran ahead of anti-colonial aspirations. The February Revolution made possible a reimagination of the political relationships present in the former empire, but it took several months for nationalist activists to push even modestly for goals of autonomy. Over the course of the year, federalism gained respect and currency as a solution that would allow for the satisfaction of many local aspirations without destroying the central state altogether. Metropolitan elites, battered by the revolutionary wave they were riding, insisted over and over again on deferring these questions until the convening of the Constituent Assembly. But those same elites kept pushing back the elections for that assembly. As patience wore thin and the weakness of the Provisional Government became more evident, the struggle for national rights broke out into the open in the summer of 1917. This battle over empire ruined the political fortunes of the Kadet Party, but it was not enough to ensure autonomy, much less independence, for non-Russians. Importantly, however, it was in 1917 that the first politically viable anti-colonial positions were taken in the metropole. Led by socialists from the borderlands who assumed important positions in the Petrograd Soviet, the left insisted on the principle of "national self-determination." Marrying this conception to the hugely popular slogan of "peace without annexations or indemnities" allowed "self-determination" to enjoy widespread support among large swathes of regular Russians, who had never been as invested in the imperial project as their elites had been. This shift wrong-footed virtually every politician in Petrograd at some point during 1917, but Lenin and the Bolsheviks used it to great effect as they rose to power in the fall of that year.

"The self-determination of nations" now took on a discursive life of its own, not just in Russia, but internationally as well. Entente leaders paid homage to it in their speeches in early 1918, and the Germans insisted on its application during the negotiations at Brest-Litovsk. The Brest-Litovsk discussions solidified the principle and made it an indispensable feature of the Versailles negotiations and the postwar order. But these conferences also demonstrated the cynical and manipulative ways that national self-determination could be deployed. The Germans forced Trotskii to recognize an independent Ukrainian delegation on the basis of self-determination and smugly occupied Estonia and Eastern Latvia by rigging plebiscites and piously claiming to be lending support to the will of the people in those regions. No one at the table—German or Soviet—was fooled. The language of force was still stronger than the language of national rights. The two sides would replay these bloody masquerades a generation later on the same terms on the eve of World War II. Still, the language had consequences, not least for the development of the Soviet state. While that state-building enterprise will be briefly addressed at the end of this concluding chapter, we should note that federal structures and the rhetoric of national self-determination were strong legacies of the revolutionary political era and probably could not have been avoided by the Bolsheviks, even had they wanted to.

STATE FAILURE

The imperial state had undergone significant changes and challenges during the half-century before the Great War, culminating in the Revolution of 1905, which called into question the legitimacy of the tsarist order and witnessed the state temporarily losing control of public order in many cities and villages. Still, the imperial state continued to function and to exert its influence throughout the territories of the empire. Where martial law was declared in 1905–1907, there was some anxiety on the part of economic actors that the bifurcation of power might cause a loss of confidence, and some state officials complained that army rule "paralyzed" civilian power.[13] But these frictions did not cause the same damage to the imperial state that martial law in the Great War did. Indeed, after the revolutionary wave had passed, state power and capacity continued to develop, most notably under Stolypin, when an era of modest reforms reigned. Stolypin's agrarian policy famously sought to destroy the old Russian commune through a wager on "sober and strong" individualistic peasants, plans to expand zemstvos more widely in the empire were developed, and serious education reform and military reform efforts were undertaken through robust inter-ministerial committees. Furthermore, Stolypin addressed imperial questions head-on, throttling initiatives suggested by non-Russian nationalists in the borderlands and forwarding a strong new vision of a Russian Empire suffused by a new brand of Russian nationalism. One could hardly call the political situation between 1905 and 1914 stable, but the Russian state was functional and growing stronger.

The declaration of martial law across the western empire at the start of the Great War began the second phase of decolonization: the process of state failure. This decree, which was intended to streamline and strengthen the exercise of state power by putting it in the purportedly efficient hands of the military, crippled imperial influence in the borderlands instead. As we saw in Chapter 1, state officials, many of them experienced in their difficult jobs, fled the western provinces, some due to fear of invasion and others due to the uncertainty of their positions. Lines of authority were confused. Bureaucrats long used to reporting through civilian chains of command now had a new boss, but that boss was largely absent. Stavka moved slowly and ineffectively to establish an office of civilian administration. As a result, a vacuum of power and authority arose in the borderlands. That vacuum was partially filled by civic leaders from the territories in question, many of whom were inclined to non-Russian nationalism. Mostly, however, the vacuum was unfilled, and

---

[13] Robert Weinberg, *The Revolution of 1905 in Odessa: Blood on the Steps* (Bloomington: Indiana University Press, 1993), 148.

manifestations of anarchy and economic disorder flowered. Much of the effort at imperial governance took place in the foreign territories occupied by the successful army, most notably in Galicia and (eventually) Eastern Anatolia. But here the new officials were not seasoned imperial administrators, but fanatics and enthusiasts of various stripes, especially Orthodox stripes. The "reunification" of Galicia to the Russian Empire in 1914 and early 1915 was thus an unqualified and utter disaster. The process of state failure accelerated in the spring and summer of 1915 as the tsar's armies retreated. Increasingly, the problems of governance faced in the west became problems experienced in the center of the empire as well. Nicholas II not only lost symbolic authority as a result of military defeat and political scandal in 1915 and 1916, but his administrators also increasingly struggled to perform their duties. State power was in a crisis situation well before the February Revolution.

If one aspect of the crisis of state power in the midst of war was a weakening of authority, another was a story of political innovation geared toward remobilizing the Russian state and Russian society. As tsarist methods of governance proved incapable of dealing with the challenges of the war, a strain of technocratic and progressive authoritarianism came to the fore on several issues. Other authors have thoughtfully discussed this matter in terms of key issues such as food supply.[14] The focus in this volume was on two other social "problems" that these progressives addressed: epidemic disease and labor shortages. Technocrats both inside and outside the government and military tackled the problem of epidemic disease through an increase in surveillance, mandatory inoculations, and an expansion of a professional corps of medical workers under the auspices of Zemgor and the Red Cross. Labor shortages also helped to expand the scope of state intervention as the war progressed. At first, military and state officials dragooned local peasants and townsmen for ad hoc projects, but over time this grew into more systematic use of forced labor. Civilians at the front could not supply all the labor necessary, so the army turned to the prisoner-of-war population and eventually to the disastrous draft of exempt ethnic groups in the Caucasus and Central Asia in 1916. The army too looked in new directions in 1916, most notably in the combat operations pioneered by General Brusilov. Brusilov was long sympathetic to technocratic authoritarianism, and his management and planning style reflected the congruence of his views with civilian progressives.

Still, there is no doubt that the decisive year for state failure and political innovation was 1917. The February Revolution and the abdication of the tsar caused a centuries-old system of authority, legitimacy, and governance to disappear, bringing liberation on the one hand, but the exposure of the serious fissures present in imperial society on the other. As the discussion of imperial challenge in 1917 suggested, the capacity of political leaders in Petrograd to influence events—much less to govern—in the periphery was quite limited, not only for the Provisional Government, but for the Petrograd Soviet too. Conditions were little better in

---

[14] See here especially Peter Holquist, *Making War, Forging Revolution* (Cambridge, MA: Harvard University Press, 2002); Lars Lih, *Bread and Authority in Russia, 1914–1921* (Berkeley: University of California Press, 1990).

central Russia. All throughout the empire, ethnic rivalries, class conflict, and party divisions hampered the ability of the state to provide security and sustenance. Crime and economic collapse began to spiral out of control as the failing state looked on helplessly. The Bolshevik coup in October represented a point of no return. Anti-communists across the political spectrum challenged Bolshevik rule. When non-violent political efforts proved useless (as during the single session of the doomed Constituent Assembly in January 1918), the Whites moved to the borderlands to organize themselves militarily. By August 1918, as we have seen, they had limited the extent of Bolshevik state power to the old Muscovite heartland. But they too were unable to organize effective systems of governance, and the result, in 1918 and beyond, was a full-blown condition of state collapse and anarchy.

The relationship of the state to violence is an intimate one. Strong states are able to manage violence effectively in order to provide security for their citizens and to protect themselves from rebellion. Weak states leave their citizens exposed to abuse, and they are vulnerable to further corrosion as disorder spreads. The Russian imperial state began the war as a fully functioning organization of power, but the violence of the war years reversed the pre-war trend toward state strengthening. Over the course of four years, it weakened, failed, and then collapsed entirely.

The engine of this transformation was combat against the Central Powers. One of the goals of this book has been to integrate the military history of the war with the social and political history of the war. Combat was crucial to the process of decolonization. Battles had consequences. When Russian troops were successful, as in Galicia in 1914 and 1916 or in the Middle East in 1916, they occupied new territories. As we have seen, the policies developed to govern and legitimate Russian rule in those new territories existed in a tense but mutually influential relationship with new governing practices adopted across the empire as a whole. In particular, economic policies and ethnic politics were affected by decisions taken by generals in their zones of influence. Likewise, military success also translated into the capture of millions of prisoners of war. The new state vision of controlling human movement, organizing and coercing labor, and of creating camps to physically (as well as conceptually) order this process was a result of military success. Battles had consequences at the individual level too. Soldiers and civilians caught in the vortex of violence became more brutal and were less likely to build or sustain bonds outside of their primary community. They became agents of imperial destruction.

Military failure brought its own consequences, especially during the Great Retreat in 1915 and during the massive military collapse from June 1917 to March 1918. As we saw in Chapter 2, the military retreat in 1915 decisively transformed the social and political fabric of the empire. Pessimism replaced guarded optimism among many regular Russians. The attempt to identify those who were responsible for the mess quickly transformed broad anti-German sentiment into anti-court sentiment. Waves of refugees flooded Russian towns and villages from Poltava to Sakhalin. Reports of severe shell shortage shocked the business community into patriotic action. And the general social peace of the first months of the war unraveled. Anti-foreign riots in Moscow and violent strikes in the Central Industrial Region demonstrated that the war had come home. All of these events had a significant impact on the political system. Party leaders came under intense pressure from cadres around the empire—especially from those near the war zone—to insist upon substantial changes in the structure of the government and the conduct of the war. The formation of the Progressive Bloc was, as a result, a direct outcome of the military events at the front. In 1917, the decisive moment in the unraveling of the revolutionary order was the failure of the June Offensive. That failure was itself related to the social and political transformations that had occurred since February. Society and politics affected combat just as much as combat affected society and politics. The headlong flight from the front sent Ukraine and Latvia into anarchy, pushed Kornilov in the direction of warlordism, and placed the revolution at the mercy of the Germans. In all of these ways, the operational history of the war proved central to the social and political histories of the war as well.

Wartime violence was not, of course, limited to combat. We have seen throughout this book that troops regularly committed violence against civilians, not only in occupied territories, but also in territories on the Russian side of the pre-1914 border. This violence was important in its own right. It deeply affected the daily life of civilians as their personal sense of security declined precipitously and as their livelihoods were transformed by the emergence of naked economic coercion. Soldiers thieved, marauded, and requisitioned for fixed prices at gunpoint. Their commanders attacked tradespeople for "speculation" and were then surprised when commerce collapsed. Wartime Russia grew more callous and more brutal with every passing day, and this was reflected in an increase in crime and in the willingness of soldiers and armed civilians alike to seek the solution to their political and social woes through the barrel of a gun.

This violence had a strong ideological component. As I have argued elsewhere, violence was central both to the imagining of the nation and the civic practices associated with it.[15] I have focused in this book on a different ideological aspect of violence: the practice of atrocity and the discourse that surrounded it. We saw in the introduction how the origins of the Great War in the decolonizing conflicts in the Balkans placed the issue of atrocity at the heart of the discussion of the war's meaning. Germany and Austria went to war with accusations of Serbian savagery on their lips. After the sacking of Kalisz and the razing of Belgium, the Entente eagerly joined in to define the war as one for civilization against German barbarism. This discourse was plainly linked to pre-war colonial discourses which justified the conquest and occupation of foreign lands if those efforts were undertaken in the name of modern civilization. At the same time, a new strain of this civilizational discourse had emerged, one that treated human rights abuses as a violation of international law. Germany's reluctance to join the other Great Powers as they created and codified new laws of war and of civilian treatment already predisposed many Europeans, including German policymakers themselves, to expect that German troops would pay little attention to "civilized norms" once the bullets started flying.[16]

---

[15] Sanborn, *Drafting the Russian Nation.*

[16] Isabel V. Hull, *Absolute Destruction: Military Culture and the Practices of War in Imperial Germany* (Ithaca: Cornell University Press, 2005), 128–9.

This powerful, but often confusing, set of commitments to "civilization" left tsarist Russia in an awkward and ambiguous position. On the one hand, Russia had long been seen as the most backward and barbarous of the Great Powers, as a land of semi-Oriental brutality and despotism, with Cossack troopers renowned across the continent for their savagery to enemy soldiers and civilians alike. Russia was the patron of the Balkan Slavs, whose bloody exploits had filled the news during 1912 and 1913, and who continued their tradition of political murder with the shooting of Franz Ferdinand. On the other hand, Russia's Ministry of Foreign Affairs and the legal thinkers associated with it had been prime movers in the development of international law.[17] Russian social and cultural elites were well known and were respected as much as they were exoticized.[18] Above all, they had contracted and would fulfill an alliance with the very French and British figures whose approval they sought. For Russia, the war was fought not only for civilization in the abstract, but also for the recognition of Russia as a full member of the civilized world. The question of atrocity would therefore have special relevance within the Russian political context.

Again, the actual practice of violence had important consequences in this regard. The Russian government worked hard to get itself on the right side of the atrocity issue. It played up the importance of Kalisz and sponsored popular films on the violation of Belgium as a way to link itself discursively with its western allies.[19] It avidly joined in the denunciations of German atrocities, documenting the abuse of Russian POWs and civilians in a fully illustrated report, hundreds of copies of which were sent to press outlets and neutral countries in June 1915.[20] The genocide in Armenia provided yet another opportunity for condemnation on behalf of civilization, and the Russian Ministry of Foreign Affairs took full advantage of the situation, coining the term "crimes against humanity" to link Russia once more to the legal humanitarian strain of the civilizational discourse.[21]

But atrocity cut both ways. The Russian invasion of East Prussia prompted the Germans to complain vociferously about Cossack atrocities, and they had a legitimate basis for doing so.[22] This allowed German propagandists to deflect the criticisms of the occupation of Belgium by arguing that the Entente was also

---

[17] This is an argument that Peter Holquist has developed in several recent conference papers and in his current book project.

[18] Modris Eksteins, *Rites of Spring: The Great War and the Birth of the Modern Age* (Boston: Houghton Mifflin, 1989).

[19] *Liliia Belgii*, directed by Władysław Starewicz, sponsored by the Skobelev Committee (1915). Included in DVD collection *Early Russian Cinema: A Unique Anthology in 10 Volumes*, vol. 3 (Harrington Park, NJ: Milestone Films, 2007–2008).

[20] Major-General Prince Orlov, introductory letter to the report of the Imperial Extraordinary Investigative Commission for the Investigation of the Violation of the Laws and Customs of War by Austro-Hungarian and German Troops (June 1915), GARF f. 601, op. 1, d. 641, l. 13.

[21] Gary Jonathan Bass, *Stay the Hand of Vengeance: The Politics of War Crimes Tribunals* (Princeton: Princeton University Press, 2000), 116.

[22] See Joshua Sanborn, "Atrocities in East Prussia," *Russian History Blog*, 16 February 2011. <http://russianhistoryblog.org/2011/02/atrocities-in-east-prussia-1914/> "Russians in East Prussia (pt. 2)," *Russian History Blog*, February 24, 2011.<http://russianhistoryblog.org/2011/02/russians-in-east-prussia-1914-pt-2/>. For another eyewitness account of pillaging and destruction, see Frenkel', 81.

responsible for massacres.[23] The oppressive occupation of Galicia by Russia in 1914–1915 did little to help the Russian case. Just as damaging in the long run were the accusations, many of them internal, of Russian atrocities on Russian territory. The most notable of these developments was the one surrounding the terror campaign launched against the empire's Jewish population. Jewish activists consciously packaged their reports of these pogroms in a way that would gain the attention of foreign audiences and, through them, to high figures in the Russian government.[24] The strategy worked. By the summer of 1915, even rabidly anti-Semitic members of the Council of Ministers were telling the military high command to stop the persecutions, in part because they were destabilizing the imperial social and ethnic order, and in part because Russia's allies were horrified by the army's campaign against Jewish civilians.[25] The political opposition to the left and the center also protested the pogroms and used the atrocities committed by the army as further evidence of the moral bankruptcy of the autocratic regime. As we saw in Chapter 5, Kerenskii would deploy this language once more when denouncing the state's behavior in Central Asia during the steppe rebellion, asking explicitly how Russia could condemn Germany when its own punitive expeditions were so bloody. And, though the political power of these accusations was well understood, they were nevertheless heartfelt and widely shared. Gor'kii's ruminations on atrocity and humanity in April 1917 reflected the strength of this discourse well into the revolutionary era.

The end of the Great War brought the end to whatever restraints had been in place regarding atrocity. The Civil War was marked instead by the valorization of violence and the open practice of terror campaigns. Both Whites and Reds utilized extralegal, arbitrary, and merciless violence to achieve political ends or simply to satisfy their desires in the territories they marched through. Enemy officers were normally shot on the spot if captured during battle. Grotesque and public torture was common. Entire villages were punished for the perceived misdeeds of the few. The Bolsheviks justified the Red Terror as a necessary mechanism of revolutionary class warfare. It would not do to treat the enemy gently, no matter what bromides to "humanity" and "civilization" had been mouthed during the war against Germany. Terror, "however arbitrary and severe," was necessary for the revolution to succeed.[26] The Whites were equally forthright. Kornilov and Markov urged the Volunteer Army on with cries of "the more terror, the more victories!"[27] Anti-Bolshevik forces in Ukraine launched a year of terror against the Jewish population

[23] John Horne and Alan Kramer, *German Atrocities, 1914: A History of Denial* (New Haven and London: Yale University Press, 2001), 79.
[24] For an example, see *The Jews in the Eastern War Zone* (New York: The American Jewish Committee, 1916).
[25] Polly Zavadivker, "Reconstructing a Lost Archive: Simon Dubnow and 'The Black Book of Imperial Russian Jewry,' Materials for a History of the War, 1914–1915," *The Simon Dubnow Institute Yearbook* 12 (2013): 3–26.
[26] Leon Trotsky, *Terrorism and Communism: A Reply to Karl Kautsky* (Ann Arbor: University of Michigan Press, 1961), 50.
[27] Cited in Viktor G. Bortnevski, "White Administration and White Terror (The Denikin Period)," *Russian Review* 52, no. 3 (July 1993): 356.

in 1919 that dwarfed the murders of the pre-war or even the war years, causing hundreds of thousands of casualties. Some Jewish communities were attacked as many as eleven times over the course of the year.[28] In Siberia, Kolchak's forces pursued a counterinsurgency campaign as brutal as any pursued by the Reds during the Civil War. Other commanders were even more grisly, as the gothic Mongolian adventure of Baron von Ungern-Sternberg can attest. The "bloody Baron" and his men shot civilians for sport, roasted them alive, and searched passing trains for hidden Bolsheviks with such vigor that travel through the area became virtually impossible.[29] If these events naturally had something to do with revolution and with the development of passionate communism and anti-communism, they also had strong roots in the period of the Great War, when politics became mortal combat and when life cheapened significantly as the result of wartime brutalization.[30]

There is no better demonstration of the fact of imperial state collapse than the rise of men like Ungern-Sternberg.[31] The preconditions for the emergence of warlordism had been set over the course of the war. The state maintained a basic monopoly on the deployment of legitimate violence through 1916, although the nature of that legitimation had become increasingly national rather than imperial. This was true not only of nationalist appeals to Russian soldiers, but also to other ethnic groups as well, who were allowed to form legions such as those that composed the so-called "Savage Division" of martial volunteers from the Caucasus. Again, 1917 was important in this trajectory. Not only did the army expand this notion of volunteer shock troops to include units of revolutionary enthusiasts and patriotic women, but the collapse of legitimate police authority after February required the formation of militias of various stripes. Whatever word can be used to describe the nature of organized force in 1917, "monopoly" is not it. As soldiers and civilians alike lost respect for and challenged the authority of central elites, warlordism became increasingly likely. Again, Kornilov was the best example of a commander who inspired devotion from some of his dedicated troops, who sought to combine political power with military authority, and came to learn the importance of local authority in a time of anarchy. He died in 1918, but he spawned many imitators in 1919 and beyond, from peasant anarchists such as Nestor Makhno to savage Cossack atamans such as Grigorii Semenov.[32]

[28] O. V. Budnitskii, *Rossiiskie evrei mezhdu krasnymi i belymi* (Moscow: ROSSPEN, 2006), 275–6; Piotr Wróbel, "The Seeds of Violence. The Brutalization of an East European Region, 1917–1921," *Journal of Modern European History* 1 no. 1 (2003): 136.

[29] Paul du Quenoy, "Warlordism 'à la Russe;' Baron von Ungern-Sternberg's Anti-Bolshevik Crusade, 1917–21," *Revolutionary Russia* 16, no. 2 (2003): 1–27.

[30] Willard Sunderland, "Baron Ungern, Toxic Cosmopolitan," *Ab imperio: teoriia i istoriia natsional'nostei i natsionalizma v postsovetskom prostranstve* no. 3 (2005): 285–98.

[31] Joshua Sanborn, "The Genesis of Russian Warlordism: Violence and Governance during the First World War and the Civil War," *Contemporary European History* 19, no. 3 (August 2010): 195–213.

[32] Jamie Bisher, *White Terror: Cossack Warlords of the Trans-Siberian* (London and New York: Routledge, 2005).

SOCIAL DISASTER

The collapse of the state and the expansion of violence thus had destructive effects upon the imperial social fabric. This third phase of decolonization—social disaster—moved from the front to the rear during the Great War and came to dominate the entire period of the Russian Civil War. Social ties weakened, and the institutions that traditionally had provided stability proved unable to do so as the war progressed. Two social problems were especially notable during the war years, each of which was intimately tied to the state crisis that grew more and more acute with each passing month: the wartime economic emergency, and the phenomenon of violent migrations.

We have only been able to touch lightly on a few aspects of the complex and extremely important history of the Russian economy in the years of the war. The imperial system was fundamentally disrupted at the outset of the war. Russia had exchanged labor and goods on the international market in large quantities prior to 1914. The major land routes to Europe were blocked when the war broke out, and the most significant sea routes were shut down when the Ottomans closed the Straits and the Germans bottled up the Baltic Sea. The only routes left open had small capacity, tenuous links to central Russia, and were hampered by extreme cold: the connections to Asia and the Pacific through Siberia, the polar shipping routes to Murmansk and Arkhangel'sk, and land traffic through Scandinavia. At first, state and military planners thought this enforced autarky might be a blessing in disguise. Perhaps, they thought, the reduction in agricultural production sure to occur with the mobilization of millions of peasants would be offset by the elimination of grain exports. In broad strokes, this was true: the grain fields of the empire produced enough to feed the population right through 1917.

However, this was too crude an understanding of the economy. It is not enough to grow grain (or to produce other goods). It must also be stored, transported, stored again, and distributed. This would require either the strengthening of the internal capillaries of the imperial market economy or the development of a new non-market form of economic production and allocation. As we saw in Chapter 1, the tsarist state steadfastly refused to do either. Fearing foreigners, Jews, and "speculation," military and governmental authorities harassed and attacked not only merchants but the very notion that trade for profit could be helpful and patriotic. Fearing communists, the same authorities supported the principle of private property and rejected the possibility of seizing the estates or enterprises of Russian proprietors to serve the war effort or the public welfare.

Thus, the economic system we might call "Stavkaism" combined a fierce hostility to market capitalism with an equally violent hatred of communism. Stavkaism was not limited to the generals governing the borderlands from Stavka. I use it here simply as shorthand for the anti-capitalist, anti-communist, and anti-Semitic political economy that dominated economic policymaking in the combat zone in the first year of the war and then extended more broadly across the empire as the war proceeded. The internal contradictions of this economic ideology were profound, as two wartime phenomena demonstrate. The first phenomenon, which has been explored in depth by Eric Lohr, was the assault on the private property rights of enemy aliens during the war. Military leaders at Stavka led the charge to first sequester and then seize massive tracts of land and huge factories, especially from German subjects. Bureaucrats and local residents then scrambled to scavenge and cannibalize the enterprises. This all occurred within the context of a long-standing debate regarding land reform and factory ownership in which moderates and conservatives had piously defended private property rights. As anxious government officials soon complained, this assault could (and did) weaken whatever principled claims to property rights the state might make in other contexts.[33] If you could take Schmidt's land to provide for the public welfare and to support the war effort, why not take Ivanov's too? The second phenomenon had to do with the image of the Jew in wartime. For adherents to Stavkaism, Jews were the prototypical capitalists: speculators seeking profit in market-oriented activities. At the same time, Jews were also the prototypical communists: the representatives of foreign contamination and political subversion. It is important to understand that this bifurcation was not the result of a reasonable assessment that some Jews were capitalists and some were communists. Instead, "the Jew" was both of these things at the same time.

Plainly, Stavkaism could not resolve the basic problems that the wartime economy generated. Indeed, it made them worse. As we saw in Chapter 1, the campaign against Jews and the widespread adoption of the *taksa* made legal trading in the war zone unprofitable and dangerous. This pushed a great deal of commerce and production into the "second economy" of the black market. Marauding and requisitions by the army (and then increasingly by civilians too) created a "third economy" based not on money but on coercion. I have traced the results of this transformation of the wartime economy throughout the book as the Great Retreat brought some of this malaise to the center of the empire. Inflation became the key day-to-day problem for Russian subjects, the topic of letters back and forth to the front and of daily conversations in battalions and in peasant huts. Shortages soon followed, as forced low prices and deep uncertainty led to hoarding and as consumer goods took a back seat to military production. The blundering supremacy of the army in the economy also made itself felt. If the war and the army always took priority, then no one could say no to military economic officials, who took more men, horses, trains, and grain than they needed and used those resources inefficiently. It was only in 1915 that the military began coming to terms with the fact that these inefficiencies, in the context of total war, hurt them directly on the battlefield. Munitions workers drafted en masse in 1914 slowly returned to their factories, where they did more good than in the trenches. Army participation in the Special Councils and in the War-Industrial Committees meant that the top brass, at least, understood that civilian–military planning and coordination had to replace simple hoarding. These bodies made significant improvements in specific areas, in

---

[33] Eric Lohr, *Nationalizing the Russian Empire: The Campaign against Enemy Aliens during World War I* (Cambridge, MA: Harvard University Press, 2003), 64–5.

particular in regard to weapons production. The shell shortages that had affected the battlefield so significantly in the spring and summer of 1915 eased considerably over the course of 1916.

Overall, however, the economy continued to collapse, as the long lines for bread and the absence of other key consumer goods in late 1916 and early 1917 attested. Russian economic officials could not adequately address these deficits either in principle or in practice. They developed plans for grain requisitioning in late 1916 but could not solve the problem of how to use coercion to enforce the policy, slowing implementation and resulting in failure.[34] They decided to move to rationing in Petrograd in February 1917, but this led to hoarding, greater shortages, and eventually the street protests that would result in the February Revolution. That revolution succeeded in forcing the abdication of the tsar, but it only made the economic problems worse. The Stavkaists had largely been discredited (though some of their prejudices remained). However, the emergence of "Dual Power" between the Provisional Government and the Petrograd Soviet made the creation of a coherent economic policy virtually impossible, as each body had quite different ideas regarding political economy and the measures necessary to revive the country's prosperity. As a result, things went from bad to worse. As 1917 turned to 1918, and then throughout the rest of the Civil War, the Whites, Reds, and warlords all failed to create the conditions of state support and personal security necessary for vibrant economic institutions to re-emerge. People were hungry and cold. Then, increasingly, they starved and froze to death. As they weakened, they sickened further. Each month saw an increase in the number of people hospitalized, and epidemic diseases became more prevalent.[35] In the summer of 1918, cholera consumed cities such as Iaroslavl. By October, the global influenza pandemic was hitting other towns in the Golden Ring such as Rybinsk and the Soviet leadership in the Kremlin alike.[36] Many Russians no sooner recovered from one disease than they were struck by the next one.[37] Cities emptied, and villages tried to survive on their own resources. The collapse of the imperial economy deeply affected Russian society.

If the economy was a central aspect of wartime social disorder, so too was the physical uprooting of millions of Russian subjects. Human migration as such is not necessarily a source of social instability. Migration indeed often strengthens social ties between the migrants themselves, and healthy societies develop institutions that allow for the inclusion of newcomers and facilitate the departure of

[34] Holquist, *Making War, Forging Revolution*, 42.

[35] B. Leont'ev (Senior Doctor of Red Cross infectious disease hospital in Minsk), Letter to Administration of the Chief of the Red Cross of the Western Front (April 1918), GARF f. R-4094, op. 1, d. 6, l. 55.

[36] "Vypiska protokola soveshchaniia Tsentral'noi Kollegii ROKK s Okruzhnymi Komissarami," (5 September 1918), GARF f. R-4094, op. 1, d. 56, l. 111-111ob.; Chair of Rybinsk Soviet Executive Committee, Telegram to Red Cross Flying Detachment (23 October 1918), GARF f. R-4094, op. 1, d. 132, l. 9; Central Collegium of the Red Cross, Telegram to V Bonch-Bruevich (Sovnarkom) (15 October 1918), GARF f. R-3341, op. 1, d. 122, l. 25.

[37] N. I. Vladimirtseva, "Iz vospominanii sestry miloserdiia F. N. Slepchenko," *Otechestvennye arkhivy* no. 6 (1994): 64.

those who temporarily or permanently emigrate. In wartime Russia, however, these migration flows were both the result and cause of violent disruption. Again, these were processes that began in the first year of the war. Millions of reservists migrated to the front and established an uneasy relationship with the colonized communities they settled amongst. Soon, fears of spying and the emergence of a toxic form of ethnic politics led to mass movement. Some inhabitants were arrested and deported, others fled as the security situation deteriorated. First tens of thousands, then hundreds of thousands of people, many of them Jews, headed eastward. In 1915, military defeat and the army's scorched earth policy caused the scope of these migrations to expand considerably. Millions of people of all ethnicities now took to the roads and the rails. Even the best-intentioned and most highly functioning state could not have dealt effectively with this influx of people. They needed food, shelter, jobs, a way to preserve their own cultural commitments, and a way to integrate with the societies they joined. Despite the labors of volunteer organizations and the remarkable good will of many host communities, these refugees suffered. At the same time, the towns and villages where they had made their homes now changed as well, not always for the better. As the empire's economy imploded, the sympathy of host communities for these extra mouths to feed "evaporated."[38]

The movement did not stop in 1915. In 1916, Muslims emigrated in droves from Russian Central Asia, in small part to the west, where unlucky men had been drafted as laborers, and in much greater numbers across the border to China. Desertion from the army, a problem from the start of the war, took on epic dimensions in 1917, when the largest episode of mass desertion in military history took place in the Russian army.[39] Deserters were far more disruptive than the civilian refugees had been. They had guns, a sense of privilege, and some wartime experience in looting. They marauded their way to central Russia in 1917, where they kept their guns and their penchant for using them. As in other respects, the experience of the Civil War between 1918 and 1921 was the culmination of these trends of collapse. People fled advancing armies, and they fled the starving cities. They hopped from place to place under rapidly changing circumstances. Train stations became swarming hives of humanity, at least until the transportation system broke down almost entirely. Finally, in one of the signature moments of 20th-century Russian history, many of them fled across state borders, creating large Russian émigré communities all over the world, in places such as Istanbul, Paris, Belgrade, Harbin, New York, and Buenos Aires. The imperial state, the imperial economy, and the imperial society had all been destroyed by the end of 1920.

---

[38] Peter Gatrell, *A Whole Empire Walking: Refugees in Russia during World War I* (Bloomington: Indiana University Press, 1999), 179.

[39] See here Joshua Sanborn, "Russian Soldiers and Refusal in the Great War," in *Accepter, Endurer, Refuser*, ed. Nicholas Beaupré, Heather Jones, and Anne Rasmussen (Paris: Les Belles Lettres, forthcoming).

REBUILDING THE EMPIRE

This book has been devoted to describing the first three stages of the process of decolonization, in which the imperial state collapsed amidst increasing challenges from the periphery, through metropolitan dissension regarding the aims and morality of empire, and via violence and social disaster. The fourth stage—that of building a postcolonial state and society—deserves its own separate study, but it merits a brief discussion here. I suggested in the introduction that this fourth stage might still be incomplete a century later, but this judgment is unavoidably normative and subjective. No state is fully capable, and no society is fully healthy. Deciding whether a process of state-building and social healing has succeeded is therefore never a straightforward enterprise. On the one hand, a Soviet state and a Soviet society were plainly formed out of the rubble of the imperial apocalypse, and they were based on avowedly anti-imperial ideals. At a basic level, then, we can say that the Soviet Union was a postcolonial state as early as 1923, when a new Union constitution was adopted, a progressive policy on nationalities was implemented, and the first two years of the New Economic Policy (adopted at the Tenth Party Congress in 1921) had eased the economic and social crisis experienced during the Civil War. On the other hand, it would be inaccurate to suggest that the Bolshevik state functioned effectively, much less efficiently. The economy remained in a parlous condition. Insecurity and fear still marked social interaction, due both to crime and to what the Bolsheviks called "banditism," a mixture of anti-Bolshevik resistance, leftover remnants of warlordism, criminality, and the indiscriminate and corrupt use of force by local officials. Still, given the extent of the catastrophe in 1918, the Bolshevik success in building a new social and political regime that governed most of the former empire by 1923 deserves an explanation. How did they accomplish this rather remarkable feat?

The story starts with the Red Army. It had begun 1918 understaffed and overextended. The victories it achieved early in the year spoke more to the weakness of the forces challenging it than to its own capabilities. As we saw earlier in this chapter, volunteer levies had been pitiful, and the revolutionaries hoping to become commanders frequently lacked the staff-room skills necessary to succeed. In addition, the regime faced not only the problem of domestic counterrevolution but also the threat of foreign intervention. Trotskii, as the commissar for military affairs, spearheaded a drive to build a new Red Army on the basis of conscription, the recruitment of old officers as "bourgeois" military specialists, and the *matériel* inherited from the tsarist armories. Lenin fully supported all of these endeavors. Neither of them had any use for the starry-eyed "military opposition" who insisted on a new "revolutionary" form of warfare. Trotskii failed at first. Young Russian men dodged the draft, bitter mid-level Bolsheviks endlessly harassed military specialists, and increasingly large enemy forces pressed in from all sides. The fall of Kazan' on 7 August 1918 to the small group of White forces attacking it demonstrated that basic weakness.

It turned out, however, that the fall of Kazan' was rock bottom. The day afterwards, the German army suffered its so-called "Black Day" in France, setting in motion the chain of events that would lead to the armistice on the Western Front in November. On 10 August, Lenin either presciently or fortuitously ordered General Bonch-Bruevich (the leading military specialist in the army) to transfer forces from the anti-German "screens" to the Volga.[40] Trotskii and Bonch-Bruevich were anxious about this move, but they obeyed the orders. The Germans did not attack. More than 30,000 soldiers arrived near Kazan' by the middle of the month. The tide turned. On 28 August, the Reds fought off a direct assault on their rail communications and Trotskii's own command train. On the next day, punitive detachments stopped a panicked flight of Red soldiers, court-martialed the deserters, and shot one out of every ten of them. On 10 September, Trotskii and his men retook the city, and much of the rest of the Volga fell to them in the following weeks.[41] By October, they controlled the Eastern Front and had more than 100,000 men in that one army group alone. The command and conscription problems faced by the Reds had not disappeared, and there would be losses as well as victories over the next two years, but there was no doubt that the Red Army at the end of 1918 was a much more formidable instrument than it had been at the start of that year.

As the Red Army advanced, it moved into the colonial borderlands where anti-imperial sentiment had developed so rapidly during the period of war and revolution. One by one, White leaders fell before the communist advance. The Volunteer Army cracked and gave way in late 1919 and early 1920 before rallying one more time, unsuccessfully, in Crimea. In November 1920, these ragged remnants sailed away from their homeland. Admiral Kolchak's arrest in January 1920 allowed the Reds to consolidate control over Siberia and to re-establish the links between the soviets in Central Russia and those in Central Asia. The Bolsheviks took, lost, and retook Kiev several times in 1918 and 1919 before finally seizing it for good in the wake of the Soviet–Polish War of 1920. Armenia, Georgia, and Azerbaijan were also annexed in 1920 in a flurry of fighting and political jostling between Russian and indigenous parties, the beleaguered Ottoman state, and Great Britain. Thus, when the peoples living in the non-Russian areas of the empire first had the chance to encounter Bolshevik rule, it was through revolutionaries of the mostly Russian working class and through the officers and soldiers of a Red Army that was also completely foreign to them.

This was the imperial dilemma faced by all of the political and military actors in the Civil War. The struggle took place mainly in non-Russian territories and was deeply affected by the benevolence or hostility of the local population, but the main combatants were not only alien but also carried the taint of years of colonial aggression. Indigenous forces did arise, and several, such as the Rada and Nestor Makhno's band of "Green" partisans in Ukraine, were extremely successful. But

---

[40] I have seen no evidence that these two events were directly connected. Bolshevik military intelligence was unlikely to have picked up on this dramatic moment and the shift in German priorities it would entail. Nevertheless, it is almost certainly the case that Lenin was aware that the German position in the West was serious enough that they were unlikely to revive hostilities in the East.

[41] Mawdsley, *Russian Civil War*, 66–7.

these groups had even less chance of finding common cause than did the similarly dispersed and disparate White armies. How, then, could the "Russian" armies operate and build alliances, given the legacy of Russian imperialism?

This was a question that the White leadership utterly failed to ask or to understand. As we saw earlier, Denikin was offended at the very thought of independent forces emerging in his beloved empire and actively thwarted any possibility of cooperation not only with Georgian and Ukrainian leaders, but also on occasion with the very Cossack governments that hosted him in the Don and Kuban regions. Kolchak was no better, and Wrangel's turnaround on this issue in 1920 was literally too little and too late.

The Bolsheviks, on the other hand, were far better positioned to respond to this dilemma. In their very first party programs, the Bolsheviks had asserted their support for national self-determination.[42] They had reaped the political benefits of that stance in 1917, when they were able to demonstrate that they were early adopters of this slogan of peace and decolonization. Now, in the Civil War, they were faced with the consequences of their centrifugal policy. A certain segment of the party had always been suspicious of forwarding a national agenda, fearing that it would sap class solidarity. That group now insisted upon abandoning the slogan and moving straight toward a post-national communist platform. Lenin, however, remained steadfast. The legacy of empire could not be eliminated in a day. Not only would other nationalities view invading and occupying Russians as an imperial force, but even "Red" Russians with guns were likely to be prone to chauvinism and to act accordingly. It would require vigilance to ensure that the communist project did not become an imperial project in fact as well as perception. At the same time, as we have seen, Lenin was at heart a centralizer. He did not actually want to see these regions determine their own leaders and their own policies in 1920 or 1921, as the experience of the Civil War had shown quite clearly that local potentates would seek to follow independent paths. The ideal solution, from his perspective, would be to have indigenous officials lead indigenous peoples to "determine" that their political future lay in accepting the leadership of the Central Committee in Moscow. Unfortunately, those indigenous leaders did not exist, at least not in sufficient numbers.

The Bolshevik solution, then, was rather ingenious. Having created a one-party state, they took advantage of what appeared to be an unnecessary duplication of party and state institutions to create a federal state bureaucracy and a unitary party organization.[43] Given that the party controlled the state (the party's secretariat chose the members who would appear on uncontested ballots in elections to the soviets and appointed the functionaries who ran local governments), this meant that power was unitary even if the state system was formally federal. Still, these

---

[42] Jeremy Smith, *The Bolsheviks and the National Question, 1917–1923* (London: Macmillan, 1999), 14.

[43] Both the Communist Party and the Soviet state had a hierarchy of offices that began at the local level with party cells and village or urban soviets and ran through district and regional levels before reaching the top in Moscow with all-Union bodies (the Central Executive Committee of the Soviets and the Central Committee of the Party).

formal measures would do nothing to lessen the danger of Bolshevik colonialism if all of the members of the ruling apparatus were ethnically alien to the local peoples they governed. Thus, the leadership resolved to create a large cadre of indigenous Bolsheviks capable of fulfilling Moscow's will and convincing their co-nationals that Soviet power was their own. This would require more than old-style imperial collaboration; it would require a whole set of new education and training institutions and a guarantee that these new leaders would have easy access to jobs and positions in the ruling strata. These goals lay at the base of the Bolshevik strategy of *korenizatsiia* (or "indigenization") that created the "Affirmative Action Empire" of the 1920s.[44]

These exercises in state-building and creative cadre-building were successful, as the strength of national party organizations right through the end of the Soviet period would demonstrate. But it cannot be said that the communists eliminated all traces of colonialism. Russian political figures and ethnographers continued to view these borderlands as "backward," benighted, and needing a strong ruling hand from the West. Economic exploitation continued too, though the creation of regional party organizations headed by politicians from the titular nationality of the region did allow for the successful lobbying of the center to create centers of industrial modernity in the former "colonies." Some of the largest projects of the ambitious First Five-Year Plan were set in non-Russian areas, such as the hydroelectric dam on the Dnipro River in Ukraine, the new railway that connected Turkestan to the Trans-Siberian Railway, and the steel plant in the Southern Urals. As the experience on the "Turksib" railway would demonstrate, these "development" projects were frequently accompanied by intense ethnic violence and clashes between workers brought in from Russia and Ukraine and those who worked close to their homes.[45] If the Soviet Union was not exactly a revived empire, it nevertheless was deeply affected by the imperial legacy.

What sort of state was it, then? It was revolutionary, it was communist, and it was postcolonial. Like other postcolonial states, it was unstable. State institutions were violently coercive but functionally weak. Social relations had been poisoned by the years of conflict, and communities suffered as a result. Ethnic groups eyed each other with wary suspicion. Poverty and disease proliferated. The more the state tried to fix the typical problems of the postcolonial mess, the more it failed. The more it failed, the more violent it became. The more violent it became, the worse the postcolonial problems got. If it would be silly to argue that all of the ills and terrors of the Soviet regime were the result of its postcolonial status, it would be equally problematic to ignore the deep imprint that the process of decolonization left upon the Russian Empire and the rulers who sought to govern it. Many of the key political processes of the Stalinist regime—economic mobilization, forced collectivization, and state terror—were deeply inflected by the experience of war

[44] Terry Martin, *The Affirmative Action Empire: Nations and Nationalism in the Soviet Union, 1923–1939* (Ithaca: Cornell University Press, 2001).

[45] Matthew J. Payne, *Stalin's Railroad: Turksib and the Building of Socialism* (Pittsburgh: University of Pittsburgh Press, 2001).

and decolonization. Veterans of the Great War and the Civil War joined the Bolsheviks in using violence to address both economic and ethnic problems. The deadly experiences of collectivization and famine in Ukraine and Kazakhstan and the terror campaign launched against ethnic elites were just two of the many examples of this poisonous mix of communism and postcolonialism. As the Soviet Union lurched toward an even greater war and to a troubled remainder of the century, the rubble of the Great War remained at its foundation, shifting slightly, and eventually causing the whole structure to crack and crumble.

Works Cited

ARCHIVAL COLLECTIONS

Library collection of "Russia Abroad" (BFRZ)—Moscow, Russia
Leonid N. Andrusov papers
Arkhimandrit Iov papers

State Archive of the Russian Federation (GARF)—Moscow, Russia
Fond 215—Chancellery of the Warsaw Governor General
Fond 217—Warsaw Province Gendarme Administration
Fond 238—Lublin Province Gendarme Administration
Fond 579—Personal Files of P. N. Miliukov
Fond 601—Personal Files of Nicholas II
Fond 1669—Lomzha Province Gendarme Administration
Fond 1791—Main Administration for the Militia and for Securing the Personal and Property Rights of Citizens of the Ministry of Internal Affairs of the Provisional Government
Fond R-3341—Central Committee of the Russian Society of the Red Cross
Fond R-4094—Administration of Representatives of the Russian Society of the Red Cross with the Armies of the Western Front and the Sixth Army

Hoover Institution Archives (HIA)—Stanford, California (USA)
Mikhail V. Alekseev papers
Nikolai N. Baratov papers
Dmitrii Heiden papers
Boris Nikolaevsky collection
Ernest Riggs papers
Russia—Shtab Verkhovnogo Glavnokomanduiushchego collection

Latvian State Historical Archives (LVVA)—Riga, Latvia
Fond 3—Chancellery of the Lifliand Governor
Fond 51—Riga City Police Administration
Fond 2736—Riga City Duma
Fond 7233—Lifliand Provincial Commissar (Provisional Government)

Military Reading Room of Russian State Library (RGB)—Moscow, Russia
Manuscripts (call #D 36/340)—Orders to the Kiev Military District
Manuscripts (call #D 156/8)—Orders to the Kazan' Military District
Manuscripts (call #D 157/20)—Orders to the First Army
Manuscripts (call #D 157/22)—Orders to the Second Army

Russian State Historical Archive (RGIA)—St. Petersburg, Russia
Fond 1278—State Duma
Fond 1292—Ministry of Internal Affairs: Administration of Affairs Relating to Obligatory Military Service

Russian State Military Archive (RGVA)—Moscow, Russia
Fond 1—Administration of the People's Commissariat for Military Affairs
Fond 79—Commissariat for the Demobilization of the Old Army

Russian State Military History Archive (RGVIA)—Moscow, Russia
Fond 1720—Staff of the Kazan' Military District
Fond 2000—Main Administration of the General Staff
Fond 2003—Staff of the Supreme Commander (Stavka)
Fond 2005—Military-political and Civilian Administration (Stavka)
Fond 2006—Administration of the Field Inspector of Engineering Units (Stavka)
Fond 2018—Administration of the Supreme Chief of Sanitary and Evacuation Units (Stavka)
Fond 2067—Staff of Armies at the Southwestern Front
Fond 2106—Staff of the First Army
Fond 2108—Administration of the Chief Engineer of the First Army
Fond 2134—Staff of the Eighth Army
Fond 2168—Staff of the Army of the Caucasus
Fond 2294—First Army Corps of the Caucasus
Fond 12651—Main Administration of the Russian Society of the Red Cross

Central State Historical Archive (Kyiv) (TsDIAK)—Kyiv, Ukraine
Fond 274—Kiev Province Gendarme Administration
Fond 315—Chancellery of the Military Prosecutor of the Kiev Military District Court
Fond 715—Southwestern Committee of the All-Russian Zemstvo Union
Fond 1439—Chernigov Province Gendarme Administration

NEWSPAPERS

The New York Times
Russkie vedomosti

INTERNET RESOURCES

"Catalog of Cemeteries." <http://www.cmentarze.gorlice.net.pl/Gorlice/Gorlice.htm> (accessed 5 June 2013).
International Committee of the Red Cross. "Convention (II) with Respect to the Laws and Customs of War on Land and its Annex: Regulations Concerning the Laws and Customs of War on Land. The Hague, 29 July 1899." <http://www.icrc.org/applic/ihl/ihl.nsf/ART/150-110010?OpenDocument> (accessed 5 June 2013).
Sanborn, Joshua. "Atrocities in East Prussia." *Russian History Blog*. 16 February 2011. <http://russianhistoryblog.org/2011/02/atrocities-in-east-prussia-1914/>
Sanborn, Joshua. "Russians in East Prussia (pt. 2)." *Russian History Blog*. 24 February 2011. <http://russianhistoryblog.org/2011/02/russians-in-east-prussia-1914-pt-2/>

FILMS

Liliia Belgii. Directed by Władysław Starewicz and sponsored by the Skobelev Committee: 1915. Included in *Early Russian Cinema: A Unique Anthology in 10 Volumes*, vol. 3. Harrington Park, NJ: Milestone Films, 2007–2008.

BOOKS AND ARTICLES

Abraham, Richard. *Alexander Kerensky: The First Love of the Revolution*. New York: Columbia University Press, 1987.

Airapetov, O. R. "Narochskaia operatsiia i otstavka A. A. Polivanova," *Vestnik Moskovskogo Universiteta* ser. 8 (istoriia), no. 6 (2001): 80–97.

Aksenov, V. B. "Militsiia i gorodskie sloi v period revoliutsionnogo krizisa 1917 goda: problemy legitimnosti." *Voprosy istorii* no. 8 (2001): 36–50.

Alekseeva-Borel', Vera. *Sorok let v riadakh russkoi imperatorskoi armii: M. V. Alekseev*. St. Petersburg: Bel'veder, 2000.

Alexinsky [Aleksinskaia], Tatiana. *With the Russian Wounded*. London: T. F. Unwin, 1916.

Allen, W. E. D. and Paul Muratoff. *Caucasian Battlefields: A History of the Wars on the Turco-Caucasian Border, 1828–1921*. Cambridge: Cambridge University Press, 1953.

An-sky, S. *The Enemy at His Pleasure: A Journey through the Jewish Pale of Settlement during World War I*. New York: Henry Holt, 2002.

Arapov, D. "'Vo vsem musul'manskom mire nabliudaetsia chrezvychainyi pod''em religioznogo i natsional'no-kul'turnogo samosoznaniia': Ministerstvo vnutrennykh del i 'musul'-manskii vopros'." *Istochnik* 55, no. 1 (2002): 61–6.

Arens, Olavi. "The Estonian Question at Brest-Litovsk." *Journal of Baltic Studies* 25, no. 4 (1994): 305–30.

Astashov, A. B. "Soiuzy zemstv i gorodov i pomoshch' ranenym v pervuiu mirovuiu voinu." *Otechestvennaia istoriia* no. 6 (1992): 169–72.

Badcock, Sarah. *Politics and the People in Revolutionary Russia: A Provincial History*. Cambridge: Cambridge University Press, 2007.

Baker, Mark. "Rampaging 'Soldatki,' Cowering Police, Bazaar Riots and Moral Economy: The Social Impact of the Great War in Kharkiv Province." *Canadian-American Slavic Studies* 35, no. 2–3 (2001): 137–55.

Bakhturina, A. Iu. *Politika rossiiskoi imperii v vostochnoi Galitsii v gody pervoi mirovoi voiny*. Moscow: AIRO-XX, 2000.

Bakhturina, A. Iu. *Okrainy rossiiskoi imperii: gosudarstvennoe upravlenie i natsional'naia politika v gody Pervoi mirovoi voiny, 1914–1917gg*. Moscow: ROSSPEN, 2004.

Banac, Ivo. "South Slav Prisoners of War in Revolutionary Russia." In *Essays on World War I: Origins and Prisoners of War*, ed. Samuel R. Williamson Jr. and Peter Pastor, 119–48. New York: Columbia University Press, 1983.

Bass, Gary Jonathan. *Stay the Hand of Vengeance: The Politics of War Crimes Tribunals*. Princeton: Princeton University Press, 2000.

Belova, Irina. *Pervaia mirovaia voina i rossiiskaia provintsiia, 1914-fevral' 1917 g*. Moscow: AIRO-XXI, 2011.

Bisher, Jamie. *White Terror: Cossack Warlords of the Trans-Siberian*. London and New York: Routledge, 2005.

Bobrinskii, N. A. "Na pervoi mirovoi voine. Iz zapisok grafa Nikolaia G. Bobrinskogo." *Dvorianskoe sobranie* no. 3 (1995): 176–90.

Bogdanovich, P. N. *Vtorzhenie v Vostochnuiu Prussiiu v avguste 1914 goda: Vospominaniia ofitsera general'nogo shtaba Armii generala Samsonova*. Buenos Aires: Dorrego, 1964.

Boleslavski, Richard. *Way of the Lancer*, in collaboration with Helen Woodward. New York: The Literary Guild, 1932.

Bondarenko, D. Ia. "Vremennoe pravitel'stvo i problema avtonomii ukrainy (iiul'-oktiabr' 1917 g.)." *Otechestvennaia istoriia* no. 1 (2006): 54–64.

Bortnevski, Viktor G. "White Administration and White Terror (The Denikin Period)." *Russian Review* 52, no. 3 (July 1993): 354–66.

Browder, Robert Paul and Alexander F. Kerensky, eds. *The Russian Provisional Government, 1917: Documents*. 3 vols. Stanford: Stanford University Press, 1961.

Brower, Daniel. *Turkestan and the Fate of the Russian Empire*. London and New York: RoutledgeCurzon, 2003.

Brusilov, General A. A. *A Soldier's Notebook, 1914–1918*. Westport, CT: Greenwood Press, 1971 [1930].

Budko, A. A., E. F. Selivanov, and N. G. Chigareva. "'V izvestnye momenty na voine ne meditsina, ne nauka, ne operatsiia igraiut samuiu vaznhuiu rol', a organizatsiia raboty': Voennaia meditsina Rossii v gody Pervoi mirovoi voiny." *Voenno-istoricheskkii zhurnal* no. 8 (2004): 57–62.

Budko, A. A., E. F. Selivanov, and N. G. Chigareva. "'Preodolevaia strakh i opasnost', Rossiiskie mediki s chest'iu vypolniali svoi dolg." *Voenno-istoricheskii zhurnal* no. 9 (2004): 42–8.

Budnitskii, O. V. *Rossiiskie evrei mezhdu krasnymi i belymi*. Moscow: ROSSPEN, 2006.

Buldakov, V. P. *Krasnaia smuta: priroda i posledstviia revoliutsionnogo nasiliia*. Moscow: ROSSPEN, 1997.

Burbank, Jane and Frederick Cooper. *Empires in World History: Power and the Politics of Difference*. Princeton: Princeton University Press, 2010.

Burbank, Jane and Mark von Hagen, "Coming into the Territory: Uncertainty and Empire." In *Russian Empire*, ed. Burbank, von Hagen, and Remnev, 1–32.

Burbank, Jane, Mark von Hagen, and Anatolyi Remnev, eds. *Russian Empire: Space, People, Power, 1700–1930*. Bloomington: Indiana University Press, 2007.

Burr, Millard and Robert O. Collins. *Africa's Thirty Years War: Libya, Chad, and the Sudan, 1963–1993*. Boulder, CO: Westview Press, 1999.

Buttino, Marco. *Revoliutsiia naoborot: Sredniaia Aziia mezhdu padeniem tsarskoi imperii i obrazovaniem SSSR*, trans. Nikolai Okhotin. Moscow: Zven'ia, 2007 [2003].

Chernev, Borislav. "The Brest-Litovsk Moment: Self-Determination Discourse in Eastern Europe before Wilsonianism." *Diplomacy & Statecraft* 22, no. 3 (2011): 369–87.

Chernev, Borislav. "'The Future Depends on Brest-Litovsk': War, Peace, and Revolution in Central and Eastern Europe, 1917–1918." Ph.D. diss., American University, 2013.

Cherniavsky, Michael. *Prologue to Revolution: Notes of A. N. Iakhontov on the Secret Meetings of the Council of Ministers, 1915*. Englewood Cliffs, NJ: Prentice-Hall, 1967.

Churchill, Winston. *The Unknown War: The Eastern Front*. New York: Charles Scribner's Sons, 1931.

Citino, Robert Michael. *Quest for Decisive Victory: From Stalemate to Blitzkrieg in Europe, 1899–1940*. Modern War Studies. Lawrence: University Press of Kansas, 2002.

Clark, Christopher. *The Sleepwalkers: How Europe Went to War in 1914*. New York: Harper Collins, 2013.

Cohen, Aaron J. "Oh, That! Myth, Memory, and World War I in the Russian Emigration and the Soviet Union." *Slavic Review* 62, no. 1 (Spring 2003): 69–86.

Cooper, Frederick. *Africa since 1940: The Past of the Present, New Approaches to African History*. New York: Cambridge University Press, 2002.

Cornwall, Mark. "Morale and Patriotism in the Austro-Hungarian Army, 1914–1918." In *State, Society, and Mobilization*, ed. Horne, 173–90.

Danilov, Iu. N. *Velikii kniaz' Nikolai Nikolaevich*. Paris: Navarre, 1930.

Davies, Norman. *God's Playground: A History of Poland.* 2 vols. New York: Columbia University Press, 1982.

Dedijer, Vladimir. *The Road to Sarajevo.* New York: Simon and Schuster, 1966.

Dekel-Chen, Jonathan, David Gaunt, Natan M. Meir, and Israel Bartal eds. *Anti-Jewish Violence: Rethinking the Pogrom in East European History.* Bloomington: Indiana University Press, 2011.

Dekrety sovetskoi vlasti. 18 vols. Moscow: Gosizdat, 1957–.

DiNardo, Richard L. *Breakthrough: The Gorlice–Tarnow Campaign, 1915.* Santa Barbara: Praeger, 2010.

Dowling, Timothy C. *The Brusilov Offensive.* Bloomington: Indiana University Press, 2008.

Durham, M. E. *The Struggle for Scutari (Turk, Slav, and Albanian).* London: E. Arnold, 1914.

Durova, Nadezhda. *The Cavalry Maiden: Journals of a Russian Officer in the Napoleonic Wars,* translated by Mary Fleming Zirin. Bloomington: Indiana University Press, 1988.

Dwyer, Philip G. "'It Still Makes Me Shudder': Memories of Massacres and Atrocities during the Revolutionary and Napoleonic Wars." *War in History* 16, no. 4 (2009): 381–405.

Eksteins, Modris. *Rites of Spring: The Great War and the Birth of the Modern Age.* Boston: Houghton Mifflin, 1989.

Eliseev, F. I. *Kazaki na kavkazskom fronte 1914–1917.* Moscow: Voenizdat, 2001.

Engel, Barbara Alpern. "Not by Bread Alone: Subsistence Riots in Russia during World War I." *Journal of Modern History* 69 (December 1997): 696–721.

Engelstein, Laura. "'A Belgium of Our Own': The Sack of Russian Kalisz, August 1914." *Kritika: Explorations in Russian and Eurasian History* 10, no. 3 (Summer 2009): 441–73.

Fallows, Thomas. "Politics and the War Effort in Russia: The Union of Zemstvos and the Organization of the Food Supply, 1914–1916." *Slavic Review* 37, no. 1 (March 1978): 70–90.

Fava, Andrea. "War, 'National Education' and the Italian Primary School, 1915–1918," in *State, Society, and Mobilization,* ed. Horne, 53–70.

Fearon, James D. and David D. Laitin. "Ethnicity, Insurgency, and Civil War." *The American Political Science Review* 97, no. 1 (2003): 75–90.

Fediuk, Vladimir. *Kerenskii.* Moscow: Molodaia gvardiia, 2009.

Fedyshyn, Oleh S. *Germany's Drive to the East and the Ukrainian Revolution, 1917–1918.* New Brunswick: Rutgers University Press, 1971.

Feldman, Robert S. "The Russian General Staff and the June 1917 Offensive." *Soviet Studies* 19, no. 4 (April 1968): 526–43.

Ferguson, Niall. "Prisoner Taking and Prisoner Killing in the Age of Total War: Towards a Political Economy of Military Defeat." *War in History* 11, no. 2 (2004): 148–92.

Figes, Orlando. *A People's Tragedy: The Russian Revolution, 1891–1924.* London: Pimlico, 1996.

Fischer, Fritz. *Germany's Aims in the First World War.* New York: W. W. Norton, 1967.

Fitzpatrick, Sheila. *The Russian Revolution.* 2nd ed. Oxford: Oxford University Press, 1994.

Fleer, M. G., ed. *Rabochee dvizhenie v gody voiny.* Moscow: Voprosy truda, 1925.

Flockerzie, Lawrence R. "Poland's Louvain: Documents on the Destruction of Kalisz, August 1914." *The Polish Review* 28, no. 4 (1983): 73–87.

Florinsky, Michael T. *The End of the Russian Empire.* New Haven: Yale University Press, 1931.

fon Shvarts, A. V. *Ivangorod v 1914–1915: iz vospominaniia komendanta kreposti.* Paris: Tanais, 1969.

Frenkel', Z. G. "Zapiski o zhiznennom puti." *Voprosy istorii* no. 1 (2007): 79–99.

Fuller, William C., Jr. *The Foe Within: Fantasies of Treason and the End of Imperial Russia.* Ithaca: Cornell University Press, 2006.

Fuller, William C., Jr. *Strategy and Power in Russia, 1600-1914.* New York: Free Press, 1992.

Gaida, F. A. *Liberal'naia oppozitsiia na putiakh k vlasti (1914–vesna 1917 g.).* Moscow: Rosspen, 2003.

Galin, V. V. *Voina i revoliutsiia.* Moscow: Algoritm, 2004.

Galitskaia golgofa: voennye prestupleniia Gabsburgskoi monarkhii, 1914–1917. Trumbull, CT: Peter S. Hardy, 1964.

Gatrell, Peter. *A Whole Empire Walking: Refugees in Russia during World War I.* Bloomington: Indiana University Press, 1999.

Gatrell, Peter. "Prisoners of War on the Eastern Front during World War I." *Kritika: Explorations in Russian and Eurasian History* 6, no. 3 (Summer 2005): 557–66.

Gatrell, Peter. *Russia's First World War: A Social and Economic History.* Harlow: Pearson Longman, 2005.

Gaudin, Corinne. "Rural Echoes of World War I: War Talk in the Russian Village." *Jahrbücher für Geschichte Osteuropas* 56, no. 3 (2008): 391–414.

Geiss, Imanuel, ed. *July 1914, The Outbreak of the First World War: Selected Documents.* New York: Charles Scribner's Sons, 1967.

General Committee of the Russian Union of Zemstvos. *Russian Union of Zemstvos: A Brief Report of the Union's Activities during the War.* London: P. S. King & Son, 1917 [1916].

Gerasimov, M. N. *Probuzhdenie.* Moscow: Voenizdat, 1965.

Glenny, Misha. *The Balkans: Nationalism, War, and the Great Powers, 1804–1999.* New York: Penguin, 1999.

Golikov, G. N. and Iu. S. Tokarev. "Aprel'skii krizis 1917 g." *Istoricheskie zapiski* 57 (1956): 35–79.

Gooch, G. P., and Harold William Vazeille Temperley, eds. *British Documents on the Origins of War, 1898–1914,* 11 vols. London: His Majesty's Stationary Office, 1926.

Gorelkina, E. V. ed. "Iz istorii rabochego dvizheniia vo vremia mirovoi voiny (Stachochnoe dvizhenie v Kostromskoi gubernii)," *Krasnyi arkhiv,* no. 6, 5–27. 1934.

Gorizontov, Leonid. "The 'Great Circle' of Interior Russia: Representations of the Imperial Center in the Nineteenth and Early Twentieth Centuries." In *Russian Empire,* ed. Burbank, von Hagen, and Remnev, 67–93.

Gorky, Maxim. *Untimely Thoughts: Essays on Revolution, Culture and the Bolsheviks, 1917–1918,* introduction by Mark D. Steinberg, trans. Herman Ermolaev. New Haven: Yale University Press, 1995.

Gothein, Georg. *Warum verloren wir den Krieg?* 2nd edn. Stuttgart and Berlin: Deutsche Verlags-anstalt, 1920.

Graf, Daniel W. "The Reign of the Generals: Military Government in Western Russia, 1914–1915." Ph.D. diss., University of Nebraska, 1972.

Graf, Daniel W. "Military Rule Behind the Russian Front, 1914–1917: The Political Ramifications." *Jahrbücher für Geschichte Osteuropas* 22, no. 3 (1974): 390–411.

Greaves, Rose Louise. "Some Aspects of the Anglo-Russian Convention and Its Working in Persia, 1907–1914 – I." *Bulletin of the School of Oriental and African Studies, University of London* 31, no. 1 (1968): 69–91.

Gudmundsson, Bruce I. *Stormtroop Tactics: Innovation in the German Army, 1914–1918.* Westport, CT: Praeger, 1989.

Hall, Richard C. *The Balkan Wars, 1912–1913: Prelude to the First World War*. London and New York: Routledge, 2000.

Hasegawa, Tsuyoshi. *The February Revolution: Petrograd, 1917*. Seattle and London: University of Washington Press, 1981.

Hasegawa, Tsuyoshi. *"Gosudarstvennost', Obshchestvennost', and Klassovost'*: Crime, Police, and the State in the Russian Revolution in Petrograd." *Canadian-American Slavic Studies* 35, nos. 2–3 (2001): 157–82.

Helmreich, Ernst Christian. *The Diplomacy of the Balkan Wars, 1912–1913*. Cambridge, MA: Harvard University Press, 1938.

Hevia, James Louis. *English Lessons: The Pedagogy of Imperialism in Nineteenth-Century China*. Durham, NC: Duke University Press, 2003.

Heyman, Neil M. "Gorlice–Tarnow: The Eastern Front in 1915." *The Army Quarterly and Defence Journal* 109, no. 1 (1979): 60–73.

Hirsch, Francine. *Empire of Nations: Ethnographic Knowledge and the Making of the Soviet Union*. Ithaca: Cornell University Press, 2005.

Holquist, Peter. "What's so Revolutionary about the Russian Revolution? State Practices and the New-Style Politics, 1914–1921." In *Russian Modernity: Politics, Knowledge, Practices*, ed. David L. Hoffmann and Yanni Kotsonis, 87–111. New York: St. Martin's Press, 2000.

Holquist, Peter. *Making War, Forging Revolution: Russia's Continuum of Crisis, 1914–1921*. Cambridge, MA: Harvard University Press, 2002.

Holquist, Peter. "The Role of Personality in the First (1914–1915) Russian Occupation of Galicia and Bukovina." In *Anti-Jewish Violence*, ed. Jonathan Dekel-Chen et al., 52–73.

Horak, Stephan M. *The First Treaty of World War I: Ukraine's Treaty with the Central Powers of February 9, 1918*. Boulder, CO: East European Monographs, 1988.

Horne, John. "Introduction: Mobilizing for Total War, 1914–1918." In *State, Society, and Mobilization*, ed. Horne, 1–18.

Horne, John. "Remobilizing for 'Total War': France and Britain, 1917–1918." In *State, Society, and Mobilization*, ed. Horne, 195–211.

Horne, John and Alan Kramer. *German Atrocities, 1914: A History of Denial*. New Haven and London: Yale University Press, 2001.

Horne, John, ed. *State, Society, and Mobilization in Europe during the First World War*. Cambridge: Cambridge University Press, 1997.

Hroch, Miroslav. *Social Preconditions of National Revival in Europe: A Comparative Analysis of the Social Composition of Patriotic Grounds among the Smaller European Nations*. Cambridge: Cambridge University Press, 1985.

Hull, Isabel V. *Absolute Destruction: Military Culture and the Practices of War in Imperial Germany*. Ithaca: Cornell University Press, 2005.

Hutchinson, John F. *Politics and Public Health in Revolutionary Russia, 1890–1918*. Baltimore, MD, and London: Johns Hopkins University Press, 1990.

Ignat'ev, A. V. "Politika soglashenii i balansirovaniia: vneshnepoliticheskii kurs Rossii v 1906-1914 gg." *Otechestvennaia istoriia* no. 3 (1997): 23–32.

Jahn, Hubertus. *Patriotic Culture in Russia during World War I*. Ithaca: Cornell University Press, 1995.

Jelavich, Barbara. *Russia's Balkan Entanglements, 1806–1914*. Cambridge: Cambridge University Press, 1991.

Jones, David R. "The Imperial Russian Life Guards Grenadier Regiment, 1906–1917: The Disintegration of an Elite Unit." *Military Affairs* 33, no. 2 (October 1969): 289–302.

Jones, Heather. "Military Captivity and the Prisoner of War, 1914–1918." *Immigrants and Minorities* 26, no. 1/2 (2008): 19–48.

Kappeler, Andreas. *The Russian Empire: A Multiethnic History*, trans. Alfred Clayton. Harlow, UK: Longman/Pearson, 2001.

Karpovich, V. D., ed. *Gosudarstvennaia Duma, 1906–1917: stenograficheskie otchety*. 4 vols. Moscow: Pravovaia kul'tura, 1995.

Katkov, George. *The Kornilov Affair: Kerensky and the Break-up of the Russian Army*. London: Longman, 1980.

Keegan, John. *The First World War*. New York: Vintage, 1998.

Keirim-Markus, M. B. "O polozhenii armii nakanune oktiabria (Doneseniia komissarov Vremennogo pravitel'stva i komandirov voinskikh chastei Deistvuiushchei armii)." *Istoricheskii arkhiv* no. 6 (November 1957): 35–60.

Kel'ner, Viktor. "The Jewish Question and Russian Social Life during World War I." *Russian Studies in History* 43, no. 1 (Summer 2004): 11–40.

Kenez, Peter. *Civil War in South Russia, 1918: The First Year of the Volunteer Army*. Berkeley: University of California Press, 1971.

Kennan, George F. *The Other Balkan Wars: A 1913 Carnegie Endowment Inquiry in Retrospect with a New Introduction and Reflections on the Present Conflict*. Washington, DC: Carnegie Endowment for International Peace, 1993.

Kerensky, A. F. *The Prelude to Bolshevism: The Kornilov Rising*. New York: Dodd, Mead, and Company, 1919.

Khalid, Adeeb. *The Politics of Muslim Cultural Reform: Jadidism in Central Asia*. Berkeley: University of California Press, 1998.

Kir'ianov, Iu I. "Massovye vystupleniia na pochve dorogovizny v Rossii (1914–fevral' 1917 g.)." *Otechestvennaia istoriia* no. 3 (1993): 3–18.

Kirby, D. G., ed. *Finland and Russia, 1808–1920, From Autonomy to Independence: A Selection of Documents*. London and Basingstoke: Macmillan, 1975.

Kirimli, Hakan. "The Activities of the Union for the Liberation of Ukraine in the Ottoman Empire during the First World War." *Middle Eastern Studies* 34, no. 4 (1998): 177–200.

Klier, Dzh [John]. "Kazaki i pogromy: chem otlichalis' 'voennye' pogromy?" In *Mirovoi krizis 1914–1920 godov i sud'ba vostochnoevropeiskogo evreistva*, ed. O. V. Budnitskii, 47–74. Moscow: ROSSPEN, 2005.

Knox, Major-General Sir Alfred. *With the Russian Army, 1914–1917: Being Chiefly Extracts from the Diary of a Military Attaché*. 2 vols. London: Hutchinson & Co., 1921.

Kobylin, Viktor. *Imperator Nikolai II i zagovor generalov*. Moscow: Veche, 2008 [1970].

Koenker, Diane P. and William G. Rosenberg. *Strikes and Revolution in Russia, 1917*. Princeton: Princeton University Press, 1989.

Kojevnikov, Alexei B. *Stalin's Great Science: The Times and Adventures of Soviet Physicists*. London: Imperial College Press, 2004.

Korzeniowski, Marius. "Rejon Zachodni Centralnego Komitetu Obywatelskiego - powstanie i początki działalności." *Studia z dziejów Rosji i Europy Środkowo-Wschodniej* 29 (1994): 29–46.

Kostrikova, E. G. *Rossiiskoe obshchestvo i vneshniaia politika nakanune pervoi mirovoi voiny, 1908–1914*. Moscow: IRI RAN, 2007.

Kotsonis, Yanni. "Arkhangel'sk 1918: Regionalism and Populism in the Russian Civil War." *Russian Review* 51, no. 4 (October 1992): 526–44.

Kotsonis, Yanni. "'No Place to Go': Taxation and State Transformation in Late Imperial and Early Soviet Russia." *Journal of Modern History* 76, no. 3 (September 2004): 531–77.

Kournakoff, Sergei. *Savage Squadrons*. Boston and New York: Hale, Cushman, and Flint, 1935.

Kozlov, V. A. and S. V. Mironenko, eds. *Arkhiv noveishei istorii Rossii*, vol. 7. Moscow: Rosspen, 2001.

Kozybaev, Manash, ed. *Groznyi 1916-i god (sbornik dokumentov i materialov)*. 2 vols. Almaty: "Kazakstan," 1998.

Kramer, Alan. *Dynamic of Destruction: Culture and Mass Killing in the First World War*. Oxford: Oxford University Press, 2007.

Ksiunin, Aleksei. *Narod na voine: iz zapisok voennogo korrespondenta*. Petrograd: Izd. B. A. Suvorina, 1916.

Kuper, Leo. "The Turkish Genocide of the Armenians, 1915–1917." In *The Armenian Genocide in Perspective*, ed. Richard G. Hovannisian, 35–52. New Brunswick and Oxford: Transaction Books, 1986.

Galuzo, I. ed. "Vosstanie 1916 g. v Srednei Azii." *Krasnyi arkhiv* 3, no. 34 (1929): 39–94.

Lalkov, Milcho. *Mezhdu vuztorga i pokrusata: Bulgariia po vreme na voinite 1912–1918 g.* Sofiia: SlovD, 1993.

Lemke, Heinz. *Allianz und Rivalität: Die Mittelmächte und Polen im ersten Weltkrieg (Bis zur Februarrevolution)*. Berlin: Akademie-verlag, 1977.

Lemke, Mikhail. *250 dnei v tsarskoi stavke: vospominaniia, memuary*. 2 vols. Minsk: Kharvest, 2003.

Lenin, V. I. *Sochineniia*. 4th ed. Leningrad: Gosizdat, 1951.

Lentsen, Iris. "Ispol'zovanie truda russkikh voennoplennykh v Germanii (1914–1918 gg.)." *Voprosy istorii* no. 4 (1998): 129–37.

Lieven, D. C. B. *Russia and the Origins of the First World War*. New York: St. Martin's Press, 1983.

Lih, Lars. *Bread and Authority in Russia, 1914–1921*. Berkeley: University of California Press, 1990.

Lincoln, W. Bruce. *Passage Through Armageddon: The Russians in War and Revolution, 1914–1918*. New York: Simon and Schuster, 1986.

Lincoln, W. Bruce. *Red Victory: A History of the Russian Civil War*. New York: Simon and Schuster, 1989.

Liulevicius, Vejas G. *War Land on the Eastern Front: Culture, National Identity, and German Identity in World War I*. Cambridge: Cambridge University Press, 2000.

Liulevicius, Vejas G. *War Land on the Eastern Front: Culture, National Identity, and German Occupation in World War I*. Cambridge: Cambridge University Press, 2000.

Lohr, Eric. "1915 and the War Pogrom Paradigm in the Russian Empire." In *Anti-Jewish Violence*, ed. Dekel-Chen et al., 41–51.

Lohr, Eric. "The Russian Army and the Jews: Mass Deportation, Hostages, and Violence during World War I." *Russian Review* 60 (July 2001): 404–19.

Lohr, Eric. *Nationalizing the Russian Empire: The Campaign against Enemy Aliens during World War I*. Cambridge, MA: Harvard University Press, 2003.

Lohr, Eric. "The Russian Press and the 'Internal Peace' at the Beginning of World War I." In *A Call to Arms: Propaganda, Public Opinion, and Newspapers in the Great War*, ed. Troy R. E. Paddock, 91–114. Westport, CT: Praeger, 2004.

Lohr, Eric. *Russian Citizenship: From Empire to Soviet Union*. Cambridge, MA: Harvard University Press, 2012.

Luk'ianov, M. N. "'Rossiia – dlia russkikh' ili 'Rossiia dlia russkikh poddannykh'? Konservatory i natsional'nyi vopros nakanune pervoi mirovoi voiny," *Otechestvennaia istoriia* no. 2 (2006): 36–46.

Luntinen, Pertti. *The Imperial Russian Army and Navy in Finland, 1808–1918*. Helsinki: SHS, 1997.

Lyandres, Semion. *The Fall of Tsarism: Untold Stories of the February 1917 Revolution*. Oxford: Oxford University Press, 2013.

Lyon, James M. B. "'A Peasant Mob': The Serbian Army on the Eve of the Great War." *The Journal of Military History* 61 (July 1997): 481–502.

Macqueen, Norrie. *The Decolonization of Portuguese Africa: Metropolitan Revolution and the Dissolution of Empire*. London and New York: Longman, 1997.

Magocsi, Paul R. *A History of Ukraine: The Land and Its Peoples*, 2nd ed. Toronto: University of Toronto Press, 2010.

Makarenko, P. V. "Bol'sheviki i Brestskii mir." *Voprosy istorii* no. 3 (2010): 3–21.

Maklakov, V. A. *Rechi: sudebnye, dumskie, i publichnye lektsii 1904–1926*. Paris: Izd. Iubileinogo komiteta, 1949.

Manela, Erez. *The Wilsonian Moment: Self-Determination and the International Origins of Anticolonial Nationalism*. Oxford: Oxford University Press, 2007.

Martin, Terry. *The Affirmative Action Empire: Nations and Nationalism in the Soviet Union, 1923-1939*. Ithaca: Cornell University Press, 2001.

Martynov, E. I. *Serby v voine s Tsarem Ferdinandom (zametki ochevidtsa)*. Moscow: P. P. Riabushinskii, 1913.

Maslovskii, E. V. *Mirovaia voina na Kavkazskom fronte, 1914–1917g.: strategicheskii ocherk*. Paris: Vozrozhdenie, 1933.

Mawdsley, Evan. *The Russian Civil War*. Boston: Allen & Unwin, 1987.

McMeekin, Sean. *The Russian Origins of the First World War*. Cambridge, MA: Harvard University Press, 2011.

Melancon, Michael. "Rethinking Russia's February Revolution: Anonymous Spontaneity or Socialist Agency?" *Carl Beck Papers in Russian and East European Studies*, no. 1408. Pittsburgh: University of Pittsburgh Press, 2000.

Melkumian, G. A. "Vrachi-Armiane na Kavkazskom fronte pervoi mirovoi voiny." *Patma-Banasirakan Handes. Istoriko-Filologicheskii Zhurnal* no. 3 (1975): 126–35.

Menning, Bruce W. *Bayonets Before Bullets: The Imperial Russian Army, 1861–1914*. Bloomington: Indiana University Press, 1992.

Menning, Bruce W. "The Offensive Revisited: Russian Preparation for Future War, 1906–1914." In *Reforming the Tsar's Army: Military Innovation in Imperial Russia from Peter the Great to the Revolution*, ed. David Schimmelpenninck van der Oye and Bruce W. Menning, 215–31. Cambridge: Cambridge University Press, 2004.

Meyer, Alfred G. "The Impact of World War I on Russian Women's Lives," In *Russia's Women: Accommodation, Resistance, Transformation*, ed. Barbara Evans Clements, Barbara Alpern Engel, and Christine D. Worobec, 208–24. Berkeley: University of California Press, 1991.

Mikhutina, Irina. *Ukrainskii Brestskii mir: put' vykhoda Rossii iz pervoi mirovoi voiny i anatomiia konflikta mezhdu Sovnarkomom RSFSR i pravitel'stvom Ukrainskoi Tsentral'noi Rady*. Moscow: Evropa, 2007.

Miliukov, P. N. "Territorial'nye priobreteniia Rossii." In *Chego zhdet Rossii ot voiny: sbornik statei*, ed. M. I. Tugan-Baranovskii, 49-62. N. p: Prometei, 1915.

Miliukov, Paul. *Political Memoirs, 1905–1917*, ed. Arthur P. Mendel, trans. Carl Goldberg. Ann Arbor: University of Michigan Press, 1967.

Mints, I. I. "Revoliutsionnaia bor'ba proletariata rossii v 1914–1916 godakh." *Voprosy istorii* no. 12 (December 1959): 23–40.

Mirotvortsev, S. R. *Stranitsy zhizni.* Leningrad: Medgiz, 1956.

Moeller, Robert G. "Dimensions of Social Conflict in the Great War: The View from the German Countryside." *Central European History* 14, no. 2 (1981): 142–68.

Molenda, Jan. "Social Changes in Poland during World War I." In *East Central European Society in World War I,* ed. Béla K. Király and Nándor F. Dreisziger, 187–201. Boulder: Social Science Research Monographs, 1985.

Mombauer, Annika. *Helmuth von Moltke and the Origins of the First World War.* Cambridge: Cambridge University Press, 2001.

Mombauer, Annika. *The Origins of the First World War: Controversies and Consensus.* Harlow, UK: Longman, 2002.

Morrison, Alexander. "Metropole, Colony, and Imperial Citizenship in the Russian Empire." *Kritika: Explorations in Russian and Eurasian History* 13, no. 2 (Spring 2012): 327–64.

Münkler, Herfried. *Empires: The Logic of World Domination from Ancient Rome to the United States,* trans. Patrick Camiller. Cambridge, UK: Polity Press, 2007.

Nachtigal, Reinhard. *Die Murmanbahn: Die Verkehrsanbindung eines kriegswichtigen Hafens und das Arbeitspotential der Kriegsgefangenen (1915 bis 1918).* Grunbach: Verlag Bernhard Albert Greiner, 2001.

Nagornaia, O. S. *Drugoi voennyi opyt: rossiiskie voennoplennye Pervoi mirovoi voiny v Germanii (1914–1922).* Moscow: Novyi khronograf, 2010.

Nastuplenie iugo-zapadnogo fronta v mae-iiune 1916 goda. Moscow: Voenizdat, 1940.

Nelipovich, S. G. "Naselenie okkupirovannykh territorii rassmatrivalos' kak rezerv protivnika: internirovanie chasti zhitelei Vostochnoi Prussii, Galitsii i Bukoviny v 1914-1915 gg." *Voenno-istoricheskii zhurnal* no. 2 (2000): 60–9.

Novikova, Liudmila G. "A Province of a Non-Existent State: The White Government in the Russian North and Political Power in the Russian Civil War, 1918–1920." *Revolutionary Russia* 18, no. 2 (2005): 121–44.

Novikova, Liudmila G. *Provintsial'naia "kontrrevoliutsiia": beloe dvizhenie i Grazhdanskaia voina na russkom Severe, 1917–1920.* Moscow: Novoe literaturnoe obozrenie, 2011.

Okey, Robin. *The Habsburg Monarchy: From Enlightenment to Eclipse.* New York: St Martin's, 2001.

" 'Okopy eti okhrainiat Varshavu, k kotoroi tak neravnodushen nemets . . .': dnevnik nachal'nika sapernoi komandy 24-go Sibirskogo strelkovogo polka praporshchika A. I. Todorskogo, iiun'-sentiabr' 1915 goda." *Voenno-istoricheskii zhurnal* no. 9 (2004): 23–8.

The Origins of the First World War: Diplomatic and Military Documents, ed. and trans. Annika Mombauer. Manchester and New York: Manchester University Press, 2013.

Orlovsky, Daniel. "Velikaia voina i Rossiiskaia pamiat'." In *Rossiia i pervaia mirovaia voina (materialy mezhdunarodnogo nauchnogo kollokviuma),* ed. N. N. Smirnov, 49–57. St. Petersburg: Dmitrii Bulanin, 1999.

Osipov, S. P., ed. *Psikhozy i psikhonervozy voiny: sbornik.* Leningrad and Moscow: OGIZ, 1934.

Otchet o deiatel'nosti meditsinskoi organizatsii komiteta zapadnago fronta Vserossiiskago Zemskago Soiuza za oktiabr', noiabr', i dekabr' 1915 g. Moscow: Vserossiiskii zemskii soiuz. Komitet Zapadnogo fronta, 1916.

Owen, Thomas. *Russian Corporate Capitalism from Peter the Great to Perestroika.* Oxford: Oxford University Press, 1995.

Paduchev, Vl. *Zapiski nizhnego china 1916 god.* Moscow: Moskovskoe tovarishchestvo pisatelei, 1931.

Pagden, Anthony. *Lords of All the World: Ideologies of Empire in Spain, Britain, and France, c. 1500–c. 1800.* New Haven: Yale University Press, 1995.

Pares, Bernard. *My Russian Memoirs.* London: Jonathan Cape, 1931.

Payne, Matthew J. *Stalin's Railroad: Turksib and the Building of Socialism.* Pittsburgh: University of Pittsburgh Press, 2001.

Pearson, Raymond. *The Russian Moderates and the Crisis of Tsarism, 1914–1917.* Basingstoke: Macmillan, 1977.

Petrone, Karen. *The Great War in Russian Memory.* Bloomington: Indiana University Press, 2011.

Pipes, Richard. *The Russian Revolution.* New York: Alfred Knopf, 1990.

Pisarev, Iu A. *Tainy pervoi mirovoi voiny: Rossiia i Serbiia v 1914–1915 gg.* Moscow: Nauka, 1990.

Podorozhnyi, N. E. *Narochskaia operatsiia v marte 1916 g. na Russkom fronte mirovoi voiny.* Moscow: Gosizdat, 1938.

Poletaev, V. E., et al., eds. *Revoliutsionnoe dvizhenie v Rossii posle sverzheniia samoderzhaviia.* 10 vols. Moscow: Izd. Akademii nauk SSSR, 1957.

Polner, Tikhon J. *Russian Local Government during the War and the Union of Zemstvos.* New Haven: Yale University Press, 1930.

Polvinen, Tuomo. *Imperial Borderland: Bobrikov and the Attempted Russification of Finland, 1898–1904,* translated by Steven Huxley. Durham, NC: Duke University Press, 1995.

Porshneva, O. S. *Krest'iane, rabochie, i soldaty Rossii nakanune i v gody Pervoi mirovoi voiny.* Moscow: ROSSPEN, 2004.

Porter, Thomas Earl. "The Emergence of Civil Society in Late Imperial Russia: The Impact of the Russo-Japanese and First World Wars on Russian Social and Political Life, 1904–1917." *War & Society* 23, no. 1 (May 2005): 41–60.

Prazmowska, Anita J. *A History of Poland.* New York: Palgrave Macmillan, 2004.

Proctor, Tammy M. *Civilians in a World at War, 1914–1918.* New York: New York University Press, 2010.

Prusin, Alexander Victor. *Nationalizing a Borderland: War, Ethnicity, and Anti-Jewish Violence in East Galicia, 1914–1920.* Tuscaloosa: University of Alabama Press, 2005.

Quenoy, Paul du. "Warlordism 'a la Russe;' Baron von Ungern-Sternberg's Anti-Bolshevik Crusade, 1917–21." *Revolutionary Russia* 16, no. 2 (2003): 1–27.

Rabochee dvizhenie na Ukraine v period pervoi mirovoi imperialisticheskoi voiny, Iiul' 1914 g.– fevral' 1917 g.: Sbornik dokumentov i materialov. Kiev: Izd. "Naukova Dumka," 1966.

Rachamimov, Alon. *POWs and the Great War: Captivity on the Eastern Front.* Oxford and New York: Berg, 2002.

Rachamimov, Alon. "The Disruptive Comforts of Drag: (Trans)Gender Performances among Prisoners of War in Russia, 1914–1920." *The American Historical Review* 111, no. 2 (April 2006): 362–82.

Radkey, Oliver H. *Russia Goes to the Polls: The Election to the All-Russian Constituent Assembly, 1917.* Ithaca and London: Cornell University Press, 1990.

Rainbow, David "Saving the Russian Body: Siberian States in the Russian Civil War." Paper delivered at the Jordan Center for the Advanced Study of Russia, New York, 28 September 2012.

Remak, Joachim. *Sarajevo, the Story of a Political Murder.* New York: Criterion Books, 1959.

Retish, Aaron B. *Russia's Peasants in Revolution and Civil War: Citizenship, Identity, and the Creation of the Soviet State, 1914–1922.* Cambridge: Cambridge University Press, 2008.

Reynolds, Michael A. *Shattering Empires: The Clash and Collapse of the Ottoman and Russian Empires, 1908–1918.* Cambridge: Cambridge University Press, 2011.

Robinson, Paul. *Grand Duke Nikolai Nikolaevich: Supreme Commander of the Russian Army.* DeKalb: Northern Illinois University Press, forthcoming.

Rosenberg, William G. *Liberals in the Russian Revolution: The Constitutional Democratic Party, 1917–1921.* Princeton: Princeton University Press, 1974.

Rossiia v mirovoi voine 1914–1918 goda (v tsifrakh). Moscow: TsSU, 1925.

Rossos, Andrew. *Russia and the Balkans: Inter-Balkan Rivalries and Russian Foreign Policy, 1908–1914.* Toronto: University of Toronto Press, 1981.

Rostunov, I. I. *Russkii front pervoi mirovoi voiny.* Moscow: Izd. Nauka, 1976.

Rozenfel'd, Semen. *Gibel'.* Leningrad: Izd-vo pisatelei v Leningrade, 1932.

S"ezdy i konferentsii konstitutsionno-demokraticheskoi partii, ed. O. V. Volobuev and O. N. Lezhneva 3 vols. Moscow: ROSSPEN, 2000.

Sanborn, Joshua. "The Mobilization of 1914 and the Question of the Russian Nation: A Reexamination." *Slavic Review* 59, no. 2 (2000): 267–89.

Sanborn, Joshua. *Drafting the Russian Nation: Military Conscription, Total War, and Mass Politics, 1905–1925.* DeKalb: Northern Illinois University Press, 2003.

Sanborn, Joshua. "Unsettling the Empire: Violent Migrations and Social Disaster in Russia during World War I." *Journal of Modern History* 77, no. 2 (June 2005): 290–324.

Sanborn, Joshua. "Liberals and Bureaucrats at War." *Kritika: Explorations in Russian and Eurasian History* 8, no. 1 (Winter 2007): 141–62.

Sanborn, Joshua. "The Genesis of Russian Warlordism: Violence and Governance during the First World War and the Civil War." *Contemporary European History* 19, no. 3 (August 2010): 195–213.

Sanborn, Joshua. "Military Occupation and Social Unrest: Daily Life in Russian Poland at the Start of World War I." In *Writing the Stalin Era: Sheila Fitzpatrick and Soviet Historiography,* ed. Golfo Alexopolous, Julie Hessler, and Kiril Tomoff, 43–58. New York: Palgrave Macmillan, 2010.

Sanborn, Joshua. "Russian Soldiers and Refusal in the Great War." In *Accepter, Endurer, Refuser,* ed. Nicholas Beaupré, Heather Jones, and Anne Rasmussen. Paris: Les Belles Lettres, forthcoming.

Sanborn, Joshua. "When the Front Came Home: The Great Retreat of 1915 and the Transformation of Russian Society." In *The Great War and the Russian Revolution: A Centennial Appraisal.* Bloomington: Slavica Publishers, forthcoming.

Sapargaliev, G. *Karatel'naia politika tsarizma v Kazakhstane, 1905–1917 gg.* Alma-Ata: Nauka, 1966.

Schindler, John. "Steamrollered in Galicia: The Austro-Hungarian Army and the Brusilov Offensive, 1916." *War in History* 10, no. 1 (2003): 27–59.

Scott, James Brown. *Official Statements of War Aims and Peace Proposals, December 1916 to November 1918.* Washington DC: Carnegie Endowment for International Peace, 1921.

Segal, Harold B. "Culture in Poland during World War I." In *European Culture in the Great War: The Arts, Entertainment, and Propaganda, 1914–1918,* ed. Aviel Roshwald and Richard Stites, 58–88. Cambridge: Cambridge University Press, 1999.

Semine, Christine D. *Tragediia russkoi armii Pervoi Velikoi Voiny 1914–1918 g.g.: zapiski sestri miloserdiia kavkazskogo fronta.* 2 vols. New Mexico: n. p., 1964.

Seregny, Scott J. "Zemstvos, Peasants, and Citizenship: The Russian Adult Education Movement and World War I," *Slavic Review* 59, no. 2 (Summer 2000): 290–315.

Shevyrin, V. M. *Zemskii i gorodskoi soiuzy (1914–1917): analyticheskii obzor.* Moscow: INION RAN, 2000.

Showalter, Dennis. *Tannenberg: Clash of Empires*. Washington DC: Brassey's, 2004 [1991].

Shubin, Aleksandr. "The Treaty of Brest-Litovsk: Russia and Ukraine." *Lithuanian Historical Studies* 13 (2008): 75–100.

Siegelbaum, Lewis. *The Politics of Industrial Mobilization in Russia, 1914–17: A Study of the War-Industries Committees* (New York: St Martin's, 1983).

Simmons, Pol [Paul]. "Anatomiia bunta: volneniia v 223-m pekhotnom Odoevskom polku nakanune Fevral'skoi revoliutsii." *Russkii sbornik* 11 (2012): 232–54.

Simpson, J. Y. *The Self-Discovery of Russia*. New York: George H. Doran Company, 1916.

Sirotkina, Irina. "The Politics of Etiology: Shell Shock in the Russian Army, 1914–1918." In *Madness and the Mad in Russian Culture*, ed. Angela Brintlinger and Ilya Vinitsky, 117–29. Toronto: University of Toronto Press, 2007.

Smele, Jonathan. *Civil War in Siberia: The Anti-Bolshevik Government of Admiral Kolchak*. Cambridge: Cambridge University Press, 1996.

Smith, C. Jay, Jr. *Finland and the Russian Revolution, 1917–1922*. Athens: University of Georgia Press, 1958.

Smith, Jeremy. *The Bolsheviks and the National Question, 1917–1923*. London: Macmillan, 1999.

Smith, Leonard V. "Remobilizing the Citizen-Soldier Through the French Army Mutinies of 1917." In *State, Society, and Mobilization*, ed. Horne, 144–59.

Sokol, Edward Dennis. *The Revolt of 1916 in Russian Central Asia*. Baltimore, MD: The Johns Hopkins Press, 1954.

Sokolova, A. N. "Iz pisem Sekretariata TsK RSDRP(b) na mesta v dni bor'by za Brestskii mir." *Voprosy istorii KPSS* no. 6 (1958): 68–77.

Solntseva, Svetlana A. "Udarnye formirovaniia russkoi armii v 1917 godu." *Otechestvennaia istoriia* no. 2 (2007): 47–59.

Solntseva, Svetlana A. "The Russian Army's Shock Formations in 1917," trans. Liv Bliss. *Russian Studies in History* 51, no. 4 (Spring 2013): 50–73.

Solskii, Vatslav. *1917 god v zapadnoi oblasti i na zapadnom fronte*. Minsk: Tesei, 2004.

Sovet ministrov rossiiskoi imperii v gody pervoi mirovoi voiny. Bumagi A. N. Iakhontova (zapisi zasedanii i perepiska), ed. B. D. Gal'perina and R. Sh. Ganelin. St. Petersburg: Bulanin, 1999.

Stepun, Fedor. *Byvshee i nesbyvsheesia*. 2nd ed. St. Petersburg: Aleteiia, 2000.

Stockdale, Melissa K. *Paul Miliukov and the Quest for a Liberal Russia, 1880–1918*. Ithaca: Cornell University Press, 1996.

Stockdale, Melissa K. "Miliukov, Nationality, and National Identity." In *P. N. Miliukov: istorik, politik, diplomat*, ed. V. V. Shelokhaev, 275–87. Moscow: ROSSPEN, 2000.

Stockdale, Melissa K. "'My Death for the Motherland is Happiness': Women, Patriotism, and Soldiering in Russia's Great War." *American Historical Review* 109, no. 1 (February 2004): 78–116.

Stoff, Laurie. *They Fought for the Motherland: Russia's Women Soldiers in World War I and the Revolution*. Lawrence: University Press of Kansas, 2006.

Stoff, Laurie. *More than Binding Men's Wounds: Wartime Nursing Service in Russia during World War I*. Lawrence: University Press of Kansas, forthcoming.

Stone, Norman. *The Eastern Front, 1914–1917*. New York: Penguin, 1999 [1975].

Stovall, Tyler. "The Consumers' War: Paris, 1914-1918." *French Historical Review* 31, no. 2 (Spring 2008): 293–325.

Strachan, Hew. *The First World War*. New York: Penguin/Viking, 2003.

Sudavtsov, N. D. "'Geroinia, protivopostavivshaia tevtonskoi zabronirovannoi sile svoiu velikuiu liubiashchuiu dushu russkoi zhenshchiny'." *Voenno-istoricheskii zhurnal* no. 3 (2002): 47–52.

Sunderland, Willard. "Baron Ungern, Toxic Cosmopolitan." *Ab imperio: teoriia i istoriia natsional'nostei i natsionalizma v postsovetskom prostranstve* no. 3 (2005): 285–98.

Swain, Geoffrey. "Russia's Garibaldi: The Revolutionary Life of Mikhail Artemevich Muraviev." *Revolutionary Russia* 11, no. 2 (December 1998): 54–81.

Thaden, Edward C. *Russia and the Balkan Alliance of 1912.* University Park, PA: Penn State University Press, 1965.

Thurstan, Violetta. *Field Hospital and Flying Column, Being the Journal of an English Nursing Sister in Belgium and Russia.* London and New York: G. P. Putnam's Sons, 1915.

Trotskii, L. D. *Kak vooruzhalas' revoliutsiia,* 3 vols. Moscow: Vysshii voennyi redaktsionnyi sovet, 1923–1925.

Trotsky, Leon. *History of the Russian Revolution,* translated by Max Eastman. 3 vols. London: Sphere, 1967 [1932–1933].

Trotsky, Leon. *Terrorism and Communism: A Reply to Karl Kautsky.* Ann Arbor: University of Michigan Press, 1961.

Trotsky, Leon, George Weissman, and Duncan Williams. *The Balkan Wars, 1912–13: The War Correspondence of Leon Trotsky.* New York: Monad Press, 1980.

Tsiunchiuk, Rustem. "Peoples, Regions, and Electoral Politics: The State Dumas and the Constitution of New National Elites." In *Russian Empire,* ed. Burbank, von Hagen, and Remnev, 366–97.

Tugan-Baranovskii, M. I., ed. *Chego zhdet Rossiia ot voiny: sbornik statei.* N.p: Prometei, 1915.

Tunstall, Graydon A. *Blood on the Snow: The Carpathian Winter War of 1915.* Lawrence: University Press of Kansas, 2010.

Uspenskii, A. A. *Na voine: Vostochnaia Prussiia—Litva, 1914–1915 g.g., Vospominaniia.* Kaunas: n. p., 1932.

Uspenskii, A. A. *V plenu (prodolzhenie knigi Na voine): vospominaniia ofitsera v dvukh chastiakh.* Kaunas: n.p., 1933.

Vakar, S. V. "'Eto vam ne universitet, a eskadron'." *Voenno-istoricheskii zhurnal* no. 2 (2000): 45–53.

van Bergen, Leo. *Before My Helpless Sight: Suffering, Dying and Military Medicine on the Western Front, 1914–1918,* translated by Liz Waters. Farnham: Ashgate, 2009.

Vasilevskii, L. M. *Po sledam voiny: vpechatleniia voennago vracha.* Petrograd: Tip. Imp. Nik. voen. akad., 1916.

Vladimirtseva, N. I. "Iz vospominanii sestry miloserdiia F. N. Slepchenko." *Otechestvennye arkhivy* no. 6 (1994): 58–72.

Volkov, Vadim. *Violent Entrepreneurs: The Use of Force in the Making of Russian Capitalism.* Ithaca: Cornell University Press, 2002.

von Hagen, Mark. "The Great War and the Mobilization of Ethnicity in the Russian Empire." In *Post-Soviet Political Order: Conflict and State Building,* ed. Barnett R. Rubin and Jack Snyder, 34–57. London and New York: Routledge, 1998.

von Hagen, Mark. *War in a European Borderland: Occupations and Occupation Plans in Galicia and Ukraine, 1914–1918.* Seattle: University of Washington Press, 2007.

von Hindenburg, Marshal Paul. *Out of My Life,* trans. F. A. Holt. London: Cassell and Co., 1920.

von Ludendorff, Erich. *Ludendorff's Own Story, August 1914–November 1918.* 2 vols. New York and London: Harper and Brothers, 1919.

Vostochno-Prusskaia operatsiia: sbornik dokumentov. Moscow: Gosudarstvennoe voennoe izdatel'stvo Narodnogo Komissariata Oborony SSSR, 1939.

Wade, Rex A. *Red Guards and Workers' Militias in the Russian Revolution.* Stanford: Stanford University Press, 1984.

Wandycz, Piotr S. *The Lands of Partitioned Poland, 1795–1918.* Seattle: University of Washington Press, 1974.

Washburn, Stanley. *The Russian Campaign, April to August 1915, Being the Second Volume of "Field Notes from the Russian Front."* New York: Charles Scribner's Sons, 1915.

Washburn, Stanley. *On the Russian Front in World War I: Memoirs of an American War Correspondent.* New York: Robert Speller and Sons, 1982 [1939].

Weber, Max. *Sociological Writings,* ed. Wolf Heydebrand. New York: Continuum, 1994.

Weeks, Theodore R. *Nation and State in Late Imperial Russia: Nationalism and Russification on the Western Frontier, 1863–1914.* DeKalb: Northern Illinois University Press, 1996.

Weinberg, Robert. *The Revolution of 1905 in Odessa: Blood on the Steps.* Bloomington: Indiana University Press, 1993.

Wheeler-Bennett, John W. *The Forgotten Peace: Brest-Litovsk, March 1918.* New York: William Morrow & Company, 1939.

Wildman, Allan K. *The End of the Russian Imperial Army: The Old Army and the Soldiers' Revolt (March–April 1917).* Princeton: Princeton University Press, 1980.

Wildman, Allan K. *The End of the Russian Imperial Army: The Road to Soviet Power and Peace.* Princeton: Princeton University Press, 1987.

Wróbel, Piotr. "The Seeds of Violence: The Brutalization of an East European Region, 1917–1921." *Journal of Modern European History* 1, no. 1 (2003): 125–49.

Yakhontoff, Victor A. *Across the Divide: Impersonal Record of Personal Experiences.* New York: Coward-McCann, 1939.

Yekelchyk, Serhy. *Ukraine: Birth of a Modern Nation.* Oxford: Oxford University Press, 2007.

Zakharova, Lidiia. *Dnevnik sestry miloserdiia: na peredovykh pozitsiiakh.* Petrograd: Izd. Biblioteka "Velikoi voiny," 1915.

Zavadivker, Polly. "Reconstructing a Lost Archive: Simon Dubnow and 'The Black Book of Imperial Russian Jewry,' 1914–1915." *The Simon Dubnow Institute Yearbook* 12 (2013): 3–26.

Zhdanova, I. A. "Problema federativnogo ustroistva v Fevral'skoi revoliutsii 1917 g." *Voprosy istorii* no. 7 (2007): 17–29.

Zhiglinskii, A. N. "'Ia gord tem, chto mogu byt' polezen Rossii': Pis'ma iz proshlogo, utrachennoe nasledie." *Istochnik* no. 3 (1996): 12–30.

Index

Maps, diagrams, and tables are given in italics.

Printed and bound by CPI Group (UK) Ltd, Croydon, CR0 4YY